A History of
Laxton

For the people of Laxton

A History of
Laxton
England's Last Open-Field Village

J. V. Beckett

Basil Blackwell

First published 1989

Basil Blackwell Ltd
108 Cowley Road, Oxford, OX4 1JF, UK

Basil Blackwell Inc.
432 Park Avenue South, Suite 1503
New York, NY 10016, USA

British Library Cataloguing in Publication Data

Beckett, J. V.
Laxton: England's last open-field village
1. Nottinghamshire. Laxton, history
I. Title
942.5′24
ISBN 0–631–15972–X

Library of Congress Cataloging in Publication Data

Beckett, J. V.
Laxton: the story of an English village / J. V. Beckett.
p.   cm.
Bibliography: p.
Includes index.
ISBN 0–631–15972–X
1. Laxton (England) – History.   2. Villages – England–
Nottinghamshire – History.   I. Title.
DA690.L299B43   1989
942.5 ′24–dc 19   88–32116
CIP

Typeset in 10 on 12 pt Sabon
by Joshua Associates Ltd., Oxford

Printed in Great Britain by
Butler and Tanner Ltd., Frome

Contents

List of Plates

List of Figures

————⟡————

List of Tables

Preface

Laxton is unique. It is the only village in England where open-field farming (sometimes known as common-field, or even as strip farming) is still practised under the oversight of a court leet. Other places as far apart as Braunton in Devon and Soham in Cambridgeshire still have remnants of the open-field system which was once found through much of the Midlands and the south of England, but only Laxton has the system – albeit in an attenuated form – still in working order. Why? Or to put it more explicitly, why was Laxton not enclosed and just what relation is there between the open-field system of the medieval village and the methods of farming today? These are the two central questions which underlie this book. Enclosure has been an issue since the 1630s, if not earlier, and even today it cannot be entirely ruled out as a possibility on some future occasion. Change has been a necessary adjunct to the survival of the open-field system. Laxton is not, and never has been, a museum; today's farmers, like their predecessors a thousand years ago, must earn their living, and if they are to do so they must bend and change with the agricultural climate. This is the story of a living village, not of a long-past community which we can reconstruct merely from close reading of documentary sources.

'Village' history has had a chequered past. Once the province of gentry and parsons who wrote in an antiquarian manner about what interested them, in the past forty years or so it has taken on board new techniques and ideas as the quantity and quality of the available records has improved. The most notable developments have been in the area of family reconstitution using parish registers, but for various reasons such a study is inappropriate for Laxton. Instead it was decided to try to exploit to the full a splendid collection of estate surveys, together with the parish records and the papers surviving in the archives of the Earls Manvers, lords of the manor of Laxton from 1640 until 1952. From these it is possible to offer answers to the basic questions posed above. However, to concentrate merely on landownership and farming economics would make an interesting academic exercise but a rather dull book.

It would also leave tantalizingly vague all sorts of other questions, among them the obvious one of what was it like to live in Laxton? How many people made their home in the village, where did they live, how did they earn a living and what was the structure of power? These are just some of the questions which can be asked and this book attempts to look at the village in all its facets to see just how it has responded to the passage of time.

The book could not have been written as it has without considerable help from various quarters. I owe an intellectual debt to the pioneering work of the late Professor J. D. Chambers, whose surviving papers suggest that he at one time proposed a study which might have taken a similar course to the present book. I would like to thank Professor Chambers's daughter, Mrs Ann Howard, for making available to me a number of his papers and a tape recording still in her possession. Alan Cameron, formerly Keeper of Manuscripts at Nottingham University, and now of the Bank of Scotland, helped me in the original planning of the project and read some of the chapters in draft. His support was greatly appreciated, as was that of Dr Catherine Delano Smith, who has taken a geographer's-eye view of Laxton over many years. She was kind enough to read several chapters in draft and to discuss with me many of the ideas in the book. I am also indebted to Dr Stephen Wallwork for undertaking the aggregative analysis of the parish registers, and to Professor Maurice Barley for drawing several of the figures and for reading the whole manuscript.

For the financial support without which the project could not have been undertaken I am grateful to the Nottinghamshire County Council Research Fund of the University of Nottingham, the Crown Estate Commissioners, and the Economic and Social Research Council. The funding enabled me to employ Dr Trevor Foulds as research assistant on the project, and his help in collecting and processing the survey and census data was invaluable. Underlying much of the analysis and many of the tables which follow is a vast collection of material and a new methodology made possible by the age of the microchip. The methodology and computer-linkage techniques were largely developed by Mrs Anne de Cogan of the University of Nottingham's Cripps Computer Centre. It was Dr Foulds who converted the possibilities into practice. I should also like to thank the staffs of the various archive repositories in which I have gathered material, and in particular Mr Adrian Henstock and his colleagues at the Nottinghamshire Archives Office, and Dr Dorothy Johnston and her staff in the Nottingham University Manuscripts Department. Others to whom I should like to express my thanks for their help at various times in the preparation of this book are Dr Sheila Aley, Dr David Crook, Dr Keith Dexter, Mr Peter Evans, Dr J. R. Fisher, Dr David Hey, Dr B. E Hill, Dr B. A. Holderness, Dr Roger Kain, Mr Chris Lewis, Mr Rowan McFerran, Mr Denzil Newton, Dr A. D. M. Phillips, Professor A. J. Rayner, Dr N. C. P. Tyacke, Dr Tim Unwin, Mr Jeremy Ware and Dr Brian Wood.

Finally, the book put me in touch with living history. I took time out to make a video about Laxton, at the behest of the Visitors' Centre Trustees, as a result of which I have had the privilege of being present on Jury Day and attending a meeting of the Court Leet. I have also benefitted immeasurably from conversations with the people of Laxton. Everyone has been obliging and helpful, but I must mention in particular Mrs Alice Bailey, Bill Bartle, Mrs Janet Cooke, Mrs Annie Cree, Colin Cree, Ron Cree, Mrs Margaret Ilyott, Michael Jackson, Graham Laughton, Reg Rose, Edmund Rose and Mrs Marjorie Sayer.

List of Abbreviations

BL — British Library

Life at Laxton — B. A. Wood, Charles Watkins and C. A. Wood, eds, *Life at Laxton: the memories of Edith Hickson* (Nottingham, 1983)

NAO — Nottinghamshire Archives Office

NUMD — Nottingham University Manuscript Department

Open Fields — C. S. and C. S. Orwin, *The Open Fields* (Oxford, 1938)

PRO — Public Record Office

TTS — *Transactions of the Thoroton Society*

Wood, thesis — B. A. Wood, 'Land Management and Farm Structure: Spatial Organisation on a Nottinghamshire Landed Estate and its Successors, 1860–1978' (unpublished Ph.D. thesis, University of Nottingham, 1981)

Acknowledgements

PLATES

The author and publisher would like to thank the following for permission to reproduce plates: Aerofilms 2.1; Professor M. W. Barley 4.1; British Crown Copyright/RAF Photograph, reproduced by permission of the Controller of Her Britannic Majesty's Stationery Office (Photograph: Cambridge University Collection) 1.1 (Map after VCH *Nottinghamshire I (1906)*); Nic Broomhead and the Craft Design Unit, Rufford Craft Centre, Leisure Services Department, Nottinghamshire County Council 11.1; Cambridge University Collection; copyright reserved 6.1, 6.4; Mrs Ann Howard 10.1; Mrs Ann Howard and the Manuscripts Department, Nottingham University Library 2.2, 2.4, 3.2, 7.1, 9.1; Mr Graham Laughton 6.5, 7.4, 10.2; Nottinghamshire County Library 7.2; Mr Reg Rose 9.2; Trustees of the Thoresby Estate 2.3; Trustees of the Thoresby Estate and the Manuscripts Department, Nottingham University Library 8.1, 8.2.

The following plates are kindly provided by the Author: 3.1, 4.2, 5.1, 5.2, 6.2, 6.3, 6.4, 7.2, 7.3, 8.3, 10.2.

FIGURES

The author and publisher would also like to thank the following for permission to reproduce figures: Professor M. W. Barley 4.1, 5.1, 8.1; *East Midland Geographer* 0.1; Dr Brian Wood 9.1, 9.2.

Introduction

———◆———

Just off the A1 in Nottinghamshire between the sleepy market town of Tuxford and the rather drab colliery village of Ollerton lies Laxton. Approaching it, as many travellers do, from the west, the road climbs steeply into the parish through the northern end of Wellow Park before flattening out across the 80-acre expanse of Westwood Common. The road bends around Westwood (or Common) Farm, on the further edge of the common, and then winds gently towards the village along Acre Edge. To the right is the Mill Field, to the left, behind the hedge, the West Field. In the distance is the church tower, which stands clear in the landscape when the sun catches it from the west on a late summer afternoon. Beyond it the eye is carried to the Lincolnshire plain in the distance and, on a clear day, to the towers of the great cathedral in Lincoln. Away to the right is the rolling hillside of Laxton's third open field, the South Field. Just beyond the entrance to Mill Field the road bends sharply to the left between two high hedges, and almost without warning the visitor comes upon the village.

Laxton is not a handsome village. Many of the houses are just one room deep, with perhaps a one-storey outshoot containing a kitchen and storehouse. Several are of eighteenth-century construction; one or two dates on gable ends testify to considerable building in the village during the century. A number are built on long narrow plots, gable end on to the street, originally in order to allow the passage of animals and machinery through to the farmyard and to farm buildings at the rear. Houses and buildings do not always look to be in good condition – there is one dilapidated cottage and several rusting corrugated-iron roofs – so that the visitor may not be aware that he is passing through a village designated a conservation area under the terms of the Civic Amenities (1967) Act. However, this stipulation has helped to ensure the retention, as far as possible, of existing buildings, and their conversion for agricultural purposes. The handful of modern buildings which have been permitted give an inharmonious look to the village.

Beyond the fork in the road where a spur separates off towards West Field,

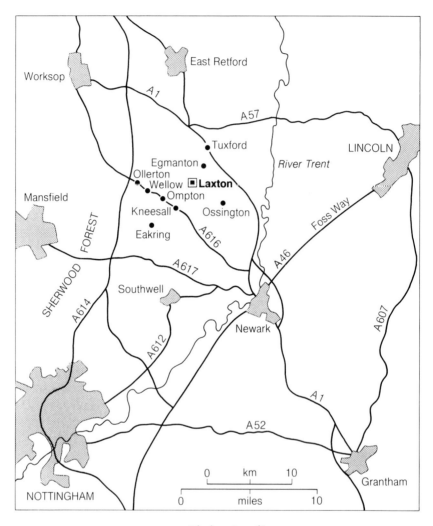

FIGURE 0.1 *The location of Laxton*

the traveller passes along the main street. On the left and right are farmhouses and cottages; the old school, now the village hall, is on the right, the village shop is on the left, on the right again the medieval church, and on the left a row of council houses dating from the 1950s. The road begins to dip, and in front is the Crosshill, a tiny village green at the junction of the Egmanton road. Now the road sweeps away to the right, past the Dovecote Inn on the left and down a gentle slope with more farmhouses and farm buildings on either side, to the junction at the southern end of the village. Here the road forks to go either to

Kneesall or Moorhouse. In a modern motor car the whole journey from entry to exit takes less than two minutes.

Laxton is a large parish for the area, spreading across 4,007 acres of farmland on a gently sloping plateau. This is a ridge of high ground, the highest in the county, between the 100 and 200 feet contour lines, which form the western edge of the Trent valley. It slopes southward from just over 250 feet in the northwest to about 197 feet in the southeast and owes its undulating aspect to a network of eastward-draining valleys. Some of these give rise to quite steep slopes, the most dramatic of which is on the north side of the castle site, where the land falls away to offer distant views over Nottinghamshire and into Lincolnshire. The plateau is of Keuper Marl (interleaved with waterstone beds which explain the stone footings to many of the village walls), giving a heavy clay. In 1862 the soil was described as varying from rich friable loam to very strong clay, which was naturally adaptable to arable or grass. Sadly, the reporter continued, much of the soil yielded 'scanty crops of grain in ordinary seasons, though generally of good quality'. The best arable was the open-field land.[1] In modern terminology Laxton is classified as class-three agricultural land.

The open fields are the main attraction luring the visitor some miles from the nearest notable country house, and from the twelfth-century minster a few miles down the road at Southwell. Laxton is neither a country house nor a cathedral, nor is it a museum; rather, it is a working example of the communal system of farming which operated over large parts of England from the early Middle Ages until at least the eighteenth century. The recommendation to visit Laxton (in, for example, the publications of the English Tourist Board), points not to the village, but to the medieval system of open-field farming preserved here as nowhere else in England.

Laxton's written history begins in 1086 but almost inevitably the coverage thereafter is patchy. The village and its fields are not especially well documented in the medieval period, although we know it flourished in the early Middle Ages when the castle was built. By the time the documentary evidence becomes more extensive in the seventeenth century Laxton enjoyed a more predictable life as just one of the thousands of open-field villages scattered across midland England. From Mark Pierce's superb map and terrier of 1635 a pen portrait can be drawn of the village at about the time of the Civil War. Areas of the open fields had already been enclosed as part of a piecemeal process which has continued down to the twentieth century. Thus, in the 1720s, demographic problems and depression in agriculture led to a reorganization of the manor in which the meadows were enclosed; land was removed from the open fields and four independent farms were laid out on the edge of the parish. In the first half of the eighteenth century enclosure 'by agreement' was common in Nottinghamshire.

[1] NUMD Ma S 16.

By 1759 about 45 per cent of the county area was already enclosed and over the following century another third was enclosed by legislation.[2]

With population falling and farming depressed, Laxton's open fields might well have been fully enclosed and turned down to pasture, as happened in many Midlands parishes on clay soils including Wigston Magna in Leicestershire.[3] However, two major reasons prevented or at least delayed enclosure. One was the lord of the manor, the second Duke of Kingston, who was lukewarm on the issue. Had he acquired the estates of Sir Bryan Broughton when they were sold in 1751 he would have owned enough land to enclose the manor even if the lesser freeholders had resisted and forced him to obtain an Act of Parliament. But he did not and the opportunity passed. The freeholders were the second reason why enclosure was delayed. Small freeholders survived most successfully in the arable claylands, where their presence, and the unfriendly nature of the soil, delayed enclosure.[4] Nationwide, freeholders were in decline in the seventeenth and eighteenth centuries, but in Laxton they increased in numbers and acreage down to 1789. The complications of tenure brought about by their presence undoubtedly delayed, even if it did not finally prevent enclosure. Nor did the situation change greatly during the Napoleonic wars. All over the country wealthy farmers enjoying growing incomes took the opportunity to invest some of their capital in freehold land. For many, including several in Laxton, the cooler agricultural climate after 1815 saw them run into considerable financial difficulties. The same downturn in the economy effectively ended the first serious negotiations designed to find a means of enclosing the parish.

Laxton is perhaps best documented during the Victorian period. A combination of government-generated statistics such as the decennial census enumerators' books and, from the 1860s, the agricultural returns, coupled with a vast collection of estate papers and accounts among the papers of the lord of the manor, provide a detailed picture of the parish and its farming community. The census returns reveal who lived in the village, where they came from, to whom they were related, and the occupations they pursued. They show that population reached its maximum figure in modern times in 1831 but then began to fall as the village offered fewer employment opportunities on the land. Enclosure negotiations in the 1840s made no substantial progress, although the hamlet of Moorhouse was enclosed in 1860. In any case, the evidence points to a relatively prosperous village in the middle decades of the nineteenth century.[5]

---

[2] Joan Thirsk, *The Agrarian History of England and Wales, volume 5, 1640–1750*, part 1 *Regional Farming Systems* (Cambridge, 1984), pp. 116, 120.

[3] W. G. Hoskins, *The Midland Peasant* (1957).

[4] Michael Turner, *English Parliamentary Enclosure* (Folkestone, 1980), p. 162.

[5] Laxton is generally well documented, the absence of an enclosure award notwithstanding! The major gap is that few records have survived relating to the farms (amounting to over 700 acres) owned by the Broughton and Savile families to the 1860s. Inevitably what follows has something of a Thoresby-eye view, since it is the records of the lord of the manor which are most plentiful.

After a series of major land exchanges in the mid-1860s the enclosure road again seemed open. It was not to be and for various reasons the issue was shelved once again. After 1873 rural England was plunged into depression. In Laxton rents fell, farmers were distressed and efforts were made to change the farming balance to concentrate on livestock farming. Many of the remaining freeholders could not compete: Earl Manvers, the lord of the manor, was the chief beneficiary as they sold up, and by 1906 he was the sole owner of open-field land. Once again the conditions seemed right for enclosure, but once again it did not follow, although in a major reorganization of the estate the open fields were considerably reduced in size and their layout was altered.

Since 1914 the village has changed considerably. Population has fallen steadily (at leat until 1981), the number of open-field tenancies has declined, and the pattern of farming has altered to fit government and EEC policies. Enclosure is no longer anticipated in quite the same way that generations of Laxton farmers must have viewed the possibility through the eighteenth and nineteenth centuries. Indeed, the emphasis has shifted: the question is no longer when will Laxton be enclosed but how can enclosure be prevented from taking place? Rev. Christopher Collinson, vicar of Laxton at the turn of the century, published a brief article in *Country Life* in 1906 in which he pointed out that Laxton was now almost unique in retaining its open fields.[6] A year later, in an important book on the English peasantry, Gilbert Slater illustrated a number of his points from the case of Laxton. Slater's lead was soon followed. In his textbook on agricultural economics published in 1923, J. A. Venn commented specifically on Slater's role in drawing attention to the historic significance of Laxton.[7] During the 1920s the correspondence columns of *The Times* carried a number of suggestions as to how Laxton might be preserved as part of the national heritage. Thus, in 1925 Montague Fordham wrote to alert readers to the possible effect on Laxton of the Law of Property Act which was to come into force early in 1926: 'for historic reasons it certainly deserves to be maintained as a national trust.' Several letters of support were subsequently published. *The Times* sent a reporter to the village, and carried an article dated from Laxton on 4 January 1926 designed to allay fears about the future. The Laxton open fields, readers were assured, would not disappear because Earl Manvers had no intention of enclosing the village, despite the fact that the farming system was uneconomic to maintain.[8]

In the years which followed Laxton's reputation grew. The British Association visited the village during its annual meeting at Leicester in 1933. A number of radio programmes in the 1930s, some made particularly for schools, were devoted to the historic role of Laxton and a film was made about the village

[6] C. B. Collinson, 'A Survival', *Country Life*, XIX, 789 (19 May 1906), 713–14.

[7] Gilbert Slater, *The English Peasantry and the Enclosure of Common Fields* (1907); J. A. Venn, *The Foundations of Agricultural Economics* (1923).

[8] *The Times*, 29, 30, 31 December 1925, 2, 5 January 1926.

and its open fields.[9] In Laxton itself the Inspector of Schools noted in 1929 that 'the Head Master endeavours to bring home to them [the children] the unusual historical significance and real interest of what otherwise might appear to them quite commonplace and colourless.' The children were taken into the open fields 'to study field strips while men were ploughing'.[10] All this activity culminated with the publication in 1938 of C. S. and C. S. Orwins's classic academic study *The Open Fields*. The Orwins had been interested in Laxton for a number of years. It was Dr Orwin who showed the British Association around the open fields in 1933, the same year that he and his wife presented maps of the village to the school. Their particular interest was in the early history of the open fields and the principal landowners, but they also provided a detailed account of Laxton based on the 1635 survey. Above all, they reiterated the importance of Laxton: 'it is the only place in England where the open-field system of land tenure and farming is still practised in all its essentials.'[11]

Laxton was now recognized as unique but its future was still uncertain. By 1952 the lord of the manor and principal landowner, the sixth Earl Manvers, was aware that when he died his successors might need to sell the manor to pay death duties. To forestall the possibility that this would lead to enclosure he persuaded the Ministry of Agriculture to buy the open-field farms and to undertake to maintain the open-field system in perpetuity. Laxton appeared to have been saved. However, in 1979, and notwithstanding the agreement of 1952, the newly elected Conservative government announced that Laxton was to be sold as part of its policy of disposing of state assets.[12] Once again the correspondence columns of *The Times* carried protests and this time the paper published a leading article reminding the government that its predecessors had acquired Laxton in 1952 in order to preserve its unique farming system. Thus, the leader thundered, unless a body such as the National Trust could be persuaded to acquire Laxton in order to preserve the village in its current form, no sale ought to take place: 'Laxton should be withdrawn from the market, and the Minister [of Agriculture] resume his agreeable responsibilities as lord of the

---

[9] *Medieval Village*, Gaumont British Instructional Ltd 1936. Later films have included *Laxton*, Hull University Audio Visual Centre, 1975, and *Heritage for Sale*, which was made by Anglia Television at the time of the sale in 1979. Laxton has frequently featured in films and television series, most recently Michael Wood's *Domesday* series shown by BBC 1 in the autumn of 1986. A video, made on behalf of the Trustees of the Visitors Centre by the University of Nottingham, is currently available.

[10] NAO SL/106/1/2.

[11] *Open Fields*, p. 69. The first edition included a black and white copy of the Mark Pierce map of 1635 and a transcription of the whole of the accompanying survey book, but this was not included in the second edition of 1954, or in a third edition of 1967 which included a new introduction by Joan Thirsk relating the Orwin's' work to more recent research. NAO DD/846/1/26. The Orwins were not the first scholars to write about Laxton. Locally the village had already attracted the attention of J. B. Firth, *Highways and Byeways in Nottinghamshire* (1916), pp. 375–81; and J. D. Chambers, 'The Open Fields of Laxton', *TTS*, 32 (1928), 102–25.

[12] Ministry of Agriculture, Fisheries and Food, Press Release, 28 November 1979.

manor.'[13] Other newspapers, on both sides of the Atlantic, featured the story; a variety of pressure groups made representations to the government urging a change of mind on the subject of Laxton and the Laxton farmers mounted their own vigorous campaign to save the open fields.[14]

The government was unrepentant, but the Ministry of Agriculture did at least insist that any purchaser would have to undertake to continue – if at all possible – the system of open-field farming. In the end Laxton did not pass back into private hands; instead it was sold to the Crown Estate Commissioners who undertook to continue the open-field system and its associated customs. The price of £1 million (less than half the expected market value) reflected the need for some form of subsidy if the system was to be maintained.[15] At least in the intermediate term, open-field farming in Laxton had been saved.

Laxton may have avoided total enclosure but it has not been immune to agricultural changes over the centuries and in the chapters which follow the primary intention is to describe how it has evolved. Despite Laxton's importance, it is a story which has never been told in detail,[16] and only now is it possible to fulfil Montague Fordham's suggestion in 1925 that at the very least Laxton ought to be the subject of proper investigation, in order that a record of its history and present features could be made.[17] One of the aims of this book is to suggest why Laxton is such a unique part of our national heritage.

---

[13] *The Times*, 28 November, 5 and 6 December 1979, 4 February 1980.

[14] *The Daily Telegraph*, 10 May 1980; *Daily Mail*, 30 November 1979; *The Observer Magazine*, 22 June 1980; *The Stars and Stripes*, 13 January 1980. Among pressure groups taking an interest was the Nottinghamshire local history society, the Thoroton Society. A file of correspondence relating to the issue is in NAO DDTS/44/5. Mr Reg Rose of Bottom Farm was particularly active on behalf of the village farmers.

[15] Ministry of Agriculture, Fisheries and Food, Press Release, 30 April 1981.

[16] Recent work on Laxton includes J. D. Chambers's official guide to the village *Laxton – the Last English Open Field Village* (London, 1964). This was reprinted with minor revisions in 1979, but is now out of print. *The East Midland Geographer*, 7, 6 (1980) carried several articles about Laxton. Also relevant is Wood, thesis, pp. 381–501. Numerous magazine articles have been published about Laxton and its open fields. The Local Studies Library of Nottinghamshire County Library, Angel Row, Nottingham, maintains an updated file of publications relating to the village.

[17] *The Times*, 29 December 1925.

Chapter One

Medieval Village

Laxton today is a pleasant village. Its houses congregate around the church, the shop, and the pub, in a manner virtually unchanged since the early seventeenth century and probably much earlier. Some of the houses, with their gables end on to the street, and their farmsteads stretching back from the roadway are, admittedly, rather different from those usually found in modern English villages, but for most visitors Laxton is not easy to distinguish from many of the other brick-built, nucleated settlements of this part of Nottinghamshire. Visitors, however, are usually interested less in the village than the surrounding fields. Many of them come because they were once taught about strip farming, and their hazy recollections from half-forgotten schooldays have left them with a romantic historical picture in which three fields, fallow years and strips, merge imperceptibly with medieval peasants, smocks and pitchforks, into a rustic landscape over which the sun seems never to set. Some visitors are almost surprised to find that Laxton is not peopled by peasant-like figures tilling the land without the help of modern technology, while others half expect to see repeated on the ground the multicoloured lines drawn in their childhood schoolbooks to depict the variegated strip pattern. Of course there is something 'romantic' about a village which still farms according to practices which appear to date back over hundreds of years, but conditions today are far removed from those in which generations of Laxton people have lived since 1086, when Domesday Book recorded a small band of men and women residing and working in the village. To understand Laxton today we must travel back in time to locate the origin of the open-field system, and to trace its vagaries and changes. In so doing we shall come across the people who have made the village what it is today – the landlords and tenants who are the spiritual, and in some cases the actual, predecessors of the men and women in modern Laxton.

Laxton or, as it often appears, Lexington – in its earliest form Lexintune – was already a thriving centre when William the Conqueror's forces invaded England in 1066. A scatter of Romano-British pottery and coins has been found in several plaes in the West Field suggesting several habitations of the first to fourth centuries AD, and at one of them the finding of building materials and Fesserae indicates a villa.[1] Other finds, including a mosaic floor behind a house at the western end of the present village, are known to the villagers but have not been investigated by archaeologists.[2] Later evidence of occupation is provided by Laxton's name, which is Anglo-Saxon, although the Danish influence on agricultural terminology (in such words as syke, toft, flatt, gate and wong) points towards a mixed society. Field name evidence suggests that much of the modern parish was once woodland, and that considerable clearance must have taken place in the early Middle Ages to accommodate a growing village population.[3]

In 1066 Laxton was the centre of an extensive estate of which the lordship belonged to an English thane, Tochi son of Outi, who owned property throughout the East Midlands. After 1066 Tochi was displaced, and succeeded by a Norman, Geoffrey Alselin. According to Domesday Book:

In Laxintune Tochi had 2 carucates of land [assessed] to the geld. [There is] land for 6 ploughs. There Walter, a man of Geoffrey Alselin's, has 1 plough and 22 villeins and 7 bordars having 5 ploughs and 5 serfs [servi] and 1 female serf [ancilla] and 40 acres of meadow. Wood [land] for pannage 1 league in length and a half a league in breadth. In King Edward [the Confessor's] time it was worth 9 pounds; now [it is worth] 6 pounds.

With an adult male population of around thirty-five, possibly 100–20 people were living in the village, perhaps in homes along what seems to have been the original village street, today running roughly south from the Dovecote Inn to the point where the Moorhouse road peels off to the left. This is a sheltered area, unlike the ridge on which most of the later village was built. It also provides a reasonable drainage slope. The Domesday entry suggests that the people of Laxton were probably cultivating about 720 acres of arable land, that they had 40 or more acres of land for mowing and woodland to provide pannage (acorns and beechmast) for pigs, fuel and building timber.

After Alselin's death the property probably descended through an heiress to be held in her right by her husband Robert de Caux. Robert became the hereditary keeper of the Royal Forests of Nottinghamshire and Derbyshire and made Laxton his administrative centre.[4] Between about 1100 and 1227 all of Nottinghamshire north of the Trent (including Laxton) lay within the bounds of Sherwood Forest; the jurisdiction of the keepership also extended into Derbyshire. The administrative centre for the whole of this vast area was Laxton Castle.

[1] A. Cameron, 'Laxton before 1635', *East Midland Geographer*, 7, 6 (1980), 222–3; *ex. inf.* M. W. Bishop.

[2] *Ex. inf.* Mrs Janet Cooke.

[3] Trevor Foulds, 'Laxton: Field Names as Evidence for the Ancient Landscape', *Nottinghamshire Historian*, 42 (1989), 4–11.

[4] D. Crook, 'The Early Keepers of Sherwood Forest', *TTS*, 84 (1980), 14–20.

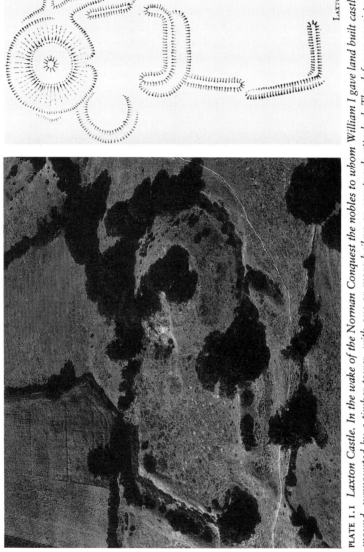

SCALE OF FEET

0   100   200   300

Laxton Castle.

PLATE 1.1 *Laxton Castle. In the wake of the Norman Conquest the nobles to whom William I gave land built castles. Most consisted of a motte or mound, surmounted by a timber tower, with one or more baileys or courtyards attached. The defences consisted of earth ramparts with timber palisading on top; the timber work was later replaced by stone walling. Residential buildings with barns, stables and the like were built in a bailey. The earthworks and ditches at Laxton can be seen in this picture taken from the east. The 'motte' and the inner and outer baileys are clearly visible from the air. The castle was allowed to decay in the late thirteenth century.*

Although visitors to Laxton expecting to find a massive, medieval, stone-built castle will be disappointed, what survives on the northern edge of the village is Nottinghamshire's best preserved, and possibly finest motte and bailey. Precisely when the castle was built is unknown. It probably dates from the late eleventh century (some authorities suggest a latest date of 1135), although it seems possible that it was constructed in two or three major phases between the Conquest and the reign of King John (1199–1216). It consisted of a ditched mound (or motte) on which a timber tower was constructed. Around the motte were two fortified enclosures or baileys, which provided the living quarters, and also protection for both people and farm animals. The castle was built on a grand scale; the substantial earthworks reveal a circumference of 816 feet and a total height of 71 feet, topped by a smaller mound 8 feet high and 147 feet in circumference. This extra mound or cone on the summit of the motte is unusual.[5] Although there is no evidence to suggest that the castle was ever the subject of military action, it was certainly not built merely for show. It was erected where the land rises to 220 feet above sea level, some of the highest land in Nottinghamshire, and consequently it commanded a good view not merely of the surrounding countryside but also of the Royal Forest of Sherwood. The view remains impressive today even if the landscape is much altered. A pleasure park also seems to have been laid out, doubtless to provide entertainment for visitors.

Whatever the chronology of building, the local impact was considerable. The people of Laxton must soon have become aware that the castle was designd as rather more than a home for Robert de Caux and his family; indeed, it became a stopping-off point for a succession of royal visitors from Henry II to Edward I. The third Robert de Caux, the last male member of the family, died about 1168, leaving an only daughter and heiress, Matilda, who was married to Ralf FitzStephen, Henry II's chamberlain. When Ralf died in about 1202 his wife's lands were taken into the hands of King John and although they were restored to her the following year, the king retained the manor of Laxton for himself, subsequently staying at the castle on a number of occasions. Repairs and alterations were carried out at his orders in 1205–7, and a new pigeon house was built at a cost of £12 in 1213–14. In 1217, after his death, Matilda de Caux secured the restoration of the manor.[6] This did not interrupt the flow of royal vistors – Henry III visited Laxton in 1225 and Edward I (withQueen Eleanor) shortly before Eleanor's death in 1290 – even though, with the reduction of the area under forest law in 1227, Laxton was no longer part of Sherwood Forest.

The keepership remained with de Caux's successors until 1286, during

---

[5] Colin Groves, 'Gazetteer of Minor Moated and Fortified Sites in Nottinghamshire', unpublished MA thesis, University of Nottingham, 1987, pp. 92–7.

[6] H. M. Colvin, *History of the King's Works* (London, 1963), vol. I, p. 120; vol. II, pp. 979–80.

which period Laxton seems to have been a thriving community. Certainly the castle, although probably having just a small garrison, must have had to accommodate substantial numbers of visitors – which may account for the extensive fishponds along Radbeck, noted in a charter of 1232, and there would doubtless have been plenty of employment for villagers. Laxton must also have had a class of salaried or fee'd officials, which would have given a larger than normal cash element to the village economy. The availability of money is clear in 1208 when the people of Laxton were able to pay £100 on demand to prevent the township from being burned down by the king. It is possible that the west–east village street was laid out in the period 1130–1230, to accommodate what may have been a substantial population, which must have been boasted – at least in part – by activities associated with the castle.[7]

Meantime the lordship of the manor had changed hands through marriage and inheritance. Matilda de Caux, who had secured the restoration of Laxton, died in 1224. She was succeeded by John de Birkin, son of another Maud de Caux, probably her aunt, and her husband Adam de Birkin. However, by 1230 the manor was held by John Birkin's daughter Isabella and through her marriage to Robert de Everingham the manor of Laxton passed into the hands of the de Everingham family, who held it until late in the fourteenth century. A charter of 1232 reveals that a sub-manor had been created within Laxton by this date, since it confirmed to Robert de Lexington various grants of land made to him by Maud de Caux and her successors in title, the de Birkins and the de Everinghams. Robert de Lexington was rector of Laxton, a prebendary of Southwell and a judge under King Henry III. He had extensive estates, including Laxton, where the fishponds on sloping ground south of the church (known as Hall grounds or Hall orchard) presumably belonged to the family together with an appropriate house. The de Lexingtons subsequently moved to Tuxford. In the late thirteenth century their sub-manor was divided between two heiresses of Robert de Lexington's nephew Robert de Markham. The elder of the two heiresses, Cecilia de Markham, married Thomas de Bekering, and her part of the property subsequently descended to Lord Vaux of Harrowden in the sixteenth century. Bertha, the younger of the two heiresses, married William de Longvilliers, and her part of the property (which included much of Moorhouse) remained in her husband's family until 1541 when it was sold to Augustine Hinde of the City of London for £360.[8]

In 1300 Laxton may well have been enjoying some of its most prosperous days. It was a substantial settlement; no fewer than forty-two separate tax-payers are recorded in the 1327 'twentieth', more than for any other settlement in Bassetlaw, and well in advance of East Retford (24) and Mansfield (36). Five years later in the 1332 subsidy return, Laxton's forty-two taxpayers found

[7] Cameron, 'Laxton before 1635', pp. 223–5.

[8] *Open Fields*, pp. 71–91, gives the descent of the manor and sub-manor in more detail than in this paragraph. The point about ownership in the sixteenth century is developed in chapter 3.

among themselves a total of 72s 6d. Adam de Everingham, Thomas de Bekering and Thomas de Longvillers (the lord and sub-lords), paid the highest rates, but the other 39 taxpayers were all paying sizeable sums. In 1334 the village was assessed for tax purposes at £5 1s 4½d on moveable wealth totalling £76. At this level it was much wealthier than neighbouring villages such as Egmanton, Wellow, Eakring and Walesby, and more on a par with the neighbouring market towns of Mansfield (£7), Tuxford (£5 2s) and Southwell (£5 9s 6½d). Although it was not in the same league as Newark (£26 0s 2d) Laxton was a considerable settlement; indeed, of 266 Nottinghamshire settlements of which there is a record, only 20 (7.5 per cent) were assessed for more than Laxton.[9]

These impressive statistics raise the obvious question of why Laxton, with its castle and populous village, did not become a town with market rights? Of course it may have had a 'prescriptive' market (although it has to be said that there is no firm evidence to support this hypothesis) but because a charter was never acquired the market declined and eventually disappeared. Possibly Crosshill, the small triangular green in the middle of the village, could have been the site of an early market.[10] This is speculation. If Laxton did have an early market no charter was ever granted, perhaps because the lords of the manor actively opposed such a grant or, in the various changes of the early thirteenth century, failed to press the case. In any case Laxton declined. The keepership passed to the de Everinghams with the estate in 1230, but the position was mismanaged by Robert de Everingham (c. 1256–87). He was imprisoned at Nottingham in 1286 for trespass of the royal venison it was his duty to preserve and stripped of the keepership by the king. Already by that time the restriction of Forest Law and the cutting back of the forest boundaries had undermined Laxton's administrative function, partly because the village was no longer within the forest. (Ironically this enabled Laxton to expand its arable to what was probably the maximum extent.)

Having lost the keepership, the de Everinghams seem to have abandoned Laxton, allowing the castle to fall rapidly into disuse. In 1287 the Inquisition *post mortem* taken at Robert de Everingham's death stated that the manor of Laxton was insufficient to sustain his son and heir Adam, then aged seven. This was despite the fact that between the 1250s and the early seventeenth century

[9] PRO E 179/159/4. I should like to thank Dr Tim Unwin for this reference to the 1327 tax. R. E Glasscock (ed.), *The Lay Subsidy of 1334*, British Academy Records of Social and Economic History (1975), pp. 227–34.

[10] Cameron, 'Laxton before 1635', p. 224. There is no evidence of prescriptive market rights in *Placita de Quo Warranto* (1818). The possibility of a market on the Crosshill is suggested on the basis of Christopher Taylor's speculations in 'Medieval Market Grants and Village Morphology', *Landscape History*, 4 (1982), 21–8. See also T. Unwin, 'Rural Marketing in Medieval Nottinghamshire', *Journal of Historical Geography*, 7 (1981), 231–51. Hallaton, Leicestershire, which did have a market, is a possible parallel: J. Hadfield (ed.), *The Shell Book of English Villages* (1980), p. 209.

the demesne land attached to the lordship was always recorded as about 250–300 acres. Subsequent Inquisitions on Adam de Everingham and his successors show that by the late thirteenth century the family preferred to live on the ancestral manor of Everingham in Yorkshire, and the castle was allowed to decay.[11] Thereafter Laxton lacked a resident lord, who might more easily have obtained a market charter than the village community acting on its own.

After 1300 the village is likely to have endured the problems caused by a general downturn in the economy, the Black Death in 1348–9, and subsequent revisitations of plague throughout the fourteenth century. The east midland counties lost at least half their population between 1348 and 1400 and Laxton was no exception; the evidence in Inquisitions strongly suggests that the village experienced many years of economic difficulty. Eighty acres of woodland were valued at 26s 8d in 1388, and the same acreage at 20s in 1433; the windmill, worth 15s in 1252, was worth only 6s 8d in 1341, 'because it is broken and ruinous', and 4s by 1388. The difference in rental between 1388 and 1433 was considerable, rents from tenants at will falling from £20 to £5. A similar picture can be drawn from Inquisitions relating to Moorhouse. In 1289 it had its own mill, but in 1352 this was described as decayed and ruinous. The picture should not however be overdrawn. No returns have survived from Laxton to the 1377 Poll Tax, but by the time of the early sixteenth-century subsidies Laxton had at least retained its relative position in Bassetlaw. It was taxed at £3 2s 4d in 1524, which was substantially more than Tuxford (£1 18s 4d) and neighbouring villages such as Egmanton, Kirton, Eakring and Wellow. However, with only eighteen taxpayers the village was obviously much reduced from two centuries earlier. Recovery from the Black Death was long and painful.[12]

Early in the fifteenth century the manor of Laxton passed from the de Everinghams into the family of John Roos, a Nottinghamshire squire whose descendants were to hold it for nearly 200 years. When John Roos died in 1458 the manor passed to his son Robert, who proceeded to settle it on Thomas Rotherham, Archbishop of York. The Archbishop founded a new College of Jesus at Rotherham in 1482–3, and appropriated Laxton to the College. Of life in Laxton at this time we know relatively little, although the village was rocked by a scandal in 1471 when the vicar, Richard Johnson, was first set in the stocks at Wellow and later gaoled in Nottingham. He was accused by William Blyton of Wellow of having had an affair with his wife. Johnson petitioned the Archbishop of York for help but although subsequently released from confinement he was obliged to quit the living.[13]

[11] *Open Fields*, pp. 99–111, gives a full description of the IPMs. P. T. H. Unwin, 'Patterns and Hierarchies of Rural Settlement in Nottinghamshire before 1700', unpublished Ph.D. thesis, University of Durham, 1979, pp. 589–92.

[12] My thanks are due to Tim Unwin for these references.

[13] R. L. Storey, 'A Fifteenth-century Vicar of Laxton', *TTS*, 88 (1984), 39–41.

With Laxton temporarily in the hands of the Archbishop of York it is not perhaps surprising to find some attention being paid to the church. There is no evidence that the village had either a church or a priest in 1086. The present church, which is dedicated to St Michael, dates from the 1190s onwards. It was remodelled and extended during the 1250s and 1260s – further evidence of the prosperity of Laxton in the mid-thirteenth century – when the chantry altar was endowed and the old chancel and aisles were enlarged. By the close of the thirteenth century it was a building of some splendour and once the present chancel was built during the fourteenth century it was larger and more elaborate than most of Nottinghamshire's parish churches, which again points to a sizeable village population. Archbishop Rotherham made further improvements. The present chancel screen was originally part of the rood screen which he erected. He was also responsible for the clerestory (the windowed upper part of the church), and the windows were enriched on the exterior by gargoyles placed between them. For the north side of the church Rotherham commissioned an effigy of himself replete with cope and mitre and holding his primatial cross. The de Everingham monuments in the church represent members of the family who died between 1287 and 1398. Adam de Everingham (d. 1341) is represented with both his first wife Clarice and his second wife Margery. The oak effigy of Margery (d. 1336) is the only surviving wooden medieval effigy in Nottinghamshire.[14]

From the late fifteenth century Laxton church was served by a vicar with the rectory and its emoluments going first to the College of Jesus and, after the Reformation in the 1530s, to lay impropriators. Moorhouse had a small chapel at some point in the later medieval period but in 1575 it was said to be in ruins: 'no services have been held since the suppression of mass.'[15]

Prior to the Reformation the priory of North Ferriby (Augustinian canons of the order of the Temple of the Lord of Jerusalem) held 68 acres in Laxton's Mill Field. Nothing is known of the date of the grant, or of the donor, but this was part of a holding which extended into several manors in mid-Nottinghamshire. The priory was suppressed on 13 August 1536.[16] There were also two chantries within the parish church in Laxton, both founded by Robert de Lexington. One was dedicated to St Edmund, the other to the Blessed Virgin Mary. Both had chaplains. John Derman was appointed chaplain of St Mary's chantry in 1490 and like his successor in the 1530s, John Herbert, he was paid to pray for Sir John de Lexington and his wife Margery, Henry III, William de Vescy and a number of other notables, a list which suggests a foundation date of 1250–60. The chaplains shared the chantry house, a messuage and an

[14] A. W. Keeton, *Laxton and its Past* (Nottingham, n.d.), pp. 15–18; H. Gill, 'St. Michael's, Laxton', *TTS*, 28 (1924), 96–105; N. Pevsner and E. Williamson, *The Buildings of England: Nottinghamshire*, 2nd edn (1979), pp. 164–5.
[15] *Cal. Patent Rolls*, 1572–5, no. 2829, p. 457.
[16] Victoria County History, *Yorkshire*, III (1913), 241.

orchard, while the chaplain of St Edmund's had the exclusive right to various
parcels of land amounting to about 40 acres.[17]

The Reformation in the 1530s, and the subsequent dissolution of the
monasteries at the behest of Henry VIII and his advisers, had repercussions for
Laxton, although the same vicar seems to have served from 1542 to 1582 without finding his faith too severely compromised.[18] More contentious was the
fate of the chantry lands. After the dissolution they were granted to Thomas
Marshe of London, gentleman, and Roger Williams of Usk, gentleman, for
£952 in 1549.[19] They may have changed hands more than once and by 1635
the land was divided between five individuals. Although their tenurial status is
not clear, they could have been freeholders who had purchased the land from
the original grantees, or their successors. (The property designated chantry
lands in 1635 belonged to freeholders in the 1730s.) Three of the chantry land
holders in 1635 had cottages in the village, but it is not certain that any of these
were the chantry house since in a lease of 1631 the lord of the manor granted to
Henry Inkersall a messuage called the Chantry with associated land.[20] Unfortunately Inkersall does not appear in the 1635 survey of the village as the
occupier of a house, and the fate of the chantry house must remain a mystery.

When Rotherham died in 1500 he directed in his will that if his niece Anne
Restwold should marry Humphrey Roos, the manor was to return to the Roos
family. Fortunately Anne must have been agreeable, or at least she must have
been persuaded to agree, and the marriage took place. Following a legal case in
Chancery in 1508 the manor was returned to the family under the terms of a
licence granted to Humphrey and Anne. Humphrey died in 1521, but not
before either he, or his son Francis (1506–78), had begun to build a manor
house in what had been the inner bailey of the old castle. It was probably
erected in stages and the only visual evidence we have relating to it is on Mark
Pierce's map of Laxton drawn in 1635. This shows a three-gabled manor
house, with stables, a brewhouse, dovecotes, a garden and an orchard. The
E-shaped ground plan of the house can still be traced on the ground.

During the sixteenth century the Rooses found themselves in financial difficulties, partly as a result of legal costs incurred during the Chancery case, and
perhaps as a result of their building activities. Their liquidity problems
increased when Francis Roos split the property at his death, bequeathing the
lordship of the manor to his eldest son Peter, but other land to the second son
Thomas. Peter Roos found himself with a far from enviable financial position

[17] *Valor Ecclesiasticus*, 1535, v, 128; *The Register of Thomas Rotherham, Archbishop of York
1480–1500* (ed.), E. E. Barker, vol. 1, Canterbury and York Society, vol. 69, 1976, p. 164;
A. Hamilton Thompson, 'Chantry Certificate Rolls for the County of Nottinghamshire', *TTS*, 17
(1913), 61–4.
[18] *Nottinghamshire Guardian*, 16 July 1949.
[19] *Cal. Patent Rolls*, 1548–9, p. 398.
[20] BL Egerton, 3660E/B355.

and immediately after his father's death in 1578 he obtained a licence to sell Laxton and Moorhouse.[21] In the event this turned out to be an unnecessary precaution, although his problems remained considerable and between 1598 and 1600 he was involved in a series of mortgage transactions designed to secure advances of money.

We know a little about Peter Roos from his efforts to help local people brought before the church courts. As a minor gentleman, who perhaps felt more in common with his tenants than more substantial landowners, he went to the unusual lengths of pleading the case of people presented before the ecclesiastical court. In 1594, for example, he intervened in the case of Margaret Lane of Laxton, who was presented for fornicating with Richard Caldwell. According to Roos, 'she is utterly undone by the evil fortune that she had in the matter wherewith she was troubled.' Being only a poor servant she had little enough money to pay for a midwife and Roos asked for the case to be dismissed without further trouble to her. Caldwell was not so fortunate; found guilty he was sentenced to do two penances in Laxton church and another in Newark 'with a white sheet about him and a white rod in his hand' – the usual penalty of the time – between the hours of 11 o'clock and 12 o'clock on 22 January 1595, 'in the presence of the whole multitude of people assembled [and] in the open sight of the congregation'.

Roos's familiarity with his tenants eventually landed him and his wife before the Archdeacon's Court. He was presented in 1603 for failing to receive Holy Communion at Easter and two years later for being present at the 'May game', a form of enjoyment with sexual overtones to which the church took exception. Worse, he had attended on the Sabbath, 'amongst others his neighbours', a sure indication that he was seen to be leading them astray. His wife, who was presented with him in both 1603 and 1605, appeared alone in December 1605, shortly after his death. She was accused of adultery with Ralph Brett.[22]

Roos's death merely transferred the family's financial difficulties to his son Gilbert, who inherited a far from enviable situation. Information contained in the feodaries survey, an analysis of the estate drawn up by an official of the Court of Wards because Gilbert was only thirteen and therefore became a ward of the Crown, reveals that Laxton was the largest of Peter Roos's various estates in mid-Nottinghamshire and they were collectively valued at just £63 10s a year.[23] In practice the income they yielded may not have been as small as this assessment implies. In wardship cases royal rights were sold to private individuals (known as 'committees') who could recover their costs out of the estate (known as 'compositions'). The wardship of a young man was

---

[21] *Cal. Patent Rolls* 1575–8 no. 2770.

[22] The Archdeaconry Court papers are in NUMD. These cases are taken from transcriptions of the Act Books held in the Department of Adult Education at the University of Nottingham and used with permission.

[23] PRO Ward 5/32/1606.

usually sold for a fixed price, with one of the conditions being that the person acquiring the wardship had the right to negotiate a marriage alliance for his charge. Property in the king's hands because of the wardship was usually leased for an annual rent, although in normal circumstances the buyer of the wardship and the lessee of the land were the same person.

In the case of Gilbert Roos the king gave custody to Lord Bruce, who transferred it to Edward Orrell, gentleman. Orrell took advantage of the wardship. In 1607, aged fourteen, Gilbert was married to Orrell's daughter Elizabeth. At his coming of age several years later, Gilbert Roos instituted Chancery proceedings in order to recover his inheritance. He was successful but it turned out to be a pyrrhic victory since he now added to the debts of his father those incurred in legal costs. His financial problems were acute; indeed, the county historian Robert Thoroton records in his *Antiquities of Nottinghamshire* a heart-rending story about Gilbert's wife being forced to go into the fields to glean for corn, so far was the family reduced.[24]

In an attempt to stave off the inevitable, Gilbert Roos borrowed from Sir John Byron of Newstead on the security of property in Laxton and Kneesall. Salvation did not lie this way, however, and in 1618 he took what may have been the only realistic course left to him and sold the manor and parsonage of Laxton, together with all the family's other properties, to George Villiers, Marquess (and later Duke) of Buckingham, for £6,000.[25] With Gilbert Roos's death in 1621 a long line of lords of the manor to whom Laxton had descended by inheritance since the Conquest came to an end, although the Roos family remained – in reduced circumstances – in the village. For the historian the change of ownership had one major benefit; the records are voluminous from the early seventeenth century and they permit a much more detailed account of the village than is possible from the rather more sparse material before 1600.

---

[24] Robert Thoroton, *Antiquities of Nottinghamshire*, 3rd edn (ed.), J. Throsby (Nottingham, 1797), vol. III, p. 209.

[25] BL Egerton 3631, f. 100.

Chapter Two

Open-Field Farming

From earliest times the villagers of Laxton practised mixed farming. Crops were grown and animals were raised with the balance between these enterprises depending as much on fluctuating demand as on the particular qualities of the east Nottinghamshire claylands. The major aim was to ensure that the essential needs of each community were supplied from its own land. In the English Midlands the arrangements by which this was achieved have come to be known as the 'classic', or 'midland' open-field farming system in which the agricultural cycle was operated in common under the oversight of a court. The fields were subdivided, with each farmer having a number of unhedged strips widely scattered through them. Meadow was also shared. It was a flexible system; additional land could be taken into cultivation or arable could be converted to grass according to local population pressure or market prices. Good and bad soils were shared, as were the risks of harvest failure through crop disease or devastation. Individual strips could be exchanged to consolidate holdings, or subdivided to provide land for new farmers. The system was not without its faults: uncooperative neighbours meant problems for everyone; access to holdings was a cause of many disagreements; and the effort expended on reaching each strip, particularly those in the farthest corners of the great fields, was a constant source of annoyance. For all these shortcomings the system worked, which is why it lasted for hundreds of years in the Midlands. It was finally undermined by the need to respond to rising demand for the produce of the land and to do so by agricultural specialization. Only in Laxton does it now survive, and no understanding of the open fields today would be complete without an appreciation of changes which have taken place in the system and its day-by-day operation through time.

THE ORIGIN OF THE OPEN FIELDS

The origin of the open-field agricultural system in England has long been a matter of discussion and Laxton has been used as evidence in support of more than one theory. The threat to Laxton in 1926, for example, sparked off a more general debate on open fields in the correspondence columns of *The Times*, and the Orwins' book was designed as a major practical contribution to what had hitherto been a highly theoretical discussion. In its classic form, with two, three or four subdivided fields farmed in common, the fully fledged open-field system was not organized until relatively late in the Middle Ages. However, it was preceded at least as far back as the seventh century by a larger number of smaller systems centred on scattered hamlets rather than a single, centralized village.[1] The early documents give little away about how the system developed in Laxton and the landscape bears the imprint of so many generations of farmers that it is impossible to discover much from more than a thousand years ago. The first reliable and detailed information we have about the Laxton open fields is from a map and terrier prepared in 1635, by which time the system was not merely mature but even ageing. For earlier centuries we can do no more than fit what little we know about Laxton into a more general picture drawn on the basis of better-documented systems elsewhere.

When William the Conqueror's clerks compiled the great Domesday survey in 1086 Laxton was reported as having six plough teams. This would suggest a total arable area of about 720 acres (customary measure) possibly divided into two fields of roughly similar size, an East Field and a Mill Field, neither yet as large as it was to become by the early seventeenth century. There would also have been permanent meadow in the low-lying parts of what is today South Field. Much of the rest of the land between these fields and the meadow and the encircling woodland (still a characteristic feature of Laxton) would have been waste, occasionally 'assarted', or taken in for temporary cultivation, and heavily used for foraging, timber cutting and free-range grazing. It was also important as a reserve of land potentially available for cultivation.

Laxton village was the main but not necessarily the only settlement. Although not singled out for mention in the Domesday survey, the hamlet of Moorhouse may already have existed. Almost certainly there were once other farmsteads in the area which is now South Field; the field name 'Harwick Closes' contains the Old English *wic* which is a common term for settlement. This, and other independent hamlets or farms, may still have existed in 1086 surrounded by their arable, and an independent farm on the eastern side of South Field seems to have survived long after 1086. Eventually the inhabitants moved into the village or Moorhouse and the farmland was reorganized into the complex system which existed by 1635.

The extension of the arable land at the expense of waste and woodland took

---

[1] H. S. A. Fox, 'Approaches to the Adoption of the Midland System', in T. Rowley (ed.), *The Origins of Open-Field Agriculture* (1981), pp. 68–88; Joan Thirsk, 'The Common Fields', *Past and Present*, 29 (1964), 3–25, and 'The Origin of the Common Fields', *Past and Present*, 33 (1966), 142–7; J. Z. Titow, 'Medieval England and the Open Field System', *Past and Present*, 32 (1965), 86–102; Robert A. Dodgshon, *The Origins of British Field Systems* (1980).

place over a long period of time. Land would have been prepared for cultivation piecemeal, to suit the demand for food and as the numbers available to sow, weed and above all harvest, increased. Ideally each block of land cleared for cultivation – known as a furlong – would have been a standard size, designed to fit into the existing pattern of shared and subdivided fields. However, in the rolling terrain of the east Nottinghamshire plateau on which Laxton sits, steep-sided slopes ensured that neither furlong size nor shape could be anything but irregular. The most crucial consideration was that the furlongs, and the strips within them, should be orientated according to the lie of the land so that surface water could run off downhill in the furrows and the gutters between furlongs.

Doubtless the early medieval farmers would have had a sharp eye for variations in the quality of terrain and have picked out for initial clearance the areas most likely to produce the best arable soils. Furlong names may hint at such variations and at the sequence of clearance. 'Honey Holes' and 'Pudding Roods' indicate sticky, rather wet land, difficult to work. Names like 'Fenmoor' and 'Shortdoles' suggest land best used as meadow, too wet for cultivation but highly valued as capable of producing a good growth of grass that could be cut, dried and stored as hay for winter feed. This was essential if livestock and plough animals were to be over-wintered. Many of the meadow names are found in a band running across the parish between what today is the southern part of Mill Field and Moorhouse. By contrast, few moor, woodland or meadow names are to be found in what is now West Field and the northern part of Mill Field, which could indicate that these areas were cultivated at an early date. East Field, which has sometimes been considered the earliest arable field to be created, is particularly notable for moor and other names suggestive of second-rate soils.

Over centuries rather than decades, land at Laxton was cleared and divided into furlongs which in turn were incorporated within the farming system. The chronology is virtually impossible to reconstruct, but at some time in the Middle Ages existing fields, meadows and moors were organized into the open-field system. Almost certainly this took place against a background of population growth in the early Middle Ages which was countered by bringing into cultivation even some of the wettest parts of the fields. In Mill Field, 'Foulsyke' – boggy land, especially contaminated by sewage – was being cropped by 1326. Following the demographic disasters of the fourteenth century this poor land was allowed to revert back to grass. Similarly 'Frearfalls', a large area of grass closes on the western side of Mill Field, was arable land in 1326 but grass closes in 1635.[2]

On the west, south and east sides of the parish and around the castle to the

[2] Trevor Foulds, 'Laxton: Field Names as Evidence for the Ancient Landscape', *Nottinghamshire Historian*, 42 (1989), 4–11.

north of the main settlement, extensive tracts of land were held in closes. Usually these were areas of poorer soils, or else they were too distant from the village for arable culture to be economic. In 1635 the four open fields totalled 1,894 acres, and the surrounding closes 828 acres. Whether all or any of the closes had ever been within the boundaries of the open fields is unknown, but the acreage in closes increased over time as the open fields were reduced in size by enclosures. As we shall see, enclosures occurred in the seventeenth and eighteenth centuries as farmers sought extra grazing land but, as with Frearfalls in 1326, the process could be reversed. In the 1790s, and again in the twentieth century, closes have been ploughed to increase the arable acreage. Consequently the existence of extensive closes outside the open fields has enabled the farmers to alter the balance between arable and livestock depending on demand. This may well be part of the reason that farming conditions in Laxton seem never to have reached a point where enclosure was an economic necessity.

In Laxton today houses and farm buildings are almost exclusively in the village. Only a few eighteenth- and nineteenth-century farmsteads stand on their own land well away from the main settlement. Attached to each village farmstead and running back from the house is a close. These once contained orchards and were used for growing vegetables or for keeping animals overnight or at certain times of the year. At the far end of these closes ran a back lane which gave access from the rear. The present layout of the village certainly goes back to the early seventeenth century, corresponding almost exactly with the layout depicted on the map of 1635.[3] Surrounding the village were the open fields. Mill Field, at 833 acres the largest of the fields in 1635, is first documented in 1189, but it may have been in existence much earlier. West Field, known alternatively since 1857 as Top Field, was 418 acres, and South Field, known interchangeably as Bottom Field since the 1890s, was 508 acres. South Field may have been the last field to have been organized since it is not named in any document earlier than 1232. In the seventeenth century Laxton had a fourth field, East Field, of 135 acres. This was operated in conjunction with West Field until it was removed from the open-field system early in the present century. Each of the open fields was bounded by a hedge or fence, designed to prevent livestock from straying when the field was in fallow, but furlongs and strips within the fields were not distinguished in any clear way. A single, hedged strip which can be seen today in South Field, dates from the early nineteenth century.[4]

In theory (although we have no way of knowing whether it was the case in practice) each farmer would have held strips within each furlong in each field. The strips at Laxton were usually ploughed into ridges known as 'lands' (see

[3] See chapter 3.
[4] Bodleian Library, MS Top Notts c.2. References here and subsequently to the 1635 terrier are taken from the reproduction in *Open Fields*, pp. 199–318. A random check shows that the Orwins transcription is reliable.

PLATE 2.1 *View of Laxton from the north-west looking across West Field towards the village, with South Field in the background. The variegated pattern in the West Field reflects the different stages of cultivation on the individual strips. Running across the field in the foreground is Radbeck, one of the largest of the Laxton 'sykes'.*

below p. 51). Broad strips might have contained as many as five, seven or even more 'lands'. In 1635 Thomas Levers farmed 28 acres altogether and had five strips in West Field. Of these one had four 'lands', one had three 'lands', two had two 'lands' and one was a single 'land'. Thus in his five strips he had twelve 'lands', each of which would have been between 6 and 8 yards wide. Altogether, Levers had 37 'lands', of which 12 were in the West Field, 10 (in five strips) in the South Field, and fifteen (in nine strips) in the Mill Field. The size of each strip, like the acreage of each holding, changed over time. Amalgamation and subdivision of strips occurred as the result of demographic and economic changes. The old system of divided inheritance was designed to ensure that each son received a fair if not equal share of land in terms both of acreage and also quality and accessibility. The long-term result was fragmentation. Other factors, such as the reallocation of holdings and individual strips over time, attempts at consolidation, and the varying nature of the soil, have all contributed to the pattern of strips found at Laxton. Thomas Levers's strips in

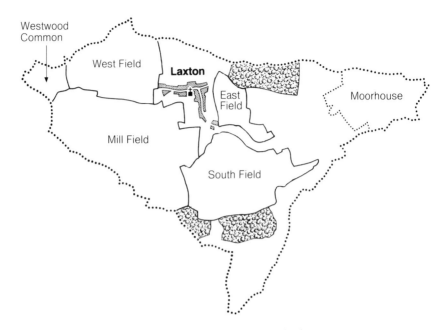

FIGURE 2.1 *Laxton, showing the open fields, c.1635*

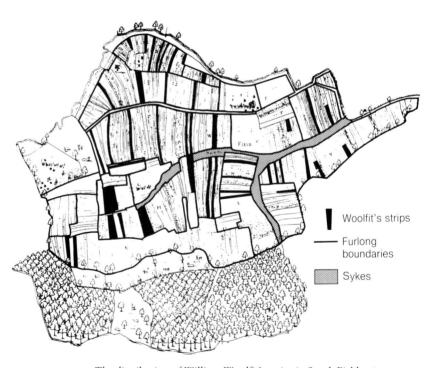

Woolfit's strips

Furlong boundaries

Sykes

FIGURE 2.2 *The distribution of William Woolfit's strips in South Field, 1635*

1635 included one of 1 rood 28 perches which was ploughed as a single 'land', and another of 1 rood 18 perches divided into four 'lands'. Today, under quite different circumstances and when all the strips are much larger to suit modern farming practices so that the variation is less marked, individual strips average 3.75 acres, but the smallest is less than one acre.

Since individual strips were unhedged, some sort of communal system of farming was unavoidable. As the expansion of arable reduced the amount of moor and waste available for grazing, the livestock had increasingly to be fed from the pasture resources of the open fields. These were considerable. In addition to odd corners of rough grass, they included after-harvest stubbles, the fallow field and the 85 acres of permanent grass in the low-lying, marshy areas known as sykes; indeed, while it is the rotation of the crops which is the best known part of open-field farming, the key to the entire system was the community's grazing requirements for its beasts. To allow free-range grazing on stubble and fallow, and to avoid the need for hurdles or fences, all the strips within a group of furlongs, if not the entire field, had to be sown and harvested in coordination. Moreover, the intricate and densely interlocking furlong and strip pattern of each field meant that access to each strip was difficult. Land was too valuable to be wasted and where furlongs met end on end, or where one furlong finished at right angles to another, the farmers agreed a permissible encroachment for turning the plough. The last $2\frac{1}{2}$ yards of abutting 'lands' came to be known as 'stintins' – areas on which either farmer might tread for the purpose of cultivating his own territory, carting manure and carrying away the harvest. It was not an ideal arrangement but it served a purpose.

Access was also gained via balks, uncultivated areas varying in width between a narrow path and a cart track, parcels of land known as headlands which were situated at the top and bottom of a furlong to give the plough team room to turn – and sykes. A heavy plough pulled by a team of oxen needed room to turn in order to go back along the 'land' and this was also why lands tended to be long and thin. In addition, the ploughman needed to approach the end of a strip at a slight angle in order to be able to turn his team within a reasonable space. This produced the reversed 'S' shape which characterized the cultivated strips, and which can still be seen at Laxton today despite the use of modern farming equipment. Turning in a syke was relatively straightforward, but half-balks, a term used frequently in the 1635 survey of Laxton, were banks formed when the narrow lands had to be ploughed obliquely to the contour. Some would have been quite small, and a few of them are still to be seen in the fields today.[5]

A communal system could function effectively only if some legal authority existed to control the activities of the individual farmers; the whole community needed to accept what was in practice a complex agricultural cycle and it was

5 Catherine Delano Smith, 'Laxton in 1635', *East Midland Geographer*, 7, 6 (1980), pp. 229–30.

vital that this should be carefully regulated so that scarce resources could be skilfully husbanded. Here the crucial role was played by the manor court, and this is what makes the survival of open-field farming unique. Other areas of open-field landscape survive in Lincolnshire, Cambridgeshire and Devon, but none are operated in the same way. Today the court meets annually in the Dovecote Inn, but this was not always so in the past. Until 1684 it met twice a year, in April and October, in keeping with medieval precedent. Occasionally, in modern times, it has failed to meet altogether, as in 1898 – when the chosen date clashed with rent day – and in 1917 and 1926. On a couple of occasions it has been postponed until after Christmas, as in 1915 and 1936, but under normal circumstances it has convened and still convenes in late November or early December. The powers exercised by the court have gradually declined. The right to adjudicate over minor social offences disappeared towards the end of the seventeenth century; the demand for fealty (a declaration of loyalty to the lord of the manor from an incoming tenant) was abolished in the nineteenth century; and under the Law of Property Act (1925) the court lost its authority over ditches and roads (although the dykes are still inspected annually by its officers). However, the court continues to control the cultivation of the open fields and even today much of its business is based on medieval precedent. Fortunately the jurisdiction of the court covered the whole parish and records have survived for most of the period since 1651.[6] From them we can gain a clear indication of how Laxton has been regulated through the centuries.

THE MANOR COURT

To appreciate the complexity of the open-field system we must first understand the role of the manor court, because this is not merely an integral part of the system but the key element. It was through the court that the day-to-day working arrangements were made, revised and enforced. 'Court' is used loosely here, since what developed was in effect a streamlined version of medieval practice with two courts rolled into one – the Court Baron, at which changes in the tenure of land were allowed and registered, and the Court Leet (view of frankpledge), at which communal manorial conduct was agreed upon. The lord of the manor may have been, and remains, in control through the Court Baron, but the extent of that control has always ben limited by the rules and

---

[6] These and subsequent references are from the court rolls. Presentment papers and court minutes have survived for most years since 1651. Those for the seventeenth and eighteenth centuries are in BL Egerton 3631, fos 131–226, and 3632, fos 1–246. Presentment papers continue in this collection to 1820, but from 1755 the court minutes are in NUMD Tallents Papers. Post-1820 presentment papers are also in this collection. The most recent court records are held by Hodgkinson and Tallents, Solicitors, of Newark. In what follows, individual references are usually given only to the Egerton Papers; those in the Tallents papers are normally identifiable by year.

regulations of the Court Leet. Constables, Poor Law officers and church-wardens are among those who have exercised jurisdictional powers in Laxton since the eighteenth century, and serious offences have been prosecuted in higher courts, but the viability of the open-field system has continued to depend on the farmers' recognition of the Court Leet's authority over the agricultural cycle.

By the seventeenth century it was unusual for lords of manors to attend their manor courts in person, but the legal standing of the court demanded the presence of the lord's steward, who presided over business. The task of calling the court fell to the bailiff or court crier, a man appointed by the lord of the manor, and responsible for collecting fines imposed by the court and for enforcing the rules of the open-field system. The Laxton manor court still requires the presence of these two officials today. They do not change often; in fact, since 1914 there have been only three bailiffs: John Dewick from 1914 until he resigned the post in 1936, 'Jack' Rose from 1936 until 1963 and his son Edmund Rose since then.

Today, business commences with the swearing in of a jury (known in the past as the homage) from among those present. Individuals have occasionally refused to serve, despite financial penalties. By contrast the death of Mr William Quibell was recorded in the jury minutes for 1883 'as a mark of sympathy' to show appreciation for his many years of jury service. The steward swears in the foreman of the field which is to be fallow (or nowadays in a forage crop) over the coming year, and then the twelve jurymen in three groups of four. Each man signifies his consent by kissing a copy of the New Testament. Women have never been on the jury, although female farmers are allowed to appoint representatives and in the early years of the nineteenth century Sarah Wright served as bailiff.[7]

Next, the bailiff 'calls over' the Suit Roll. All occupiers of land and property in Laxton are on the Suit Roll of the manor – a list of those who use common rights in Laxton and Moorhouse – and they are summoned to the court. It is usually only tenants of the open-field farms and one or two others with farming interests who attend. As a result numbers have fallen. In 1755 67 out of 90 people on the roll attended but numbers declined during the nineteenth century and in recent times have seldom exceeded fifteen to twenty. Women could, and often did attend; Martha Clark, Kezia Quibell, Jane Peatfield and Elizabeth Bagshaw were among the twenty-eight villagers present in 1881. Absentees are fined for 'default of suit of court', and 2p is paid by the bailiff for each of them.[8]

In the past the next task of the court was to appoint officers, first for Laxton

[7] NUMD Tallents Papers, 29 November 1813.

[8] A number of Suit Rolls of the manor court have survived among the court papers in NUMD Tallents Papers.

and then for Moorhouse. The open fields in Moorhouse were enclosed in 1860, but until then, with the exception of a bailiff, the hamlet had its own court officials. A bailiff was not required because the Moorhouse farmers attended the Laxton court. The most important court officer was the pinder. The job involved rounding up stray stock and driving them into the village pound or pinfold. The pinder was entitled to collect a fee when the offending farmer reclaimed his stock. For sheep the fees were doubled in 1843, from 2d to 4d for every score or part of a score – double for people living outside the village. Even so, in 1869 John Dixon offered his resignation as pinder on the grounds that the fees were insufficient. The pinder was subject to the jurisdiction of the court and in 1668 William Chadwick had to pay 1s 6d 'for not performing his office as being pinder'. Anyone attempting either to remove impounded stock from the pinfold without paying the fine, or to rescue his stock from the pinder while it was being driven to the pinfold, could also be fined. 'For taking his sheep from Moorhouse pinder' – in other words for removing them from the pinfold to which they had been conveyed as strays – without permission Edward Betney was fined 1s in 1679.[9] In modern times the posts of bailiff and pinder are combined because stray cattle are less of a problem, although the present holder of the post, Edmund Rose, can recall being woken at 2.30 a.m. in the morning to take charge of cattle wandering loose in the village.

Still in its role as a Court Baron, the next task of the court, until towards the end of the nineteenth century, was to admit new freeholders and tenants. Traditionally the Court Baron was concerned with copyhold property, but this form of tenure had disappeared in Laxton by 1650. Thereafter heirs succeeding to a freehold, purchasers of a freehold and tenants entering a holding under the lord, were expected to attend the court to swear 'fealty' to the lord, a traditional custom designed to show that they recognized the lord's authority within the manor and cemented by the payment of a fee of 3s 4d. This practice was abandoned only in 1890, when it was 'resolved that in future new tenants should not be required to do fealty'. Robert Shipton, one of the largest of the Laxton freeholders in 1635, died in the 1650s leaving no heir, and the property descended to a distant relation. At the April court in 1659 'Richard Shypton of Chelsea in the County of Middlesex, yeoman' was admitted by the court. Clearly Laxton was not to the new owner's taste and he decided to sell the property. The land was divided and in 1665 five people were admitted by the court as the new owners of what had previously been a single holding.[10] The number of admissions of this type varied through time. Between 1658 and 1700 the average was two a year, but between 1726 and 1731 they totalled 63, giving an average of five a year for the eighteenth century. By contrast, from

---

[9] BL Egerton 3631, fos 178, 204; 3632, f. 6.
[10] BL Egerton 3631, fos. 162, 187.

1801 until the ending of the practice in 1890 the yearly average was again between two and three.[11]

Finally the court considers presentments for offences committed within its jurisdiction. Today the Court Leet deals only with offences relating to the open fields and the presentments are all brought by the jury. In the past the range of powers was much wider. The Court Baron 'presented' serious social offenders to the Sheriff to be brought before Petty or Quarter Sessions, while the Court Leet dealt with minor breaches of the peace and enforced the law relating to the sale of bread and ale. Individuals were regularly fined 6d 'for breaking the assize of bread and ale'. The powers permitting the court to take action in cases of breach of the peace were still used in the seventeenth century. In 1651 Peter Roos, gent, was fined 12d 'for an affray upon Lawrence Bretton'. The following year John Cooke of Moorhouse was fined 3s 4d for 'making a fray upon Rebecka Pye of Moorhouse, widow'. In 1656 John Tompson and Francis Morton, both of Moorhouse, were each fined 3s 4d for making an affray upon each other, while in 1660 Leonard Browne was fined 6s 8d for 'making a fray in the alehouse'. Sadly the brevity of the entries means that the details of these offences are left to the imagination, although there is some evidence to suggest that violence among neighbours was more marked in the seventeenth century than in more recent times.[12]

Arising from its role in maintaining law and order, the Court Leet appointed the village constable and his two deputies (known as thirdboroughs) until 1754, and occasionally other village officers (including two overseers of the poor in 1659). In the course of the seventeenth and eighteenth centuries, however, social matters passed out of the court's hands, and by the 1720s the constable and the overseers of the poor and the highways were working under the jurisdiction of the parish vestry. On the other hand, the court was still empowered to act in cases where village life was threatened with disorder: in 1780 Joseph Pierce was presented 'for keeping a servant girl contrary to the laws of our court when she is likely to become chargeable to the parish and he has been admonished and told of the same by William Cocking, by order of the officers.' The fine was set at £1 19s 11d 'if he dont turn her away before old Michaelmas day next'.[13] Court bye-laws were periodically drawn up to aid the jury in its decision making, as in 1686, 1688, 1789 (revised 1821), 1871, 1908 and 1959. Among the regulations in 1789 was a bye-law that anyone caught stealing in the village should be punished 'as the law directs at the expense of the parish and the informer to have five shillings to be paid by the constable of the parish for the information'.[14] The powers may have passed away but the jury still wished to make clear its theoretical right to prosecute offenders.

---

[11] *Open Fields*, pp. 153–4.
[12] BL Egerton 3631, fos 131, 137, 152, 168; L. Stone, 'Interpersonal Violence in English Society, 1300–1840', *Past and Present*, 101 (1983), 22–33.
[13] BL Egerton 3632, f. 204.
[14] *Open Fields*, pp. 172–81.

To maintain order in the village the court also exercised powers over the roadways. Villagers were punished for damaging or obstructing the roads in some way. In 1652 Edward Allicock was fined 1s 'for not removing his wood out of the Townes Street' even after being ordered to do so at the previous court, and Robert Skaith was presented in 1662 'for laying wood in the town street in hindering the highway'. Considerable time was spent checking access to the open fields and making sure that drainage was as efficient as possible. Since stock were grazed on the fallow field, and on the other fields between harvest and sowing, there must also have been considerable movement of animals around the village. When the open fields were broken after harvest, for example, it is possible that anything up to 3,000 animals would be driven into the fields, and another substantial movement must have taken place around 23 November when horses, cattle and excess sheep were removed from the new fallow field prior to winter. The implications for wear and tear were considerable and it is hardly surprising that the lanes linking the village to the fields had to be broad and direct, hence the wide verges which still separate the modern roads from the adjoining fences.[15] Since the 1920s the main village roadways have been the responsibility of the County Council, but paths and access roads in the open fields are still the concern of the court.

Presentments for social offences were followed by presentments to the court for contempt. Sir Bryan Broughton, Lord Halifax and Edmund Hinde, gentleman, were all fined 2s 6d in 1683 for failure to attend and to do fealty. Such men were unlikely to appear in person before a village court; Halifax, who lived at Rufford, owned only a handful of acres in Laxton, and the Hindes, as we shall see, regarded themselves as above such matters. It is not even clear if they paid their fines! Fines were imposed on individuals who did not appear when summoned for jury service. In 1768 William Woolfit was fined 1s 6d 'for not attending the Jury when public notice was given', and Francis White was fined 5s in 1820 'for not attending upon the Jury'.[16] Fines of this nature seem to have become more common as the nineteenth century progressed. Samuel Pinder, butcher, was fined 5s in 1824, and in 1828 he, Benjamin Rose and John Wombell were each fined 5s. Some offenders were unrepentant. Seth Cole, a publican-farmer in Moorhouse, was fined 4s for non-attendance in 1843, 5s in 1844, and 2s in 1846. He seems later to have changed his ways and he was sworn in as a juryman at the 1856 court and later served as overseer of the poor.

The court has powers to waive fines when good cause is shown. In 1850 Thomas Bagshaw was excused a fine imposed the previous year and John Cree was let off a 2s 6d non-attendance fine in 1915 and excused future attendance

---

[15] BL Egerton 3631, f. 176; J. A. J. Gell, 'Laxton – Network Analysis of an Open-field Parish', unpublished BA dissertation, University of Nottingham, 1977, pp. 21–8.

[16] BL Egerton 3632, f. 245.

at the court on account of his delicate health. On the other hand late attendance at court was unacceptable; William Johnson's 5s fine in 1868 seems to have stood, even though the record is endorsed 'arrived at 12.20'. Leaving the court before business was completed could constitute an offence; John Hopkin was fined 5s in 1741 'for departing from the Court in contempt thereof', while in 1909 George Newboult was fined 2s 6d 'for not staying till business was over'. Finally, questioning the rights of the court was an offence, hence the fine of no less than 39s imposed on Thomas Shipton in 1654 'for saying the jury was foresworn', and 6d four years later on Robert Shipton 'for privately hearkening the jury when they was about the court matters being not allowed by them'.[17]

The most important presentments, and the ones which are still brought today, relate to offences committed in the open fields. To understand these properly some account is needed of the Laxton jury system. A new jury is sworn in each year at the manor court, consisting of twelve men, chosen from among

PLATE 2.2 *The jury setting off to inspect the open fields, late 1950s. Left to right, back row: Ernie Kent, Wilf Rayner, Jack Cree, J. F. Hoare (Ministry of Agriculture agent), Sidney Johnson, Wilf Saddington, and Oliver Laughton (driving tractor); front row, George Woolhouse, Rev. Richard Camenisch, Ted Sayer (partly hidden), Jack Rose, Reg Rose, Jimmy Price. Ernie Kent, Ted Sayer and Reg Rose still farm in the village today.*

[17] BL Egerton 3632, f. 173; 3631, fos 143, 160.

villagers named on the Suit Roll, and a foreman. Traditionally, the foreman was elected by the jury, but today three farmers hold the office in rotation (one for each of the three fields). Together with the bailiff they are responsible for organizing any necessary work in the open fields, including the maintenance of roads, gates and ditches. However, the jury sworn in at the court early in December is for the *following* year. Its terms of reference relate to the field currently in fallow (or nowadays a forage crop) and due to become the winter wheat field in the next cycle. Consequently the main business of each court sitting is to deal with presentments brought by a jury sworn in twelve months earlier. The duties of the jury end after the court has met. An obvious problem arising as a result of this system is that since the court appoints a jury with the specific role of looking after a particular field, rather than the manor as a whole, separate arrangements are needed to ensure that offences elsewhere are observed and reported. Nowadays this is not regarded as a serious problem, but in the past the court appointed burleymen to report incidental offences. They were occasionally presented for failing to carry out their duties.[18]

Although offences during the year are reported to the jury, its major task occurs a few days before the court is due to meet. On what is called Jury Day, usually a week or so before the date fixed for the court, the outgoing jury inspects its field. By this time, following its year in fallow, the field has been ploughed and sown. The jurors assemble in the yard of the Dovecote Inn at 10.30 a.m. Two of the twelve are detailed to walk the dykes and the rest are taken – nowadays on a tractor and trailer provided by the field foreman – to the field. There they check boundary markers, replace any stones or stakes that have been moved, look for any ploughing encroachments into roads and sykes, and ensure that the rules relating to the maintenance of fences, hedges, gates and ditches have been observed. Stakes are hammered in to mark the boundaries between the strips and the edges of the sykes and roadways.

Great care is taken to check that farmers have not ploughed into the pathways which provide access to the open fields. At the 1935 court questions were raised about the proper width of these tracks and it was suggested that steps needed to be taken to lay down the rights and obligations of the occupiers. The Thoresby agent walked the grassways with the three foremen in June 1936, as a result of which it was decided to stake out all the access routes in each of the fields that year. Roadways were to be 15 feet in width and the foremen were instructed to be stricter about encroachments in the future. Since then, fines for over ploughing have been common and today the roadway widths are carefully checked with a tape measure to forestall dissension.

The inspection over, the jurors return to the Dovecote Inn. Lunch is provided, partly paid for from the proceeds of fines levied at the previous year's court. Since in the past this was never sufficient to provide suitable fare for the

---

[18] BL Egerton 3632, f. 101.

jurymen the Thoresby estate normally made an additional contribution. After lunch the jurymen discuss the level of fines to be recommended for the offences they have noted. Their decisions are recorded on the 'Presentment Paper'. Today the whole business is more of a social occasion than a formal meeting, but this was not necessarily so in the past. At the beginning of the century when John Bagshaw of Town End Farm was one of the foremen, he always ordered everyone except the jurors from the room before business commenced, and all decisions were taken in confidence.[19]

The offences themselves often seem petty when discussed today, but they are still punishable. This is seen as a means of reinforcing the social discipline necessary to run the open-field system. The stakes define the layout of the field until it is next inspected in three years time. Today they often disappear in the interval, but in the past it was a serious offence to remove them. Edward Herren was fined 10s in 1708 'for taking up the mearstone [the precedessors of today's stakes] the jury had set down'.[20] Fines are still regularly levied for ploughing into the sykes and common balks, or for encroaching on a neighbour's 'land'. Failure to clear up loose earth, lime or manure is also liable to incur a penalty, particularly since the 1730s because of the need to keep the sykes clear for mowing. In 1968 Reg Rose of Bottom Farm was fined the relatively substantial sum of 30s for depositing manure on Long Syke in the South Field.

Where 'lands' abut a road and where boundary hedges come down to a road on either side, as between West and Mill Fields, fences have to be maintained. Failure to look after hedges and fences, or even leaving open a gate, can incur a fine. In 1653 Becki Pye and John Cooke were fined two shillings 'for not locking up their gates in the corn field', while John Edmundson incurred a one shilling fine 'for breaking William Kirklies hedge and throwing in the ditch in Brockley's Close'.[21] Dykes and streams also have to be kept clean. After the court appointed two jurors to inspect all sewers and watercourses in 1860, eleven individuals were fined, and when Robert Weatherall objected to his 9d fine it was increased by 4s 6d. These inspections were regularly repeated.

Farmers presented before the court today are usually fined for a single misdemeanour but multiple offenders were not unknown in the past. John White was fined a total of £1 1s 6d in 1760 for 'removing the stakes belonging to the commons (10s) [. . .] ploughing up the commons (5s) [. . .] for going over Mr Doncaster's Ingar and Newdikes (5s) [. . .] [and] for not paying the jury's fees (1s 6d)'.[22] Although today's farmers have an interest in maintaining the system where their predecessors often sought to gain advantages, fines are still levied,

[19] *Ex inf.* Ron Cree.
[20] BL Egerton 3632, f. 97.
[21] BL Egerton 3631, f. 141.
[22] BL Egerton 3632, f. 197.

usually of fifty pence or a pound, occasionally rising to £5 for a more serious misdemeanour. Half the fines go to the lord of the manor, the rest towards the cost of the following year's jury lunch.

Finally, how did the court enforce its decisions? It is tempting to see the court as a village democracy, particularly as it was clearly no respecter of persons – the Duke of Portland was fined in 1887 'for leading soil off the common', and in 1915 the lord of the manor himself suffered the indignity of being fined £1 by a manor court in his own jurisdiction, because one of his employees had put soil and stones in Radbeck Syke. Earl Manvers's agent, R. W. Wordsworth, paid the fine and solemnly recorded the fact in the estate accounts. However, it would be misleading to read too much into such entries in the records. The court depended for its legal authority on the lord of the manor. Quite apart from appointing the steward and the bailiff, the lord could instruct the court about its duties. In 1884 a letter was read from Wordsworth, to the effect that since Manvers had undertaken to clean and enlarge Cundy Rood Dyke, running from the South Field into Moorhouse, it was now the duty of the jury to ensure its upkeep. The lord of the manor's help also had to be invoked when trouble occurred. In 1680, as we shall see, it was to the lord of the manor that the villagers appealed when the jury inadvertently signed away to Moorhouse rights of common to which the smaller settlement had not previously had access.

Towards the end of the nineteenth century the court was increasingly held in contempt by offenders who refused to pay their fines. Why this was so is not known, although some farmers probably resented being subject to an anti-quated system of obligation, particularly those with little or no land in the open fields. The court officers sought help from the lord of the manor (in the person of R. W. Wordsworth). In 1891 John Frow was fined 2s 6d for failing to clean out his meadow dykes and when this was still outstanding two years later and he refused to pay 'the default was reported to Mr Wordsworth who undertook to obtain payment.' Six years later, in 1899, Frow was found by the jury to have committed a trespass. This time he wrote to the court saying that he could not attend due to a prior commitment at Mansfield, that in any case he was not guilty and that he would not pay the fine. Four months after the court met he paid the ten shilling fine, not because he accepted the jurisdiction of the court but 'as Mr Wordsworth wishes it to be so although it is not just and not pleasant'.

Nor have things changed greatly in the twentieth century. George Saxelby's fine of one guinea in 1927 was eventually remitted, but not until the steward had commented that 'he is a difficult man to deal with and it will not be easy to extract £1 1s from him.' The Thoresby agent commented in 1936 that 'the trouble at Laxton is, that sometimes fines are ignored and not paid. I think it would be a good plan in future, for a list of all fines not paid to be sent to this office [Thoresby] and I would then put pressure on the offenders to pay the fines.'[23] Refusal has continued to be a problem, despite the efforts of the court's officers. On the very day that Horace Hennell refused to pay a fine in 1951 the steward sent him a letter pointing out that it was his duty to pay. Nowadays the system depends on good will and fines have been halved or reduced to avoid trouble, but this has not prevented lively debates at the court – despite the relative smallness of the sums assessed.

THE COMMONS

An important subject on which the court had to pass judgment was the question of common rights. Here a distinction needs to be made between common grazing rights in the open fields, and areas of land known as the commons. The latter were the remnants of former wastes after open fields and enclosures had been taken in, and until recently Laxton had two major areas of common grazing: Westwood Common (also known as Cocking Moor), which is about 80 acres; and the much smaller East (or Town) Moor Common. Rights in the commons were traditionally reserved for inhabitants of the village who occupied little more than a house and close and probably did not have land in the open fields. There are 104 such rights, each one attached to a 'toft' in the village. Toftholders using their rights had to conform to rules laid down by the court. Individuals fined for failing to ring their swine before turning them out on the commons included Rebecca Pye in 1658, and the earliest bye-laws of which a record survives (1686) include a clause requiring everyone to ring their swine on penalty of 3s 4d. Others were fined for failing to look after the commons. Rowland Dickinson was fined 6d in 1662 'for not felling his part of thistles in the Town Moor'.[24]

Those people with toft rights were permitted to graze animals on the commons on the general principle that they did not keep more during the summer than they could support through the winter. This did not stop people trying. Those caught were fined. Francis Roos was fined six shillings in 1667 'for overcharging the commons with his sheep having more in summer than he maintains in winter'.[25] In the course of time the problem grew. By 1870 a number of toftholders with little land in the village were abusing the system. In the words of John Horncastle, the Thoresby agent, they had acquired 'the habit of procuring large quantities of sheep merely for the purpose of turning on the Commons during the season, to the great injury and almost exclusion of other toft holders who have larger quantities of land, and keep a regular flock of sheep the year through'. This led to overstocking, and hungry sheep were

[23] NUMD Ma 2C/183/610.
[24] BL Egerton 3631, fos 160, 176; *Open Fields*, p. 158.
[25] BL Egerton 3631, f. 198.

breaking through the fences in search of food. Several of the toft owners decided that the time had come to take action to limit the use of the commons, both because overstocking was reducing their value, and also because of ill feeling in the village resulting from these sharp practices.[26] A meeting was convened at the beginning of March 1871 to discuss the future of commons and the more general issue of grazing rights in the open fields.

Grazing rights in the open fields were also controversial. The first documented dispute followed a meeting of the manor court in October 1680 which discussed the rights of Moorhouse farmers to the common grazing in Laxton. At that court an agreement was drawn up by William Scrimshaw, the steward, Francis Green, the bailiff, and Mr Augustine Hinde, the major landowner in Moorhouse. The jurymen were told to sign the agreement, which they did 'out of fear of Mr Hinde', even though they had not been acquainted with the details. Within hours they were appalled to find what they had done, and John Roos was asked to petition the lord (or in this case lady) of the manor, asking her to overturn the agreement because Hinde had mistakenly been granted 'right of common in our best field without limitation'. The details of this agreement are shrouded in mystery. Roos argued that Green, the bailiff, had connived in what was a breach of the known rules, 'and not only the jury (except Moorhouse men) but 19 parts of 20 of the whole town are much grieved now they understand the contents of the agreement'. Green was quick to defend himself and to take the side of the Laxton men, and after depositions had been taken from tenants and freeholders with long memories of the village it was clear to Green 'that Moorhouse has no right of common with Laxton'. While some Moorhouse men had a right of common in Laxton as a result of holding land there others did not. As for Mr Hinde, who had caused the trouble in the first place, 'we think has had the worst case of them all for his farm in Moorhouse can pretend to no more right of common with Laxton than any other farm there'. The jurors also swore an affidavit to the effect that they had been forced to set their hands to a document with many inaccuracies in it, and finally the lord of the manor accepted the case and declared the agreement invalid.[27] It was not, however, the only occasion that the men of Laxton and Moorhouse clashed over such rights.

The commons, and more generally common rights, were the subjects for discussion at the meeting in March 1871. The vicar took the chair and Horncastle attended on behalf of Manvers. Others present were twelve farmers, five freeholders, three freeholder/farmers, the miller, the butcher, the tailor and six cottagers. First, it was resolved that 'the quantity of stock turned out on the commons should be limited.' The principle established, it was up to the meeting to decide the terms and conditions of future limitations. William Pinder

[26] NUMD MaB/217/46.
[27] NUMD MaB/201/1,3,5.

proposed a motion, which was carried, that no toft owner in the village should turn out on the commons at one time before the breaking of the open fields more than twenty sheep. Individuals with such rights were permitted to graze twenty sheep or an agreed equivalent in beasts or horses.

The meeting then turned to the subject of common grazing rights. It was agreed that from the time animals were allowed into the wheat field after it had been harvested the number of horses, cattle and sheep on the commons should be unlimited until October 15, or 28 days after the field was opened for stubble grazing, whichever was the earliest. Similar rules applied for the spring corn field except that unlimited stock could remain on the field until 23 November, at which date the limit of twenty sheep for each toft owner was to recommence. The same pasturing rules were to apply to the summer fallow field as for the commons, until 8 October each year, after which stock could be transferred to the field which was to become fallow during the following season. The meeting also agreed that no sheep should be allowed on the commons and into the fields unless they had been dressed, as a preventive for scab, and that every sheep turned out was to be dressed before the breaking of the fields. No ram was to be allowed to run in the open fields from their breaking until 15 October. It was agreed to publish the new rules, and to circulate copies to each toftholder. A committee of six was appointed with powers to enforce the rules by presenting offenders at the court.[28]

It was only a matter of time, however, before common rights again became a problem. With an increasing number of cattle being kept in the village by the end of the nineteenth century, as farmers sought to find a way of making a living when arable prices were falling, friction was almost inevitable. The Thoresby agent was accused of abusing the system in 1879 when he let a common right to Mr Merrils, junior. Laxton's freeholders complained that a man ought to live in the house on a particular toft in order to exercise a right of common. The agent responded that it was not the cottage or house which gave the right, but the land belonging to it or on which it had once stood. He dismissed the freeholder's argument on the grounds that it implied that 'a person however many Common Rights he possessed could never exercise more than one.' In Horncastle's view, while ever a person possessed premises (either as owner or tenant), he or she was entitled to enjoy the benefits of a common right. Despite Horncastle's vehemence on the subject he seems to have stepped outside the existing rules, since it had been agreed in 1871 that each toftholder should be permitted to exercise rights for one toft only, however many they might possess.

The new rules also assumed that the 104 holders of rights in the common enjoyed pasturage in the open fields at certain times of the year. Horncastle took exception to this regulation: 'Common Right owners must stick to their

[28] NAO PR 4093, 4095; *Open Fields*, pp. 178–9.

Commons. I shall object to any one (whether a tenant of Earl Manvers or not) exercising any right as to stocking these open fields unless he is an occupier of land.' Wordsworth, who became the agent in 1883, took a more lenient view of the situation and it was not until the opening decade of the twentieth century that common rights again became a source of controversy. Wordsworth called a meeting in April 1907 'to discuss the question of what Commons should be let out at the annual letting', and to consider 'a number of complaints made to me with regard to the exercise of common rights'.[29] To the vicar he wrote in more forthright terms: 'The rules drawn up in March 1871 at a vestry meeting held in the school have been reduced to a farce, and we must try to come to some better understanding, satisfactory to all freeholders, and see that it is stuck to.'[30] He argued that the original right to graze the two commons had been reserved to the toftholders, or those with no other land to pasture, and

1. The open Fields are to be grazed by Earl Manvers' Tenants only. No Tenant, who has no unenclosed land, is to be allowed to turn any stock into the Fields.

2. A Tenant, whose holding does not exceed a total of 40 acres, may turn into the open Fields under the following regulations, though he may not have unenclosed land in *each* of the three Fields. Tenants holding over 40 acres can only turn into the Fields in which they have unenclosed land.

3. The Fields are to be stocked as follows :—

    (a) **The Wheat Field.**—Unlimited stock from the breaking up of the Field to the 15th October in the same year.

    (b) **The Bean and Clover Field.**—Unlimited stock from the breaking up of the Field to the 23rd November in the same year.

    (c) **The Fallow Field.**— From the 23rd November in one year to the 8th October in the following year, twenty Sheep by each Tenant. No Cattle or Horses to be allowed in this Field during the time named.

4. All stock so turned in to be the bonâ fide property of the Tenant, and no joist stock to be allowed under any circumstances. Anyone transgressing this Rule will be liable to be fined by the Jury.

5. No Sheep to be turned into the open Fields until they have been properly dressed, such dressing to be done before they are turned in.

6. No tup to be turned in to the open Fields before the 15th October, or to be allowed to remain there later than the 23rd December, in any year.

7. The Foremen of the Juries, and the Parish Pinder, are to see that these Rules are carried out, and are to report anyone breaking them to the Thoresby Estate Office at once, and anyone so reported may, after one caution, be given notice to quit his Farm.

Lord Manvers appeals to his Tenants, in their common interests, to help him and the Foremen of the Juries to carry out the above. He asks them specially to be careful to shut the Gates on the Commons when passing through them, and also the Gates on the lands which he has lately inclosed.

R. W. WORDSWORTH,

AGENT FOR EARL MANVERS.

Estate Office, Thoresby Park,

April, 1908.

PLATE 2.3 *Rules and Regulations for Grazing Laxton Open Fields, 1908. The right to common grazing in the open fields was contended from the 1870s onwards, and finally settled only by the new regulations issued from Thoresby in April 1908. Since Earl Manvers now owned all the land in the open fields, he was able to introduce and enforce regulations which excluded cottagers (with rights to use Westwood Common) from grazing their animals in the fields. The regulations were printed and circulated to all the Laxton tenants.*

[29] NUMD MaB/193/17, Ma 2C/162/535.
[30] NUMD Ma 2C/162/538.

their grazing was regulated under the terms drawn up in 1871. Gaits, or the right to turn out stock on the open fields, had been reserved to those with land in the fields. This excluded both the smaller tenants or freeholders with no strips, and the few tenants of enclosed farms who had no gaits. Some freeholders with common rights, but no land in the fields, had taken to turning unlimited stock into the fields, a right which he did not accept: 'I maintain that a common right is confined to the commons, and that the open fields, which are now wholly Lord Manvers', form no part of the common right.'[31] People possessing no rights had been putting stock both on the commons and in the open fields, and the 1871 regulations were not being observed.

It was clearly time for an authoritative judgement but when counsel's opinion was taken the result was not particularly satisfactory. He found that no one without land in the open fields had any right to turn stock into them. This was Wordsworth's line of argument, but in law the decision was said to be not very firmly based.[32] After further discussion a new agreement was finalized in April 1908. The common lands in the village were defined. A distinction was drawn between the two commons (Westwood and East Moor) and other common lands (22 acres) which were let on an annual basis. The proceeds of the lettings were divided between the 104 owners of common rights, Earl Manvers (97), and the freeholders J. Bagshaw (3), the vicar, G. Bagshaw, S. Bartle and W. G. Quibell, one each. The Bagshaws, Bartle, Quibell and the vicar also had the right to turn animals on to East Moor Common between 1 May and 15 November each year. Only Lord Manvers's tenants were permitted to turn stock into the open fields (because he owned all the land in the open fields).

Some of these rules were slightly amended before the regulations came into force. Tenants with more than 40 acres could graze only the open fields in which they had a strip or strips, but those with less than 40 acres could turn out stock into each field as long as they had at least one strip. The rule was changed in 1958 when it was agreed that unlimited stock could stay in the wheat field until 20 October or an earlier date if the season permitted. By 1967 demand for common grazing in the open fields had almost entirely disappeared.

In regard to Westwood Common it was agreed that Lord Manvers should be able to offer his rights first to his smaller tenants with no land in the open fields, but in the event of their declining to exercise them, to tenants with open-field land. An agreement signed by the freeholders a year earlier in regard to the commons was torn up, and the juries of the several fields, in conjunction with the pinder, were empowered to see that the rules were obeyed.[33]

Since 1908 the commons, and common rights in general (although these will

---

[31] NUMD Ma 2C/162/542.
[32] NUMD Ma 2C/162/576.
[33] *Open Fields*, pp. 180–1; NUMD Ma 5E/148.

be discussed in more detail below) have become less important to the Laxton economy. The reservation of the commons to toftholders permitted the survival of landless cottagers in the village into the twentieth century – a point of some significance in any consideration of the advantages and disadvantages to Laxton from the failure to enclose. By the 1920s the smallholders were fewer in number and, coupled with a relaxation of pressure on grazing land as the acreage in permanent pasture increased, demand for the commons began to slacken. John Cree, of Old Vicarage Farm, used to put animals on Westwood Common, but by the 1930s drivers were increasingly inclined to leave open the gates that enclosed the commons as they motored through the village. Not surprisingly animals escaped, but rather than lay cattle grids the villagers abandoned the common and by 1939 few animals were being grazed. In 1941 the common was requisitioned for cropping.

When the County Agricultural Committee was ready to return the common at the end of the 1949 harvest, Lord Manvers almost immediately began to take steps to enclose it and to extinguish the remaining common rights. A meeting was held in the village in May 1950, when it was pointed out that while it was requisitioned the land had produced quite good crops. On this basis the Minister of Agriculture, who was responsible for the requisitioning, took the view that the common should continue in arable despite the fact that under the terms of the original agreement in 1941 the Ministry had agreed to seed the common with grass before giving it up. After a long debate and much correspondence it was finally agreed that Lord Manvers should be empowered to buy out the freeholders, close the commons, and allocate the land to farms which the estate was retaining. On 9 June 1950 Manvers agreed to pay £30 for each of the six common rights he did not already own. Manvers retained ownership of the common when he sold the manor to the Ministry of Agriculture in 1952, but it was not until early in 1953 that he acquired all 104 rights, and advertisements were placed in a number of newspapers to the effect that the common was to be closed. Shortly afterwards the land was added to Westwood and Crosshill Farms, and today it is all part of Westwood Farm. The sight of oil seed rape growing on what was once Westwood Common is a reminder of how some parts of the Laxton agricultural cycle have changed out of all recognition.[34]

East Moor Common retains the features of common land. Eight grazing rights are attached to specific properties within the village. The tenants of these holdings have the right to graze an animal on the common between 1 May and 23 November each year. However, the Court Leet in 1935 accepted that it had no right to impose fines for stocking the common beyond the proper date because it was effectively outside the jurisdiction of the open-field system after 1908.

[34] NUMD Ma 3E/2218–65; Acc. 508 Meeting 31 May 1950; C. M. Fordham to A. Cowdry, 21 June 1951.

THE FARMING YEAR

Perhaps the most vital role of the court has been to oversee the farming year. Any study of an open-field village must assume some appreciation of the agricultural cycle. Considerable changes have taken place over the centuries and there is a natural tendency to focus on the annual round of labour in more recent times, or, at least, the period before the great technical changes of the past few decades. Laxton today preserves traditions which may derive from the beginnings of open-field farming, and in what follows we are trying to describe the cycle through the eyes of present day participants while contrasting their testimony with documentary evidence of what happened in the past. The aim is to give an indication of what the farmers are doing at any given point in the year. We have three main guides: Edith Hickson, who lived in Laxton at the end of the nineteenth century; Ron Cree, who farmed in the village from the late 1920s until the 1970s; and Annie Cree, a farmer's wife in Laxton for nearly forty years.[35] Their testimonies, together with evidence drawn from a variety of documentary sources and from a number of other individuals, enable us to piece together a picture of the sequence of events in the farming year which have continued year in and year out in approximately the same form for centuries.

Today's Laxton farmers till the soil and (most) keep some animals. The rent is paid, and the farmer's profit is taken, from the sale of wheat and of the animals and their products. Consequently each farmer has always had to keep a delicate balance between looking after the health and welfare of his cattle, sheep, pigs and poultry, and cultivating his fields. So every day provides a variety of activities.

The day starts early for a Laxton farmer. When Edith Hickson lived on her father's farm (Bar Farm) between 1893 and 1903 the working day began sometime after 4 a.m. when the cows and horses were fetched into the farmyard. The cows had to be milked (by hand) and fed, and the horses prepared for the day's work, by 6 a.m. The hours had slackened a little by the time Ron Cree started working in Laxton for his father, John Cree, at Old Vicarage Farm in 1924. Their farm was 101 acres. Four years after Ron Cree began work his father was offered the tenancy of Step Farm, to be worked in conjunction with Old Vicarage Farm. John Cree's eldest son (Ron's brother), also John Cree, who had started life in farm service, came home to break some horses in, and he agreed to take Step Farm. The father died two days before John Cree took over Step Farm, effectively leaving his two sons, John and Ron (the latter at only 17) to run the farms. Ron Cree's 101 acres included ten strips in the open

---

[35] *Life at Laxton.* Interviews with Mr Ron Cree, 25 May 1988, and Mrs Annie Cree, 2 June 1988.

fields – three in West Field, three in Mill Field (of which he was foreman for a dozen years) and two in South Field – and a number of enclosures. He also had two strips in enclosed areas, which were still worked as strips but no longer subject to the court. Other parts of his land were in grass. In the south of the village beyond Brockilow he had 36 acres of grass, and since water was laid on he could put his cattle out there to graze.

When Ron Cree first started to farm the day began at 6 a.m. when the horses and cows were fetched. The cows were milked and returned to the fields in time for breakfast at 8 a.m. After breakfast the horses would be in harness ready to pull the plough or any other appropriate gear to one of the strips. Ron Cree had thee horses, of which two were used in ploughing. One might be in foal, and it was only during the busy summer months when the binder was in operation that he needed all three in harness. There would be a short break about 11 a.m. for bread, cheese and beer, or in Ron Cree's case a jam pasty and cold tea (no sugar or milk). Work continued until about 2 p.m., which was theoretically the time needed to plough an acre. The farmers and their hired hands then retraced their footsteps back to the village in time for their dinner. After the meal the horses would be fed and turned out into the fields (or into the stable in winter), the plough would be cleaned, the animals would be fed, and the cows would be milked. Work ended for the day at about 6 p.m.

In winter, working days tended to be rather shorter to fit in with daylight hours, and in summer, particularly during haytime and harvest, they were usually longer, sometimes extending from dawn to dusk. The animals might be taken out into the fields early in order to enjoy the coolest hours of the day, and because the men stayed longer in the fields either they took their dinner with them or their wives brought it out to them so that no time was lost. Ron Cree's sister-in-law, Annie Cree (née Moody) married John Cree of Step Farm in 1929. She would carry a cooked meal out to her husband even, in her younger days, while pushing a pram. The meal eaten she would take the dirty plates and cutlery back to the house, and then make a second journey to the field with tea, which she carried in a milk can. Summer and winter alike it was a six day week, and if Sunday was the day of rest the cows still had to be milked and the animals tended. Ron Cree recalls that on Sundays and holidays such as Christmas Day it was normal to keep work to a minimum and to have a rest in the early afternoon. Such days were few and far between because the business of making a living demanded long hours of routine manual labour, which went on day in and day out with little change.

On each farm the proportion of crops to animals varied. John Cree at Step Farm had about twelve cows in the early 1930s but no sheep. Ron Cree had both. Usually he had five or six milking cows, which, in the days before machinery, was about as many as could comfortably be milked morning and evening by hand, leaving time for the rest of the business of the farm. He had twenty ewes to run in the fallow field through the winter. He would expect them to produce thirty lambs or so. A few would be kept to replace the flock while some of the older ones were taken to market. Both older ewes and lambs would be sold at Retford Fair on 2 October. In return it was possible to buy a ram which would be put to the ewes. Lambing began in late February, and the sheep were sheared in May. Before shearing they were washed. The sheep-wash was on the village stream where the water was damned to form a wash stead and the reluctant sheep were passed through it to clean their fleeces and their bodies. They were then sheared with sharp-pointed shears, which were later replaced by mechanical clippers which did the job both more quickly and more neatly. The fleeces were taken to the wool sales at Retford. Bullocks were sold at Retford and Newark Fairs. Ron Cree always had a pig or two and usually about 100 chickens. He would buy the latter in February and keep them until they had finished laying, about eighteen months later.

The rotation of crops in the great open fields, perhaps the most familiar aspect of the system, was designed partly to maintain the fertility of the soil, partly to clean the land and partly to provide additional grazing for the animals. By tracing the agricultural cycle from one summer to the next we can see how the rotation operated, in a cycle which has changed only marginally since the seventeenth century (table 2.1).

TABLE 2.1 *The rotation of the open fields in Laxton*

Cycle Year	Winter-sown corn	Spring-sown crops	Fallow (grass)
One	South	Mill	West
Two	West	South	Mill
Three	Mill	West	South

The first major event of the agricultural year was haymaking, which began in June and lasted for three to four weeks (table 2.2). The hay crop was vital to the village economy because, in the absence of turnips and clover, it provided the essential winter feed for the animals. The best hay was cut in June since by July it was going to seed and the animals did not like it as well. The grass was laid in swathes on the ground with a scythe and then left for a day or two before being turned by hand. When it was dry it was raked into cocks and carted home to the stackyard to build a rick ready for winter use. Eventually the scythe was replaced by a grass cutter, which would be pulled by two horses. Everyone joined in at haymaking whether cutting or turning the hay. The children would help to make the cocks, and on at least one occasion a Sunday School treat was cancelled to ensure that they were able to continue with the work.[36]

---

[36] *Life at Laxton*, p. 14.

Key:

⬛ Winter sown corn, usually wheat.

▨ Spring sown crops, barley, peas, beans etc.

☐ Fallow (or, today, a forage crop)

West Field   Laxton   East Field

Mill Field   South Field

Year one

West Field   Laxton   East Field

Mill Field   South Field

Year two

West Field   Laxton   East Field

Mill Field   South Field

Year three

FIGURE 2.3 *The rotation of crops through the open fields*

TABLE 2.2 *The Laxton farming cycle*

Date	Event
Late June	Haymaking
Late June/early July	Letting of the gaits and commons by auction (syke grass)
6 July	All animals to be cleared from sykes (before 1730)
10 July–1 August	Mowing of the sykes (since 1730)
1 August	Haymaking in the meadows completed and meadows opened for grazing (before 1730)
August	Beginning of harvest – winter corn field harvested
Late August/early September	Winter corn field 'broken' – stock allowed to graze the stubbles. Farmers begin harvesting spring corn field
15 October	Spring corn field 'broken' – stock moved from wheat field to graze stubbles
October/November	Fallow field ploughed, harrowed and sown with winter corn
1 November	Meadows closed (before 1730)
23 November	All animals to leave open fields, except 20 sheep per farmer on the fallow field
Late November	Jury Day – new wheat field inspected and restaked
Early December	Court Leet held
21 December	Syke grasses paid for (since 1730)
November/December	Preparation of new spring corn field for planting in following spring
March	Spring corn field sown
April	Stock turned out into sykes (before 1730) and closes
Spring	Lambing, calving, farrowing of sows

Nowadays the hay is mown from enclosed fields and in recent times some farmers have kept ploughed land in the spring corn field for clover. When this practice began the clover was mowed first so that farmers could sow a second crop on the land. The situation was rather different in the past. In the seventeenth century the majority of hay came from the village meadows. Laxton then had four areas of meadow land, each of which was fenced, and when George Marshall and John Cooke failed to maintain their section of fencing they were both fined by the court in 1653.[37] Until Lammas time, 1 August, the meadows were closed so that grass could grow and the hay crop could be harvested. This had to be completed by 1 August when the meadows were 'broken' – opened for animals. Turning out animals too soon or breaking the restrictions on stock incurred fines. Twelve individuals were each fined 4d in

[37] BL Egerton 3631, f. 141.

1651 'for putting horses in the Long Meadow contrary to a pain'.[38] Because the meadows were in low-lying areas they were too wet to use after 1 November, and in any case many farmers would have sold their surplus livestock by then. As we shall see in chapter 4, the meadows were enclosed at the end of the 1720s and turned into closes which were let to individual tenants.

The closure of the meadows increased the value of the syke grass. These were a significant resource in the parish; even today the sykes run to about 26 acres in the West Field, 18 acres in the Mill field and 33 acres in the South Field. In the seventeenth century livestock which could be tethered – effectively cattle and horses – was grazed on the sykes. Individual sykes were earmarked, either for mares and foals or for stallions or cows or oxen. All animals had to be cleared from the sykes after Old Midsummer (6 July) to avoid the possibility of damage to the harvest on the surrounding strips. Failure to heed this rule could incur a fine. The tenants' rights to such grazing was determined by the number of stints, or gait rights, in their possession. There were 312 of these and they were closely guarded. They were often bequeathed in wills. Katherine Allicock, who died in 1633, left to her daughter Katherine the lease of the property she held and the reversion of four gaits, while in 1647 Thomas Taylor left ten gaits each to his three godchildren. Even in the twentieth century they have been a cause of disputes. After Elizabeth Bagshaw's death in 1930 the freehold purchased by her husband in 1892 was divided between the daughters, one of whom told the Thoresby agent that 'we have a dispute between Mrs Bennet, Mrs Cree and myself. Can you tell me how many gaits belong to the small holding which I have.'[39] No outsider was permitted grazing rights on the village sykes; anyone caught letting their gaits to a non-villager was fined by the court, hence Richard Woolfit's 2s fine in 1711 'for letting gaits out of town'.[40]

Grazing stock in the sykes was an uneconomical and wasteful use of an important resource. After the meadows were enclosed the practice developed of auctioning the grass for hay and dividing the proceeds between the 312 gait holders. As in many other villages, Laxton followed the custom of auctioning grass along the road sides. This took place at the annual vestry meeting on Easter Tuesday, and part of the proceeds went towards the upkeep of the village roads. From 1730 the syke grasses were also auctioned, but on a separate occasion in June or early July, when the farmers would have had a chance to see how the grass was growing before putting in their bids. The first letting took place on 13 June 1730, and annually ever since the syke grasses in the wheat and spring corn fields have been sold by lot to anyone who lives (officially 'puts up smoke') in Laxton. (Since the fallow was abandoned in 1967 it has also been possible to sell the syke grass from the third field. Previously no distinction

[38] BL Egerton 3631, f. 131.
[39] NAO Will of Katherine Allicock, 1 June 1633; NUMD Ma 5E/116/6.
[40] BL Egerton 3632, f. 101.

could be made.) The grass has to be mown and carried away by fixed dates varying between 10 July and 1 August.

Control of the grass sales is in the hands of the clerk of the gaits and commons. As far as we can tell, from the eighteenth century this position was held by the schoolmaster or the parish clerk (sometimes the same person). Between 1934 and her death in 1940, the former schoolmistress Miss Barbara Willis held the post. Since the school closed in the 1940s a number of people, including on one occasion the vicar, have held the clerkship, but since the 1950s it has been in the hands of Mr Reg Rose, the brother of the current bailiff. Receipts from the sale are used to pay the auctioneer and the clerk, to pay for the hire of the village hall, to pay for the stakes used by the jury and, nowadays, the jury lunch in the Dovecote Inn. Any remaining balance goes towards improving the roadways in the open fields. In 1730 the receipts of £27 11s were used for poor relief, and later the proceeds were recorded as being 'for the use of the town'.[41] Once these expenses have been met any balance remaining is divided between the 312 gait holders.

The receipts have varied considerably depending on the demand for grass in the village. Between 1847 and 1900 they seldom fell below £100, and on occasion (as in 1855, 1860, and several years between 1868 and 1876) they topped £200. As a result, in the 1880s gait rights were worth between 7s and 10s each a year. In the late nineteenth and early twentieth centuries the acreage under permanent grass in Laxton increased and demand for the syke grasses declined. By the 1930s receipts seldom topped £50 a year, and in 1937–8 and 1943–4 they fell below £4. Today they vary according to the hay crop, but with less permanent grassland in the village receipts have again risen. The record in recent years is £1,100, and in 1988 the farmers bid more than £900 in a sale which lasted just fifteen minutes.[42] The use to which the gait money should be put was disputed early in the present century and in 1908 it was agreed that any additional proceeds were to be divided among the owners of the gaits (Manvers 299, J. Bagshaw 5, the vicar, G. Bagshaw, S. Bartle, W. G. Quibell, 2 each) with the proportions subject to a deduction of 10 per cent 'for the maintenance of the dykes and gates which Lord Manvers hereby agrees to maintain'. The farmers pay for their purchases on 21 December.

Haymaking was usually completed two or three weeks before the harvest was ready. Traditionally harvest began with a first fruits service held in the church one morning early in August. The farmers and their labourers would attend, leaving their scythes, rakes and forks at the church door. The service no longer takes place, although the custom continues of taking the first sheaf into the church at the beginning of harvest.

By tradition the first field to be harvested is the winter corn field, although

---

[41] NAO PR 4103.
[42] NAO PR 4102; personal information.

Ron Cree recalls that in his day winter oats were usually the first crop to be harvested. They might be in the spring corn field or in an enclosed field. The oats would be mown and then left to dry for – so the saying went – three Sundays, before being raked into stooks. Corn was cut with reaping hooks, bound into sheaves and built into stooks. The fields wee mown with a scythe or sickle, usually by teams of two men and a boy. Many years later Bill Beckitt recalled his childhood before the first World War:

I was the boy in this team, which was made up of a chap called George Engleton, who swung the scythe all day from 8 a.m. until dark. My uncle Sam was the man who raked the corn together with a three pronged rake. He raked it into bundles of sheaves while my job was to make bands out of straw to tie up the bundles into sheaves. If we worked hard all day then we could clear an acre per day. We had to stack the sheaves up in tens, five a side, to let them ripen and keep dry.[43]

We know that Beckitt was recalling the wheat harvest because although the weather might determine whether barley or wheat was mown first, barley was stooked in fours and wheat in tens. The crops were left in the field for ten days and then carted home to the stackyard by the end of September. Harvest Thanksgiving was celebrated when the last load of corn was safely in, traditionally on the Thursday of Laxton Feast week. Annie Cree would celebrate by cooking her family a dinner of beef and plum pudding.

By the early years of the twentieth century some of the hardest physical labour was being taken out of the harvest by the introduction of the horse-drawn reaper. Edith Hickson was among the men, women and children who gathered in the East Field to watch the first demonstration of the new machine. It was pulled by two, three or four horses depending on the crop and on the soil texture and slope. At first the machine was mainly used to lay the crop in neat swathes ready for the binder. Until this was followed by the self-binder even the smallest children continued to help out in the harvest fields. The teams of Irish labourers hired in for the harvest disappeared from the countryside as man power gave way to horsepower.

Next came threshing days. A well-filled stackyard at the close of harvest has always been a source of pride and admiration. It suggests a good season and good husbandry. However, the grain was there to be used, and from the end of harvest until the following May each farmer needed a number of threshing days in order to separate grain from straw. For centuries the grain had been threshed by hand with a flail. This was slow and tiring work which took place on odd days through the winter, especially when the weather prevented outdoor work. The coming of the steam threshing machine at the end of the nineteenth century greatly speeded up the work. Ron Cree could thresh all his corn in about four days, but ten or eleven men were needed to operate the machine and

[43] William Beckitt and Jack Cook, *Open Field Recollections* (Laxton, n.d.), p. 8.

everyone helped their neighbours. One or two men would be throwing sheaves on to the drum, others would be stacking straw, carrying water for the engine or moving coal. Usually, on his own farm, Ron Cree threshed on three or four separate days through the year, calling in the contractor when he needed more feed or straw for the animals.

Threshing took place periodically from late October until May. Meanwhile stacks had to be well battened down to survive the winter. Even building them was an art which Ron Cree admits he never fully mastered. Some farmers liked to keep a stack for threshing just prior to rent day. The major aim was to clear the stackyard by the time the animals were turned out into the fields at the end of April or early May. The corn was ground at the village mill until 1916, but since then wheat has sold out of the village for milling.

Once all the corn was gathered after harvest the fields would be 'broken', and stock could be run on the stubbles. First the bailiff and the field foreman would agree a date for breaking the winter corn field. Their decision would be announced by the ringing of the church bell at six o'clock on the appropriate morning. Those eligible were permitted to turn out unlimited stock to run on the stubbles until 15 October. Some farmers could not wait for the official announcement and the court was forever dealing with people who had jumped the gun – presumably because they had run out of feed, or to save their grass for the future. Among hundreds of offences of this nature John Skaith was fined in 1662 'for putting sheep into the stubble field before the usual time'; George Broughton was fined 3s 4d in 1696 'for turning his horses loose in the stubble field before the field was broken'; and in 1866 George Lee incurred the court's displeasure for 'tenting cattle in the open fields before the time of breaking'.[44]

Once harvesting in the winter corn field was finished the farmers began work in the spring corn field, which they would hope to complete early in October. The spring corn field was then 'broken', usually on 15 October, and the stock moved from the stubbles of the outgoing wheat field to the stubbles in the spring corn field. This mass movement of animals was brought about to enable the farmers to begin preparing the old wheat field for its forthcoming spring corn crop. Animals were permitted in the spring corn field until 23 November, since this was to be the new fallow field. From 23 November all cattle and horses had to be removed to enclosed pastures or farmsteads, but until the following October, when wheat sowing on the fallow would commence, each farmer was permitted to keep twenty sheep in the field. The more frequently land is cropped the greater the accumulation of weed, and the purpose of the fallow year was to control the weeds. Sheep were put into the field to clean it by eating the weeds, and incidentally to provide a small amount of manure. In this way the land was cleared for ploughing and the effect of the sheep trampling over the field was to lay a good seed bed for the following year.

[44] BL Egerton 3631, f. 176; 3632, f. 63.

By 1967 demand for common grazing in the open fields had virtually disappeared: artificial means were available of undertaking the cleaning work of the fallow jacks; the boundary hedges were no longer animal proof; and in any case Laxton had fewer sheep. This had a number of repercussions. With little demand for stubble grazing the fields no longer needed to be cleared of their crops by a certain date to allow for the pasturing of animals. More critically, in 1967 the farmers agreed to a change which effectively brought to an end the tradition of keeping one field fallow. By the mid-1960s most of the farmers had a herd of milking cows but the area under permanent grass was declining. Demand for hay was considerable. Consequently the farmers agreed that the fallow field ought to be put to more productive use by undersowing the spring corn with a hay crop for the following year. A special meeting of the court was convened in April 1967 at which it was decided that grazing rights on the fallow should be withdrawn between the end of February and 1 July. By the latter date the forage crop would have been cut for hay or silage. The field would be open again for grazing from 1 July, or as soon as the crop had been gathered until it was time to sow the winter wheat.

The decision to abandon the fallow field was much debated in the village. The late Oliver Laughton of Ivy House Farm fully appreciated the farming difficulties which led to the change of practice, but like Ron Cree – who still has doubts about the decision twenty years on – he was not sure that open-field farming had any real legitimacy in Laxton without the fallows.[45] Ironically these doubts have been partly justified by changes in farming practice. Initially the decision seemed to make sense, especially when Laxton had an outbreak of foot and mouth disease in the winter of 1967–8. In 1967 the parish had 464 sheep, but this number fell to 72 in 1968 and to just three in 1970. Only Colin Cree at Step Farm restocked, and although one or two other farmers now have a few sheep, numbers are still below the (low) levels of the 1960s and barely sufficient to undertake the traditional work of the fallow jacks. In addition, the substitution of a fodder crop for bare fallow enabled farmers to plough up temporary grass in enclosed areas to increase the area under cereals. In 1968 the cropped acreage in Laxton exceeded 2,000 acres for the first time, with a considerable increase in barley. However, since 1970 most of the farmers have stopped milking, and much of the hay grown in the old fallow field is now sold for horseculture.

Both today and in the past farmers were not short of work once the harvest was over in late September. Root crops had to be pulled by hand, topped and tailed, and the fallows had to be ploughed. Four or five times during the year was adequate, but six was the ideal. On a fine day 8 or 10 ploughs might be at work, and Bill Bartle remembers counting now fewer than 17 at work in South Field on one occasion in the 1930s. Ploughing took place in such a way as to

---

[45] *Farmers Weekly*, 12 September 1969.

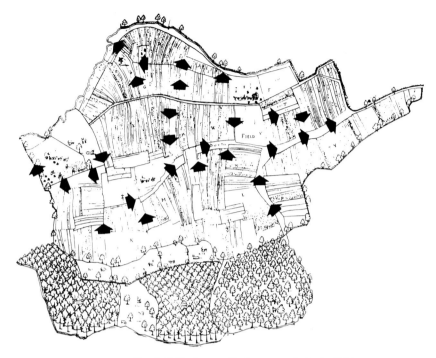

FIGURE 2.4 *South field, the runoff of water to drain the field*

bank up the lands in the strips in ridges (or as Laxton farmers call them 'riggs') separated by furrows. Ploughs used at Laxton, as in so much of midland England, were mouldboard ploughs often pulled by a pair of oxen and a lead-ing horse. The mouldboard turned the soil over, usually to the right. Since the farmers ploughed round the central opening furrow the soil of the whole 'land' tended to be heaped into a ridge anything up to three feet high. The ridges were deliberately created to improve drainage by speeding up the runoff of surface water. The furrows acted as gutters. Today the ridges have almost all been eradicated. Relicts or shadows of the corrugated effect which ridge and furrow gives to much of the Midlands landscape where the land has not been ploughed since enclosure can be seen in a handful of places in modern Laxton. Stub-ends along the edges of some of the sykes and balks in the open fields, which were used for turning, are a reminder of one of the most characteristic visual features of an open-field landscape.[46]

[46] S. G Upex and B. A. Wood, 'A Survey of Relict Open-Field Landscape Features at Laxton', *East Midland Geographer*, 7, 6 (1980), 245.

Although the fallow field would have been ploughed before harvest, it was still necessary to harrow it to break up large lumps of soil and to level the surface ready for sowing. In the seventeenth century wheat and barley were probably grown in the same field, but in modern times the winter corn field has been in wheat. The seed was sown broadcast and harrowed in before the Field Jury inspection in November. Sowing began immediately after Feast Sunday, which was on or near 11 October, and in the next few weeks anything that was to be over-wintered had to be sown, whether it was wheat, or oats and winter beans elsewhere in the manor. Sowing was by hand from a hopper, a bag which would be slung with straps from the shoulders of the sower. The motion of scattering the seed involved a highly skilled action that only a practised man could achieve. The seed drill did not come into widespread use in the village until the Second World War. After sowing, movement was restricted, and taking a horse and plough over the field could incur a fine – as both George Weatherall and Thomas Quibell found to their cost in 1888.

Once Jury Day and the Court Leet were over, winter was approaching. Whatever the weather, there was still plenty to do. Hedgecutting was one task. Hedges were cut with a slasher, but it was a time-consuming job, and it was not always possible to cut all the hedges on a farm each year. As Ron Cree recalls, it was a question of doing what you could. The outgoing wheat field had to be ploughed in preparation for the following year's spring corn crop. Ploughing needed to be completed in time to allow the land to be broken by frost and rain before sowing commenced in March. On Laxton's rather heavy Keuper Marl soils it was not long into winter before the plough became immobilized, first through damp, later through frost. Work on the land came to a standstill, although the farmstead remained a hive of activity. Hay had to be fed to calves, cows and horses. Muck-leading and cleaning out calf pens and hen roosts provided other tasks.

With spring came a new set of jobs. It was time to sow the spring corn field with barley, oats, beans or peas, usually to provide winter feed for the livestock. In the village, attention focused on lambing and calving, and farrowing sows. Once the animals were turned out into the (enclosed) fields late in April or early in May it was time to clear up the yards and cart the manure to the strips. It took time to cart the muck, and three or four loads a day would be good going. The muck had to be forked into the carts and then spread, with the fork, over the field. If the earth was hard-baked (clotted) it might be broken with a mallet to cover the manure.

Perhaps because it was so physically demanding, most of the farm work was done by men. In Edith Hickson's day, girls were sent out to service as soon as possible, and those still at home were expected to do domestic duties such as making and mending clothes. Annie Moody went as a maid to the vicarage in 1916, when Rev. James Tunbridge came to the village, and there she stayed until her mother died two years later and she moved back home to look after her father and brother. Women helped out in the fields only at haytime and harvest, and at other times during the year they hoed sugar beet and picked potatoes, fruit and the produce of the kitchen garden – much of which they turned into jam and wines. At other times they milked the cows and fed the calves and poultry, collected eggs, plucked and dressed chickens, and weeded the land. After the pig was killed – everyone seems to be able to recall without much affection the awful noise of this macabre event – the butcher would cut it up and the women would cook the meat and make pastry for the pies. They spent long hours in the dairy, separating the cream from the milk in order to make butter. Everything of market value was the responsibility of the farmers' wives, who also reared the animals – and the children.

It was only on market days that the farmers and their wives regularly left the village. Some of the cattle were sold at the Monday market in Tuxford, partly because the alternatives of Retford and Newark were further to travel. Cattle which had to be sent a distance went on the railway from one of the two Tuxford stations. Sheep and horses could be walked to Retford, while pigs would be taken in a muckcart. Ron Cree went to market most weeks, usually to Retford where he banked and where he sold his cattle, but it was the women who were the most regular market attenders because they had to sell the produce of the dairy and farmyard.

In Edith Hickson's day many of the farmers' wives had a stall at the weekly market in Tuxford. They set off on board the carrier's wagon early in the morning since, when conditions under foot were poor, it could take two or three hours to travel from Laxton. The Laxton women arrived when others were already trading, but they rented tressles in the market and most had regular customers who could be relied upon to come and buy butter and eggs, and even a chicken if this had been ordered in advance. Although the women sold poultry and occasionally flowers, butter was their main commodity and much of the farm economy depended on the price at which they could sell. Their goods sold, the women purchased necessities for the week to come and travelled home. When Annie Moody moved to Step Farm after her marriage to John Cree in 1929, she found herself with very similar tasks, although by this time Tuxford had declined and she went by bus each week to Newark market. She too had regular customers for her butter and eggs, and any butter remaining at the end of the day was sold to wholesalers. By the 1930s all this was changing. The farmers' wives stopped going regularly to market and instead gathered outside the village shop with their butter. Frank Sampson would take it on his horse and dray to Mansfield or Chesterfield, and would pay the women on his return. Butter became less important as the farmers started to sell liquid milk.

This is to run ahead, and in any case to emphasize change is to forget the essential continuity of the past. Year in and year out the manor court has overseen the activities of the Laxton farmers. It still combines the dual functions of a Court Baron and a Court Leet, and it retains the power to fine offenders who transgress the rules of common husbandry. It has of course changed. No one would refer to the jury today – as the bailiff did in 1680 – as 'a company of ignorant men who could scarce any of them write their names', who for fear of one of the freeholders 'unadviseably subscribed' to an agreement they admitted to not understanding.[47] Moreover its powers today are more nominal than real. The Thoresby agent wrote in 1915 that 'there is no doubt that the court does a lot of good and if possible the custom should be upheld,' but in 1939 the steward described it as 'largely a nominal matter for the purpose of preserving the tradition'.[48] The traditions survive, but Laxton is not caught in a time warp, and it is to the evolution and development of the village since 1635 that we must now turn in more detail.

[47] NUMD MaB/201/3.
[48] Hodgkinson and Tallents, Solicitors, Newark, H. Argles to H. Tallents, 4 December 1915; H. Tallents to GB Instructional Films Ltd. 27 July 1939.

Chapter Three

The Village in the Early
Seventeenth Century

Seventeenth-century visitors to Laxton would have found themselves in a village which, in layout, had changed relatively little over the past 350 years. Approaching the village not along the line of the existing main road but of an older 'green lane' – an unsurfaced pathway – which is still used for access to the West Field, the first house a visitor would come across was a cottage on the left-hand side of the road just past the entrance to West Field. In 1635 this was occupied by William Skaith, a tenant of the lord of the manor, with a holding which totalled nearly 8 acres. This was divided between $2\frac{1}{2}$ acres in a close at the rear of his house, a couple of holdings in the South and Mill Fields, and several others in the meadow lands. Moving along the North Row our visitor would find houses with their attached crofts on both sides of the road. Naturally the buildings would have looked rather different from their twentieth-century successors, since they would have been constructed of mud and stud on a timber frame, with a thatched roof. Brick arrived in Laxton only towards the end of the seventeenth century. If the materials with which they were constructed were different from those of the twentieth century, some of the tofts on which they stood have hardly changed in shape, and a number of the surrounding hedges certainly date back at least to the 1630s.[1]

Continuing along the main street – known in the 1630s as North Row – on his left our visitor would pass the track which led to the Hall and the site of the castle. At the Crosshill he would have found a road layout which has hardly changed, and as today he could turn either to the left, along the road towards Egmanton, past what was known both then and now as the Bar (one of several gates separating the village from the open fields), or right into East Row. If he took the latter course he could walk down the hill following the line of the present Kneesall road. However, he could not have reached Moorhouse, as he might today, since in those days the hamlet was approached along a green lane

---

[1] J. O. Rieley and P. R. Tomlinson, *Woods, Hedgerows and Grasslands of the Parish of Laxton, Nottinghamshire* (Nottingham, 1987).

PLATE 3.1 *Main Street, looking north, and showing the crofts and tofts stretching back from the farm buildings running along the street, towards the back lane. This layout is virtually unchanged from Mark Pierce's map, and some of the hedges shown here may be even older. Many Nottinghamshire villages had layouts similar to Laxton, where the principal steet was flanked on either side by footpaths or back lanes providing access to the open fields.*

which formed a back lane to East Row. This path is no longer in use. What was the main road to Kneesall in the seventeenth century is today merely a trackway through the Mill Field. What condition the roads were in is more difficult to tell. This is one of many gaps in our knowledge, but the omissions are far fewer than in the medieval period and we can paint a reasonably comprehensive pen portrait of the village and its inhabitants early in the seventeenth century.

THE LORDSHIP OF THE MANOR

Visitors in the seventeenth century were almost certainly fewer in number than in the days when kings and courtiers passed through the village. Laxton, by 1600, was a purely agricultural village, distinguished from its neighbours only in being rather more populous than many of them, and even this was less noticeable than it had been even a century earlier. Where Laxton's tax rating in

1524 was substantially in advance of Tuxford's, in the 1621 subsidy Laxton's seven taxpayers were assessed at 19s 4d, while the nine taxpayers in Tuxford paid £3 2s 4d.[2] The prosperity of the early Middle Ages had left only a few marks, among them the physical presence of the – somewhat dilapidated – church. This did not mean that the village was unchanging; indeed, it was passing through a period of transition as the result of turnover among the major landowners. Gilbert Roos's sale of the lordship in 1618 to the Duke of Buckingham was just one of several transactions with significant repercussions for the village community.

Buckingham had no intention of living in Laxton. As James I's court favourite he accumulated a substantial fortune between 1616 and 1620, much of it in landed property. Laxton, and other land he acquired from Gilbert Roos, were minor interests within an expanding empire which reached its peak when he acquired Burley-on-the-Hill in Rutland in 1621.[3] Since Buckingham's main interests were in his native Leicestershire it is not surprising that the Nottinghamshire properties did not play a part in his longer term planning, and in 1625 he sold out to Sir William Courten.[4] Courten (1572–1634) was the son of a Flemish refugee who had settled in London and traded in silk and linen. He went to Haarlem as a young man, acting as a factor in his father's firm, and there married the deaf and dumb daughter of a Dutch merchant, who brought him a dowry of £60,000. In 1606 he went into partnership with his brother and, despite a Star Chamber prosecution for trading irregularities in 1619, both men were knighted. Their capital was estimated in 1631 at £150,000. Sir William owned twenty vessels trading with Africa and the West Indies, and he was a pioneer of settlement in the West Indies. In England, his main interest was in the acquisition of land and by the time of his death he had accumulated estates yielding £6,500 annually. Among them were Laxton and Kneesall, but Courten, like Buckingham before him, almost certainly bought Laxton as an investment, and his family retained the manor for less than twenty years, selling out in 1640 to the Earl of Kingston.[5]

Meantime what of the sub-manor which had been divided between the two daughters of Robert de Markham back in the thirteenth century? By the sixteenth century one part had descended through Cecilia de Bekering into the hands of the family of Vaux of Harrowden. In 1612 it was held by Edward, fourth Baron Vaux (1588–1661). The Vaux family was Catholic, and the fourth baron was committed to the Fleet prison in 1612 for refusing to take the Oath of Allegiance. Recusancy fines gradually impoverished the family, until

[2] P. T. H. Unwin, 'Patterns and Hierarchies of Rural Settlement in Nottinghamshire before 1700', unpublished Ph.D. thesis, University of Durham, 1979, pp. 600–1.

[3] Roger Lockyer, *Buckingham: the Life and Political Career of George Villiers, First Duke of Buckingham, 1592–1628* (1981), pp. 61–3.

[4] BL Egerton 3599, fos 32–56.

[5] *Open Fields*, pp. 82–3. For the sale to Kingston see chapter 4.

by the time of his death the fourth baron left his younger brother little more than an empty title.[6] Most of the estate had been sold piecemeal including the Laxton property, which Vaux parted with to Peter Broughton of Lowdham, a younger son of the Broughton family of Broughton in Staffordshire. He was probably a brother of Sir Thomas Broughton (who had married Mary Roos). The full extent of the Roos–Broughton connection is difficult to reconstruct, but Bryan Broughton, gentleman, was an executor of the will of Mary's brother Thomas Roos (d. 1610). Among the possessions bequeathed in Thomas Roos's will were 'all such household stuff as I have in Staffordshire'.[7]

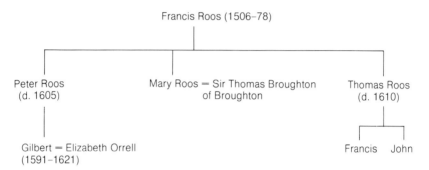

FIGURE 3.1 *The Roos–Broughton connection*

The second part of the sub-manor had come through a series of transactions into the hands of the Hinde or Hynde family. Augustine Hinde, liveryman of the Clothworkers' Company and Alderman of the City of London, purchased the property in 1541. At his death in 1554 he was Lord Mayor elect of the City, but his successors preferred the country to the life of the capital. Augustine Hinde (1574–1647), his grandson, was living in a substantial house in Moorhouse by 1635. It was recorded in 1674 as having six hearths, one of the largest houses in the village; the present Church Farm may well stand on the same site. Augustine Hinde was a man of some substance. His will, drawn up in 1644, included bequests totalling £200, although his signature is barely legible. Hinde, and several generations of his successors, are buried in the parish church.

By 1635 Courten, Broughton and Hinde were the largest landowners in Laxton, but they were by no means alone. In 1612 'the owners of Laxton town'

[6] The whole, rather sad story, is told in Godfrey Anstruther, *Vaux of Harrowden: a Recusant Family* (Newport, 1953).

[7] *Open Fields*, p. 88. The Orwins are incorrect in asserting that the sale to the Broughtons took place during the sixteenth century. An additional complication to this rather difficult family reconstruction is the link between the Roos family and the Vauxs. The third baron Vaux borrowed £200 from Peter Roos in 1589: Anstruther, *Vaux of Harrowden*, p. 215.

included thirteen men, headed by Lord Vaux, Gilbert Roos, esquire, and his cousin Francis Roos, gentleman, and Augustine Hinde.[8] By 1635 the first three of these men did not own property in the village (table 3.1), and the most substantial landowner was the lord of the manor, William Courten, who had succeeded to the estate at his father's death the previous year.[9] In addition to the property acquired from the Duke of Buckingham in 1635, between 1629 and 1631 Sir William Courten had bought from Francis Roos a 66-acre farm, which included one of Laxton's windmills. The first written record of a mill in the village dates from the thirteenth century but there are several mill mounds in the parish.[10] Roos had inherited the property in 1610. Whether this was the extent of Francis Roos's holdings is not known; although his widow held one of the largest farms in 1635, she was not a freeholder. By 1635 Courten had also acquired property from two of the other freeholders recorded in the 1612 list: he bought at least 300 acres of land from Augustine Hinde in 1634, for which he paid £442, and which cut Hinde's overall holding in Laxton by half; while on a smaller scale Edward Snow sold him a farm of 6 acres.[11] These purchases gave Courten 60 per cent of all the property in Laxton.

TABLE 3.1 *Landownership in Laxton in 1635*

Owners	No.	Acreage	%
Lord of the manor	1	2329	60.3
Major freeholders	2	1116	28.9
50–99 acres	2	145	3.8
20–49 acres	4	116	3.0
10–19 acres	3	38	1.0
5–9 acres	3	21	0.5
1–4 acres	6	15	0.4
Under 1 acre	4	3	0.1
Other	3	78	2.0
	28	3861	100.0

Source: Bodleian Library, MS Top Notts c.2. The figures for Moorhouse total 333 acres, which suggests that land in adjoining parishes may have been included in the analysis.

[8] Robert Thoroton, *Antiquities of Nottinghamshire*, 3rd edn (ed.), J. Throsby (Nottingham, 1797), vol. III, p. 210.
[9] PRO Ward/7/89/246; BL Egerton 3631, f. 100.
[10] *Open Fields*, pp. 92–7.
[11] NAO PR 4805/1; BL Egerton 3631, fos 105–6.

The rest of the property was more widely dispersed, although Peter Broughton (754 acres) and Augustine Hinde (362 acres) held nearly one-third of the manor between them. In addition to acquiring Vaux's estate Broughton had also bought a number of freehold closes totalling 74 acres from Gilbert Roos, and he was easily the second largest landholder in Laxton. Of the other freeholders, Robert Shipton (76 acres) lived in Laxton and, like most of the farmers, had his property scattered between the different fields and meadows, but James Bacon (69 acres) lived in Wellow.[12] His holdings primarily consisted of closes in the west side of Mill Field, once the property of North Ferriby Abbey. Five of the lesser freeholders had no residence in the village. Among them were Fulk Cartwright (9 acres), lord of the manor of Ossington (and brother-in-law of the first Earl of Kingston), and the Countess of Shrewsbury (6 acres) who lived at Rufford. The others lived and worked in Laxton. Some could have let their land to unnamed tenants, while others may have been people like William Treswell, who held '10 lands belonging to Egmanton' (2 acres) in the West Field, and lived in the adjoining village. Finally there were the church lands. The 20 acres in Moorhouse in possession of the Dean and Chapter of Southwell was a freehold they retained until the 1850s and, as we have seen, the chantry land may already have been in the hands of freeholders.

The division of landownership accounts for the complex structure of tenure in 1635. Of the 89 households in the village 48 were leased from the lord of the manor, 16 from Broughton, and 7 from Augustine Hinde. Fourteen properties including two half messuages were in the hands of freeholders, while one house was owned by the village and the other three were part of the chantry lands. Of the 22 houses in Moorhouse, 11 were leased from the lord of the manor.

THE VILLAGE

The extent to which the villagers were aware of these changes of lordship and landownership, and the views that they expressed about them, have gone unrecorded. However, one connected development cannot have escaped their attention. In 1625 the Duke of Buckingham employed Francis Watson and William Mason to undertake a survey of his property. We know that they made some progress, but that their work remained incomplete when Buckingham sold out to Courten. Within a few years of acquiring the lordship, and after he had made a number of additional purchases, Courten decided to revive the survey. To complete the work Watson and Mason had begun he employed Mark Pierce, a surveyor already known for his work in Northampton, Essex, Hertfordshire and Kent. This commission, and the subsequent survival of both the book of survey (the terrier) and a superb map of the manors of Laxton and

---

[12] NAO PR 4805/1.

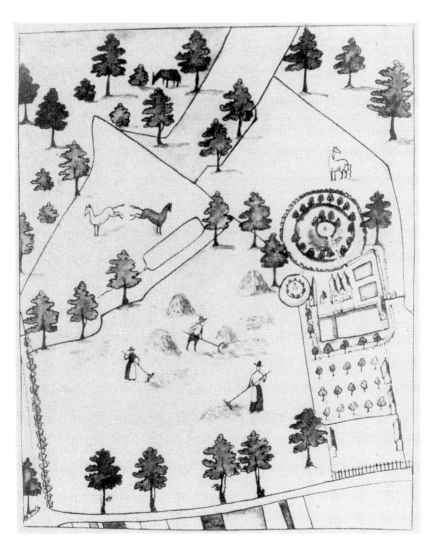

PLATE 3.2 *Haymaking in Laxton, 1635. This detail from Mark Pierce's map of 1635 shows one of the many harvesting skills drawn by Pierce. Like some of the others, including broadcast sowing and reaping, the techniques had not greatly changed by the 1930s. The picture also shows Pierce's depiction of the site of the castle and, in the inner bailey, the sixteenth-century manor house built by the Roos family. This went out of use in the seventeenth century but its outline can still be traced today.*

Kneesall, provide a detailed picture of the village as contemporaries would have known it in the 1630s. The map recorded every house, building and enclosure, together with all the strips of ploughland in the open fields, and every dole or grassland in the meadows. Pierce numbered the parcels of land for easy identification in the terrier, or to be more accurate he numbered nearly all of them, since he includes two number 11s but is unclear about the location of numbers 12–15, 69–80 and 113–17. The total number of parcels came to 3,333. Visually the map is superb, although it is also misleading because Pierce depicted a continuous expanse of unhedged strips and some grassland, while omitting a number of significant details such as closes and enclosures in the open-field furlongs as well as headlands between the furlongs. These can be reconstructed only by careful use of the terrier in conjunction with the map.[13]

Despite these caveats, Pierce's survey and map are a mine of information from which we can quarry in assembling our picture of Laxton in the early seventeenth century. We can start with the village itself since the first part of the terrier covers 'the site of Laxton town', and details 86 houses and cottages, together with two half messuages. The other 38 entries in this section are for crofts, closes and tofts without dwellings on them. Only one of the houses enumerated in this part of the schedule was not actually in the village; a cottage on Westwood Common in the tenure of Edward Harrison. Later in the terrier Pierce noted an additional house near to Westwood Common, so that altogether there were 89 households in Laxton, and 22 in Moorhouse.

Pierce was mainly concerned with property ownership, and he does not name the occupants of each house. Fortunately there is enough information in the terrier, when coupled with other contemporary sources, to work out with a fair degree of accuracy how many people lived in Laxton, where they lived and what they did. Historians accept a mean household size of 4.25–4.75 for the early seventeenth century.[14] If all 111 houses were occupied the population of Laxton in the mid-1630s must have been between 470 and 530. We can test this conclusion against other sources. Calculations based on the parish registers, which date – with gaps – from the 1560s, suggest a population of around 450 in the mid-sixteenth century. Natural increase would have pushed this figure steadily upwards through the sixteenth and seventeenth centuries, but adjustments need to be made for migration from the village.[15] The population of England was increasing steadily through the sixteenth century, and Laxton was no exception, at least until the 1570s. After this there was almost

[13] Bodleian Library, MS Top Notts c.2. Unless stated otherwise, material in the rest of this chapter is taken from this terrier.
[14] Peter Laslett, 'Mean Household Size in England since the Sixteenth Century', in P. Laslett and R. Wall (eds), *Household and Family in Past Time* (Cambridge, 1972), p. 126.
[15] These and subsequent references to population figures for Laxton are explained and graphed in the appendix, pp. 324–6.

certainly some reversal of the trend to a low point in what are now regarded, nationally, as the crisis years of the 1590s.

Recovery set in rapidly with an increase in baptisms at the end of the 1590s, and in a Church Visitation of 1603 John Cadman, the vicar of Laxton, recorded 310 communicants and non-communicants. This suggests a population in the range of 470–500. Although there was then a further minor crisis, with burials peaking at 25 in 1603, a population figure of around 490 in the early seventeenth century seems reasonable. The empty tofts depicted on Pierce's map may indicate a decline in numbers from an even higher point at an earlier date. Locally, only Kneesall, with perhaps 420 people, could approach Laxton in size, and to find larger settlements it was necessary to look towards the market towns of Tuxford, East Retford and Southwell.[16]

From Mark Pierce's map we know that almost everyone in the parish lived in houses more or less on the same sites, in both Laxton and Moorhouse, on which properties can be found today. Many of the tofts and crofts are unchanged since the early seventeenth century, but the houses have changed. In 1635 the villagers would have lived in mud and stud structures built on a timber frame. These were less permanent buildings than brick-built houses, although the frame would doubtless have been used many times over, and in some parts of Nottinghamshire they were eventually incorporated into brick structures. Mud and stud did not disappear from the village completely until the present century, although by then surviving buildings were outhouses and sheds rather than dwellings. One advantage of mud and stud was that the buildings were relatively easy to erect and maintain. Most villagers, with a little help from neighbours, would have been able to keep their property in repair, or even overhaul it completely, when needed. Timber was available in the lord of the manor's woodlands; the village had a plentiful supply of clay for packing the walls; the waterstones thrown up in the Keuper Marl were used as footings to give a good base; and reed was locally available for thatching.

Over much of England houses were growing larger in the sixteenth and early seventeenth centuries,[17] although this was not necessarily to accommodate more people. English households have traditionally supported only the nuclear family of parents and children, together with any servants or ancillary workers, and not the extended families found in other parts of the world. Laxton was no exception to this pattern. Furthermore, if houses were larger this did not mean that they were any less cluttered. In her will of 1649 Bridget Nicholson set about disposing of a houseful of beds: the featherbed on which she lay dying was to go to her daughter Joan; while another daughter, Anne, received 'one bedsted in the parlour, as also one featherbed with all the furniture thereunto belonging'.

---

[16] Anne Whiteman (ed.), *The Compton Census of 1676: a Critical Edition* (1986), p. 583; A. C. Wood, 'An Archiepiscopal Visitation in 1603', *TTS*, 46 (1942), 11.

[17] W. G. Hoskins, *The Midland Peasant* (1957), p. 186; K. Wrightson and D. Levine, *Poverty and Piety in an English Village: Terling 1525–1700* (1979), p. 37.

Anne Taylor of Moorhouse, who died in 1661, listed all her possessions, and the names of who was to receive each of them after her death. In doing so she provided a picture of the inside of her house. To her son-in-law Lawrence Urry she left 'one feather bed, one linsey wolsey pillow and one other pillow, one blanket, one coverlet green and yellow, one pair of hempin sheets, one pair of hardin sheets', a pan and two pewter dishes. To her granddaughter Mrs Taylor left 'a seiled bedstead with a teaster over it', two pewter dishes, two brass pans, a pillow, a towel, two napkins, 'and my best weaving coat and one filled chest'. Her grandson's legacy included 'one linen sheet, a towel and one napkin'. Edmund Woolfit, who died in 1660, was mainly concerned with disposing of his agricultural goods, but he also took care to designate the future owners of 'one round table', his best bedsteads, 'a new feather bed and bolster, two blankets (and other bedding)', as well as his pewter, brass and linen. Other will makers were concerned about particular family heirlooms, including silver spoons and, occasionally, 'all my silverware', although this was a rarity in Laxton.[18]

Wills offer a hint of the quality of village life, and there are a number of other pointers in this direction. Despite the state of the roads, there is ample evidence that people did move into and out of the village, and as a result Laxton is likely to have been affected by events occurring well beyond the parish boundary. Traditional village life was convivial. It centred around the alehouse, annual feasts and festivals and, in the interests of maintaining neighbourliness, villagers were generally tolerant of heavy drinking, swearing and fornication. It was the kind of culture which came into conflict with the new puritan ethic of late sixteenth- and early seventeenth-century England, which emphasized piety and thrift, discipline and sobriety. The clash of cultures is now well established for some areas of the country, and is seen as a vital element contributing to the civil wars of the 1640s. Of course Laxton may have escaped all this, particularly with so many changes of landlord. We do not know whether the puritan fanaticism found elsewhere in England reached the village, but the people of Laxton were probably not especially devout. One indication is the state of the medieval parish church. Worshippers in the seventeenth century would have found it rather drafty and probably in a poor state of repair. Complaints about the fabric and the churchyard were frequently taken to the church courts; in 1603, for example, the churchwardens were presented for failing to carry out proper repairs, and six years later their successors were given six months to repair the church fence. William Woodrow left £3 in 1646 'towards the mending of the glass windows about Laxton church', and in the 1660s it was found to have major defects in the walls, pavements and porches.[19]

---

[18] Here and below the evidence is taken from wills proved in the Archbishopric of York and currently housed in the Nottinghamshire Archives Office.

[19] These and subsequent cases are from the church court Act Books (see chapter 1, n. 13). W. A. Pemberton, 'Studies in the Ecclesiastical Court and Archdeaconry of Nottingham, 1660–89', unpublished Ph.D. thesis, University of Nottingham, 1952, chapter 3, p. 18.

Neglect of the church implies a lack of interest in spiritual life, and this may also explain the regularity with which Laxton people appeared before the church courts in the early years of the century. Grace Doncaster was the cause of many a man's downfall. On 14 January 1602 she was accused of fornication with William Pawson and George Sampson. She pleaded not guilty to an association with Pawson but guilty with Sampson, who also pleaded guilty when presented the following month. In March Richard Harpham and no lesser person than the vicar, John Cadman, were also presented on suspicion of fornication with the seductive Miss Doncaster, although neither man was found guilty. Not a great deal is known about cases in the civil courts because for seventeenth-century Nottinghamshire only Minute Books have survived, which are relatively uninformative, but in 1616 Hugo Clark was presented for bad conduct and for threatening the vicar, William Rooke.[20] He was doubtless not the only villager to appear before the justices, although the majority of disputes are likely to have been settled in the village.

On the other hand we should not tar all the villagers with the church court brush, and it may be that we can see evidence of a greater religious commitment in some of the tortuous wording of will preambles. Grace Hasland of Moorhouse, in her will of 1646 bequeated her soul to God 'hoping to be saved by the merits of Christ Jesus my only redeemer'; while William Woodrow of Laxton went even further, bequeathing his soul 'into the hands of Almighty God my creator, hoping to be saved only by the merits, death and passion of Christ Jesus my blessed saviour and redeemer'. This was going rather beyond the standard form of simply bequeathing one's soul into the hands of Almighty God, which was all Robert Dickinson thought necessary in 1657. On the other hand folklore and superstition were still rife in the village. Robert Wildsmith and Robert Dickenson were presented before the church courts in 1602 'for charming of Richard Sa[l]mon's daughter of the fever'.[21]

OCCUPATIONS

Most Laxton people in the early seventeenth century earned their living from the land, but precisely what this meant could vary considerably. Courten's property can be roughly divided into a number of categories. First, there was the demesne property, 295 acres, predominantly in the vicinity of the manor house, of arable and meadow lands divided into closes – the land which would

---

[20] H. H. Copnall (ed.), *Nottinghamshire County Records of the 17th Century* (Nottingham, 1915), p. 44.

[21] Wrightson and Levine, *Poverty and Piety*, pp. 156, 158. From about 1610 the church courts were predominantly concerned with presenting individuals for non-attendance, and Dr N. G. P. Tyacke, who has worked extensively on these later records, assures me that the number of prosecutions for sexual and other offences declined.

have been worked for the lord of the manor by the village peasants in the medieval centuries – together with 292 acres of woodland. In 1635 all the arable and meadow was let to tenants.[22] Second, came the tenements, farms owned by the lord, but traditionally leased to rent-paying tenants. This land was divided between 58 tenants in the village and a further 10 in Moorhouse. Their holdings ranged between Thomas Taylor with 99 acres, and 34 tenants with less than 5 acres each. Finally, the properties recently acquired from Hinde, Roos and Snow were still administered separately and let to 7 tenants. Broughton retained in hand a property known in the 1635 survey as 'the Great Farm', and leased the rest of his Laxton property to 25 tenants. Hinde leased about 100 acres to 12 tenants.

The largest farms were those of Peter Broughton (433 acres), Augustine Hinde (254 acres), and Samuel Stanford (243 acres). Broughton's 'Great Farm' consisted of former demesne land, acquired from Gilbert Roos, and property bought from Lord Vaux. Much of it was in closes on the eastern and southern borders of the parish beyond the open fields, although it included closes, meadows and arable and pasture in the open fields. The property, together with his 51 acres in Moorhouse, must have been administered by a bailiff. Hinde retained 202 acres in hand in Laxton, which included some large closes towards the edges of the parish.

Few household inventories have survived for Nottinghamshire before 1689, and consequently we do not know whether Laxton enjoyed the general improvement in living standards which occurred nationwide over the period 1540–1640.[23] The larger farmers are the best documented. Samuel Stanford was the most substantial non-landowning farmer, a yeoman-farmer in the parlance of the sixteenth and seventeenth centuries – although the term is notoriously difficult to define and while most Laxton farmers who left a will were described as husbandmen, those in Moorhouse were usually described as yeomen. Stanford had the characteristics of a yeoman: he was Courten's steward, and his farming interests included manorial and demesne property. In addition, he carried the authority derived from his tenure of the manor house; Mark Pierce's terrier attributes to Stanford 'Laxton Hall, or the manor house, with the gatehouses, brewhouses, stables, cowhouses, two dovehouses, court, garden, mount orchard, vineyard orchard, two barns, one hemp yard, and the hall land'. This was a substantial holding, but he is also recorded as the tenant of another house in the village, and since by 1640 the Hall was let to Henry Inkersall, he may have moved out. Perhaps this was a temporary arrangement, since early in 1641 Inkersall released the hall to Thomas Batchelor, described as 'of London, yeoman', Stanford's son-in-law.[24] In his will, made in December

---

[22] However, a surviving rental of 1521 gives only tenants by lease of years and does not include these properties: BL Egerton 8446.

[23] Hoskins, *Midland Peasant*, p. 186.

[24] NAO PR 4805/1, 4802, f. 60.

1641, Stanford included a plea: 'if my son John do come home and have a mind to live on the hall living at Laxton, then he shall give to my son Samuel for his goodwill of the said hall £30.'[25] Stanford held 123 acres of Courten's demesne, 51 acres attached to the parsonage (and leased from Courten jointly with Humphry Hopkinson), 68 acres in a farm which had been purchased from Augustine Hinde, and 2 acres in the Mill field leased from Broughton – in total 101 separate holdings through the village.

Stanford's partner, Humphry Hopkinson, was also an energetic farmer. In 1621 he leased 67 acres from Buckingham, but by 1635 he had considerably expanded his interests. With Richard Whitlam he had become tenant of a 97-acre farm acquired by Courten from Augustine Hinde; with Stanford he had acquired the lease of the parsonage lands and the tithe collection; and in his own right he had also rented 24 acres from Broughton, a total holding of 239 acres divided into no fewer than 260 parcels.

These were the most substantial holdings, but two other farmers worked more than 100 acres and probably deserve the appellation of yeoman: Thomas Taylor, with 38 acres of demesne held jointly with Widow Harpham, a 99-acre farm leased from Courten, and 4 acres in the village which he owned; and William Woolfit, who leased 50 acres from Hinde, and 55 acres from Broughton. Thomas Taylor was the son of another Thomas Taylor, described as husbandman, who died in 1631. Although Thomas Taylor senior left all his Laxton property to his eldest son Thomas, he also bequeathed a house in Kneesall to a nephew, and a house in Newark to his son Alexander and daughter Anne. Significantly his will was witnessed by two of Laxton's other substantial farmers, Samuel Stanford and Humphry Hopkinson, suggestive perhaps of a farmer hierarchy. Less is known about William Woolfit (see figure 3.2), but Edmund Woolfit, who was certainly a relation of William's and farmed a substantial holding, died in 1660. Leaving no heir he chose to divide his effects between his various surviving relations. His standing crops included 2 acres and 1 rood of barley, half an acre of wheat and 1 acre and 1 rood of peas. The crops could be claimed only after the next harvest. He also bequeathed his cattle (6 are mentioned), sheep (20), horses (2), as well as 2 bacon flitches and his 'new cart, one plough, and a pair of harrows'.[26]

Others, with substantially fewer acres in Laxton may have had land in adjoining manors which would have placed them on a par with these men. This may have been the case with Thomas Green who died in 1640. In 1635 Green owned a cottage and yard in the village with 1 rood and 4 perches of land, but he also leased Copthorne close from Courten (13 acres 2 roods), a further three 'lands' in West field 'which is in question for freehold', and another 14 acres from Broughton, a total holding of 28 acres. At his death the cottage passed to

[25] NAO PR 4143, Will of Samuel Stanford, 11 December 1641.
[26] NAO Will of Edmund Woolfit, 22 April 1654 (proved 1660).

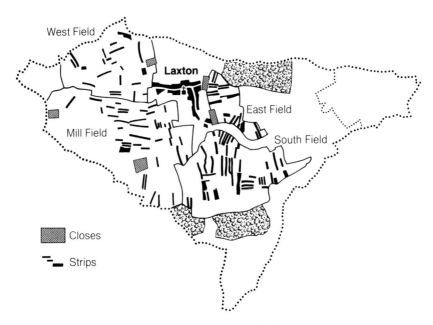

West Field

Laxton

East Field

Mill Field

South Field

Closes

Strips

FIGURE 3.2 *William Woolfit's land holdings in 1635*

his eldest son Francis (though it was tenanted by Ralph Gascoigne), who also
received his horse, gear, harness and best cart. Green left to his grandson
Thomas Milner one heifer and the crop of barley growing on an acre of arable;
and to his granddaughter Margaret Milner one heifer calf and the wheat growing on half an acre of arable. These legacies were to be delivered into the hands
of Samuel Stanford, to use them for the benefit of the grandchildren. Ostensibly
Green does not appear as one of Laxton's more substantial farmers, but his will
was administered by Samuel Stanford, and the bequests point to a man of some
wealth since they included five shillings to a female servant, and one shilling to
John Jepson 'for ringing my passing bell and digging my grave'.[27]

Table 3.2 shows the variety of farm sizes in the parish. Two-thirds of the
cultivated acreage was in the hands of 20 individuals, while more than 100
people occupied less than 30 per cent of the acreage. Seventeen of the smaller
freeholders owned (or in one case rented) a house in Laxton or Moorhouse, and
most farmed only the land they owned, including Robert Shipton, John
Chappell and Bryan Smith. Others, including Thomas Green, owned so little
that it is not surprising to find them renting additional property. Who worked
the land owned by some of the non-resident freeholders is not clear. A few

[27] NAO Will of Thomas Green, 7 January 1639/40.

TABLE 3.2 *Size of farms in Laxton, 1635*

Acreage	Number	Total acreage	Non-waste (%)
100+	5	1077	32.2
51–99	15*	1131	33.8
21–50	15	519	15.5
11–20	10	167	5.0
6–10	21	174	5.2
1–5	34	99	3.0
Under 1	27	12	0.4
Dean and Chapter, Chantry		21	0.6
Closes (joint tenures)		142	4.3
	127	3342	100.0

* One of these farms was jointly farmed by Humphry Hopkinson and Richard Whitland, so Hopkinson appears twice in this group.

people owned or leased just the house and yard in which they lived, among them Cecily Arrall, Anthony Salford, James Taylor and James Smalley, all Courten tenants; Robert Dickinson, the blacksmith (holding of Broughton), William Doncaster (holding of Hinde), and two Moorhouse freeholders, William Dickinson and Richard Pye. Most people, however, held other land in the village from Courten, Broughton or Hinde.

How much land was required to support a family is not clear. Some of the very smallest holdings certainly look to have been farms. Charles Cawdaile, for example, held a cottage and yard in the village, 2 lands and 1 'gore' in the West Field, 5 lands and 2 gores in the South Field, 9 lands in the South Field, and 3 doles of meadow in South Lound meadow. The whole amounted to slightly less than 5 acres, which he rented from Courten for 8s a year. Other smallholdings were probably worked by village craftsmen, but many must have been in the hands of people who sold their labour in the village. Eight people leased nothing more than a house and yard, while John Bullivant must surely have struggled to make a living from his house and yard, 2 'lands' in the West Field and one in the South Field, a total holding of less than 2 acres. Peter Broughton's Great Farm included a house in the village which he presumably leased to a bailiff or to labourers, although Mark Pierce did not record such information. If the characteristic open-field farm was a family concern, several of the larger Laxton holdings must have required hired hands at least during busy seasons of the year. Many of those with holdings of 5 acres or less may have supplemented their income by labouring for other farmers.

The number of people who were primarily craftsmen in early seventeenth-century Laxton is not clear from Pierce's survey since he gives little away about how individuals made a living. John Brook was the miller, Nicholas Taylor was a tanner, Nicholas Pawlthorp and Francis Smith were tailors, and Henry Inkersall seems to have been the village baker.[28] Robert Dickinson was the blacksmith. At his death in 1661 he left 'all the tools, implements and goods belonging to my shop' to his wife and son. Most craftsmen combined their work with a small agricultural holding. Thomas Bee, a weaver who died in 1631, left to his son Theophilus 'my shop with my two looms and all the gear and furniture thereunto belonging', and to his two daughters shares in his 'brown heifer'. Nicholas Pawlthorp held just 2 acres in 1635, but other crafts-men had substantial holdings although not large farms. Christopher Betney, described in his will as a joiner when he died in 1640, farmed 23 acres in 1635, while Nicholas Taylor held 17 acres. Robert Dickinson held only a house and croft in 1635 (leased from Broughton), but by the time he died he had acquired 'a little portion of arable land' and a small flock of sheep. The parish registers record the burial of a carpenter in 1638, a glover in 1640, and in 1642 a weaver and a mason. Among will-makers were Thomas Parker, glover (1652), William Greete, weaver (1662), Robert Joules of Moorhouse, carpenter (1667), and Peter Allicock, wheelwright (1667).

Close examination of Mark Pierce's survey also shows that no occupier is recorded for a number of houses in the village. For the 111 houses in Laxton and Moorhouse, occupiers can be reasonably ascertained for only 95. Some of the village's more substantial farmers are named as tenants of more than one house, among them Robert Roos with three, and Humphry Hopkinson, Robert Shipton and William Woolfit with two each. Who lived in the 16 houses for which no occupier is given by Pierce? They could have been tenants of the manor for whom Pierce does not record a residence, or tenants of some of the absentee freeholders, or even individuals sub-letting from substantial farmers such as Hopkinson and Woolfit. Alternatively they could have been labourers or cottagers renting a house while they were employed in the village. We cannot be sure, but there is evidence to suggest that the turnover of individuals (and to a lesser extent families) in the village was considerable, and some of these houses could have been occupied by people on short-term contract work in the village.

The Protestation Returns were compiled in 1641–2 to assess the strength of religious conformity.[29] All males of 18 years and over were recorded, and for Laxton and Moorhouse this produced 153 names. Coming so soon after the 1635 survey, the overlap of names with the terrier ought to be significant, but

---

[28] BL Egerton 3660E/B355.
[29] W. F. Webster (ed.), *Nottinghamshire Protestation Returns 1642–3* (Nottingham, 1980), pp. 18–19.

when the lists are compared some surprising results emerge. Only 57 people can be identified with any reasonable certainty as appearing in both the survey and the Protestation Returns, while 91 appear only in the Protestation Returns and 76 only in the survey. This turnover requires some explanation.

Part of this discrepancy in numbers is relatively easy to account for. In the first place, since the Protestation Returns recorded all males over 18 they must have included a number of sons living with their fathers and not having an establishment of their own who would not have shown up in the survey; after all, a young man of 18 in March 1641–2 would have been only 11 or 12 in 1635. Second, various people recorded in the survey would not, for one reason or another, have turned up in the Protestation Returns. These included women (13 owners or occupiers in 1635), institutions – among them the Dean and Chapter of Southwell – and male freeholders and tenants not resident in Laxton (20). In half a dozen cases there is reason to believe that since 1635 a son had come of age and taken over the management of the property from a widowed mother. This was the case with Francis Roos, recorded as church-warden, who in 1635 was 17 and living with his mother, Widow Roos. The death of the father probably accounts for another half dozen or so cases where a surname is common to both the 1635 and the 1641/2 lists but the christian name has changed. Finally, families came and went in the seventeenth century with surprising frequency. A handful of substantial families had been in the village for anything up to a century before Mark Pierce began his work, and some were to remain for many generations to come. They included the Chappells – still living in the parish as late as 1854 – the Hazzards, the Salmons and the Taylors. However – and this will become clearer in later chapters – these were the exception rather than the rule, and particularly among young men seeking contract employment, and among labouring families looking for work, the turnover of surnames was considerable, often over short periods of time. Children were expected to make their way independently in the world by their early teens.

None of this helps to fill the houses. However, since virtually no evidence of sub-letting occurs in the terrier it looks as if a substantial number of agricultural labourers were living in the village, many of them only for a short time. Some were almost certainly hired by the year to undertake work on behalf of one of the larger farmers. Annual service was common among males aged between 15 and 24 from the seventeenth century. As a result, young men would regularly be arriving in the village for a short stay before moving on again, but they were likely to leave little record of themselves. Usually they would have lived with their employer, although there is no reason why a substantial farmer should not have boarded them in a separate property. The evidence of their presence in the village can perhaps be inferred from the Protestation Returns. The occurrence of surnames such as Furnace, Gurnell, Hill, Quickfall, Reddish and Stevenson, which appear in no other contemporary lists, may well pinpoint who these young men were. In addition the burial registers for Laxton 1635–42 record a further eleven surnames which appear in neither the survey nor in the Protestation Returns. Four of these are of females, possibly young girls who died while in service as domestic servants.

FARMING

Open-field farming enabled most households to provide the majority of their own needs. Barley supplied food and drink, while the hundreds of acres of wheat, rye, peas and beans which were grown annually offered sustenance for both man and beast. The wheat was ground at one of the mills. The main village mill was, predictably, in Mill Field in 1635, and the site can still be seen today, but there was also another mill in South Field which was probably used mainly by the people of Moorhouse. Most families kept poultry, a pig, a few sheep and one or two cattle. The animals provided food, bacon, butter and cheese, as well as wool for turning into cloth to supply the demand for sheets, towels and ordinary garments. Some fuel could be obtained from the woodlands. Our knowledge of farming practice in this period is, however, relatively thin, but we do know that some if not all of the Laxton farmers must have been enjoying relative prosperity. This is not surprising as conditions everywhere were favourable in this period, but for Laxton we can measure something of what it meant from the level of rents and the efforts to enclose.

One of the reasons why Pierce was apparently inconsistent in the information he included in the terrier is that Courten commissioned the survey with a particular aim in mind. Although he wanted a full survey of ownership, his main concern was with those properties which he owned, and for this reason these are the only ones for which rental information was included (see table 3.3). When Francis Bushie surveyed Peter Roos's estate in 1606 in connection with the wardship of Gilbert Roos, he valued Laxton at just £13 6s 8d which suggests that despite a century or so of rising prices and rents in England the Roos estate was yielding a relatively poor return.[30] A rental of 1621 named 42 leasehold tenants of the lord of the manor in Laxton and 12 in Moorhouse, paying a total of £95 1s 4d in rents.[31] Francis Roos's rent was £4 0s 4d. His widow was paying the same amount in 1635 for 97 acres held on a two-life lease (the only example of this form of customary tenure in 1635) with remainder to her 17-year old son Francis. Other examples of similarities between the lists could also be given, although there is evidence to suggest that some attempt had already been made to push up rents; Nicholas Pawlthrop, for example, was paying 8s 2d in 1621, but £1 5s in 1635.

[30] PRO Ward/5/32/1606.
[31] BL Egerton Roll 8446.

TABLE 3.3 *The Laxton rental in 1635*

| | Rental | | |
	£	s	d
Chief rents	1	6	2
Laxton demesne lands	104	15	8
Laxton tenements	253	13	10
Moorhouse tenants	9	16	0
	369	11	8

Source: C. S. and C. S. Orwin, *The Open Fields* (Oxford, 1938), p. 148.

Courten's intention was to introduce economic rents in place of the customary ones which were being paid, particularly on the manorial lands. These had traditionally been under-rented because tenants also paid fines. In Laxton, although the fines had disappeared, rents remained low. From 1,407 acres of manorial land Courten was receiving just £254 rent (3s 7d per acre), which included the rents of the farms newly purchased from Hinde, currently let for £73, whereas the 295 acres of demesne which he let yielded £105 (7s 1d per acre). In two cases the terrier noted that the rents could be raised on the expiration of the current lease. In Moorhouse William Urry's farm was rented at £3, but valued at £15 in 1635; Widow Hazard's, rented at £3 10s, was valued at £5; and Anthony Taylor's, rented at 19s, was valued at £3. In Urry's case the rent had been £1 18s 4d in 1621. The day of the low rent was clearly numbered.

By 1642 the lord of the manor's rental looked rather more impressive. Between 1635 and 1642 15 of the tenancies had changed and 13 new tenants were listed who had not appeared in the 1635 list. Only 13 tenants enjoyed an unchanged rental since 1635, while 36 were paying more rent and just one was paying less. Some consolidation also appears to have taken place, particularly in regard to the demesne property (no longer designated as such). Most of the 1635 demesne tenants are not in the 1642 rental, while Thomas Batchelor had succeeded his father-in-law Samuel Stanford as one of the lord of the manor's most substantial tenants, paying £43 6s a year rent. Most significant of all was the increase of rent, from £369 in 1635 to £648 13s 2d in 1642.[32]

The willingness of tenants to pay improved rents was a reflection of prosperity. The desire of the farmers to enclose parcels of land was another indication of rising wealth. By 1600 somewhere in the region of 47 per cent of the land of

[32] BL Egerton 3562, fos 10–11.

England was enclosed, but none of the Midlands counties were either wholly or even heavily enclosed.[33] Laxton was probably not untypical. Pierce listed twenty-eight 'Laxton Freehold Closes', totalling 478 acres, and a further 40 acres of closes in Moorhouse. They may once have been within the open fields, but by 1635 they were outside the boundaries. Possibly they had never been within the fields both because of the practical disadvantages of taking in new furlongs at such great distances, and also declining need as pressure on land slackened at the end of the Middle Ages. Whatever the reason, Laxton enjoyed a relatively high degree of enclosure by the seventeenth century; in a survey of 1691 the proportion of enclosed land in Laxton was higher than in any of the other five Nottinghamshire parishes covered.[34]

The process of consolidation had begun long before 1635. The charter of 1232 licensed Robert de Lexington 'to make exchanges of land with his men in *Lexingtun*, both free and bond', apparently in recognition of the advantages to farming derived from strip consolidation and exchange. This is perhaps the earliest evidence of the slow but persistent practice of enclosure and consolidation which has continued in Laxton ever since. Almost certainly consolidation occurred when marginal land cultivated in the prosperous years of the late thirteenth and early fourteenth centuries fell out of use. The 1635 map shows quite clearly that poor land on the periphery of Mill Field, and several areas of South Field, were no longer cultivated in furlongs. Fig. 3.3 shows the extent to which closes had been made on the edges of the West, Mill and South Fields. It is almost impossible to date these enclosures, but their importance can be demonstrated statistically. According to Mark Pierce the area of the four open fields totalled 1,894 acres (see p. 22 above), but the closes and enclosures within them totalled 465 acres. When this is allowed for the true acreage farmed in common is reduced to 1,429 acres (see p. 316), divided roughly equally between the fields (taking West and East Fields together).

With a growing population and rising prices, energetic open-field farmers in sixteenth-century England looked for ways of consolidating strips in order to operate farms more efficiently. Since it was the price of animal products which rose most rapidly some farmers looked to enclose arable land to convert it to grass, in order to keep more sheep and cattle and thereby to increase the production of either wool or meat, while others sought communal agreement to enable them to lay down some of their open-field strips as grass leys on which livestock could either be penned in or tethered. Successive governments did their best in the course of the seventeenth century to enforce the laws against

[33] J. R. Wordie, 'The Chronology of English Enclosure, 1500–1914', *Economic History Review*, 36 (1983), 489–90.

[34] G. E. Mingay, 'Landownership and Agrarian Trends in the Eighteenth Century', unpublished Ph.D. thesis, University of Nottingham, 1958, p. 367.

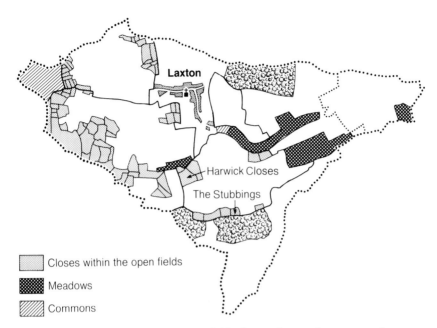

Laxton

Harwick Closes

The Stubbings

☐ Closes within the open fields

▦ Meadows

▨ Commons

FIGURE 3.3 *Closes within the open fields, the meadows and commons, 1635*

enclosing and engrossing, and a last attempt was made by the Crown in the 1630s. During this sweep, in May 1631, five Laxton farmers were reported. Robert Shipton had enclosed 2 acres, while Humphry Hopkinson, Thomas Taylor, Thomas Hunt and Alexander Taylor had all 'attempted to enclose' parcels of land varying between 1 and 3½ acres. The view of the justices, appended in a note to their report, was that, far from being prejudicial, such enclosures contributed to the maintenance of tillage, particularly, it would seem, as all were in the more remote parts of the fields. Although these were the men caught out, the 1635 map provides ample evidence that they were not alone. In East Long Lands furlong (South Field) Peter Broughton had just acquired one 'land' 'in exchange for land in West Crofts', in order to complete a sizeable block of 5 lands totalling about 1 acre. Broughton was almost certainly making closes within the open fields. In West Field numbers 608–12 in Westwood Closes are described as 20 lands 'enclosed'.[35]

These examples show that there were farmers in Laxton who were well aware of the advantages arising from consolidation. Courten's decision to complete the survey which had been started a decade earlier so that he could

[35] PRO SP/16/192 f. 94; C. Delano Smith, 'Laxton in 1635', *East Midland Geographer*, 7, 6 (1980), 226–8; cf. *Open Fields*, pp. 130, 135.

raise rents was a recognition of prosperity in the village. It also raises the more awkward question of why was enclosure not taken further? The most obvious explanation would be in terms of the continuation of copyhold and other ancient forms of tenure in the village – which were widely recognized as a hinderance to enclosure – but with one exception these had effectively disappeared in 1635. On the other hand enclosure by agreement, which would have been the form required, was not always achieved without considerable trouble, especially when the land was divided, as it was in Laxton. Courten may well have considered that in order to avoid damaging and quite likely costly opposition, he needed to buy out some of the smaller freeholders, and either to negotiate purchases from Broughton and Hinde, or to arrange agreements with them. Since almost all of the smaller holdings, the Broughton property and a sizeable slice of Hinde's land changed hands over the following century the lord of the manor certainly had the possibility of bringing about enclosure, but the opportunities were not seized. The extent of the land in closes ensured some flexibility in farming which possibly lessened the need for enclosure, while the structure of ownership and occupation actually grew more complex in the century after 1635. This had the effect of deterring would-be enclosers. The long-term consequences of these various pressures will become clear in later chapters.

Overall there is plenty of evidence that Laxton enjoyed the sort of buoyant financial conditions experienced by many communities in these years. The number of agricultural male, and female domestic servants is one indication, while another is the evidence available in wills. Several mention sums of money either owed or owing, and large sums of cash were obviously available in the local economy. Thomas Cawdwell, described as yeoman, who died in 1654 owing £62 was owed £25, while when Ann Graisbrooke, widow of the butcher, died in 1662, her monetary bequests totalled more than £140. These may not have been typical, but they point to a relatively wealthy village in the middle years of the seventeenth century.

Most of the farmers, whether they had large or small holdings, would have been concerned primarily with supplying food and other necessaries for their households, but few would have been true subsistence farmers. Virtually everyone in the village needed to sell some of their produce in the market place if they were to be able to pay their rent and their tax assessments (both local and national) and to purchase goods not available in Laxton. Among these were coal. In his will of 1654 Thomas Cawdwell instructed his son to 'give unto Mr Brittayne of Laxton the fetching home of one load of coals from the coalpits the said Mr Brittayne paying for the coal at the pits'; while William Urry of Moorhouse left instructions in 1662 that his daughter Anne was to have the chamber over the parlour in his house as her lodging room, and that if the tenants of the farm did not keep the downstairs fire well stoked they were to give Anne 'every year . . . a load of coals, and a chimney to burn them in to her own use'. Money was also needed to hire the services of the village craftsmen, the wheelwright and blacksmith, the baker and the miller.

Laxton people almost certainly favoured Tuxford, or the ancient and declining market at Ollerton. Both were within reasonable walking distance. Tuxford, just under 5 miles away, had a Monday market dealing in cattle, sheep, pigs and hops, and fairs were held on 12 May and 23–8 September. Market day was on Friday at Ollerton, which specialized in cattle and sheep, pedlery and hops, and fairs were held on 1 May and 18 October. The September and October fair dates may have been too early for the winter sale of animals, in which case Laxton farmers may have needed to travel to Newark for cattle sales in November and December. Farmers are traditionally thought to have travelled further to obtain good prices for livestock, and Laxton people were probably ready to go to Southwell and Mansfield fairs, but this is speculation.

Travelling to market also provided an opportunity to meet people beyond the narrow confines of the village. Young people could look for employment and, of course, marriage partners. For the whole period 1629–1700, 520 marriages were recorded in the parish registers. Many involved two people from within the village, but altogether 162 of the partners came from 62 places outside of the parish. Of these 46 (28 per cent) came from no more than 3 miles away, and only 23 (14 per cent) travelled 13 miles or more. Quite how people got to know each other over such distances is itself an interesting question; how, for example, did Laxton people come to marry partners from Gainsborough (2), Lincoln, or the village of Wollaton, which is close to Nottingham? The fact that 21 of the partners (12 per cent) came from the two local market towns may be an indication of where courtships began. Others probably met on the journey to or from market. To reach Tuxford, villagers from Eakring, Kneesall, Ossington, Norwell and Ompton would have had to pass through Laxton, and collectively they provided 37 marriage partners. Marriage often produced movement into or out of the village. It is usually assumed that girls married in their home church prior to moving out of the village if their husband had a farm elsewhere. If they had met, and intended to marry, an agricultural male servant hired to the village for the year, the ceremony is likely to have occurred in October or shortly after the annual hire came to an end at Michaelmas (29 September). Males, by contrast, were likely to marry in other parishes.[36]

The picture which can be drawn of Laxton life in the early seventeenth century is a partial one. The documentary sources fail us when we try to find out what sort of conditions people lived in, and how they viewed their neighbours and their lifestyle. For later periods we shall be able to provide more

---

[36] J. A. J. Gell, 'Laxton – Network Analysis of an Open-field Parish', unpublished BA dissertation, University of Nottingham, 1977, pp. 33–6.

evidence, but the helplessness of the historian when the documents fail can be demonstrated from a single example. In the 1640s the English countryside echoed to the tune of civil war. Laxton was not immune, because in 1645 Charles I quartered troops in the village.[37] Just what the villagers thought of this intrusion, or of the fall out from the Scottish troops during the seige of Newark, is impossible to know; probably they hoped, like communities elsewhere, that the Civil War would go away, and Francis Smith the tailor, the only recusant recorded in the Protestation Returns in 1643, may have found himself in a particularly difficult situation. With the first civil war over the County Committee for Nottinghamshire deemed William Rooke, the vicar of Laxton, disaffected and unsuitable for the post. As a result he was probably ejected; certainly he had gone from the living by 1650 although his successor did not take up the post until 1651.[38] Laxton was not isolated from the events of the Civil War, and we may perhaps assume that it was not isolated from the cultural ebb and flow of English society in the decades before 1660. There was doubtless much discussion, particularly of the departure of the vicar, but none of this was recorded, and as a result we can merely hint at events rather than being able to discuss them more fully.

[37] C. H. Firth (ed.), *Memoirs of the Life of Colonel Hutchinson* (1906), p. 435.
[38] A. C. Wood, *A History of Nottinghamshire* (Nottingham, 1948), p. 199.

Chapter Four

Prosperity and Depression, 1635–1736

A century after Mark Pierce compiled his map and terrier another surveyor, George Capps, was employed to go around the parish and the fields and to make a record similar in detail and content. Considerable changes had taken place in the meantime. Some alterations were obvious: there was no longer a resident lord of the manor and the manor house had been allowed to fall down; the village was beginning to take on a striking new appearance as brick-built houses replaced the old mud and stud dwellings; the meadow lands had been enclosed; part of the woodlands had been cleared; and new farmsteads had been laid out on the edges of the parish. These changes could not hide the fact that Laxton had not fared well. Down to the end of the seventeenth century, and in the first few years of the eighteenth, Laxton was a prosperous, populous village; during the 1720s the village passed through difficult days, partly reflecting national economic changes. The population of England reached a peak of 5.3 million in the mid-1650s, a figure which was not surpassed until the 1720s. With population static, and sometimes falling, wages rose and rents declined, particularly in the arable vale lands of midland England.[1] Even where rents stayed steady until the 1690s few further increases took place before the mid-eighteenth century. Prices were stable or in decline from the 1650s, and during the 1730s and 1740s agriculture was severely depressed. Landlords complained of unpaid rents and bankrupt tenants, and Laxton was not immune to these difficulties. The response varied, but by the time George Capps followed Mark Pierce's footsteps the landlord had brought about a major change – nothing less than partial enclosure.

PEOPLE

In the 1630s the village population stood at about 490. Thereafter it grew considerably, but in the 1720s it fell back to about the same level as the 1630s.

---

[1] Margaret Gay Davies, 'Country Gentry and Falling Rents in the 1660s and 1670s', *Midland History*, 4 (1977), 86–96.

The increase in numbers can be measured in various ways. Calculations based on the 1676 returns of Bishop Compton's ecclesiastical survey produce a figure of 471 by that date,[2] but this may be too low because a rather higher figure seems likely on the basis of the Hearth Tax returns (table 4.1). The total of 127 households recorded in 1664 was 16 more than Mark Pierce had counted 40 years earlier. The total was only 102 in 1674, a fall in line with what was happening elsewhere in the county. This was partly a reflection of demographic difficulties, but it was also a result of careless recording of house numbers. Although a few houses may have been demolished in the 10-year interval, country-wide the assessors seem to have been less conscientious about record-ing exempt households in 1674 than their predecessors a decade earlier. Con-verting Hearth Tax household figures into population is notoriously difficult, but on the basis of 127 households a population of between 540 and 590 seems not unreasonable.[3] An increase of between 10 and 20 per cent in the number of people, and of 14 per cent in the number of households, would also stand favourable comparison with national trends.

TABLE 4.1 *Laxton and Moorhouse Hearth Tax returns*

	Households		
Number of hearths	*1662*	*1664*	*1674*
7	1	1	–
6	–	–	2
4	1	2	2
3	2	2	3
2	8	7	32
1	82	80	51
	94	92	90
Not chargeable	No record	35	12
		127	102

Sources: PRO E/179/254/27, 29; E/179/160/322.

[2] Anne Whiteman (ed.), *The Compton Census of 1676: a Critical Edition* (1986), p. 583.
[3] These figures are calculated according to the following formulae: 1 The number of houses is inflated by 25 per cent to take account of under-registration. Laxton had 102 houses in 1674. Inflated by 25 per cent this produces a total of 127, which is multiplied by 4.25 to total 540. 2 Chargeable households are assumed to represent 65 per cent of the true total of houses. Laxton had 90 assessed houses, suggesting a real total of 138, and a population (multiplied by 4.25) of 587, or *c.*590. These formulae are explained in my introduction to W. F. Webster, ed., *Notting-hamshire Hearth Tax, 1664: 1674* (Nottingham, 1989).

These figures can be compared to calculations based on recorded baptisms and burials. Aggregative analysis of the parish registers shows a rise in numbers to 550 at the end of the 1660s. The village apparently experienced something of a crisis between 1667 and 1674, with burials exceeding baptisms almost for the first time since records began in the mid-sixteenth century. Our analysis of these figures suggests that total population may have fallen back to below 500, and it helps to explain the fall in recorded households between 1664 and 1674. It is also in line with the national trend in these years.[4] From 1673 baptisms again began to exceed burials and some recovery took place in total numbers. However, there was a further setback in the late 1680s, with total numbers falling below 500 by 1690. After this, the pattern was one of improvement, and by 1715–20 numbers probably exceeded 560.

In the course of the 1720s the upward trend in population came to an abrupt end, and went into reverse. Nationally the later 1720s were years of bad weather and poor harvests which brought the second most severe percentage decrease in population for the whole period 1541–1870. In Nottinghamshire burials reached a peak between 1727 and 1729 as harvest failures and epidemics sent the upward growth of population into reverse.[5] Laxton was badly hit, although the extent of the crisis is obscured by a gap in the baptism register for 1726–7, and in the burial register for 1727. However, in 1728 and 1729 there were 40 and 37 burials respectively, three times the usual average. It is probably no coincidence that there were more fealties sworn at the manor court in these years than at any comparable time; 14 in 1726, 8 in 1727, 4 in 1728, 10 in 1729 and 12 each in 1730 and 1731. The village population may well have declined from about 560 to around 500 in these difficult years. By 1730 the worst was over, although across the county there were further reversals in 1736 and 1741–2. Laxton was slightly affected by the first of these but seems largely to have avoided the second, as numbers recovered to about 520 by 1740. By this date, however, there is other evidence against which these figures can be compared.

The survey undertaken by George Capps during the 1730s is directly comparable with Mark Pierce's work. Where Pierce had recorded 89 households in Laxton and 22 in Moorhouse, Capps counted just 80 houses in the village and 17 in Moorhouse. We shall see that another 4 ought to be added to this total to account for the outlying farms. If this is a reasonable assumption it would suggest a considerable contraction in houses since the 1670s, and a population of about 480 (using the normal multiplier for this period of 4.75). This compares reasonably well with estimates drawn from the parish registers.

[4] The most authoritative account of English population is in E. A. Wrigley and R. S. Schofield, *The Population History of England 1540–1871* (1981).

[5] J. D. Chambers, 'The Vale of Trent, 1670–1800: a Regional Study of Economic Change', *Economic History Review* supplement (1957), 29; Chambers, *Nottinghamshire in the Eighteenth Century*, 2nd edn (1966), p. xii.

Comparison of the two surveys shows that 7 sites in Laxton had been deserted since 1635 (and the two half messuages converted into one), while in Moorhouse 4 of the lord of the manor's cottages had gone, and since 1635 one of John Roos's two houses had also disappeared. Capps's survey confirms the evidence of declining numbers, and so do the Suit Rolls of the manor court, which recorded all those in the village liable to appear at the court. In 1680 there were 112 names on the Roll, but by 1738 only 88, a decrease of 27 per cent.[6] The number of tenants also declined. In 1687 the lord of the manor had 71 rent-paying tenants, but just 68 in 1691, 69 in 1705 and 62 in 1728 – no detailed rentals survive for the intervening years. Of these 62, 22 leased farms, 25 leased cottages, 1 leased only a house and 14 leased land.

Two other counts from this period suggest an even greater decline in numbers than do these calculations. A terrier prepared by the vicar and churchwardens in 1743 recorded for Laxton and Moorhouse 82 houses, 62 orchards, 27 dovecotes and 71 crofts liable to tithe.[7] A figure of 82 houses, assuming they were all occupied, is substantially fewer than the number recorded by Capps, and suggests that population had fallen below 400. At the time of Archdeacon Herring's visitation of the village in 1743 the vicar, John Warrell, reported that there were 60 families in Laxton and a further 12 in Moorhouse, which would point to a population of only about 340.[8] These figures confirm the trend of falling numbers, but they suggest a level of catastrophe which is not born out by the parish registers and the Capps survey.

We know from the Poll Tax returns of 1667 that Laxton was a relatively wealthy village in the mid-seventeenth century. Its assessment of £20 3s was more than the market town of Tuxford (£18 17s), and not a great deal less than East Retford (£23 4s). On these figures it was also better off than many of its neighbouring villages, even if it was in a different league to more substantial settlements such as Southwell (£50 13s).[9] Hearth numbers are also a pointer towards house sizes and, by implication, wealth (see table 4.1). In 1664 the largest property in terms of hearths was Mr William Roos's house, with 7 chimneys; John Roos and Augustine Hinde (the latter in Moorhouse) had 4 chimneys; and William Stanford and William Woolfit 3 each. Seven houses had 2 chimneys; 80 had a single chargeable hearth; and 35 were not chargeable. For rural Nottinghamshire this was by no means an unrespectable total of larger houses.

Ten years later, chargeable households had declined by two but a significant shift had occurred in the number of hearths per household. The houses of both Augustine Hinde and William Roos were rated at 6 chimneys, and while there

    [6] BL Egerton 3632, fos 246–61.
    [7] NAO PR 4065; DR/1/3/2/1.
    [8] P. C. Walker and S. L. Ollard (eds), *Archbishop Herring's Visitation Returns 1743*, Yorkshire Archaeological Society, Record Series, 77 (1930), IV, 88–9.
    [9] PRO E/179/160/325.

were still only 7 houses with 3 or more chimneys, 32 were now recorded as having 2 chimneys. While one or two householders might have extended their homes in the meantime, and added a new chimney, the most likely reason for this change was stricter assessment procedures; although slightly contradictorily the number of households excused payment had fallen, probably because of lax counting.[10] What we do know is that householders with more than one hearth were automatically liable to assessment, and could not be excused on the grounds of poverty, so that the recorded figures are likely to provide an accurate guide to the larger houses in the village.

Hearth numbers tell us little about the houses they represent, and unfortunately there seems to have been no fixed relationship between the number of hearths and the number of rooms in a house. In late seventeenth-century Cambridgeshire, single-hearth houses might have between 1 and 6 rooms, although 2 to 4 were most common, and two-hearth houses anywhere between 2 and 10 rooms. The simplest house would be a hall, parlour and service room with an upper chamber over the hall or parlour. Parlours, contrary to present-day terminology, were rooms for sleeping, while upstairs chambers might be bedrooms but they were just as likely to be rooms for storing corn and ripening cheeses, partly because until the later eighteenth century few houses had a cellar. Most Laxton houses seem to have had more than the basic minimum of rooms. Although we would expect to find labourers living in houses of 1 or 2 rooms, and husbandmen and craftsmen in houses of 5–7 rooms, a straightforward correlation cannot be assumed.[11] The Chappells, a long established freeholding family in the village, seem to have had a relatively small house, but this may have been because they had grown wealthier without either moving or adding to the property. Other families may have overtaken them, since it was common practice in the Trent valley to extend houses by adding a new parlour with a chamber over it. Francis Green extended his house before he died in 1712, and in 1727 William Taylor's inventory recorded goods found by the appraisers in his new parlour and new chamber.

The problem of relating house sizes and wealth can be illustrated by looking at the inventories of a number of late seventeenth-century Laxton men and women. Inventories were drawn up at, or just after, the death of a householder, and although there are many well-known problems with interpreting the information they contain, they tell us a good deal about individual households. Nottinghamshire inventories do not usually survive before 1688, so that direct

---

[10] These points are made at greater length in my introduction to *Nottinghamshire Hearth Tax*.

[11] M. W. Barley, *The English Farmhouse and Cottage* (1961), pp. 203–10; Margaret Spufford, 'The Significance of the Cambridgeshire Hearth Tax', *Proceedings of the Cambridgeshire Antiquarian Society*, LV (1962), 53–64. The Laxton probate papers used through chapters 4 and 5 are to be found in the Archdeaconry of Nottingham collection now housed in NAO. Individual inventories have not been separately referenced since they can be found by name and date in the collection.

comparisons cannot be drawn with the Hearth Tax returns. However, they continued to be compiled down to the middle of the eighteenth century, and 63 inventories have survived for Laxton, covering the period 1688 to 1787. Some of the later ones – while giving gross values – are perfunctory documents revealing little about the household, or the individual items constituting the overall inventory. As a group however they provide a mine of information relating to the seventeenth- and eighteenth-century village.

Since appraisers usually recorded household goods on a room-by-room basis, inventories include information about both the number of rooms in particular houses, and also their contents. Inventory evidence confirms the Hearth Tax figures – most of Laxton's farmers lived in houses of a similar size. Humphrey Hopkinson, described as husbandman, came to Laxton in the 1680s, where he rented a 66-acre farm from the lord of the manor, of which nearly 46 acres were in the open fields. The rent was £22 10s in 1681, but it came down to £18 in 1684 at which it stayed. Hopkinson's home consisted of a hall, a great parlour (which was a bedroom), a kitchen and dairy, two chambers over the parlour (both of which were bedrooms), and a chamber over the house in which wheat and bacon were stored. Hopkinson was obviously a wealthy man; at his death in 1691 the gross value of his inventory was £260, which included £101 purse and apparell, and £61 in bonds and money due to him. This was probably a typical household for a later seventeenth-century husbandman. John Freeman (d. 1688), similarly described, and the father of Richard Freeman, who was leasing 54 acres from the lord of the manor in 1691, lived in a house with a hall, a parlour (in which there were 3 bedsteads), a dairy and kitchen, and two chambers, one over the parlour with the beds, and the other over the hall. In the latter he was storing wheat, peas, oatmeal, beef, bacon and cheese.

Hopkinson and Freeman were substantial farmers, but their homes were no larger than those of men whose inventories suggest they were somewhat less well off. Nicholas Woolfit left an inventory of only £19 in 1708, but his home consisted of the usual hall, parlour and kitchen with chambers over the parlour and hall; similarly Peter Dickinson of Moorhouse left an inventory of just under £30 in 1709, and lived in a house with hall, parlour and buttery on the ground floor, and parlour and hall chambers. If it is possible to generalize, parlour chambers were bedrooms and hall chambers were storage areas because warmth rising from the hall below kept them dry. Dickinson, for example, had corn and other goods in his hall chamber. It may have been only the poorest members of the community who lived in very basic houses, and they were unlikely to have had inventories taken. Prior to 1730 just one inventory survives for a labourer, Augustine Johnson of Moorhouse (1725), and he lived in the most basic of houses with a hall and parlour.

What of the more substantial dwellings in the village? The most tantalizing evidence relates to the house in which William Roos was living. He was the tenant of the 7-hearth house recorded in both the 1662 and 1664 returns (table 4.1), and one of the 6-hearth houses in 1674. It is possible that this was the old manor house, but Roos died in 1678 and although his will refers to the house in which he lived it gives no further details. The earliest Laxton rental is for 1678, after Roos's death. Rent 'for the Hall' was paid by Ann Green and her son Francis. However, in 1674 they were rated for two hearths and one hearth respectively. Various explanations are possible: the hall may have been divided into tenements which, because they record households rather than individuals, would not show up in the returns; or it may have been partially occupied perhaps as a result of dilapidations; or the Greens may simply have moved in after Roos's death. Possibly this was the point in time when it was finally vacated, but the evidence is inconclusive. What we do know is that in the course of the seventeenth century it was allowed to decay, and finally to be demolished. Some of its stone materials were re-used for building in the village; the farm-house at Ivy House Farm may contain timbers and stone from the old hall.

Francis Green was tenant of 'the hall homestead' in 1691, which was a $7\frac{1}{2}$-acre holding. At that date he rented a cottage from the lord of the manor, but by the time he died in 1712 he was a substantial farmer. He lived in perhaps the largest house in the village. The inventory mentions a kitchen, a brewhouse, a cellar and a parlour, the 'middle house', the 'nether house', five chambers, garrets and a kilnhouse. It may be that this was two houses, or a large house divided into two parts, since he left to his son John 'my old house I now dwell in and the new garretts with all the outhouses belonging', and to his widow 'that new building wherein I dwell except the garretts'. This could have been the house with 16 windows, for which a Mr Wilson paid the window tax in 1771, but there is no way of knowing.

Among the other larger houses was the property occupied by the Hinde family in Moorhouse, assessed at 2 hearths in 1662, 4 in 1664 and 6 in 1674. These figures may have represented improved assessment procedures but it is also clear that the Hindes had been building. From Edmund Hinde's inventory drawn up in 1691 we know that this house consisted of a hall and parlour with chambers over (both of which were bedrooms); a servants' chamber – this was the only house in the parish with designated servants' quarters – three chambers 'in the old building' (bedrooms); 'the old garretts', which housed a salting tub and a cheese press; and a kitchen, brewhouse, dairy, buttery and closet. Hinde of course was a gentleman, but some of the yeomen also had substantial properties, including William Challand. When Challand died in June 1716 he was tenant of a farm of 51 acres which he had leased from the lord of the manor since the 1690s at £19 10s annual rent. His house consisted of a hall, kitchen, dairy, pantry, and parlour on the ground floor, and four chambers and a garrett above. The garrett and kitchen chamber were used for storing farm produce, and Challand's local standing is witnessed by £108 in purse and apparell.

Possibly the most significant change in Laxton houses during this period was the appearance of the first brick building. The earliest dated brick house still surviving in the village is from 1703 (figure 4.1), but it may not have been the first. Edward Harrison, who died in 1702, was described as 'brickmaker'. He lived in a substantial house with hall, parlour, cellar (containing 'a few barrells and ale'), a dairy, a kitchen, and chambers over the hall, parlour and kitchen. He farmed in a small way; his inventory lists 2 cows, 1 calf, a sow, some pigs and a mare, as well as an acre of barley and 2 acres of peas in the field. This was clearly not his only interest. By far the greatest part of his inventory consisted of malt and wheat at Ollerton and Markham. Together with the cellar contents this suggests he was brewing on a substantial scale; but even this was not all – 'brick in the forest Markham and Tuxford', £60, indicates his major interest. The brick pit occupied two 'lands' in the South Field, owned by Francis Green until they were sold to the lord of the manor in 1728. In sketches prepared for the 1736 survey George Capps labelled these 'lands' as 'brick holes'.[12]

Although the number of rooms in a house was not necessarily indicative of the wealth of the family, we can learn more by examining the contents of the rooms. Although some of the inventories give only sparse detail most allow us a glimpse into what the inside of Laxton homes must have looked like had we been able to walk around them. Usually houses had a standard set of equipment supplemented by odds and ends, and items used for work which took place in the home. Richard Freeman, husbandman, who died in 1709 was not untypical. His house had seven rooms and his inventory totalled £159. Consequently he was a man of some substance although he left only £1 in purse and apparell. The main room, the hall, contained fire irons, 13 dishes and 14 plates (all pewter), 3 tables, a cupboard, a long settle, 5 chairs and a number of other small items. The adjoining parlour housed 3 bedsteads and 7 chairs. The kitchen was full of pots and pans, 2 brewing tubs and 2 scuttles of coal. It was perhaps as well that cooking did not take place in seventeenth-century kitchens. In the dairy were 5 barrels and 3 shelves. Upstairs in the hall chamber was a chest, a cheeseheck (a rack for cheeses) and cheese. The chamber over the parlour had 2 bedsteads, 2 chests and other furniture, while there was corn in the chamber over the kitchen.

Freeman's was not a cluttered house, but his appraisers leave a number of questions unanswered because they used phrases such as 'other small things'. One of the three appraisers was Francis Green, who had been doing this job for many years; indeed, of the eighteen inventories surviving for the period 1688 until his death in 1712, Green was an appraiser in twelve cases. Maybe with Richard Freeman's house he was simply not as conscientious as when he and three other village farmers examined John Freeman's house in 1688. This was a

[12] NUMD M.4513, f. 67; MaB/222/22.

BAR FARM: AL1703

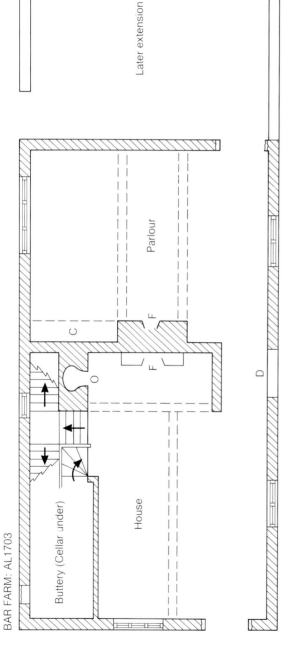

Built by A.L., who has not been identified (see plate 4.1) It was well built, with a compact plan. When surveyed in 1950 it was largely unaltered; the original entrance (D) in the south front, facing the farmyard, had been blocked and a new entrance made in the gable end. The living room (called 'house' or 'hall') had been heated by a hearth fire under a large brick hood; there was a bread oven (O). By 1950 a modern fireplace had replaced the hearth fire (F). In c.1800 a third room had been added at the east end. The western half of the house had always been divided to provide a buttery with a cellar under it; upstairs, there were two chambers over the hall, one of them with a ladder up to the loft and a larger one over the parlour. The house has recently been restored with some alterations which are not shown.

FIGURE 4.1 *Bar Farm, 1703, the oldest brick house still surviving in the village*

typical six-roomed house, and the contents of each room could have been found in many other houses. In the hall were the usual fire irons, a cupboard, a table, 2 forms, 4 stools, 5 chairs, 10 pewter dishes, 2 flagons, 6 cushions and a number of other odds and ends. Next door in the parlour were 3 bedsteads, 2 feather beds, a bolster, 2 pillows, 5 flock pillows, 2 sets of hangings with other furniture for the three beds, and a table. In the dairy were 5 barrels, 2 churns, 5 kitts (round wooden vessels used for milk or butter), 5 bowls and other milk vessels. The kitchen contained coal, 5 brass pans, 2 pots, a copper, 2 cunbells (wooden tubs) and 3 looms (tubs or buckets). Upstairs, the chamber over the parlour had a bed with associated furniture, 2 chests, 3 coverlets, 15 pairs of sheets with linen, and the hall chamber contained wheat, peas, oatmeal, beef, bacon and cheese.

Other inventories give a similarly detailed picture of the house contents, but the pattern was normally the same give or take a few particular trinkets. Warming pans were found in several houses, and the occasional clock. Brass candlesticks turn up in what presumably were wealthier households. William Urry left brass candlesticks in 1662, Humphrey Hopkinson left two in 1691, and John Chappell another two in 1692. Edward Harrison had a looking glass (1702). In 1692 Edmund Hinde had silver plate valued at £16, three guns, a clock, and – a rarity in Laxton – books. Alexander Taylor left a bible and some silver in his will proved in 1661, while Francis Green left a silver tankard in 1712. Edward Freeman had three silver tumblers (1702), and the contents of his cellar suggest that his house was an inn. William Taylor, who died in 1727 had a 'drink house' with two barrels and other equipment, as well as a dovecote chamber in which he stored corn. A number of individuals also had brewing equipment in their kitchens including Hugh Carpenter in 1709 and Thomas Salmon in 1728. Larger houses might have a brewhouse – as in the case of Francis Green – or even a buttery. Edmund Hinde had both, with seventeen barrels in the buttery.

Just occasionally we can follow the progress of a house and its contents through a series of inventories. The Challands were a substantial yeoman farming family throughout this period. In 1674 Widow Challand lived in a two-hearth house and her son William Challand in a one-hearth house. He almost certainly moved into the larger house, on the site of the present Crosshill farm, following her death. Although described as a cottage it was a substantial building with at least ten rooms, and was let to the family by the lord of the manor together with a 51-acre farm.[13] Three inventories survive for the house, from 1710, 1716 and 1735, and they show how descriptions, and possibly room functions, varied through time. The dairy is recorded only in 1710 and 1716; while the kitchen and back kitchen of 1710 were presumably the kitchen and pantry in 1716 and the kitchen in 1735. The parlour contained 2 tables and 14 chairs in 1710, 2 tables and a cupboard in 1716 and unspecified furniture in

1736. The parlour chamber of 1710 with its clock and looking glass, was probably the best chamber of 1716; while the kitchen chamber contained a bed, table and 5 chairs in 1710 and furniture in 1736, but wheat and cheeses in 1716.

The inventories also offer some indication of wealth. The hearth and Poll Tax figures for the 1660s and 1670s suggest a village enjoying some prosperity. Thirty-three inventories have survived for 1688–1736, with a gross value of £5,651 and a mean of £171. Eighteen of the thirty-three (55 per cent) exceeded £100 in gross value, while seven exceeded £250. Francis Green's inventory, appraised at £812 in 1712, was far and away the largest. The village clearly contained some wealthy farmers. On the other hand, in relative terms, Laxton may not have been increasing in wealth. In the 1667 Poll Tax it was assessed at £20 3s, twice as much as Eakring; but in 1697 it was assessed at £23 to Eakring's £25 10s. In terms of wealth it stood only fifth among the villages of the South Clay division of Basstlaw Hundred by the 1690s.[14] Also missing from Laxton inventories is evidence of credit. In some parts of the ocuntry it was normal to find quite considerable sums held in bills and bonds,[15] but this was unusual in Laxton, even among the more substantial farmers. Possibly local practice was to exclude such items. Peter Dickinson, in his will drawn up in 1705, itemized what was to happen to a sum of money he had lent on mortgage when it was repaid, but there is nothing in his inventory about this particular debt, although since he did not die for another four years it could have been redeemed in the meantime.

Finally, the probate records offer a few other insights into village life. Here we read of family tragedies and difficulties. John Harpham, who died in 1668 left his cottage to his son John with the instruction that he should maintain his elder brother William 'while he lives'. Richard Sudbury, who died in 1709, went into considerable detail in his will about what was to happen to his unborn child, leaving alternative instructions depending upon whether it turned out to be a boy or a girl. Perhaps most revealing of all is the low level of literacy. Of forty wills for the period 1662–1735, a mere seven were signed by the testator, and three of these were sufficiently shaky to suggest that the man involved was either not used to using a pen, or was at death's door. It confirms Francis Green's comment in 1680 that the jury that year were a company of ignorant men 'that could scarce any of them write their names', although in point of fact four of the twelve jurymen on that occasion were able to manage a tolerable signature.[16]

[14] PRO E/179/254/35.

[15] B. A. Holderness, 'Credit in English Rural Society before the Nineteenth Century, with Special Reference to the Period 1650–1720', *Agricultural History Review*, 24 (1976), 97–109. Credit is now well attested for English rural society in this period, and its absence in Laxton inventories is unexpected and, at present, inexplicable.

[16] NUMD MaB/201/2, 3.

We shall return to the question of prosperity in the village, but first we can present a profile of the people of Laxton in this century. A comparison of the Pierce and Capps surveys shows that only a handful of houses in the village were occupied by individuals with the same surname as a century earlier.[17] There were still Taylors in no. 2, Hunts in no. 39, Taylors in no. 49 (although they were tenants now, having sold the property to the lord of the manor), Wouflets or Woolfits in no. 67, Pinders in no. 89, Chappells in no. 107 and Cawdwells in no. 121. In Moorhouse the Dickinsons and Harphams were still in the same properties occupied by their families a century earlier. Other instances of continuity may have occurred when descent through the female line had taken place, as with the cottage owned by Thomas Cullin in 1635, which together with all his freehold was in the hands of Edith Skaith a century later. Similarly Francis Green's family still owned but did not live in the cottage in which Thomas Green had occupied in 1635.

Obviously the significance of the turnover of names in individual houses should not be exaggerated. What seems to have happened is that there had been considerable movement around the village, and many families still survived from a century earlier. Of fifty-eight separate surnames recorded in 1635, and forty-nine in 1736, nineteen were common to both. Even where families had retained the same house over the century their farms had sometimes changed considerably. The Woolfits at number 67 farmed 104 acres in 1635 but just 66 acres in 1736, whereas at number 89 the Pinders farmed 51 acres in 1635 but 220 acres in 1736, and at number 121 the Cawdwells farmed just 6 acres in 1635 and 72 acres in 1736. Where farms had been taken over the acreage was also likely to have changed. William Doncaster leased numbers 59 and 60 in 1736 (Crosshill Farm) and worked 182 acres; but a century earlier these had been separate holdings in the hands of William Grasbrough (9 acres) and Robert Roos (26 acres). The idea that houses and farms were passed on intact from generation to generation is clearly a false one in the case of Laxton.

As in 1635 there were a number of houses in the 1730s for which no tenant is known. Capps recorded eleven cases of multiple occupancy: five individuals with 3 properties and six with 2 properties in Laxton (i.e. 27 properties); and in Moorhouse three cases of double occupancy (6 properties). Assuming the named person lived in one of these houses this would account for fourteen out

---

[17] The Capps survey does not exist in a single version. Capps worked from the Pierce survey, which he annotated as he went round the village. This provides one version of his survey. Secondly there are lists of freeholds in Laxton, 1732, and Kingston tenants, 1736, probably prepared by Capps in conjunction with the survey: NUMD M.4907–8. Thirdly a rough and undated copy of the whole survey is in BL Egerton 3631, fos 33–90. The three sources have been used together through this chapter.

of the thirty-three houses and leave nineteen unaccounted for. These properties may have been empty but it seems more likely that, as in 1635, they housed sub-tenants or labourers, or that they were used by servants in husbandry resident in the village.

Most villagers were farmers in one way or another, even if they combined agricultural work with alternative occupations. Open-field farming was not synonymous with small farms; indeed, as we have seen, at Laxton in 1635 there were half a dozen farms in excess of 100 acres and the range of holdings was also found in other open-field villages. The next survey which provides an indication of farm sizes and holdings in Laxton is from 1691, but it covers only the 1,944 acres of land leased to tenants by the lord of the manor and is not therefore a complete survey of the parish. Of this land, 1,480 acres (76 per cent) was let in 20 farms of 51 acres or more, the largest being Widow Roos's 105 acres (most of which was probably the same holding as in 1635). John Woolfit and his son, also John, held farms of 96 and 93 acres each – the Woolfits were not tenants of the lord of the manor in 1635 – while other substantial farms were almost certainly held by descendants of 1635 tenants, among them William Salmon (88 acres), George Urry (87 acres), Thomas Hunt (84 acres), George Pinder (67 acres), Thomas Hazard (59 acres), Richard Freeman (54 acres), William Challand (51 acres) and several of the Taylors. The major newcomer was Francis Green (87 acres), although the proliferation of Woolfits (three in this group but six altogether), Salmons (three) and Taylors (three out of nine leasing from the lord of the manor) may hide family dispersion which cannot now be traced. The twenty-one tenants of these twenty farms shared fourteen surnames all of which were present in the village in 1635.[18]

These were among the most substantial Laxton farmers at the end of the seventeenth century, but there were still plenty of small, and perhaps part-time farmers. The rest of the lord of the manor's leased property in 1691 was let to forty-nine tenants with holdings varying from a handful of perches to 50 acres. In many cases this must have been part of a larger holding while some of the lesser tenants seem to have been the successors of people who were once doing rather better. Mr William Stanford, descended from Samuel Stanford, Courten's steward, appears in the 1674 Hearth Tax return living in a house with fourth hearths. By 1691, however, he had just a cottage and some pasture land totalling 3 acres. Maybe he had gone through bad times, or perhaps this represented semi-retirement.

George Capps's survey in the 1730s covers the whole parish and is directly comparable with Pierce's work (table 4.2). It shows an increase in the number of large farms. Eleven farmers were working in excess of 100 acres and Widow Pinder topped the list with 220 acres. This increase in large farms had been achieved even though the Broughtons no longer farmed in Laxton and the

[18] BL Egerton 3564, 1691 survey of the Duke of Kingston's Laxton estate.

TABLE 4.2 *Laxton farms in 1635 and 1736*

	1635			1736		
Acreage	Number	Total acreage	%	Number	Total acreage	%
100+	5	1077	32.2	11	1526	43.6
51–99	15*	1131	33.8	14	1082	30.9
21–50	15	519	15.5	8	299	8.6
11–20	10	167	5.0	11	145	4.2
6–10	21	174	5.2	22	180	5.2
1–5	34	99	3.0	28	102	2.9
Under 1	27	12	0.4	7	4	0.1
Other		163	4.9		158	4.5
	127	3342	100.0	101	3496	100.0

* One of these farms was in the joint tenure of Humphry Hopkinson and Richard Whitlam, with the result that Hopkinson is counted twice in this group.

Sources: as table 3.2 and n. 17 to this chapter.

Hindes held only 50 acres. Overall the proportion of the parish worked in farms of 51 acres or more had risen from two-thirds to nearly three-quarters. This had been achieved partly at the expense of farms in the 21–50-acre category. Numbers were relatively unchanged in the lower groups with the exception of the very considerable decrease in people with less than 1 acre. It is this reduction which largely accounts for the overall decline of twenty-six in the number of tenants and helps to explain why Laxton was a smaller village in 1736 than in 1635. The increase in the number of large farms had taken place over a period of time (judging by the 1691 figures) and as a result of a major reorganization between 1727 and 1732 to which we shall return below.

There had also been a turnover of personnel. The Rooses now held only 14 acres in the village while the Urrys had disappeared altogether having been a substantial farming family in the seventeenth century. The Taylors still proliferated – twelve of them occupied land in 1736 – but perhaps the best indication of change is the number of large farms worked by men whose surnames do not appear in the village a century earlier. Among those with more than 100 acres in 1736 were John Birkett, Edmund Blighton, Samuel Dobb, John Herring, Thomas Skinner, John Watson and Francis White. Families came and went regularly despite the fact that tenancies could usually be passed on by will, a right carefully guarded by testators. Some wills went to great lengths to describe the tenancy. If others were less detailed the intention was none the less clear. Augustine Johnson of Moorhouse left his son one shilling and divided his 3 acres equally between his two daughters, 'and I also hope Mr Green [the bailiff] will be so kind as to accept of my son [in law] John Young for a tenant as well as I have been for I hope he will make no worse a tenant'.[19]

Not everyone in Laxton was a farmer, or at least not everyone was a full-time farmer. Between 1688 and 1736 probate papers survive for eight craftsmen. We have already met the village brickmaker Edward Harrison, and the others included a cordwainer (shoemaker), a wheelwright, a mason, a gelder – literally one who castrates animals – a weaver and two blacksmiths. Francis Hopkin, who died in 1694 was the village shoemaker. He lived in a one-hearth house in 1674, which was a typical Laxton property with a hall, parlour and dairy, topped by two chambers. The dairy however contained 'one wool wheel

PLATE 4.1 *Bar Farm in 1949. This is the earliest dated brick building in Laxton, although brick may have been in use as a building material before 1703 since Edward Harrison, brickmaker, died in Laxton in 1702. The initials AL on the house, and the date 1703 are formed in the gable with dark header bricks; compare the plan, fig. 4.1. There have been minor alterations to window openings. The house has been separated from its land and is now known as Bar Cottage. It was threatened with demolition after the Ministry of Agriculture took over the Laxton open-field farms, and in recent times it has accommodated animals. Today it has been restored and is in private hands.*

[19] NAO Will of Augustine Johnson of Laxton, 1729.

and reel' valued at 2s 6d, while his tools were valued at £1, and there was a quantity of wool stored in the chamber over the parlour. Hopkin was clearly proud of his work since he left 'my best hat and a brown suit of clothes' to his brother William. Nicholas Gascoigne, the village wheelwright, died in 1704. His inventory gives little away, mentioning only 'carpenters tools' valued at £1, which in his will he bequeathed to his son-in-law. Inventories do not always mention tools; no details are given in the cases of Thomas Adwick, the mason, Nicholas Woolfit, the gelder, and Hugh Cartwright, who was the weaver.

More is known of the village blacksmiths, the Johnsons. Thomas Johnson had two smithies, one in Laxton and the other in Moorhouse, but he still had time to keep poultry and a pig, as well as to do some farming in the fields. His workshop in Laxton was leased from the lord of the manor for £3 18s a year, and contained in 1726 two smithies, bellows, iron and other tools valued at £12 1s, while his shop book was valued at £30. The Moorhouse shop also contained bellows and other tools, valued at £3. At his death in 1726 he left the majority of his goods to his son John, who succeeded him in the business. John Johnson was also to fall victim to the demographic difficulties of these years. He was sick and weak of body when he made his will in August 1729, and was particularly concerned with the fate of his unborn child, who, if a son, was to be 'put to a trade at the expense and charge of my executrix'. An inventory of his possessions recorded some of the items which had appeared less than three years previously in his father's name. The shop book was still valued at £30, though the shop tools were given as £20. There is no mention of a smithy in Moorhouse.

Other individuals almost certainly participated in some form of craft work, while the craftsmen, whatever their official status, were also part-time farmers. Francis Hopkin leased a 7-acre close from the lord of the manor, and by far the largest item in his inventory was his ten cows valued at £31. He also had a number of calves, a pig, a ewe, a swarm of bees and some poultry. The inventory was made in April and the absence of standing crops suggests he may not have farmed open-field arable. Nicholas Gascoigne's inventory is fairly basic. It mentions corn and other goods, manure in the yard and corn growing. From this it is hard to tell the extent of his business, although since the 1690s he had rented 6 acres of close and meadow land for £1 10s a year. The three craftsmen for whom no tools were recorded were obviously active farmers. Thomas Adwick's inventory records hay and corn in the barn, a pig, 3 horses, 2 cows and other beasts, corn sown and ground prepared to sow. Similarly Nicholas Woolfit's lack of tools was not matched by a lack of agricultural produce, including cows, calves, a pig, and barley, peas and wheat in the ground. Hugh Cartwright's main concern in his will was the disposal of his land in Egmanton, while his inventory recorded barley, oatmeal, oats, hay and peas, 8 horses, 4 beasts, 4 pigs, 24 sheep, and wheat and barley in the field. Despite his two smithies Thomas Johnson found time to farm in the fields. At his death in August 1726 there was wheat and barley in the barn, as well as clover hay, while his animals included 4 horses, 3 milk cows, 2 rearing calves, 2 pigs and some sheep. His son, who died three years later, also farmed. His inventory included horses and cattle, barley, wheat and peas.

LOCAL GOVERNMENT

Changes in the lordship of the manor after 1618 had repercussions for the running of the village. Absentee landlords were hardly likely to be found, as Peter Roos had been, dancing round the village maypole and defending local people presented before the church courts. Francis Green, bailiff of the manor court, complained during the dispute over common rights in 1680 that 'the lords of the manor having lived at a distance for many years, and no person of any considerable quality living amongst us, have given the town of Moorhouse opportunity to encroach upon us'; while the members of the jury who so unwisely agreed to the decision in favour of Moorhouse at the 1680 manor court claimed that Mr Augustine Hinde had been allowed rights of common in Laxton 'for nine or ten years past [. . .] because he was an eminent man and we could not dispute it with him'.[20] Complaints were also voiced about Francis Green, who seems to have been a young man in a hurry.

In the absence of a resident lord, local government began to take on a more sophisticated form. By the time records began in the 1720s, five authorities exercised jurisdiction in Laxton: the manor court, the overseers of the high-ways, and of the poor, the constable, and the churchwardens. In a community the size of Laxton it was inevitable that there would be overlap between personnel. The holders of the different posts kept separate accounts, several of which survive for a number of years in the 1720s and 1730s.[21]

The overseers of the highways, appointed under the terms of sixteenth-century legislation, were responsible for road and bridge maintenance, but their efforts seem to have been kept to a minimum. In the 1720s they were spending no more than £2 or £3 a year, and concentrating almost entirely on infilling holes in the roads with stones. Most of their income was raised by the sale of roadside grasses for hay.

Expenditure on the poor was met from voluntary contributions or by raising a poor rate, levied according to the Elizabethan statutes of 1597 and 1601. Few willmakers took much interest in the poor, although Ann Graisbrooke left ten shillings for the poor of the parish in 1662, and in 1692 John Chappell left £1 to 'eight of the poorest widows in Laxton (to be nominated by the ministers

---

[20] NUMD MaB/201/1, 3.
[21] The following paragraphs are based on the accounts for this period in NAO PR 4102–3.

and churchwardens thereof) half a crown a piece'.[22] Usually, however, it was the overseers who had to finance outlay on the poor. In addition to paying out maintenance money, they met the cost of daubing and thatching houses, and buying shoes and coal for poorer members of the community. They also had to search out fathers in bastardy cases. At Quarter Sessions in 1678 William Taylor of Laxton was ordered to pay one shilling a week for seven years towards maintaining an illegitimate child 'by him begotten upon the body of Catherine Moss'. In 1705 the overseers petitioned Quarter Sessions about the settlement provisions for an illegitimate child of Eleanor Flint. They lost, and were ordered to pay Kirton overseers 15s as well as to maintain the child. The role of overseer could be a frustrating and time-consuming job. Outgoings averaged £26 a year between 1726 and 1736.[23]

The churchwardens' prime responsibility was for the fabric and artefacts of the church, and they spent the church rate on communion wine, coal for heating the church in winter and surplices for the clergy. Costs averaged £29 a year between 1725 and 1737, partly because of the constant struggle to keep in good working order the five church bells and the clock, since both played a vital role in the smooth running of the community. The bells cost £9 in 1725–6, and 'casting the second bell' £12 in 1731–2, an entry which hides what must have been a particularly troublesome episode for the churchwardens, since the bell had to be 'cast the second time'. Finally, the constable spent money on a variety of town-related matters, including the movement of prisoners, compensation for losses in fires (sadly, a frequent occurrence), and poor travellers through the village. 'A man that had his hand shot off' received 6d in 1728, though whether this had anything to do with the substantial amounts of gunpowder purchased in 1727 (a purchase repeated in 1729) is not known. Income came from the constable's levy, and also from rent received for township properties, and expenditure averaged £14 a year between 1725 and 1736.

All accounts had to be passed and signed by leading members of the community and when disputes occurred appeal could be made to a justice. The 1727 accounts were endorsed two years later by Edward Decker, JP, to the effect that he had heard a complaint from several local people about the accounts of Thomas Skinner and Gervase Cullen, overseers of the poor for 1727, particularly in relation to sums of £2 and £3 paid, and said to be paid, to John Hunter and John Keyworth. Decker found these outgoings 'not justly charged', but paid 'upon their own actions', and disallowed the payments, so that Skinner and Cullen were ordered to repay the money into the overseers' accounts. Not only was village office time consuming, it was also financially unrewarding.

---

[22] NAO Will of John Chappell, 1692.
[23] NAO QSMB 1678, 1704–9; PR 4779/5–18.

THE LORDSHIP OF THE MANOR AND THE MARKET IN LAND

So far in this chapter the lordship of the manor has received only scant attention, and yet the change of ownership in 1640 had important long-term repercussions for the village. At the time of Mark Pierce's survey, the ownership of the manor was in the hands of William Courten. He proved to be of a rather different mould to his entrepreneurial father and he quickly ran into financial trouble. To relieve his debts Courten borrowed £10,000 from Robert Pierrepont, Earl of Kingston, on the security of the manors of Laxton and Kneesall, but this was not the end of his troubles. For a further consideration of £7,200 he sold the property to Kingston in June 1640. Three years later he went bankrupt.[24]

The new lord of the manor was a prominent member of the aristocracy with Nottinghamshire connections which went back to the early fourteenth century. In the later 1620s Robert Pierrepont was one of the richest men in England, and he bought the titles of Viscount Newark, and Earl of Kingston-upon-Hull for £8,000. To consolidate his position he and his successors planned a series of judicious marriages, and in the course of the seventeenth century the family acquired lands in Derbyshire, Shropshire, Lincolnshire, Somerset, Wiltshire, Hampshire and Yorkshire, as well as increasing their Nottinghamshire holdings. The family wealth was recognized with the award of a dukedom in 1715. The manor of Laxton was one of the purchases of these years, and it was destined to remain in the family's hands until the 1950s.[25] The family seat was Thoresby Hall, several miles west of Laxton. Originally built during Charles I's reign, it was one of the largest houses in the county in 1674, but it was remodelled in 1685–7, and replaced in the eighteenth century. In turn the eighteenth-century house was succeeded by the present Hall in the 1870s.

In the 1630s Sir William Courten had recognized the need not merely to rack up the Laxton rents – to maximize income – but also to consolidate the property. Even so, the Pierreponts found that as lords of the manor they owned only 60 per cent of Laxton's landed acreage. Like Courten before them they set about buying up any small properties which came on to the market. This was a policy pursued by landlords throughout the arable vale lands of midland England in the period 1650–1750. It had the effect of squeezing out the smaller owner-occupiers and farmers, and paving the way for enclosure.

The obvious starting point for the lord of the manor was to target the properties owned in 1635 by the lesser freeholders. To this end the Pierreponts

---

[24] BL Egerton 3533, fos 45–57; 3599 f. 357. See also Charles Hamilton, 'The Bridgewater Debts', *Huntington Library Quarterly*, XLII (1978–9), 217–29.

[25] The family interests were divided for part of the seventeenth century: Keith Train, *Nottinghamshire Families* (Nottingham, 1973), p. 20.

purchased property in 1641 from William Cook, which he had acquired from Augustine Hinde since 1635. It was the following decade, however, before the policy made consistent headway. In 1652 the Pierreponts purchased just under 9 acres from William Cartwright, Esq, which was the freehold owned by his father, Fulk Cartwright of Ossington, in 1635. A year later they acquired Rowland Taylor's 6 acres, and the family then proceeded to pick up a number of other properties sold by Hinde since 1635; 37 acres from George Marshall 'some part thereof lately Mr Augustine Hinde's'; and the 18-acre Knapeney Close which Hinde had sold to William Rogers. Altogether between 1635 and 1736 the Pierreponts acquired 45 acres from the Hindes. To these acquisitions they added James Bacon's 69 acres in 1664 – at a cost of £633 – and Nicholas Taylor's single acre in 1665. Bryan Smith's 20 acres came to the family via Thomas and William Hunt in 1677.[26] A number of other holdings, including several properties and about 12 acres of land, were also acquired betwen 1656 and 1671–2. Not all the transactions of these years are documented, but by 1736 the lord of the manor had also acquired the tiny 1635 freeholds of Ann Hazard, John Hurst and William Taylor, totalling just under 3 acres. As a result, by 1736 the Pierreponts had acquired the property of seven of the twenty-two lesser freeholders of 1635, and in the process had extended the family property by about 160 acres.

Unfortunately for the long-term success of this policy the Pierreponts had not managed to buy a number of other properties that came on the market. Most of the small freeholds in 1635 had changed hands a century later, except for John Chappell's property in Laxton and William Dickinson's in Moor-house. In almost all cases the property was divided at sale, and although the Pierrepont usually picked up part of the acreage they were unable to acquire the whole. Among the properties divided in this way were Robert Shipton's 75 acres,[27] John Roos's 31 acres, George Salmon's 29 acres and the 54 acres of chantry land in 1635 (which, as we have seen, may already have been free-holds). Of these 189 acres the Pierreponts acquired only 22 acres, while another 50 acres of Hinde property also passed into other hands. Moreover, almost invariably the properties they failed to purchase were divided at the time of sale: 14 individuals benefitted from the Shipton sale, 10 from the Roos and 9 from the Salmon sales, 15 from sales of the chantry land, and 16 from the Hinde sales. Finally the Pierreponts had acquired just 3 of William Bedam's 15 acres, and 3 of Richard Lee's 13 acres.

The details of these various transactions may not be easy to grasp, but the main point is that while the Pierreponts appear always to have been in the market for land – and from what we know of their fortunes must always have been in a position to buy – they failed to acquire more than a share of the free-

---

[26] BL Egerton 3631, fos 109, 111, 113, 121; 3533, fos 52, 53, 56; NAO PR 4805/1.
[27] BL Egerton 3631, f. 187.

hold property which came on the market during this century. Why this should
have been the case is impossible to pinpoint, although there was clearly a flourishing market in small freeholds and some sort of formal or informal cartel may
have operated among the freeholders. Whatever the case, in the longer term the
repercussions were considerable, in particular the fragmentation of landownership in the village, since this greatly complicated the task of enclosing Laxton.

The complete process of fragmentation cannot be traced at this distance in
time, but the situation as it existed in 1736 is known. The 1650–1750 period
was a century when the small owner-occupier in midland England was largely
bought out, so it comes as a surprise to find that in 1736 the number of freeholders in Laxton with 99 acres or less had more than doubled from 22 to 47
over the century since 1635 (table 4.3). Much of the land involved had changed
hands in small parcels. Between 1707 and 1717 John Skaith paid £23 to
Thomas Adwick for 17 'lands' (totalling 3 acres) in the open fields, £42 to
Edward Herring for a close of 1½ acres, 4 'lands' in Moorhouse and 3 in West
Field (2 acres), and £78 to Richard Lee of Ossington for 39 'lands' (8 acres) in
the open fields.[28] In this manner, one or two families picked up substantial
amounts of property, notably the Greens (39 acres) and the Adwicks, but
in total 34 individual families had acquired property from the 1635 owners in
Laxton and another 12 in Moorhouse. Omitting from this list Hinde (7 acres in

TABLE 4.3 *Landownership in Laxton, 1635 and 1736*

Owners	1635			1736		
	No.	Acreage	%	No.	Acreage	%
Lord of the manor	1	2329	60.3	1	2497	64.5
Major freeholders	2	1116	28.9	2	974	25.1
50–99 acres	2	145	3.8	1	55	1.4
20–49 acres	4	116	3.0	4	134	3.5
10–19 acres	3	38	1.0	3	56	1.4
5–9 acres	3	21	0.5	13	91	2.4
1–4 acres	6	15	0.4	19	45	1.2
Under 1 acre	4	3	0.1	6	4	0.1
Other	3	78	2.0	2	16	0.4
	28	3861	100.0	51	3872*	100.0

* As a result of different surveying techniques the overall acreage of the village differs according to
the source used.

Sources: as table 4.2.

[28] NAO DDT/66/8–11.

Laxton and 1 in Moorhouse) and Broughton ($\frac{1}{2}$ acre in Laxton), and allowing for purchases in both Laxton and Moorhouse by Green and Adwick, 42 families had benefitted from freeholder sales over the century.

Among the more substantial freeholders by 1736 the two most interesting families are the Greens and the Adwicks. At his death in 1640 Thomas Green left his farming interests to his eldest son Francis. In 1665 Francis Green purchased land from John Cooke, but his own will of 1670 suggests that the property had not been greatly expanded. He left his sheep to his daughter Jane, the lease of a small farm to his son William and the rest of his property to his wife Anne and then to his son Francis. The property was described as a cottage, 'my part of the parsonage', and all leases. Francis Green junior seems to have made rapid progress. By 1680 he was steward of the court and rent collector for Thoresby. He had little time for what he regarded as the ignorant villagers, and he set about increasing the family holding in Laxton. By 1691 he leased 87 acres from Pierrepont the majority of which was enclosed, and which included the $7\frac{1}{2}$-acre 'hall homestead'. By 1705 his annual rent of £48 made him the largest Pierrepont tenant (by rent), and suggests a farm of perhaps 140 acres. Nor was this Green's only holding. He had been active in the land market, purchasing property from fifteen individuals. By the time he died in 1712 his property totalled 116 acres; of this he left 53 acres to his son John, 51 acres to his son Francis and $11\frac{1}{2}$ acres to his widow. He lived in probably the largest house in Laxton as well as owning a cottage in Moorhouse and, further afield, property in Mansfield. He was the most substantial farmer in Laxton.

Green was a man of considerable importance in the village, hence the number of occasions on which he was called as appraiser, but the family fortunes were not sustained after his death. By 1723 the farm leased from Pierrepont was in the hands of his son John, but he seems to have given it up by 1725 and it may have been divided after that. Unfortunately the rentals are incomplete at this point in time. The brothers also decided to sell off part of the property. John Green moved out of Laxton, and his older brother, Francis, died, leaving daughters to inherit the property. In 1726 and 1727 John Green sold a number of parcels of land from both holdings to the Pierrepont estate trustees, and these appear in the 1728 rental as 'land purchased of Mr John and Mr Francis Green', renting at £5 18s 6d a year. Further sales followed in 1730, 1741 and 1742.[29] By 1736 Francis Green's heiresses owned about $55\frac{1}{2}$ acres and John Green 9 acres. As we shall see, this was all sold during the following decade.

The Adwicks arrived in the village during the seventeenth century – a Francis Adwick appears in the Court Leet records for the first time in 1658.[30] In the 1670s Thomas Adwick was leasing 2 acres from the lord of the manor, and

---

[29] BL Egerton 3528.
[30] BL Egerton 3631, f. 159.

presumably other land elsewhere. Thomas Adwick, described as a mason, died in 1707, and his will mentions land in Tuxford, which he bequeathed to his son Thomas. By the 1720s Thomas Adwick junior's rent had risen from 10s a year to £2 1s, and further increases to £10 18s in 1725, and to £14 by 1728 resulted from the family leasing four closes totalling 27 acres in the vicinity of the old manor house from the lord of the manor. In addition, the Adwicks had begun to acquire land (table 4.4).

TABLE 4.4 *Thomas Adwick's freehold in 1732*

Owner in 1635	Number of parcels	Acreage		
		a	r	p
Hinde	25	22	3	30
Courten	13	8	3	06
Chantry	9	7	2	01
Smith	7	5	1	20
Bedam	2		2	15
Cartwright	1		2	07
Chappell	1	2	0	09
Lee	1			31
Town	1		1	12
Doles for meadow			2	1	11
	60	50	2	22

Source: NUMD M.4892, 1732 survey.

The complexity of business in the Laxton land market is clear from the way in which the Adwicks came into possession of some of these holdings. The property owned in 1635 by the Hindes had been purchased during the seventeenth century by William Cooke, and was bought by Thomas Adwick for £325 in 1706 from William Smithson, widower of Cook's granddaughter Mary. However, details of the transaction show that the 1706 purchase consisted of nearly 60 parcels of land amounting to more than 32 acres apart from holdings in the meadows, which suggests that part of the land was later resold. Another of Adwick's purchases was from John Green, in 1727, for £93 10s, although again the documents are not entirely consistent since they detail land to the extent of only 6½ acres whereas in an undated list of Green's sales Adwick is quoted as purchasing 14 acres. The town land was probably a close bought in 1732 for £12 from John Woolfit, while the Bedam and Lee holdings may have passed through Pierrepont hands. In February 1731 Adwick negotiated an exchange whereby he acquired 12 adjacent holdings in the East Field which he turned into a close, mainly in return for meadow holdings. Of the 12, 6 were in Courten's hands in 1635, 2 were chantry lands and the other 4 belonged to lesser freeholders.[31]

Who else was entering the Laxton land market? Some individuals were already substantial farmers. Widow Pinder bought nine individual holdings of about 5 acres. Her total ownership was just over 6 acres, but with rented land she farmed 220 acres in total. William Doncaster owned 15 acres, of which nearly 8 were purchased from freeholders, and he farmed 182 acres altogether. Francis White had purchased about $1\frac{1}{2}$ acres and owned $9\frac{1}{2}$ altogether, out of a farm of 141 acres. Samuel Dobb, John Jepson and Richard Woolfit, were further examples of substantial tenant farmers who had made small purchases from freeholders. However, many of the purchasers occupied or owned nothing more than the acquisition they had made from one of the freeholders who had sold out, among them George Pinder, Edmund Woolfit, Widow Harston, Mr Moseley, Henry Cauthern, William Skaith and Mr Markham in Laxton, and Thomas Brandritt and John Herriott in Moorhouse. Not all were apparently resident in Laxton, including George Pinder. Edmund Woolfit had just his house.

Nor was it just newcomers who had been active in the land market. The Chappells retained a freehold through the century, but it was not quite the same in 1736 as it had been in 1635. Twenty-two of John Chappell's thirty-five holdings had been in the family in 1635, but since that date 5 properties had been disposed of, including 2 to Francis Green, while 2 new ones had been acquired from Hinde, 4 from Bedam, 3 from the chantry estates and 3 (2 of which were to help form a close) from the lord of the manor. Nine separate meadow doles had been converted into a single close in the Long Meadow. The family's overall holding had declined by 3 acres but, with the lease of a close, they farmed a total of 45 acres.

The most striking conclusion to emerge from this discussion is that the free-holders' tail in Laxton was lengthening. As in 1635, twelve individuals owning 10 acres or more possessed 96 per cent of the manor. Most substantial was the lord of the manor with 2,329 acres in 1635 and 2,497 acres in 1736; he was followed by the Broughtons (now owning 727 rather than 754 acres) and Hindes (277 rather than 362 acres). The real scramble had gone on for small properties. Only two of the other freeholds in the 1730s can be positively identified as being in direct line of descent from those in 1635, and the process of fragmentation had largely taken place below the 10-acre level. Whereas in 1635 Laxton had 13 owners with 9 acres or less, by 1736 this number had risen to 38, and the overall number of freeholders with up to 99 acres had more than doubled from 22 to 47. In 1635 the 22 owners of 99 acres or less held collect-ively 338 acres or 8.7 per cent of the manor; in 1736 the 47 owners of 99 acres or less owned 385 acres or 10.1 per cent of the acreage. In other words the number of owners in this group had increased by 114 per cent, while the acreage had increased by just 14 per cent, representing just 1.5 per cent of all the land in Laxton. As we shall see, these lesser freeholders turned out to have gained a well-established foothold, which was to have considerable long-term significance for Laxton.

FARMING

The division of landholdings which occurred between 1635 and 1736 had important repercussions in the farming conditions of midland England between the mid-seventeenth and mid-eighteenth centuries. For agricultural communities across the Midlands making a living from the land was far from easy. Even where rents stayed steady until the 1690s few further increases took place between then and the mid-eighteenth century. Prices were static or in decline from the 1650s, and tenants had difficulty paying their rents. Laxton was no exception. The Pierreponts' rental remained almost unchanged around £660 from the 1690s until the estate was reorganized at the end of the 1720s. Moreover, these figures hide evidence of substantial arrears in particularly bad years. Both 1709 and 1710 are known to have been years of appallingly bad harvests nationwide, and the impact is clear from arrears of £217 and £224 respectively in 1710 and 1711. Nearly half a year's rent went unpaid in 1715 and 1717, and it was reported in 1716 that 'the tenants are under great fears of the advanced rents and advanced taxes . . . which they are told by other lords' tenants to expect.' By the 1720s rental arrears, which had once been a rarity, turned up annually in the accounts, and in 1728 the tenants could not pay their rents after three successive bad harvests.[32]

Inventories tell us something about the type of mixed farming in which the people of Laxton were engaged, although they do not adequately reflect the farming conditions of the period, and there are many problems in interpreting the data: for instance a farmer dying in winter was likely to leave rather less in terms of stock and crops than one dying just after harvest. On the other hand, since it was normal for appraisers to list crops in the barn and on the ground, we may have a better record of arable than of pastoral interests. Such problems apart we can use the inventory evidence to reconstruct something of the farming cycle in the seventeenth and early eighteenth centuries.

---

[32] NAO DDSR/30/74; BL Egerton 3530, f. 31r. Annual rentals and estate accounts for the Pierrepont estate, including Laxton, have survived in almost unbroken sequence from the 1670s to 1950. They are now in NUMD M.4197–4612, and subsequent unlisted volumes. Where the NUMD collection has gaps, these can usually be filled from BL Egerton, 3563 fos 47–51 (for 1687), and 3613–15 (for the period 1782–97). Here and in subsequent chapters material drawn from the rentals is not necessarily referenced by individual year, but can be assumed to relate to these collections.

First of all the inventories confirm the significance of mixed farming in the village. Virtually every inventory records arable crops and animals. Exceptions included Thomas Johnson the blacksmith and Edward Harrison the brick-maker. Both these men limited themselves to animal husbandry, doubtless finding that this permitted them sufficient free time to pursue their alternative interests. Otherwise, the relationship between animal and arable husbandry is clear from inventory valuations. On the larger farms the total value for live-stock was about twice the total value of crops. This is hardly surprising since a similar proportion was found in another midland open-field parish, Wigston Magna in Leicestershire. But livestock seldom represented more than two-thirds of the total value of animals and crops, by comparison with 84 per cent in the more animal-dominated parts of the West Midlands.[33] When William Challand died in 1735, field crops on his farm were valued at £69, and his animal stock at £140, 67 per cent of the overall value of his stock and crops accounted together. Few farms in these years had crop valuations in excess of £69, the major exception being Francis Green. When he died in August 1712, his crop of wheat, barley, oats and peas was valued at £236.

Second, the inventories give us a good idea about the division of arable produce in the open fields. Clayland tends to favour peas and barley, but to be inappropriate for oats and rye. It has proved impossible to match the acreages of crops recorded in the inventories with what is known of holdings from rental and survey lists. The inventories are not usually worded in such a way that a clear distinction can be made between a farmer's arable and grazing land, while vague phrases such as 'corn on the ground', or 'corn growing', reveal very little about the farm in question. Acreage in the fallow field is not always recorded, although land ploughed ready for sowing is occasionally listed as 'clotts', liter-ally lumps of hard or baked clay which were sometimes broken up with a mallet after the land was manured.

However, the most detailed inventories give some indication of how the land was divided. Most farmers had a combination of wheat, barley and peas 'on the ground' at the time of their death. The pattern of distribution suggests that wheat and barley were grown in the same field, perhaps in separate furlongs, with peas in the second field. Thomas Salmon, who died in 1727, had 3 acres of wheat, 10 acres of barley, and 13 acres of peas. With suitable variations these figures were not untypical. Peas and barley were also the most common crop 'in the barn'. What may well have happened was that the farmers sowed the winter wheat in the autumn, the peas (in the second field) in January or Feb-ruary, and barley – in the wheat field – in March or April. Wheat, barley and rye (although the latter was mentioned in only one inventory) were probably grown in one field; peas, beans, (although these are not specified in inventories)

[33] W. G. Hoskins, *The Midland Peasant* (1957), p. 159; David Hey, *An English Rural Com-munity: Myddle under the Tudors and Stuarts* (Leicester, 1974), p. 166.

PLATE 4.2 *Adjoining strips, South Field. In the spring, and particularly in the spring corn field where farmers may plant different crops, it is possible to see the boundaries between the strips quite clearly. Although the strips have been enlarged to suit modern farming techniques, the division between the strips is not a straight line. The medieval plough team followed a course which formed what appears to be a backward 'S' curve. This was to facilitate turning the ploughteam. It can still be seen even though the farmers now use tractors and modern equipment for ploughing.*

and oats in the other. Values and yields would probably help to flesh out this picture but we know little about them and the – perhaps inadequate – acreage data is our chief guide to the distribution of the crops.

Third, while most inventories record animals, not every farmer had a full complement of sheep, horses and cattle. Of the thirty inventories for the period 1688–1736 all except one (in which little detail is given) record cattle, ranging between 1 and 22 (median 12.5). This is rather more than we might expect to find; the average farm in Wigston carried six or seven, which was sufficient to meet the demand for milk, butter and cheese.[34] Few Laxton farms carried more than half a dozen cows for millking (the mean is 3.9 for the inventories in which the evidence is comparable). The additional animals were usually calves or heifers which were being fattened for the market. The total numbers of cattle increased over time, and the appraisers went to greater lengths by the 1720s to distinguish between rearing calves, and the ages of the animals being reared. This may have reflected the general Midlands shift towards animal husbandry in response to the prevailing economic conditions.

Sheep, often thought of as indispensable to open-field farming, are recorded in just seventeen out of the thirty inventories which detail farm stock (57 per cent), but these included some fairly large flocks of 80 (in two instances) and 140. Inventories lacking sheep do not necessarily date from the winter months. William Challand, who died in June 1716, had as many cattle as anyone in the village, but no sheep. In the twelve inventories which give the number of sheep, flocks ranged between a single animal and 140, with a median of 35. Twenty-two inventories record horses, ranging from 1 – presumably, as in the case of Thomas Bull who died in 1702, a single mare to carry the farmer around the parish – to 19 on one of the largest farms, which must have supported several plough teams. The median number was 6. None of the inventories mention oxen, so that horses were presumably the only animals used for pulling the plough. Twenty-three inventories record pigs. While smallholders might have a single pig, 7 and 9 were not uncommon. It seems reasonable to assume, although the inventories do not make it clear, that in these cases piglets were being recorded. Only seven inventories record poultry, but chickens were part of the farmer's wife's empire, and may have been deliberately omitted. Three inventories record swarms of bees.

Most inventories note farming gear, usually including carts – two or three of the wealthier farmers also had waggons – harrows and ploughs. Only those men farming on a very small scale would have needed to borrow equipment. Such an explanation seems likely in the case of Nicholas Woolfit. He died in 1708 with an acre of barley, half an acre of wheat, and an acre of peas 'on the ground', valued at £3 10s 6d in a total inventory of under £20, and with no farming equipment. Similarly the inventory of Peter Dickinson of Moorhouse,

---

[34] Hoskins, *Midland Peasant*, p. 159.

who died in 1709, listed corn, peas and oats in the fields, but no farm equipment. Others may have needed to borrow specific pieces of equipment since not every inventory mentions a combination of carts, ploughs and harrows. Cooperation at this level reflected the need for everyone in the community to make a living.

THE PARTIAL ENCLOSURE OF 1726–1733

Sixteenth-century enclosure in Laxton had produced closes permanently in grass. After about 1650 the economic pressures increased to speed up conversion from arable to permanent grass. Grain prices were static or falling, but the prices of dairy products and meat held firmer, thereby encouraging landlords to concentrate on livestock farming. Arable vale lands were suitable for such a change of practice, but for landowners the problem was to find sufficient pasture. Many found the answer to be the enclosure of open-field land. This was the case in Laxton, where the erosion of the open fields continued after 1635. In 1635 1,429 acres were farmed communally in Laxton's four open fields; by 1725 piecemeal enclosure had reduced the total to 1,313.[35] An opportunity to hasten this trend came at the end of the 1720s.

In 1726 the first Duke of Kingston died, leaving his estates to his 15-year old grandson Evelyn Pierrepont. For the next six years, until the second duke's coming of age in 1732, the estate was in the hands of trustees (strictly speaking guardians) headed by Lord Cheyne, and they saw it as their responsibility to reorganize the property on sounder financial lines and to improve the condition of the estates. The dead duke's debts were paid, including nearly £20,000 outstanding on mortgages, and the estate management was reorganized and improved. Under the first duke the administration of the property had been relatively casual. Various receivers collected the rents and kept accounts in whatever way seemed most adequate. From 1726 a new regime was imposed. Individual receivers were instructed to keep their accounts in a standard form, and to submit questions of importance to a central office in London, which was run by Thomas Cromp. Cromp had gained experience from supervising the young duke's expenditure while he was at Eton, and in auditing the receivers' accounts, and he was to remain in overall control of the family properties until his death in 1747. Although initially based in London, doubtless at the behest of the trustees for whom the capital was the most convenient meeting place, the office was moved to Thoresby after the second duke came of age. As a result of the trustees' efforts, net income from the estate rose from under £14,000 in

[35] See p. 316.

1726 to nearly £19,000 in 1731, and to £22,000 by the end of the 1730s – a considerable achievement during a period of agricultural depression.[36]

Laxton was caught up in this flurry of activity, and the village was to experience more change during the guardianship than at any other time before the twentieth century. In particular, Laxton was partially enclosed, but the obvious question arises of why not full-scale enclosure? The answer lies at least partly in the pattern of landownership which had evolved in Laxton by 1635. At a meeting in October 1726 the trustees considered an offer from John Green that they should buy his estate in Laxton. Their response, as recorded in the minutes, is revealing:

> the purchase being large and no improvement to be gained thereby and there being so many freeholders there that there is no prospect of making the Lordship entire they think not fit to purchase the whole but agreed with him for some parts thereof already enclosed with his Grace's land and other small parcels that lie convenient to complete some other enclosures.[37]

It was this decision which led to Green's estate being divided at sale.[38] In effect, the trustees were not prepared to spend large sums of money on buying property, because they saw no immediate prospect of controlling sufficient land in the manor to make enclosure possible. This did not stop them from acquiring parcels of land to round off existing territories. Altogether they spent £374 on nine separate property purchases.

The trustees may have been cautious about purchasing land in Laxton but they were quite prepared to tackle some of the practical farming problems in the village. In the eyes of the trustees, measures were needed to ration the use of common pasture and to increase the available pasture by piecemeal enclosures from the open fields. Pasture closes, which permitted the keeping of greater numbers of stock, were at a premium, because the prices of stock and of dairy products held firmer than those of grain. It was almost certainly to tackle this problem that the trustees decided to enclose part of Laxton between 1728 and 1732. In so doing they ensured that it was one of the many Nottinghamshire villages to experience 'voluntary' enclosure during the course of the seventeenth and eighteenth centuries. These included partial enclosures in other Pierrepont manors, among them Eakring during the 1740s.[39]

The overall aim was to increase and make better use of the existing grasslands, and to lay out a number of independent farms on the edges of the parish. The whole operation took five years to complete, and was undertaken in three

---

[36] G. E. Mingay, 'The Duke of Kingston and His Estates', unpublished BA dissertation, University of Nottingham, 1952, pp. 2–4; Mingay, *English Landed Society in the Eighteenth Century* (1963), pp. 67–70.

[37] BL Egerton 3529, f. 66.

[38] NUMD MaB/185/751.

[39] Mingay, 'Duke of Kingston', p. 87.

separate stages. In 1727 a large acreage of woodland was cleared to increase the area of grassland, and areas of rough grazing were made into closes (figure 4.2). In 1635 the woodlands covered 292 acres, but this area was reduced to 121 acres as the result of a clearance programme in 1727. Two separate places were involved. From East Park Wood, on the north side of the village adjoining the parish boundary with Egmanton, 106 of the existing 136 acres of woodland were enclosed, cleared, and converted into what became known as East Park closes. A total of seventeen separate holdings were laid out, ranging between 3 and 10 acres, and let to sixteen tenants. At Bollam Becks, the most easterly part of the woodlands on the southern border of south Field, 65 acres were cleared and divided into seven closes of between 4 and 18 acres. These were let to three separate tenants. The new enclosures were rather more regular in size and shape than older enclosures in the parish.

The rough grazing lands enclosed in 1727 were the properties known as Frearfalls, 66 acres purchased by the Pierreponts from James Bacon in 1664,

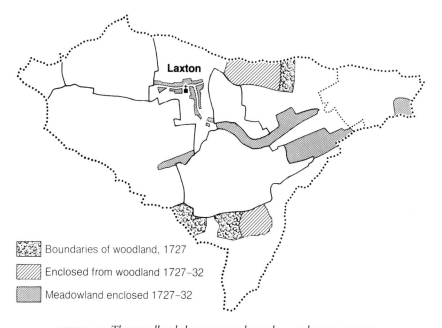

Boundaries of woodland, 1727	
Enclosed from woodland 1727–32	
Meadowland enclosed 1727–32	

FIGURE 4.2 *The woodland clearances and meadow enclosures, c.1730*

and Knapeney closes, 32 acres acquired indirectly from Augustine Hinde during the 1650s. Frearfalls, on the west side of the parish, was divided into nine closes ranging between 4 and 13 acres, and let to seven tenants; while Knapeneys, on the east side of the village, was divided into six closes of between 2 and 10 acres, initially shared between three tenants but quickly incorporated within Knapeney Farm. Altogether 270 acres of woods and rough grazing were reclaimed for agricultural purposes, probably the largest intake of land for agricultural purposes since the early Middle Ages.

The second part of the reorganization took place over the following two years and involved the laying out of four new farms. One of the major problems with open-field farming from a central village was that in a large manor such as Laxton the distance some farmers had to travel to reach their furthest strips was considerable. The presence of a house on a close on the far side of West Field in 1635 suggests that it was already considered sensible for at least one farmer to live out of the village. This, or a replacement, still survived in 1712,[40] and there may have been a separate farm at Copthorne, on the east side of Laxton towards Moorhouse. Katherine Taylor, widow, was described as 'of Copthorn house in the parish of Laxton' in her will drawn up in 1708. She left most of her estate to her grandson Richard Sudbury, and when he died two years later his address was given in the same form. No other outlying farms are known, but it is hardly surprising that the trustees saw a possible solution to some of the village problems in laying out larger farms on the fringes of the manor. The difficulty for the trustees was that whereas with the woodlands they were dealing with land already in hand, any attempt to lay out distant farms inevitably called for land exchanges if compact units were to be created. In the end four farms were laid out, and each provided the surveyor with separate problems.

Westwood Farm was where it might have been anticipated, on the west side of the village adjacent to Westwood Common. In 1736 it totalled 135 acres, and was let for £41 a year. It was composed of a number of closes including 1 on Westwood Common and 2 which were part of the Frearfalls enclosure of 1727, together with 26 'lands' in the West Field, and 94 in Mill Field (figure 4.3). Brockilow Farm, in the south of the parish, incorporated land from the southern part of Mill Field which was already predominantly in closes, together with a group of 40 'lands' which were enclosed to become part of the farm; and 53 'lands' and 2 small closes in South Field. The total acreage was 121 acres and the rent £36 a year. Where Brockilow took in land from the west side of South Field, Knapeney and Copthorne consisted of amalgams of land from the east and southeast of the field, together with closes beyond the open field. Knapeney was 101 acres in total and included 67 'lands' from the South Field, while Copthorne was 130 acres and included 38 'lands' together with a variety of closes some of which were among those newly enclosed from the woodlands at Bollam Beck. The respective rents were £35 for Knapeney and £52 for Copthorne. Quite what independence meant in this context is not entirely clear since in 1736 only Brockilow and Copthorne are recorded as having homesteads, and the latter may have been using the old house rather

---

[40] NAO Will of Francis Green, 1712.

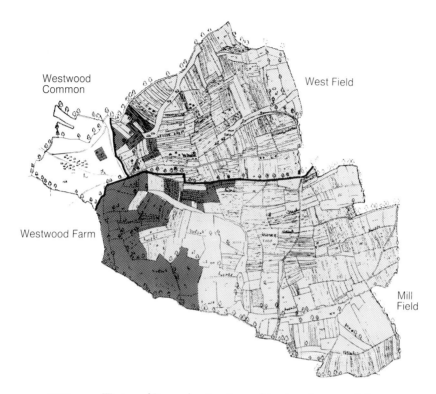

FIGURE 4.3 *Westwood Farm, showing the combination of strips and closes*

than a new building. Where Edward Freeman and Thomas Skinner, the farmers
of Westwood and Knapeney, lived is not clear.

   In each case the farm consisted of 'lands' still worked as such in the open
fields, together with 'infields' specifically enclosed from a number of strips to
become part of the farm. Altogether 169 acres of strips came out of the open
fields to become part of the new farms, reducing West Field from 318 to 300
acres, South Field from 428 to 335 acres, and Mill Field from 433 to 374 acres,
an overall reduction of about 15 per cent. Moreover, changes of this nature
involved considerable adjustment to landholdings. The enclosures brought
about to produce infields for the four farms were possible due to land purchases
or exchanges. They reveal the significance of the Pierreponts' purchasing policy
over the previous decades. Closes attached to Westwood, Brockilow and
Copthorne all included land purchased from Robert Shipton since 1635, and
Westwood and Brockilow included former chantry property. The Pierreponts
acquisition of 13 acres from Shipton and 8 acres of former chantry property

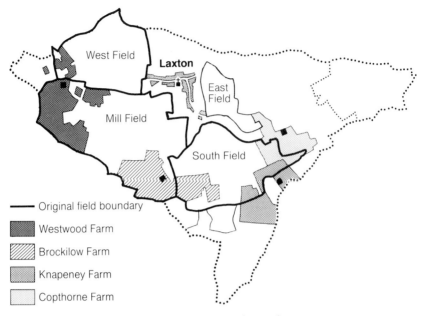

FIGURE 4.4 *The four new farms of 1729*

proved to be well invested. Brockilow infield was created after a series of exchanges and purchases, and although six parcels were specifically said to have been brought together for an enclosure at Copthorne, one was possible only because of the acquisition from Shipton and another by offering a tenant alternative land.

The third part of the reorganization plan involved enclosing the Laxton meadow lands (see figure 4.2), and this was carried out in 1731–2. It made no sense for the farmers at Westwood and Brockilow to have shares in the meadow lands, from which they were physically distant. Equally, there was little point in maintaining the existing division if the meadow lands could be more usefully employed in closes. Presumably also, although for this we have no evidence, the farmers were agreed that the return on the grass crop from the meadow was not sufficient in its current form to make it worthwhile maintaining the farming system. With so many freeholders involved in the transactions necessary to bring about change there must have been agreement in principle since the landlord would have had great difficulty imposing his will. Sadly, the Court Rolls do not provide us with the minutes of any debate which preceded this change. All we can be sure of is that it transformed the meadows into closes.

In 1635 Laxton had several meadow lands, each of which was divided into a number of doles distributed among the freeholders and the manor tenants. Shitterpool or, as the prudish Victorians renamed it, Skitterpool, was 15 acres divided into 80 doles and 3 closes in 66 different holdings; Long Meadow (88 acres) was divided into 328 doles, 25 roods, 16 'acres' and four meadows in 256 separate holdings; South Lound Meadow (36 acres) was divided into $77\frac{1}{2}$ doles, 22 'acres' and 2 closes, in 71 separate holdings; and East Kirk Ing (39 acres) was divided into 133 doles, 4 pieces of meadow and 20 'acre' pieces, divided between 110 separate holdings. Altogether 178 acres of meadow land were divided into 503 separate holdings variously described as doles ($618\frac{1}{2}$), closes (5), roods (25), 'acres' (58) and meadows (8). This must have been extremely complex to administer, and the reform of the system seems to have been a crucial consideration at the end of the 1720s.

To enclose the meadow land an exchange of properties was necessary. A series of deeds, almost all of them dating from 25 March 1731, have survived in the Manvers papers and from them we can piece together something of the operation involved. On that date John Chappell made over to Thomas Cromp, acting on behalf of Kingston, 6 doles in Long Meadow, 4 in East Kirk Ing and 2 in South Lound, together with 1 'land' in the East Field. Altogether he parted with about 2 acres which had been in his family's possession for at least a century, and in return he received one of the new closes being laid out in Long Meadow (1a 2r 23p) and five 'lands' in the West Field, totaling 3r 26p.[41] This was a relatively straightforward transaction; many of the others were much more complex, and it would be tedious to examine them in any detail. However, to give some indication of the complexity it is worth looking at the case of John Green, who negotiated with Cromp on behalf of the daughters of his late brother, Francis. From Shitterpool Meadow, Green made over to Cromp five doles. In return he received a parcel of land of just over 3 roods, on the east side of the meadow. This had previously been five separate doles. Next he exchanged two doles in East Kirk Ing for a small close in the South Field which the Pierreponts had purchased in the 1660s from William Cartwright. Finally he made over twelve doles in the Long Meadow in exchange for one of the new enclosures in the meadow (2a 2r 36p).[42]

The result of these complex negotiations was a transformation of the meadow lands into new enclosures. Long Meadow, a 70-acre holding previously divided into more than 250 separate parcels, became twenty-two separate enclosures, almost all of them between 1 and 5 acres; South Lound Meadow was divided into twelve separate holdings – two of which were attached to Knapeney Farm – and East Kirk Ing into seven closes ranging from less than 1, to more than 10 acres. Finally, South Lound, a 46-acre holding

---

[41] BL Egerton 3631, f. 14.
[42] BL Egerton 3630, f. 110.

which was in open field in 1635, was divided into a further eight closes, a substantial proportion of which became part of Copthorne Farm; indeed, one-third of Copthorne's acreage came from new closes. When all the exchanges were completed 270 acres of woodlands and rough grazing and 209 acres of meadow had been enclosed – in effect, ninety-four new closes had been carved out of 480 acres. Finally, to ensure that the loss of the meadow lands did not produce a grass shortage elsewhere in the village, the old system of grazing the sykes was abandoned in favour of the syke grass auction.

Almost everybody in the village must have been affected to a greater or lesser degree by the events of these years. In all, 270 acres had been reclaimed from wood and waste, 130 or so acres of meadow had become closes (at an outlay of £38),[43] and four substantial farms were laid out on the edge of the village which, among other things, reduced the acreage in the open fields by about 15 per cent. All of this was possible because of land exchanges between the freeholders and the lord of the manor. The reorganization was also accompanied by an 11 per cent rise in rents between 1728 and 1735, but it did not ensure that the tenants could afford to pay. Half a year's rent was foregone in 1733 when the tenants were in difficulties and arrears totalled £660. Significant sums of rent went unpaid in every year during the 1730s.

Laxton in the mid-1730s was a depressed village. For all the efforts to increase farm sizes and to reorganize the estate on to more efficient lines, our chapter ends on a note of gloom. Population was declining, rents were static, and the village was experiencing all the outward symptoms of depression common to much of the Midlands in this period. Not surprisingly the landlord sought relief through reorganization of the land. What is interesting, however, is that the Kingston trustees did not go further than they did, and in this context the proliferation of small freeholders in the village must have been significant. The Pierreponts purchasing policy had failed to make enough inroads into the 40 per cent or so of the manor that they did not own to make full enclosure possible. The relatively high proportion of land in the manor already enclosed provided some flexibility in the face of adversity but for all the efforts of the trustees Laxton's economic problems had not been cured. It is of course mere speculation to suggest that had they owned more land they would have reorganized more extensively, but the number of freeholders in Laxton was always an obstacle to enclosure and the proliferation which took place between 1635 and 1736 did not make it any easier. Here is one of the longer-term reasons why the village remained unenclosed.

---

[43] Mingay, 'Duke of Kingston', p. 49.

Chapter Five

Opportunities Missed, 1736–1790

The reorganization of Laxton under the trustees was not the signal for an immediate return of prosperity. During the 1730s and 1740s much of midland England endured a prolonged spell of agricultural depression. Prices fell, rents went unpaid and tenants departed. Enclosure of open-field land for pasture farming continued apace, and when the limits of agreement were reached Parliament looked favourably on enclosure by legislation. As a result, the forty years or so to the outbreak of the Napoleonic wars in the 1790s were a period of intense enclosure as many of Nottinghamshire's open-field parishes were turned down to grass. More than half of all enclosure by Act of Parliament in the county took place before 1793, by comparison with the national average of 38 per cent. Nor were landlords deterred by the recovery of prices as two decades of depression came to an end during the 1750s. To the people of Laxton, however, these trends were relatively insignificant. No further enclosure took place, and the farmers did not become victims of a rapacious landlord anxious to rack up rents in order to benefit from inflation; indeed, by 1789 the village could be described as relatively neglected, and a possible opportunity to enclose the open fields had been allowed to pass by when the Broughton estate came on to the market in 1750. If the Duke of Kingston had purchased it the lord of the manor would have controlled sufficient acreage to enclose the village by Act of Parliament if not by agreement. This of course is hypothetical; the historian has the benefit of hindsight where contemporaries must act according to the conditions prevailing at the time, but as this and following chapters will show the opportunities missed in this period helped to shape the long-term future of Laxton.

PEOPLE AND HOUSES

The village was almost certainly no larger in 1790 than fifty years earlier. From the parish registers we can calculate that following a low point of about 498 in

1730, the population increased in 523 by 1745. A terrier of 1743 recorded 82 houses in the village, which was a considerable decline since the 1670s.[1] Each household must have averaged 6 people. Between 1745 and 1765 population declined to a low point of about 480. The vicar recorded 80 families in 1764, again implying 6 people to a household. Seventy-three individuals paid Window Tax in Laxton in 1771. By the late 1760s the population was probably smaller than at any time since the early seventeenth century. From about 1770 recovery set in, and with occasional setbacks (in the mid-1780s for example) numbers climbed to 513 at the time of the first census in 1801. In 1789 there were still only 82 houses – 69 in the village and 13 in Moorhouse – but thereafter a number of new houses were built to bring the total up to 108 in 1801, when the ratio per household had fallen to 4.75.[2] Analysis of the parish registers gives a population figure of 528 in 1801, which is too high, reflecting the inaccuracy of the methodology, but it is sufficiently close to suggest that the trends are correct. It was not until 1811 that numbers again exceeded the figures reached prior to the demographic crisis of the later 1720s.

The continuity of names and families in the village was greater during this shorter period than between 1635 and 1736, but the turnover was still significant. A comparison of the 1736 survey with one drawn up in 1789 reveals that there were still Taylors in no. 2, Pinders in 6, Hunts in 41, Adwicks in 42, Johnsons in 44 and Taylors in 47, Doncasters in 59, Johnsons in 65, Merryweathers in 66 and Pecks in 76, Hopkins in 82, Pinders in 89, Moseleys in 105 (though they sold out in 1794), Chappells in 107, Taylors in 108 and Newsteads in 120. However, only the Chappells had occupied the same house since 1635. Of the thirty-eight separate surnames among the householders in 1736, half survived in 1789 when there were forty surnames. In Moorhouse there were still Neales in 3065, Whites in 3079, Harphams in 3081 and Jepsons in 3090, with only the Harphams in the same house as in 1635. Only four of the twelve surnames in the hamlet in 1736 survived among the nine present in 1789. Court Leet fealties also point to continuing turnover among tenants. They averaged 4.8 a year in the years for which the record is complete between 1737 and 1789. In many cases fealties must have been sworn by sons, daughters or widows surviving fathers or husbands, but from 1779 the record was more carefully kept, and of 49 admissions during ten of the years 1779–89, 21 (43 per cent) were surname successions and the rest involved a change of name.

In social composition the village had hardly changed. The majority of people continued to make their living either wholly, or in the case of the village craftsmen partly, from farming. Thomas Butler, for many years the village blacksmith, rented only the smith's shop, which suggests he did not farm. Samuel

[1] NAO PR 4065.
[2] Robert Lowe, *General View of the Agriculture of the County of Nottinghamshire* (1798), p. 175, gives a figure of 480 for 1793, but this must almost certainly be too low.

Dobb, the butcher who died in 1763, does not seem to have had any other occupation, unless he was the Samuel Dobb who was paying £50 6s 11d rent for a Pierrepont farm until 1748. Most of the other craftsmen combined their work with farming. Robert Weatherall's inventory was appraised in 1751 at £193. He was a weaver, and 'the shop that is a weaver's shop' was valued at £12 13s. However, he also leased 65 acres from the Broughtons, and his goods included cows and sheep, and crops 'on the ground'. Thomas Taylor, a carpenter who died in 1763, leased a cottage, land and the windmill from the lord of the manor for £12 15s a year. Robert Skaith's possessions in 1766 included 'three looms and other weaving utensils in the shop'; John Hunt a wheelwright, died owning goods valued at £41 7s 6d 'stuff or stock in trade'; and William Wright, who died in 1772, was a 'tailor and staymaker'. John Scott, weaver, died in 1781 with a small farm rented from Pierrepont for £5 12s a year. Usually the business was handed on: Robert Skaith bequeathed the tools of his trade to his son-in-law; John Hunt left his to his son John; and William Wright left his business to his son William.

Physically, the village gradually assumed a new appearance as the rebuilding in brick continued. In the village today there are dated buildings surviving from 1734, 1742, 1748 and 1760, and the Pierrepont accounts show that between 1734 and 1767 one and a quarter million bricks were made in the kiln in South Field. Since the number of houses did not change between the 1740s and the 1780s, these bricks, if they were all used in Laxton, went into rebuilding rather than new construction. After 1789 houses were built on new sites (or old sites reoccupied). Other buildings surviving from the mid-eighteenth century are not dated, including the main structure of the present Crosshill farmhouse (figure 5.1). The mixture of styles in the village as rebuilding proceeded is typified by the vicarage. In 1770 it was described as chiefly brick, the roof had some tile but was mostly thatch, and the adjoining barn and cowhouse were built of mud and stud.[3] This must have been a very typical combination well into the nineteenth century.

House structures changed little judging by the evidence of inventories, which continued to record individual rooms down to about 1770. What is striking in this period is the absence of reference to new or additional rooms. These would have been largely the responsibility of the landlord who, as we shall see, took little interest in Laxton. In addition, it may be that economic conditions militated against extensions, or that with whole houses being rebuilt it was not necessary to refer to parts of them as new. Rebuilding or not, most houses must have been of a very similar size (as in the seventeenth century). In the 1771 window tax return for Laxton, 73 households are enumerated of which 54 (74 per cent) had either 6 or 7 windows. Only 5 houses had 10 or more windows.

---

[3] NAO DR/1/3/2/1.

CROSSHILL FARM

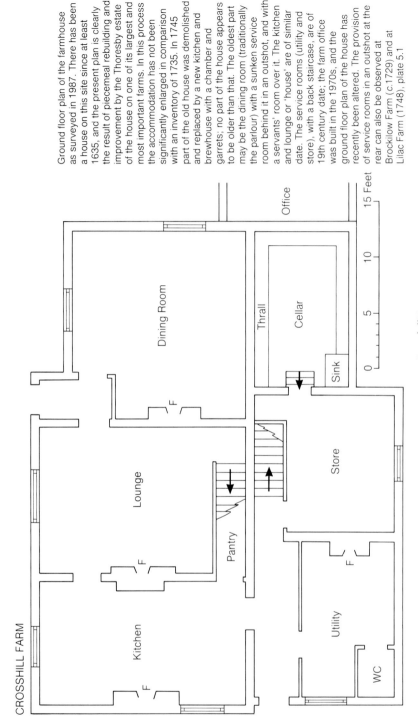

Ground floor plan of the farmhouse as surveyed in 1987. There has been a house on this site since at least 1635, and the present plan is clearly the result of piecemeal rebuilding and improvement by the Thoresby estate of the house on one of its largest and most important farms. In this process the accommodation has not been significantly enlarged in comparison with an inventory of 1735. In 1745 part of the old house was demolished and replaced by a new kitchen and brewhouse with a chamber and garrets; no part of the house appears to be older than that. The oldest part may be the dining room (traditionally the parlour) with a sunken service room behind it in an outshot, and with a servants' room over it. The kitchen and lounge or 'house' are of similar date. The service rooms (utility and store), with a back staircase, are of 19th century date; the farm office was built in the 1970s, and the ground floor plan of the house has recently been altered. The provision of service rooms in an outshot at the rear can also be observed at Brockilow Farm (c.1729) and at Lilac Farm (1748), plate 5.1

FIGURE 5.1 *Crosshill Farm*

The adverse economic conditions which produced six people to a house is reflected in the relative infrequency of luxury items in inventories. Most houses were still full of beds and bedding, kitchen utensils and basic furniture, with the occasional bed-warming pan and candlesticks. Robert Taylor, who died in 1741, left a clock valued by the appraisers at £1 15s, but for the most part the villagers' houses were filled with necessities, and there is little sign from their house contents that they were becoming wealthier. Thomas Adwick, one of Laxton's more substantial inhabitants in the mid-eighteenth century, mentioned two silver tankards in his will of 1755; and it is likely that other wealthy families such as the Doncasters and Woolfits, for whom no inventories survive from this period, would also have owned 'luxury' items.

The implication is that with the exception of one or two families Laxton was no better off in the eighteenth century than it had been in the later seventeenth. For the period 1737–90 there are 30 inventories with a gross value of £4,027 and a mean of £134, rather less than the £171 mean for the period 1689–1736. Thirteen of the thirty inventories exceeded £100 in gross value (43 per cent, by comparison with 55 per cent for the earlier period); and just four exceeded £250 (13 per cent compared to 21 per cent for the earlier period). Too much should not be read into these figures but together with the population estimates, and evidence about house building and house contents, and also the virtual absence of bills and bonds in inventories, they paint a rather sombre picture of the village. It is certainly in sharp contrast with the increasing wealth found in inventories for north-west England at this time – where there was relatively little depression in the 1730s and 1740s[4] – and the absence of a credit network is also striking. Of course the picture is marred by the non-survival of inventories for some of the wealthier families; William Doncaster, who died in 1755, left legacies of more than £2,000, and his will refers to mortgages and bonds, bills, notes, and securities for money.

VILLAGE LIFE

No papers of any village family have survived for this period, apart from those of the landlord. To some extent this must have reflected the level of literacy. Even men farming on a considerable scale were illiterate if failure to sign their own will is an acceptable guide, although a much higher proportion of individuals could sign their name than in wills made prior to 1736. The inventories of Francis White of Copthorne, who died in 1737, and Thomas Hunt, who died the following year, were appraised at more than £150, but they

---

[4] J. D. Marshall, 'Agrarian Wealth and Social Structure in Pre-Industrial Cumbria', *Economic History Review*, 33 (1980), 503–21; J. V. Beckett, 'The Decline of the Small Landowner in Eighteenth- and Nineteenth-Century England: Some Regional Considerations', *Agricultural History Review*, 30 (1982), 97–111. See also ch. 4, n. 15.

marked their wills. Both, admittedly, were sick in body at the time. Of 40 wills surviving for the years 1737–87 26 testators signed rather than marked the text (65 per cent), but two or three of these were clearly struggling with a pen. None of the four women testators in this period signed their wills.

The increase in the number of signatures suggests that education was more widely available in Laxton (although not for women) than in the past. This was because in the 1730s, and perhaps earlier, Augustine Gilbert was teaching English, writing and accounts. He charged only one penny a week, but the number of children attending for instruction seldom exceeded forty. When Gilbert came to Laxton is not known – he was not married in the village although the surname is by no means uncommon – but he occupied a cottage more or less opposite the church and 12 acres leased from the Broughtons. During the 1730s he wrote (and sometimes executed) many of the parish wills. He was described variously as parish clerk and, as in John Chappell's will, schoolmaster. He died in 1743. The details of his days as schoolmaster are sparse, and it is not clear whether he benefitted from the legacy of £40 which had been left to help provide education for the poor children of the parish. In 1743 this sum was being administered by the churchwardens until they could invest it in land.[5]

After Gilbert's death the position of village will maker and schoolmaster was assumed by his son Robert. For the next forty years Robert Gilbert's distinctive hand is on many of the wills, until his own, drawn up in 1785, which is rather less legible than some. Possibly Gilbert did not find teaching remunerative; he is referred to as a farmer in wills drawn up from about 1770, and the visitation records for 1764 mention neither a school nor a schoolmaster in the village. The vicar, Rev. William Walker, who had taken up his post in 1762, was probably offering some form of instruction; his duties included catechizing the village children each Sunday in Lent.[6] A terrier of 1777 records a wage to the schoolmaster, but this appears to have been discontinued by the time of the next terrier in 1781.[7] No other teacher is known until John Truswell took up the post in 1793.

If the level of education was such that few written records have survived, probate papers still offer some hints about village life. Family quarrels can often be detected in the provisions of wills. Augustine Gilbert seems to have had various contingencies in mind when he prepared his will in May 1743. He appointed his wife Mary and son Robert as joint executors, but added that 'if it should so happen that my dear and loving wife and son cannot be agreeable to live together', then Robert was to pay his mother £2 yearly, and 'thirds of what land I possess', as well as allowing her to enjoy the parlour and furniture in the

---

[5] P. C. Walker and S. L. Ollard (ed.), *Archbishop Herring's Visitation Returns 1743*, Yorkshire Archaeological Society, Record Series, 77 (1930), IV, 88–9.

[6] Borthwick Institute, Laxton BP.V. 1764/Ret, Archbishop Drummond's Visitation, 1764.

[7] NAO DR/1/3/2/1.

family house. Gilbert was an educated man, and it is not easy to be sure whether this smooth veneer was a cover for family disharmony. When George Peck made his will in 1774 he was more direct; he set aside £100 to be paid by his son and executor to another son Thomas, provided that Thomas

> shall think proper to stay with [Joseph], shall find unto him sufficient meat, drink, apparell and other necessaries; and no money shall be paid to him so long as they can agree to live together, but in case that they cannot agree then I order and command that my son Thomas Peck's legacy shall be paid to him one year next after such quarrel or separation.[8]

Testators usually made provision for their wives, often instructing their executor to allow them a room in the house and sufficient food and drink for their natural lives.[9] Some also provided a maintenance allowance in case the living arrangement did not work out. This was Robert Skaith's policy in 1765, perhaps because he was leaving his weaving business to William Collingham, his son-in-law, and could envisage future friction. Others took a rather harsher view of their widows' future. When Joseph Hunt died in 1770 he left instructions for his son and executor Benjamin that he was to pay his mother £3 a year for her natural life, and to give her the bed and furniture 'which we commonly lay on', various other artefacts and a wagon load of coal annually. 'But', he added ominously, 'if she will not keep unmarried' the pension and coal allowance were to cease, although she could still have the furniture. Was Hunt anxious to restrain his wife's freedom of action? Or was he reacting to some unrecorded village scandal of a widow remarrying and continuing to enjoy financial benefits which might have been meant for the eldest son? Whatever the case, similar prohibitions were included by William Wright in his will of 1772 – with instructions to the effect that in the event of his widow remarrying the household goods left to her were to be redistributed among his daughters – and by Francis White in the will he drew up in 1783.

LOCAL GOVERNMENT

We know less about how the village was governed in this period than we do for the 1720s. What little evidence survives relates to the poor and is found for this period mainly in settlement certificates, bastardy and apprenticeship papers. Few apprenticeship indentures for pauper children have survived, although in 1736 and 1737 respectively Richard Green and John Butler were apprenticed for husbandry training to William Woolfit and Richard Salmon.[10]

---

[8] NAO Will of George Peck of Laxton 1774.
[9] NAO Wills of John Chappell 1757 and John White 1771.
[10] NAO PR 4789/6, 7.

The fullest records relate to settlement cases. Under the terms of the 1662 Poor Law legislation, individuals were only entitled to poor relief in the parish in which they had a settlement, which was usually where they had been born, or where they had lived for some years, served an apprenticeship, or paid the poor rate. The parish registers contain a number of orders relating to Laxton-born individuals with settlements in nearby parishes. These included Richard Harpham, of the Moorhouse family, who was recorded in 1740 as having a settlement in Upton.[11] Settlement cases average about one a year over the whole period with as many as four in 1740, 1752 and 1777, but none at all in many other years. Almost invariably they refer to individuals settling in neighbouring villages, among them Ossington, Eakring, Edwinstowe, Weston, Bothamsall, Kneesall, Sutton-on-Trent, Egmanton, Wellow and Norwell. Just occasionally individuals turn out to have moved further afield, including Joseph Powell, who had a settlement at Harborne in Staffordshire in 1740 and John Dobb, at Ancaster in Lincolnshire in 1753.

Occasional examinations survive, resulting from the overseers bringing an applicant for relief before a JP. At least one of these gives some indication of the life of a young man. John Megget of Laxton, described as husbandman, swore an oath in 1777 that he had been born and brought up in Laxton. In 1772 he had been hired to Thomas Newstead of Dunham, where he had served for eleven months before returning to his father's house as a result of illness. Two years later he had been hired to John Waters of Great Markham, and than to Robert Womble of Wellow. At Christmas 1774 he 'fell lame' and returned to Laxton for eleven weeks to recuperate before resuming his employment at Wellow. The following Christmas he was hired to Samuel White of Ossington.[12] Megget had been working out of the village for the best part of five years, but he was never far away, and always returned to his family in the event of illness.

Bastardy was another problem for the overseers. Most bastardy papers record the efforts of the parish to ensure that the fathers of illegitimate children were traced and persuaded to maintain their offspring. Elizabeth Cawdwell, delivered of an illegitimate boy in October 1743, swore to William Blighton of Wellow as the father; Hannah Oldham named Abraham Taylor of Laxton as the father of her child in 1757; and in 1769 Elizabeth Taylor named William Quibell of Ragnall as the father of her child.[13]

These were rare instances, but from the second half of the 1770s the number of bastardy orders increased considerably. The parish registers confirm that the number of cases was rising, and in some instances attempts seem to have been made to cover up infelicities of this type. In November 1771 it was claimed that

[11] NAO PR 4779/20.
[12] NAO PR 4783/2.
[13] NAO PR 4787/1, 3, 4.

Thomas Todd, natural son of Isabel Todd had been born at Laxton, but that the relevant entry had been expunged from the register by the clerk of the parish William Wright. Miss Todd named the father as Thomas Butler of Laxton, and was permitted lying in and poor maintenance in 1772.[14] Whether the increase in illegitimacy was due to an outbreak of profligacy or simply to a greater willingness to have things out in the open, especially where former employers were concerned, is not clear, but the quality of the named fathers does seem to have risen. When Ann Wright found herself pregnant in 1781 she returned from service in Ossington to live with her mother in Laxton and named Thomas Godson, churchwarden and overseer of the poor in Ossington as the father.[15] Nor is there any evidence of once bitten twice shy. In 1776 Elizabeth Stanniland named William Wainwright as the father of her child, and nine years later she had a further pregnancy by William White of Copthorne.[16] Elizabeth Antcliffe named William Morton of Ordsall in 1782 and William Merrils of Laxton in 1785, before John Rous of Ossington made an honest woman of her in 1786.[17]

There is one will from these years which describes something of the web of illegitimacy which was developing in the village. George Chappell, 'commonly so called, otherwise George the Eligitimate Son of Elizabeth Hazard', labourer, died in 1775. Himself illegitimate, he had lived for some years with Esther Woolfit, and they had two children, Elizabeth and William. Chappell prepared his will only days before he died in June 1775, and he left his property to Esther with the proviso that on her death it was to be divided between the two children. Although he was described as a labourer, Chappell's goods were appraised at £46, and included sheep, cattle, pigs and a horse as well as crops on the ground. Esther may have been less enamoured of the state of their relationship with George, since within three months of his death she married John Brownlow.

THE CHURCH

It is impossible to be sure whether or not this impressionistic evidence of growing illegitimacy in the village represents a slackening of the hold of the church. Perhaps because they lacked a resident landlord to oversee their attendance at church worship, the people of Laxton were not particularly devout. John Warrell, a Cambridge graduate, was instituted as vicar in 1729. At the time of Archbishop Herring's visitation in 1743 he read the public service twice each

[14] NAO PR 4784/1; 4788/2. The register does not appear to have been tampered with at this point.
[15] NAO PR 4787/8.
[16] NAO PR 4787/5, 11.
[17] NAO PR 4787/10, 12.

Sunday and administered the sacrament five times a year. The number of communicants capable of receiving the sacrament was put at 180, but only 30 or 40 normally attended, with 60 at Easter. The village had two dissenters, one described as a Dipper (a sarcastic way of referring to a Baptist), and the other a newly arrived Roman Catholic. Both were female. Twenty years later, for Archbishop Drummond's visitation of 1764, Rev. William Walker prepared a further statement about the parish. He 'performed Divine Service' twice each Sunday, and administered the sacrament four times a year. About 100 people in the village were entitled to communicate, of whom about 50 attended at Easter. Everyone in the village was baptized and there were no dissenters, but there is certainly no indication here of the villagers turning up in large numbers to Sunday worship.[18]

Few wills by this period contain a religious preamble, and only William Dickinson, who died in 1758, made a specific bequest to the poor. Possibly the church itself was offputting; Warrell recorded a legacy of £5 towards church repairs, but in the 1790s John Throsby commented that it was in a state of 'impious neglect',[19] a situation which does not seem to have changed until the middle of the nineteenth century. What is not clear is whether the villagers had simply become apathetic, or whether they were actively hostile towards the church, perhaps because of one of the great conflicts in rural England, the payment of tithes.

It is hard to underplay the role of tithe in English village life. The rights to tithe must have been an endless source of discussion and heated argument in the public houses, with consequent overflow into the attitude local people adopted towards both the vicar and the church in general. The church, or a lay impropriator, had the right to one-tenth of the yearly produce of the land. Rectorial, or great, tithes consisted mainly of the produce of the corn lands, and in Laxton they were collected by the lord of the manor (although not in Moorhouse where they went to the vicar). Vicarial, or small, tithes were levied primarily on livestock and minor crops, and the vicar was entitled to these in both Laxton and Moorhouse. Tithes of all orchards and dovecotes, and of all wool, in both settlements, were payable to the vicar.[20] By the early eighteenth century most tithes were paid by a money rent, but some were still due in kind (goods). The rates at the beginning of the eighteenth century were as follows:

for house duties every man pays three half pence duty for his house, offerings two pence for every person that is above sixteen years of age. A new milched cow three half pence, for every Old Milched Cow or Stropper one halfpenny. For every dole in the meadow one halfpenny. Mamport, three half pence each. Each Oxgang four pence. Bees each

[18] Borthwick Institute, Laxton BP.V. 1764/Ret.

[19] Robert Thoroton, *Antiquities of Nottinghamshire*, 3rd edn, ed. J. Throsby (Nottingham, 1797), vol. III, p. 312.

[20] NAO PR 4071.

swarm one penny. For every young Foal one penny. For every Sheep Skin that dies between Candlemas and Clipping time one halfpenny, each servant five pence per pound for the wages. Plaster one shilling for every ten tons if taken in kind the fifth part. The windmill to pay two shillings. If any sheep etc bought into the parish before clipping time to pay fourpence per score per month. If any sheep be sold between Candlemas and Clipping Day to pay one penny for each Sheep. If they be couples to pay one penny half penny each couple. Tithe eggs for every cock three eggs and for every hen two eggs. If the hen sits she is payable. Herbage for depastured cattle.

The payments for milch cows, stroppers and foals were moduses, sums of money agreed at an earlier date, which would take the place of 'kind' on the small farms. Mainports were small tributes, often loaves of bread, which the parishioners in some places paid to the incumbents of their churches.

In much of eighteenth-century Nottinghamshire the right of tithe was attached to the estate and incorporated in the rent, so making the land tithe free and ensuring that tithes did not form an obstacle to improvement.[21] In Laxton, however, a permanent arrangement was arrived at when in 1741 the Duke of Kingston agreed to pay the vicar a composition fee of £40 a year and also to pay the £20 Land Tax due annually on the vicarage. He became entitled to one-tenth of all the produce of the fields, the enclosures, orchards, gardens and yards, and he let the tithes to freeholders and tenants in the village for a total of £217 a year. The first £40 annual composition for the small tithes of Laxton and all the tithes of Moorhouse was paid to Mr Warrell at Lady Day 1742. This sum was later raised to £50 in 1794 and to £110 in 1801.[22] It was an arrangement with which Warrell was far from pleased. He wrote to Thomas Cromp in June 1741 complaining of his 'great disappointments', as a result of which 'my wife cried all day.' His letter is informative:

I have let every one the tithe of Moorhouse, at 1s 6d the hay, and 2s 6d the arable, which raises more money than it will do by pound rent, or a shilling an acre for all the grass ground, and two the arable. This is with your own consent, so what the owners will like as well as your tenants, and the very most of the mowing ground of Laxton is worth 2s an acre especially all the meadows (the worst of which is doles), Ingar, Hall Grounds and crofts which is 67 acres, besides other good closes which may all be marked out, a week after mowing, and if you place half a crown an acre upon the arable, it will please better than your first proposal because they have all along had the pasture land tithe free. Moorhouse is badder land than Laxton, the rental of it will be above twenty pound a year. Laxton vicarage twenty one pounds.[23]

The way the new arrangement worked can be seen from table 5.1. Out of the gross sum of nearly £214, the Pierrepont estate paid £40 to Warrell, and Land

[21] Lowe, *General View*, pp. 15, 141–2.
[22] G. E. Mingay, 'The Duke of Kingston and His Estates', unpublished BA dissertation, University of Nottingham, 1952, pp. 72–3; NUMD MaB/166/91.
[23] NUMD MaB/166/107.

TABLE 5.1 *Tithe payments from 1741*

Tenants	Number	Sum payable £	s	d
Duke of Kingston's tenants in Laxton	44	122	15	8
Duke of Kingston's tenants in Moorhouse	6	7	7	0
Sir Bryan Broughton's tenants	17	41	6	6
Small freeholders in Laxton	35	19	2	$10\frac{1}{2}$
Small freeholders in Moorhouse	15	11	7	6
Mr Hinde's tenants	4	11	19	3
		213	18	$9\frac{1}{2}$

Source: NUMD MaB/166/107.

Tax (£20 on a 4s rate), leaving the rest as clear profit to the lord of the manor. The gross sum was revalued upwards in 1790 to £296, although the total slipped to £289 in 1802. The record then fails. By 1835 the vicar was receiving £180 in lieu of tithes, and in the 1880s £137 6s after tax. Other changes obviously took place from time to time. An agreement from 1773 notes that the four leading tenants of Sir George Savile in Laxton 'do for ourself and the rest of the said Sir George Savile's tenants in Laxton bargain and hereby take the Great and Small tithes of all and each of our respective farms and lands in Laxton for the term of three years from Lady day last past at the yearly rent of £50'. The money was a composition to be paid to the Duke of Kingston's steward, on a three-year lease.[24]

THE SALE OF THE BROUGHTON ESTATE

In village after village through the midland counties economic difficulties similar to those experienced by the people of Laxton in the middle decades of the eighteenth century produced enclosure, but not on the Pierrepont estates. We cannot hope to understand the events of these years without some appreciation of what was happening at Thoresby where, with much rejoicing, the second Duke of Kingston came of age in 1733. The efforts of the trustees had ensured that most of the first duke's debts and legacies had been paid. Unfortunately for the family and for the estate, the second duke's lifestyle proved beyond even his substantial means. By the early 1740s he was already in

[24] NUMD MaB/192/1164.

deep financial difficulties, and further land acquisitions were rendered more or less out of the question. This did not curtail his spending. After the old mansion at Thoresby was destroyed by fire in 1745 the duke set about building himself a new home. This was costly, as was his stud at Holme Pierrepont, the development of his urban property in Bath, and his occasional visits to London – a fortnight in the capital during the summer of 1752 cost him over £2,000.

The duke financed much of his outlay by borrowing; by 1737, just four years after he came of age, he had borrowed £26,000 on the security of the estate. Property sales in Wiltshire and Hampshire enabled him to pay off his bankers, Hoares, but by 1740 he had borrowed a further £19,000. Together with the proceeds of the sale of Sturton in Nottinghamshire this money was used to purchase a London house – which had to be sold in 1770 when his debts became excessive. Estates valued at £16,000 were mortgaged in 1742, and by 1745 the duke's debts exceeded £66,000. Retrenchment and further sales followed, but the credit mountain grew inexorably, to reach £70,000 by 1755. Marriage to a rich heiress might have helped to relieve his problems, but the duke waited until 1769 – when he was 58 years old – and chose a notorious rather than a wealthy bride. Elizabeth Chudleigh had first married in 1744, but due to what was widely rumoured to have been an illicit affair with Kingston, her husband, the sixth Earl of Bristol, obtained a divorce *a mensa et thoro* early in 1769. She married Kingston shortly afterwards, and when Kingston died four years later he left most of his estates to his widow. After his death it became known that the divorce decree had not actually annulled the original marriage, and technically Elizabeth Chudleigh had married Kingston bigamously. In April 1776 she was tried before the House of Lords and found guilty. Although she escaped sentence by pleading her privilege as a peeress, the duchess found it prudent to retire abroad. As a result, the Pierrepont estates were in the hands of an absentee owner until she died in August 1788, after which they passed to the duke's cousin, Charles Meadows. He took the family name of Pierrepont, and was created Baron Pierrepont and Viscount Newark in 1796, and Earl Manvers in 1806.[25]

The second duke's finances, and the situation between his death and the accession of Charles Meadows, were hardly circumstances conducive to efficient estate management. Kingston, it is true, did buy a number of properties in Nottinghamshire shortly after coming of age, including four houses and various parcels of land in Laxton which cost £885. Exchanges were also negotiated with several freeholders in the village, but this was in the days when Thomas Cromp was still in charge at Thoresby. After his death in 1747 there seems to have been a marked decline in efficiency, and no further purchases are recorded after the mid-1740s; indeed, some of the increase in Pierrepont acreage between 1736 and 1789 (table 5.2) may be more apparent than real, as

[25] Mingay, 'Duke of Kingston', pp. 128–47.

TABLE 5.2 *Landownership in Laxton, 1736 and 1789*

| | 1736 | | | 1789 | | |
Owners	No.	Acreage	%	No.	Acreage	%
Lord of the manor	1	2497	64.5	1	2672	67.1
Major freeholders	2	974	25.1	1	689	17.3
50–99 acres	1	55	1.4	3	241	6.1
20–49 acres	4	134	3.5	5	128	3.2
10–19 acres	3	56	1.4	11	160	4.0
5–9 acres	13	91	2.4	6	41	1.0
1–4 acres	19	45	1.2	14	34	0.9
Under 1 acre	6	4	0.1	3	1	
Other	2	16	0.4	1	17	0.4
	51	3872*	100.0	45	3983*	100.0

* As a result of different surveying techniques the overall acreage of the village differs according to the source used.

Sources: as table 4.3; NUMD M.4899–4900 supplemented where necessary from the survey of 1803 at M.4907–10.

a result of different surveying techniques. Kingston was in no position to bid for land which came on the market; had his economic circumstances been healthier he might well have been able by the middle of the century to acquire sufficient land to enclose the village.

In 1751 Sir Bryan Broughton sold all his property in the manors of Laxton and Bilsthorpe to Sir George Savile (c.1727–84) of Rufford Park.[26] The Saviles had lived at Rufford since the house was built in the seventeenth century, and they had a long-standing interest in Laxton. Sir George Savile had inherited the handful of acres belonging to the Countess of Shrewsbury in 1635 consisting of three small closes, and several 'lands' in the open fields, normally let by the early eighteenth century to a single tenant on a 21-year lease.[27] We do not know why the Broughtons decided to sell the 700 or so acres they owned in Laxton, and nor do we know why the Saviles bought the property nor what sum they paid.

What we do know is that as a result of the acquisition Laxton became one of a number of Nottinghamshire villages in which the Pierreponts and Saviles were the major landowners, among them Eakring, Gedling, Carlton and Stoke Bardolph. Initially the two families seem to have been on amicable terms. At

[26] Cheshire RO Delves-Broughton Papers, Covenant to produce deeds, 27 February 1751.
[27] NAO DDSR/207/271–2; NUMD M.4565.

Laxton various 'lands' were exchanged in the open fields in order to consolidate individual holdings,[28] but later the acquisition was used by the Saviles as a bargaining counter with the Pierreponts in an attempt to bring about exchanges in Laxton and Eakring preparatory to an enclosure. Eakring had many of the characteristics of Laxton – two large landowners (Pierrepont and Savile), and many freeholders (37, owning 633 acres, in 1737).[29] The history of the two villages was similar, and in various ways their fate was dependent upon each other. In both cases enclosure was delayed by Pierrepont indifference, by the number of freeholders, and then by disagreements between the Pierreponts and Saviles which were not resolved until the 1860s.

None of this might have happened if Kingston had been able and willing to purchase the Broughton estates in 1751. Unfortunately the documentary evidence fails us at this point, and we cannot even say if Kingston was given the opportunity to bid for the property. What we do know is that had he bought out Broughton, it would have given him ownership of roughly 85 per cent of the village, and even if the other freeholders had refused to consider enclosure he would probably have had relatively little difficulty obtaining legislation.

PLATE 5.1 *The eighteenth-century rebuilding. Lilac Farm (1748), with associated barn (1760), was part of the rebuilding in brick during the eighteenth century. It is no longer a separate farm. Stuart Rose, who lives in the house, works with his father Reg Rose at Bottom Farm, and the barn is scheduled to become a museum.*

[28] NUMD MaB/171/254.
[29] Mingay, 'Duke of Kingston', pp. 51–3.

Kingston could not have known it in 1751, but by the 1760s and 1770s Parliament normally demanded the agreement of four-fifths of the property owners by value when passing enclosure legislation. As far as can be ascertained Kingston made no move to acquire the Broughton estate in 1751. Had he bought the property Laxton's later history might have been quite different; as it was the property remained divided and disagreements between the two families delayed enclosure in both Laxton and Eakring.

THE SALE OF THE HINDE ESTATE

The Broughton sale was a straight transaction between two major landowners but when, in 1789, the Hinde estate was sold neither Charles Meadows nor the Saviles was a purchaser. Instead the property was divided among the village freeholders. In many parts of England during the eighteenth century small freeholders were under pressure to sell out to larger landowners. In Laxton the position was rather different. Whereas in both 1635 and 1736 just 12 people owned 10 acres or more, by 1803 the number had risen to 21. While in 1736 Laxton had 47 owners of 99 acres or less, in 1803 the number had slipped slightly to 42, but the overall acreage had risen from 385 acres to 605 acres, in other words from 10 to 15 per cent of the total land area. Among those with 10 acres or more, four surnames were not found among landowners in the village in 1736, while most of those appearing in this group who were owners half a century earlier had increased their acreage. When we look for reasons why this was the case it is clear that Laxton was subject to conflicting forces from outside and from within the village, and also that the maintenance of this pattern helped in the longer term to delay enclosure.

The willingness of some of Laxton's more substantial inhabitants to purchase land became clear when Francis Green's freehold property was sold in the late 1730s (table 5.3). John Green sold his 33 acres in the 1730s in nine separate parcels, and left the village. However, as trustee of the daughters of his late brother Francis he was responsible for selling their estate in 1741. Two of the three daughters had married and all three had left the area, two moving to Mansfield and the third to Manchester. When the land was put up for sale thirteen individuals shared little more than 54 acres between them. The property not acquired at the sale was bought by Kingston for £190.[30] It included a house and malthouse, a dovecote and an orchard. These were subsequently let (together with other parcels of land) to John Reynolds on a 9-year lease. Some of the purchasers seem to have been speculating because various parcels of land soon changed hands again. In 1743 Kingston bought out Richard Salmon for £81, Richard Woolfit for £86, and Timothy Wright for £26, and added these

---

[30] BL Egerton 3533 f. 49; 3528 f. 19.

TABLE 5.3 *The sale of Francis Green's estate, 1741*

Place	Purchaser	Acreage		
		a	*r*	*p*
Laxton	Thomas Taylor	7	3	09
	William Taylor	5	1	15
	Robert Skaith	4	3	19
	Thomas Adwick	1	0	00
	John Hopkin	1	3	20
	Daniel Fletcher	3	2	25
	Richard Salmon	6	0	00
	Richard Woolfit	6	0	00
	Augustine Gilbert	2	2	00
	Timothy Wright	2	0	00
	Jane Johnson	1	0	00
Moorhouse	John White	3	0	13
	Richard Maples	9	0	17
Not sold		3	3	02
		58	0	00

Source: NUMD MaB/171/249.

holdings to John Reynolds's farm. Daniel Fletcher sold the land he purchased to John Hunt.[31]

Several of these purchasers were already men well established in the village, including Richard Woolfit, Richard Maples and Richard Salmon, who held three of the largest farms. However, Woolfit, with $1\frac{1}{2}$ acres, was the only one who already owned land. None of the other purchasers farmed much more than 20 acres in the village, and only two were freeholders without any rented land. Daniel Fletcher was the village blacksmith. He leased his workshop from the lord of the manor, and his acquisition of $3\frac{1}{2}$ acres seems to be the first agricultural land he held in the village.

The Hinde sale offered similar opportunities to the farmers and freeholders. In the seventeenth century the Hindes were probably Laxton's most substantial resident family. Edmund Hinde, who died in 1691, left property in Wellow, Boughton and Grimston in addition to his estate in the village. Edmund Hinde's eldest son, also Edmund, was only 12 when his father died in 1691. He was born and buried in Laxton, although surviving family details suggest that he lived much of his life in Newark. Certainly it was 'of Newark, gent' that his

[31] BL Egerton 3533 f. 49; 3528 f. 29; NUMD MaB/211/16; MaB/171/249.

only surviving son Edmund (1711–83) described himself at his marriage in
1758. The third Edmund Hinde's wife was Ann Waldegrave of Newark, and
she had a marriage portion of £2,000. In return, as part of her jointure, Hinde
settled two farms and a cottage on his Laxton estates rented at £87 a year.
These were described in detail in 1788.

The largest holding had originally been the home farm attached to the family
house when the Hindes lived in Moorhouse. It consisted of a series of closes
and open-field land in Moorhouse and the eastern edge and southern tip of
Laxton. There were twenty-nine separate properties, totalling 199 acres, and
including what was still one of the largest houses in the parish when it was
assessed for 11 windows in 1771. The rent was £60 a year. John Herring, the
tenant until his death in 1756, left goods appraised at £560, the highest value
of a Laxton inventory between 1735 and 1790. After his death the tenancy
reverted to his widow, and from her to their daughter Mary. In 1777 Mary
married George Pinder and he was the tenant in 1788. The second farm, rented
by William Taylor in 1758 but by John Hunt in 1788, consisted of closes and
open-field land almost entirely within Laxton. The twenty separate properties
totalled 69 acres. Finally, the cottage holding, let to Anthony Pearce in 1758
and to John White in 1788, consisted of twelve separate holdings within
Laxton totalling 11 acres. Altogether, the three settled properties totalled 279
acres.

Edmund Hinde of Newark died in 1783, 'an honest man' according to a
plaque on the south wall of the parish church. He left the property to his widow
who died in 1788. Since there were no children, under the terms of Edmund's
will (drawn up in 1782), Samuel Twentyman and Henry Worrall were
appointed to sell the property in Laxton, Moorhouse and Ossington, at public
auction. The money raised was to be used for the benefit of Hinde's devisees,
the children of his three cousins.

The auction took place in April 1789 although no specific details of the
event have survived.[32] Piecing together the outcome is complicated. An
undated, early nineteenth-century document lists seven purchasers, who paid a
total of £4,976 for the property[33] (table 5.4). The accuracy of this list is open to
some question. Both William Pinder and Charles Doncaster acquired land.
From the 1790 Land Tax Assessments it is known that their share of the tax
'for land late Hinde's' increased by £3 6s 3d and £2 13s 2d respectively. On
the other hand, another source suggests that Doncaster paid £1,335 for land
from the estate.[34] Harpham, Boulton and Thompson all appear in the Land
Tax Assessments for the first time in 1790, and Thompson's purchase
amounted to 27 acres on which he paid 17s 4d land tax. At this point, how-

[32] BL Egerton 3630, fos 120, 123, 140–52.
[33] NUMD MaB/168/114.
[34] NUMD M.5548.

TABLE 5.4 *Purchasers of the Hinde estate, 1789*

Name	Sum paid (£)
William Pinder	1575
Charles Doncaster	1075
Valentine Harpham	730
William Cook	660
Thurston Bolton	438
Richard Thompson	473
Francis White	25
	4976

Source: NUMD MaB/168/114.

ever, the scent dries up. No one by the name of William Cook appears in the 1790s Land Tax Assessments, but a William Taylor appears as holding former Hinde property (14s 10d) and Thomas Adwick (14s 11d) and Francis Skinner (£1 13s 4d) both appear as holding former Hinde property in addition to their existing lands. To complicate the issue still further the Land Tax Assessments record a total of £12 14s 6d tax payable on former Hinde property, but in 1785 Hinde's assessment was only £5 8s 5d.

Other people may also have benefitted from the sale. From the tithe records we know that in 1789 20 individuals in Laxton and 10 in Moorhouse were liable for small freeholds. There were 4 common to both, making a total of 26. The 1790 list shows considerable change. All except 1 of the 20 Laxton freeholders were still included, but a further 18 individuals now held freehold land in the village, 3 of whom had previously been tenants of Hinde. Of the Moorhouse freeholders, 9 reappeared (the other, Robert Lee, is included in the Laxton list), but a further 6 freeholders were added, 2 of whom were also in the Laxton list. There were now 38 freeholders in Laxton and 15 in Moorhouse, of whom 6 held land in both settlements. Individuals admitted at the manor court to parts of the Hinde estate included William Pinder, William Wright and George Lee in 1789, and Robert Pinder and John Hunt in 1790. Only William Pinder of this group is named in the anonymous list of seven purchasers. Possibly the compiler confused Pinder's role, attributing to him purchases totalling £1,575, when some of this property pased through his hands as a legal representative. He acquired land on 4 April 1789,[35] but the same day he was party to deeds of conveyance whereby Thomas Adwick of Kelham paid £354

[35] NAO PR 4802 f. 166.

for land in Laxton and Richard Thompson of Rufford paid £599.[36] Six days later he was party to a conveyance of Hinde property to Robert Pinder of Ossington, butcher. Robert Pinder paid £355 for 37 acres, part of Stubbins closes.[37] He was paying 15s 1d land tax in 1790, but the Land Tax Assessment does not record whether or not this was former Hinde land. The evidence is inconsistent, but the complexity of the transactions may well have been because the old farms on the Hinde estate were broken up at the time of sale. The three properties sold to Richard Thompson – Breck Wong Close (22 acres), and two Westwood Closes (4 and 2 acres) – had each been part of different farms in 1788.

THE LAXTON FREEHOLDERS

The Land Tax Assessments provide an indication of the landownership pattern in the village during these years although the information is not always consistent with other sources. When the rate was levied at 4 shillings in the pound the village was assessed at £204 11s, divided as shown in table 5.5. Among the freeholders in 1748 were Hinde (4 tenants), 25 owner-occupiers, and 6 lessees from other freeholders. John Hunt was assessed separately as a freeholder and as a tenant of Hinde, hence the discrepancy.[38] No further lists survive until 1781, by which time the Pierrepont estate had transferred the burden of the tax to the tenants. The Lady Day accounts for 1774 include the laconic comment

TABLE 5.5 *Land Tax Assessment evidence, 1748–1790*

	Kingston tenants				Savile tenants[a]				Freeholders			
		Payment				Payment				Payment		
Date	No.[b]	£	s	d	No.	£	s	d	No.	£	s	d
1748	–	131	7	4	–	35	12	00	32	37	11	8
1781	47	122	1	5	12	38	11	10	31	42	5	1
1785	48	124	4	5	12	38	11	10	31	42	4	8
1790	47	124	12	5	12	38	11	10	40	42	6	1

[a] In 1751 Savile and his tenants shared the land tax in equal portions. Later practice is not known.
[b] Some overlap occurs in the numbers column because individuals could be paying as both tenant of Kingston or Savile, and as a freeholder.

Source: NAO Q/DDE/1/4.

[36] NUMD M.5507; NAO DDT/66/2–3.
[37] NUMD M.5784.
[38] NUMD MaB/203/43.

that henceforth the land tax would be collected and paid by the tenants, and despite some opposition this was the case. By 1781 the balance had shifted slightly, but the really significant change came in 1790 following the sale of the Hinde estate. In the 1785 list, 20 of the freeholders were paying as owner-occupiers, and 31 of the 40 in 1790 were paying as owner-occupiers. The effect of the Hinde sale was to increase both the number of freeholders in the village, and the size of the individual holdings.

The consolidation of their position by the freeholders during this period was accompanied by a further development which was to be of considerable long-term significance for Laxton. Table 5.6 outlines the pattern of landholding in Laxton from 1635, and shows that among owner-occupiers a significant change occurred in the nature of tenure. Whereas in 1635 and 1736 roughly two-thirds of the lesser freeholders had occupied only the acreage they owned, and a further quarter leased additional land, in 1789 only one-third occupied only what they owned while nearly half rented additional land. The sale of Francis Green's land in 1741 had aided this trend: eight of the thirteen purchasers became owners of land (as opposed to lessees) for the first time. This trend almost certainly continued thereafter, and may have been facilitated by larger farms and better-placed farmers. In 1740 George Pinder owned only 3 of the 143 acres he farmed in Laxton, and Widow Pinder just 6 of her 86 acres; by contrast at the end of the century William Pinder owned 86 acres but occupied 327. Similarly William Doncaster owned 15 of his 181 acres in 1740, while his son Charles owned 65 acres out of a total holding of 273 acres. In 1740 53 individuals were renting land; 12 others were renting land in addition to their freeholds; and 20 were just freeholders. None of those in this final group held more than 8 acres. By the 1790s 8 of the freeholders in the village were farming more than 100 acres, and in every case they were renting land to make up the difference between the acreage owned and the acreage they farmed. The Chappells owned the same land in 1789 as in 1736, but they now rented 34 rather than 15 additional acres.

TABLE 5.6 *Landownership and occupation in Laxton, 1635–1789*

	1635	1736	1789/1803
Occupying only land owned	16 (67%)	33 (67%)	15 (35%)
Occupying *more* land than owned	6 (25%)	13 (27%)	20 (47%)
Occupying *less* land than owned	2 (8%)	3 (6%)	7 (16%)
Unknown			1 (2%)
	24	49	43

Sources: as tables 4.3 and 5.2.

By 1790 the pattern of tenure in Laxton was increasingly inimical to enclosure. In the majority of Nottinghamshire villages enclosed without an Act of Parliament during the eighteenth century, the small freeholders were generally bought out in advance.[39] Although legislation enabled larger owners to overcome opposition from their lesser neighbours, an act could usually be acquired only if two-thirds to three-quarters of the owners *by value* were in agreement. Even then the complications inherent in sorting out the tenurial problems when there were large numbers of freeholders, often renting additional land, were immense. These people were unlikely to support any scheme that would damage their interests, and any enforced enclosure by legislation would have been both complex and costly.

The land-market evidence also points to another significant development in the village, the rise of a handful of wealthy families who became leading inhabitants. In the seventeenth century the most powerful were the Hinde family, and Francis Green the steward. By the mid-eighteenth century the Greens had sold up and left the village, and the Hindes had moved their interests to Newark. The precise pecking order which developed as a result is not clear but with no resident landlord several families were able to exercise a dominant influence on village life. John Warrell, the vicar, hinted in 1741 at the hierarchy. Any proposed change in the tithing customs should, he suggested to the Thoresby agent, be put initially to two particular men: 'You should use your authority with Doncaster and Woolfit if opposite to your measures. They have both good farms, and if they be a little sullen will come to themselves. If they conform, the whole parish conforms.'[40] William Doncaster was one of the most substantial farmers in the village and lived at Crosshill, but there were several Woolfits, among them William Woolfit with 84 acres and Richard Woolfit with 100 acres. Warrell was probably referring to Richard Woolfit, who, with Doncaster, was a churchwarden in 1743.[41] Both Doncaster and Woolfit appear as appraisers of inventories, although this was a job which seems to have been shared around by the leading farmers. On the other hand the Woolfits were on their way down, whereas the Doncasters were one of three families that stand out in this period together with the Adwicks and the Pinders.

The Doncasters arrived in Laxton in 1719 when William Doncaster of Ollerton married Elizabeth Skaith and came into several properties purchased by her father between 1707 and 1714. Two years later Doncaster paid £23 10s to William Taylor for 2 acres of land in the West, South and East Fields, and he leased additional property from the lord of the manor, for which he was paying £7 4s 3d rent in 1723. By 1736 William Doncaster owned 15 acres, and

[39] J. D. Chambers, *Nottinghamshire in the Eighteenth Century*, 2nd edn (1966), p. 198.
[40] NUMD MaB/166/70.
[41] NUMD M.4895; NAO PR 4787/1.

farmed 182 acres, having taken over the tenancy of Crosshill. This carried with it one of the largest farmhouses in the village with 13 windows in 1771. He was still on the look out for land and he paid John Green £192 for 8 acres of meadowland in Moorhouse.[42] In his will of 1755, Doncaster, yeoman, left estates in Normanton to his eldest son John – described as 'of Nottingham, hosier' – bequests totalling more than £2,000 to his three daughters, and his real estate in Laxton, Egmanton, Wellow and Ollerton to his younger son and joint executor, Charles. In turn Charles Doncaster continued to build up the family holding in Laxton. He was one of the most substantial purchasers in the Hinde sale, paying £1,335 for property, and by 1803 the family owned 65 acres in the village, as well as renting considerable property.[43]

The Adwicks, as we have already seen, had arrived in Laxton in the mid-seventeenth century, and had proceeded to build up a sizeable interest in the village. They also owned land further afield; at his death in 1707 Thomas Adwick devised land in Tuxford to his heir. By 1736 Thomas Adwick, described as 'of Laxton, yeoman' owned 48 acres. Four years later this had increased to nearly 54 acres, and Adwick was the most substantial owner-occupier in the village. The holding had been pieced together in a number of purchases: 32 acres in 1706, $6\frac{1}{2}$ acres in 1727, 7 acres in 1733, and various other parcels. Adwick bought 14 acres from John Green, and paid £31 1s for his purchase from Francis Green's estate.[44] Together with the 30 acres he leased from the lord of the manor this gave him a total holding of nearly 85 acres. At his death in 1755 Adwick left most of the property in Laxton to his daughters Audrey and Mary, with land in Moorhouse going direct to his son Thomas, described in the probate papers as 'of Kelham, grazier'. The property included the house in which he lived, which was left to his widow, and after her death to his daughter Audrey, another cottage left to his second daughter, Mary, and a house in Moorhouse, currently let, which he left to Thomas. These were obviously substantial properties; Mr Adwick's house had 11 windows in 1771, and Mrs Adwick's was one of eight in the village with 9 windows. In turn, Thomas built up the property by further purchases including 12 acres in the Hinde sale, until the family owned 101 acres in 1803. From 1756 their holding also included the 20 acres of Dean and Chapter land in Moorhouse, which they held on a series of renewable leases until 1847.[45] By this time they had left the village; in 1789 their house was let to Thomas Swinbourne, presumably because Thomas junior preferred to live in Kelham after his father's death. It was here that he made his will in 1791.

The Pinders were not a new family, but they were increasingly influential in the village. Thomas Pinder, husbandman, who died in 1757, left goods

[42] NAO DDT/66/12–15, 67/1; NUMD MaB/185/751.
[43] NAO DDLK/108/4; NUMD M.5548.
[44] NUMD MaB/185/751; M.5507.
[45] NUMD M.5498; NAO DDSP 21/1–18.

appraised at £298, the majority of it tied up in farm stock. This was one of the most substantial overall totals in an eighteenth-century inventory, but he was unable to sign his will. When his widow Elizabeth died in 1770, her inventory was appraised at £399 and, like her late husband, she had the majority of the money tied up in farm stock. The Pinders purchased at least 26 acres from the Hinde estate as part of a policy which increased their land owned from 9 acres to over 100 during the same period. George Pinder was tenant of the major Hinde farm before the sale of 1789, while William Pinder was the largest farmer in Laxton by the 1790s. In 1736 the various branches of the family farmed a total of 321 acres in the village; by the 1790s this had increased to 575 acres.

FARMING

The second Duke of Kingston's financial problems and his penchant for an extravagant lifestyle were hardly propitious circumstances for efficient estate management. His attention to business was not all it might have been. Major decisions were submitted to him for approval, although in many cases this must have been a formality. In his efforts at keeping estate costs to a minimum, the duke preferred to rely on part-time agents who were usually substantial tenant farmers, a policy contemporary agricultural writers condemned as likely to encourage inefficiency. The overall result, hardly unexpectedly, was that during the fifty-five years between his coming of age and the death of his widow the Pierrepont estate drifted. Kingston interested himself only in what he could extract from his tenants, and not in how he could improve their position. Charles Meadows inherited estates which had been neglected, and perhaps not surprisingly he ordered a new survey to assess the state of his inheritance and the possibilities for improvement, particularly of rents. Under these circumstances we would not expect to find significant agricultural progress during these decades. For many Nottinghamshire estates the post-1750 price rise brought with it rental increases and in some instances enclosure. Almost nothing occurred on the Pierrepont estates: rents hardly moved; spending on repairs was kept to an absolute minimum; and management was poor.

Farming practice in Laxton changed little. Every farmer for whom a detailed inventory has survived was combining crops and animals. The balance varied, partly depending on the time of year. Usually stock was one of the largest items in the inventory. When Elizabeth Pinder died in 1770 her 8 working horses were valued at £80, 3 foals at £15, 15 head of cattle at £39, and pigs and sheep at £5 2s, a total of £139 which represented 35 per cent of her appraised goods. The proportion could be even higher. Robert Taylor's inventory, taken in January 1756, totalled £73 5s 6d, of which £42 10s was for cattle, sheep and horses. In a few cases the value of stock was rather less than the value of crops and, by contrast with the earlier period, in only a handful of cases did the value of stock reach twice the value of crops. In the twenty-four inventories for this period which include comparable information, animals represented an average of 59 per cent of the total value of stock and crops. Half a dozen farmers left crops appraised at £75 or more, which may represent rising prices, or a shift in the pattern of farming, for which there is no corroborative evidence.

The inventories confirm the division of arable produce in the open fields. Thomas Hunt died in September 1738 at just about the start of harvest, and his inventory gives a good insight into the farming pattern. His crops were divided between 14 acres of wheat and barley – and the wording of the inventory suggests they were in the same field – 14 acres of peas and oats (presumably in the second field), 14 acres of hay, probably in a close, and 16½ acres of fallows. This total of 58½ acres is rather less than the 79 acres he was occupying in 1736, and suggests he may have had other land, kept for pasturing animals, not recorded in the inventory. Thomas Pinder (1757) had 16 acres of wheat and barley, and 20 acres of peas. When set alongside Hunt's inventory this would seem to confirm the normal crop division between the fields: wheat and barley in one field, peas and other crops such as beans and oats in the second field, although oats were only rarely grown. Thomas Hunt was one of just two farmers whose inventories recorded oats, and this is not surprising in view of Robert Lowe's comment in the 1790s that in the claylands 'scarce any oats are grown'.[46]

The most notable omissions from inventories are the new crops which were being introduced into English farming by the early eighteenth century, and which were sometimes found in the open fields. Claylands were inappropriate for turnip husbandry, but it was possible to grow legumes and grasses; Francis White's inventory of 1737 refers to 13 acres of peas and clover, but he was farming at Copthorne, one of the independent farms with less than the average land in the open fields. Elizabeth Pinder's crops in 1770 included a 'clover stack', but whether this was cropped from the open fields or from a separate close is not known. In 1908 the spring corn field was known as the 'bean and clover field', but as late as the 1770s there is little evidence of new crops having been introduced into the open fields. The one alternative crop for which there is some evidence is hops. Robert Lowe noted in the 1790s that hops were

a considerable article of produce in this district, principally in the part about Retford, and some about Southwell and its neighbourhood. They are generally known among traders, by the name of North Clay hops; they are much stronger than the Kentish, going almost as far again in use; but those who are accustomed to the latter, object to their flavour as rank.[47]

---

[46] Lowe, *General View*, p. 38.
[47] Ibid., p. 38.

Laxton was one of the places mentioned as having a hop plantation, and the earliest reference to hops in the village dates from 1707. In his will, drawn up during February 1707, Thomas Adwick left to his wife 'my part of the hop ground and polls'. Later evidence is sparse, but there are occasional references in the Thoresby estate accounts to hop poles. Receipts from woodlands sales in 1733, for example, included £476 'for hop poles, brush wood, timber bark and cordwood out of Middle Spring Wood'. John Herring of Moorhouse had a hopyard valued at £20 in his inventory of 1756. Unfortunately little additional evidence has survived about Laxton hop growing. Possibly the produce was sold at Doncaster hop market.

Every farmer for whom an inventory was taken during this period owned cattle. The median number of animals was 10. All but two had horses (median 5) and – by contrast with the earlier inventories – sheep. Most had pigs. Depending on the time of the year when the inventory was appraised the number of animals could be considerable. John Herring of Moorhouse died in July 1756. His inventory recorded 64 sheep, 8 cows, 7 feeding beasts, 6 calves, 5 2-year old beasts, 5 yearling beasts, 3 2-year old colts, 3 yearling foals and 6 carthorses. Herring's 8 cows were an exception; most farmers had between 3 and 6 cows, and a number of cattle they were rearing for the market. Even farmers dying in winter could leave a substantial stock. Francis White of Copthorne died in February 1737 when he had 60 sheep, 'ten beasts or cows and a bull', 'eight horses and mares', 'heifers and calves', together valued at £8, and 'two yearling foals' at £3. Herring and White probably had the largest flocks. However, while the cattle were almost always carefully detailed in the inventories, sheep were often recorded rather vaguely. John Taylor's appraisers in 1756 simply wrote 'a parcel of sheep'.

Farmers continued to maintain their own gear, although later inventories are much more peripheral in recording such detail. Elizabeth Pinder, in 1770, had 2 waggons and a cart, 3 ploughs and 4 harrows, but she was farming on a substantial scale and others may not have kept quite so many pieces of equipment. Perhaps the most detailed account is recorded in Robert Taylor's inventory of 1747. In his yard were to be found a waggon, 2 carts, 4 harrows, 2 ploughs, a swaith rake (used between rows of corn or hay to collect loose stalks or ears on to the swathes or rows), 2 ladders and several stand hecks (for storing fodder).

It would be a mistake to assume that this picture necessarily reflected ignorance or conservatism on the part of the Laxton farmers. That may certainly have been the case, but English farmers were more likely to promote improved farming if they were encouraged by energetic landlords and competent land agents. There were various ways of offering 'encouragement' through lease covenants and inheritance customs, or via rental and farm-size policies, but little change in any of these took place at Laxton during the eighteenth century.

PLATE 5.2 *High Street Farm. One of the smallholdings in Laxton today, but the layout is typical of an open-field farm. The house is gable-end on to the road to allow livestock and farm machinery into the yard and through to the buildings and stackyard behind. The tall, partly hidden, barn on the right, has stone footings, and may date from c.1700.*

The terms and conditions under which Laxton farmers held their farms were typical of Nottinghamshire, where land was generally let 'at will'. In the 1790s Robert Lowe commented that 'in general tenants do not feel themselves uneasy under this tenure and frequently succeed to their farms father to son for generations.'[48] Few if any Laxton tenants were evicted for poor farming. The normal practice was for tenancies to be handed on to whoever the deceased person designated in his will. Usually this meant first of all the widow, and then the eldest son. When the eldest son was already of age it was not unusual for the widow to be passed over in the succession. In 1757, John Chappell left his wife Sarah an annuity of £3, and decreed that all his estate should pass to his eldest son John. However, John was to allow his widowed mother the use of the little parlour and the furniture in it, as well as the adjoining garden. He was also to provide her with coal. Usually the eldest son inherited the farm. In his will made in 1766 Edward Freeman left sums of money to his four daughters, one of whom was already married, and appointed three trustees to look after his property until his son Robert reached the age of 21.

[48] Ibid., p. 16.

No evidence has survived of any written tenancy agreements on the Pierrepont property, but a few months after the Saviles bought out the Broughtons in
1751, they drew up new agreements for their tenants. Although the 6 acres
which the family had owned since at least 1635 were still let on a 21-year lease,
the rest of the estate was let on standard 'at will' agreements permitting either
party to terminate the contact at 6-months notice. The husbandry covenants
merely requested the tenants to keep the land 'in good heart and order', and to
use all manure, dung and ashes on the farm. Permission to plough up any
meadow or pasture land had to be obtained from Savile, and John Eyre was
granted leave to plough up a 5-acre close in 1763 on condition that he followed
a rotation of rape seed, barley, beans and peas, and wheat.

From the circumstances described so far it is hardly surprising to find that
farm rationalization was not being actively canvassed. Some families had no
children, and the tenancy was allowed to change hands at the discretion of the
landlord. This did not necessarily lead to property being amalgamated.
Timothy Wright held a cottage in the woods near Brockilow farm until his
death in 1752. In his will he appointed a trustee to sell up all his effects and
invest the money for the benefit of his widow. The tenancy was transferred to
John Moseley and no land amalgamation occurred. On the other hand the
Pierrepont rentals occasionally describe instances of rationalization. Whitmore
New Close was put together in 1759 for the benefit of Mr Shering's farm. It
was said to be 'constructed from all the farms with a deducted rent', of which
there were ten.[49]

Normally rationalization was less a question of adding holding to holding
than of breaking up a single tenancy between several existing farmers. When he
died in 1741 Joseph Hunt senior was paying £4 9s 7d rent. His widow chose to
retain only a house, two closes and 3 acres of arable, rented at £2 10s. Edward
Taylor vacated a cottage and land during 1742, and his properties, together
with those not required by Widow Hunt, were added to existing tenancies.
William Doncaster leased land from Taylor and Hunt which he rented at
£6 1s 4d. Later he added the Hall and 'Birkett's cottage and land', collectively
rented at £65 10s 6d, and land – by rent – of £3 12s 3d in 1743, £3 4s in 1744
and £6 11s in 1745. By 1747 his rent was nearly £85 a year, although this may
have stretched him too far since in 1761 it was reduced to £83. Even so, with
Laxton rents at about 8s an acre, Doncaster was probably farming in the region
of 200 acres by the 1760s in addition to his freehold.

A similar division took place in 1770 after the death of William Woolfit. No
inventory has survived, but Woolfit died with considerable arrears of rent and
his goods were auctioned. A cow, 'the blind mare', two fillies and a foal
together fetched £27 2s, while John Gabbitas of Walesby paid £93 4s for his
corn – which he agreed to thresh on the premises. From the £120 raised, £105

49 NUMD M.4589.

was rent arrears, and after distress and sale costs had been met, the acting constable handed over £6 15s to his widow.[50] Woolfit's rent had been £47 13s a year, and the farm was divided between fourteen existing tenants and four newcomers paying rents of £17, £23 12s, 2s and 18s annually. While increasing the number of tenants, this also had the effect of pushing up the overall rental since the separate parcels were let in such a way as to produce an overall increase in rent when the various parts were totalled.

Minor changes along these lines also occurred on the Savile estate. Comparison of an (incomplete) list for 1751 and a full rental of 1796 shows that while four farms had remained exactly the same, two had increased marginally in size, two had increased more significantly and a couple had disappeared. In 1751 George Pinder had the largest farm, with nearly 134 acres; by 1796 the farmer was Mary Pinder but she now had 161 acres. Five of the other farms were of between 65 and 92 acres.[51]

Finally, little attempt was made to 'encourage' tenants through rent increases. This was a policy beloved of some contemporary aricultural writers including Arthur Young, but between the 1730s and 1790s rents on both the Pierrepont and Savile estates remained virtually static. In Thomas Cromp's day at Thoresby the rental rose slowly to £787, mainly because of the additional parcels of land bought by Kingston in the later 1730s and early 1740s. After Cromp's death in 1747 only a few minor alterations were made in the rental. Between 1766 and 1773 rents were increased across the Pierrepont estate, but the changes in Laxton took place only as a result of farm reorganization, which brought the rental up to £827. No further changes took place until 1789. Consequently, in forty years from the end of the agricultural depression the Pierrepont's Laxton rental increased by a mere 5 per cent – at a time when prices and rents are acknowledged to have been rising significantly in Nottinghamshire.[52]

Even this was achieved through reorganization rather than by any systematic policy. Westwood Farm first appears separately in the 1729 rental when it was let for £37 14s to Francis Woolfit. This was raised to £40 18s 1d in 1731, and the following year to £41 1s 5d, when land was added with a rentable value of 3s 6d. The rent increased to £41 8s 5d in 1743 when Edward Freeman, who took over as tenant the previous year, rented an additional acre after Thomas Johnson's cottage holding was broken up. This sum was consolidated at £41 9s in 1751, at which it stayed until George Lee succeeded Freeman in 1769 at a rent of £42. This increased to £43 2s when Lee added land rented at £1 2s a year from the Woolfit farm in 1770. No further change took place until 1790. In fifty years the rent hardly changed except when land was added.

[50] NUMD MaB/206/13–14.

[51] Sandbeck Park MSS HM 3270/EMR 20, pp. 7, 15; NAO DD.SR/9A, 1751 tenancy agreements.

[52] J. V. Beckett, *The Aristocracy in England, 1660–1914* (Oxford, 1986), p. 196.

The picture was similar at Copthorne, one of the other independent farms. Francis White took the tenancy in 1729 at a rent of £44 a year, rising to £47 16s 8d in 1731, and to £52 16s in 1732. In the latter case this was partly because meadow and arable renting at £2 19s 6d was added to the farm. It remained at this until 1803, except for the addition of 2s a year from 1770 when land was added from the old Woolfit farm. We know a little about the Whites. Francis White was succeeded by his son John in 1738, a man with the reputation of being the heaviest and strongest man in Nottinghamshire. Said to weigh 33 stones, he had 'on many occasions displayed an equal preponderance of power in the exercise of which he once took up a load of wheat in his hands and threw it from him over a waggon which his servants were loading'.[53] John White married Elizabeth Harpham in 1737 and they had three sons. The oldest, John, moved to Sheffield, where he died in 1806. The second and third sons, Francis and William, farmed locally, and William succeeded his father at Copthorne in 1771. At the same time John White senior made a will apportioning the land that he owned between the two sons. He was leaving nothing to chance.

Less detail has survived about the Savile estate but what evidence there is points to a static rental. A comparison between the tenancy agreements of 1751 and a rental of 1796 shows that on the farms which remained the same in size the rents did not change, and any alterations occurred only where farm sizes differed. Even in these instances the figures suggest a straight transfer of rent rather than any increase in the sums payable.

In the difficult years before 1750 Kingston may have found that he could keep tenants only by nurturing them, but when conditions improved he simply ignored the estate. In very bad years, particularly during the 1740s, rent abatements or allowances were made and sometimes spending on repairs and improvements increased. It was unusual to spend more than £30 a year on repairs in the 1730s, but the total dropped £100 each year between 1742 and 1745. In 1745, the peak year, £159 was spent, of which £99 was for 'pulling down part Mr Doncaster's old house and building a new kitchen and brewhouse with chambers and garretts', while another £16 went towards '29,850 bricks delivered to several tenants for repairs to houses and buildings'.[54]

Although arrears did not rise substantially, and Kingston does not seem to have had problems keeping tenants, we have already seen that these were difficult years in the village. Quite apart from the demographic and financial problems, in the second half of the 1740s Laxton farmers were affected by a nationwide cattle plague in which thousands of animals had to be slaughtered. William Hazard, tenant of one of the Kingston farms in the village, was presented at Quarter Sessions in January 1747 for obstructing the local

[53] White's *Directory of Nottinghamshire* (Sheffield 1844), p. 731.
[54] NUMD M.4562.

inspector of cattle from performing his office, 'and refused to suffer him to kill a cow in Hazard's custody which was infected with the distemper'. Hazard was fined £10 (half to the informer, Robert Weatherall, a Broughton tenant, and half 'to the poor of the parish of Laxton'), and when he refused to pay the constable was ordered to distrain goods to the value of £10. Such an incident seems likely to have caused a scandal – after all, Hazard had been a church-warden as recently as 1743 and was therefore a man of standing in the village – and it is perhaps not surprising that his tenancy lapsed shortly afterwards.[55]

As agricultural conditions improved after 1750 Kingston became increasingly reluctant to finance repairs to tenants' properties. Between 1750 and 1789 no more than £47 was spent in any single year; indeed, between 1775 and 1785 only £86 was spent in total. Since this trend was repeated in his other manors, it is not surprising that Charles Meadows found the estate neglected when he inherited in 1788. Kingston and his widow could presumably ignore costs of this nature because tenants were available and rents came in. No arrears are recorded at Laxton between 1756 and 1779, and only £108 between then and 1789 (although this may have been an accounting technique since we have already seen that William Woolfit had difficulties with his rent).

Kingston could not dictate farm sizes across the parish, but the policies dictated from Thoresby and Rufford ensured that the number of tenancies remained relatively constant, with a few farms increasing in size (table 5.7). The tithe accounts record 41 tenants in Laxton and 6 in Moorhouse for Kingston year in and year out between 1753 and 1769. The number in Laxton rose to 43 in 1770 when Woolfit's farm was divided. Hinde's property was divided between 4 tenants until the sale of 1789, while the Broughton/Savile property had 20 tenants in 1749. After the sale of 1751 one tenant was made responsible for tithe, and the number of tenancies cannot be established again until the 1790s when just 12 are recorded. Although progress had not been rapid, the trend was towards larger farms, and by the 1790s more than half the parish was in twelve substantial farms of 100 acres or more. The number and proportion of farms of 21 acres or more remained almost unchanged.[56]

The most notable change came among the smallholders. The 1789 survey records only 14 occupiers of 5 acres or less, which is a remarkably low figure compard with 1736 (35) which was itself a considerable fall from the 61 in 1635. However, numbers were much higher in 1812. Either there was a resurgence (which, as we shall see, is not out of the question) or the figures are an aberration. A comparison of the 1736 and 1789 surveys shows that nineteen occupiers of land recorded in the latter survey apparently did not have a house in the village. Apart from Robert Pinder of Ossington, who obviously

---

[55] NAO QAD/1/1–2; PR 4787/1.

[56] Tithe records among the Pierrepont accounts and rentals cover the period 1743–1822: NUMD M.4557–4624; Ma2/R6–R41; MaR/23–27. Later rentals also carry some tithe material.

TABLE 5.7 *Farm sizes in Laxton in 1736 and 1789*

	1736			1789		
Acreage	No.	Total acreage	%	No.	Total acreage	%
100+	11	1526	43.6	12*	1843	51.3
51–99	14	1082	30.9	10	797	22.2
21–50	8	299	8.6	13	433	12.0
11–20	11	145	4.2	13	200	5.6
6–10	22	180	5.2	21	185	5.2
1–5	28	102	2.9	8	21	0.6
Under 1	7	4	0.1	6	1	
In hand					112	3.1
Other		158	4.5		1	
	101	3496	100.0	83	3593	100.0

* Francis and John White farmed 129 acres together, but they are also recorded as having separate farms of 81 and 4 acres respectively, which are included in the relevant groups.

Sources: as table 5.2.

lived in the neighbouring village, and Thomas Adwick, whose house was let, there is no evidence to suggest that these people were absentees. Possibly because the surveyor was predominantly concerned with Pierrepont holdings he overlooked some of the smallholdings, but the evidence is inconclusive.

In parishes where the land was divided enclosure was always complex. Only five of the Nottinghamshire manors in which Kingston owned property were enclosed by agreement in the course of the eighteenth century, which suggests that the freeholders were able to delay radical changes, at least until enclosure by legislation became a possibility in the second half of the century. By then Kingston was less interested in his estates, and enclosure on the Nottingham-shire properties was delayed until the 1790s. Between 1788, when Charles Meadows inherited the estate, and 1798, thirteen parishes in which the Pierre-ponts had an interests were enclosed by Act of Parliament. In Laxton, not only did the Pierreponts have to negotiate with a substantial landowner – the Saviles – by the time the Hinde property had been sold the complexity of tenure was enough to deter even a determined encloser like Meadows. During his lifetime almost all the Nottinghamshire manors in which the family had an interest were enclosed and one of the few larger estates to be passed over was Laxton. It may not have been a thriving and expanding village in the mid-eighteenth century, but it had come to be dominated by a number of substantial yeomen families, some, such as the Doncasters and Adwicks, with interests well beyond the village. These people were in a position to acquire significant freeholds and, together with the land they leased, worked sizeable holdings with extremely complex tenurial arrangements.

Chapter Six

Wartime Revival, Peacetime Recession: 1789–1840

With the death of the Duchess of Kingston in 1788 the long hiatus at Thoresby came to an end. Charles Meadows, the heir who took the name Pierrepont, was of a different ilk to his predecessors. He lived at Thoresby and took a keen interest in agricultural improvement; in 1803 the Society for the Advancement of the Arts awarded him its Gold Medal in recognition of his agricultural work.[1] He inherited an estate which had been largely neglected over the previous two decades and, in the case of Laxton, had hardly been touched since the partial enclosure sixty years earlier. The potential was obviously considerable, particularly as his accession coincided with two decades of prosperity for agriculture with high prices and rising rents during the wars with Revolutionary and Napoleonic France. By the time the new lord of the manor died in 1816 the estate had received considerable attention and for the first time serious discussions had taken place about the possibility of enclosing Laxton. By 1816, however, conditions were changing; a depression overtook agriculture in the aftermath of the war years and, despite some recovery during the 1820s, many tenants found themselves in renewed difficulties during the 1830s. By 1840 the worst was over, but Laxton remained unenclosed. In this chapter we shall examine the swings and roundabouts of fortune during the fifty years or so from Charles Pierrepont's accession, taking as our finishing point the acrimonious dispute over tithe apportionment in the years 1839–43, since this is another date at which we can take a bird's-eye view of the village.

PEOPLE AND HOUSES

The prosperous conditions of these years brought a surge in population. After the decades of static and sometimes falling numbers in the middle of the

---

[1] G. E. Mingay, 'The Duke of Kingston and His Estates', unpublished BA dissertation, University of Nottingham, 1952, p. 147.

eighteenth century the population reached 513 by the time of the first census in 1801, and 561 in 1811. It continued to increase rapidly, to 615 in 1821 and to 659 by 1831, the highest recorded figure in modern times, and an increase of 28 per cent in three decades. Although some of the figures are conjectural, Laxton in 1831 seems to have been approximately one-third larger than sixty years earlier. The total had fallen slightly to 641 by 1841, perhaps reflecting the agricultural difficulties of the 1830s.

Changing numbers were reflected in the turnover of families. From the Land Tax Assessments to 1830, the tithe apportionment of 1839 and the 1841 census we can gain an impression of the level of continuity. The 1790 Land Tax Assessment contains 57 surnames (owners and occupiers); the 1830 Assessment contains 59 surnames; and a combination of the tithe apportionment and census gives 67 surnames. There were 35 surnames common to the 1790 and 1830 lists, and 37 common to the lists of 1830 and *c.* 1840. At each point more than one-third of the surnames were unique to the particular list. Twenty-three surnames appear at all three dates. This is a slightly fictitious exercise because the Land Tax Assessments record the names of owners and occupiers of land, while the combined tithe-apportionment/census list records everyone in the village. The two lists may not coincide exactly, but they certainly suggest that Laxton had a core group of long established families while others passed rapidly through the village. Even established families did not stay forever. Among those who faded from the scene in this period were the Jepsons, who were resident in the seventeenth century, and the Adwicks and the Doncasters, both of whom moved to other villages. Other families first appear in the records during these years, and stayed to play a major role in village life, among them the Keyworths, the Moodys, the Quibells, the Wombells and the Saxelbys. Only the Chappells and the Harphams – Richard in Laxton and Robert in Moorhouse, both farmers – could trace their ancestry back to the great survey of 1635, though names still extant in the village in 1840 which were to be found in 1736 included Birkett, Hopkin, Johnson, Merryweather, Newstead, Peck, Pinder, Taylor and Wright. In addition, there were Rooses in 1635 and 1736, Rooses and Roses in 1789, and Roses in 1840. Despite a corruption of the name there was probably a family link, but no continuity of ownership or occupation.

The census enumerators' books survive only from 1841 but private listings drawn up at the time of the 1811, 1821 and 1831 censuses shed valuable light on the early nineteenth-century village. As table 6.1 shows, it was predominantly a young village. The figures have to be treated with some caution because in the early censuses the enumerators were asked to provide specific ages only for children up to the age of 14. Those aged 15–19 were to be recorded as 15, those of 20–24 as 20 and so on. The enumerators did not necessarily abide by these rules, but the information gathered is not likely to be entirely reliable. Despite the 20-year gap between the two sets of figures in table

TABLE 6.1 *Laxton age profile, 1821 and 1841*

Age	1821		1841	
	Number	%	Number	%
0–5	101	16.4	94	14.6
6–10	68	11.0	75	11.7
11–19	131	21.3	139	21.7
20–29	95	15.5	94	14.7
30–39	67	10.9	67	10.5
40–49	51	8.3	50	7.8
50–59	48	7.8	58	9.0
60–69	34	5.5	35	5.5
70–79	14	2.3	24	3.7
80+	6	1.0	5	0.8
	615	100.0	641	100.0

Sources: NAO PR 4796, copy of 1821 census return; PRO HO 107/850 Census Enumerators' Books, 1841.

6.1, the age groupings varied little in the village. Roughly a quarter of the village consisted of children below the age of 10, while the next largest single decadal group was the 11–19 age category, which was because of the number of servants (female domestic and agricultural male) in the village. The similarity of numbers in the later lists is also interesting. In 1831 there were 165 males of 20 years and more,[2] as compared to 159 in 1821. The proportions clearly did not vary much over time.

Where did these people live? From the published census returns we know that the number of houses in Laxton and Moorhouse increased from 109 in 1801 to 114 in 1811, fell back slightly to 113 in 1821, increased again to 126 in 1831, and declined to 119 in 1841 (although, as we shall see, this figure may reflect building as well as demolition). Almost certainly the housing stock did not keep pace with population. Except in 1801 the number of families in the village always exceeded the number of houses (130 families and 126 houses in 1831, for example), and household size was evidently on the increase. In 1801 there were 4.75 people to every house in the village – the national average – but this figure rose steadily to 4.96 in 1811 and to 5.44 in 1821. With 13 new houses constructed in the village between 1821 and 1831 the ratio fell to 5.23,

[2] NUMD MaB/174/334.

PLATE 6.1 *The village layout. Although from the seventeenth century onwards mud and stud buildings were gradually replaced by brick, the fundamental layout of the village has remained unchanged since at least 1635. This is a recent aerial view taken by the Cambridge Aerial Photography Unit. A similar effect could be obtained by substituting any of the other Laxton maps, 1635 (see cover), 1789, 1812, 1820, 1834, 1862, etc.*

but with only 119 houses recorded in 1841 it had returned to 5.4 despite a fall in the population.

The presence of bricklayers in Laxton (see table 6.2) is a reminder not merely of the increase in housing stock, but also of the continuing process of change in the appearance of the village. By the 1830s it contained a motley collection of buildings from different time periods. Mud and stud stood alongside brick; pantiled rooves beside thatched. Richard Keyworth, farming 148 acres (at what is now Town End Farm), lived in a brick and thatched house which was out of repair, while outside in the yard was a new brick and tiled barn, a carthorse stable, a granary and dovecote, and a wagon shed. Smaller farmers were often living in mud and stud cottages, although a few were fortunate enough to have brick and thatch, or even brick and tile. At least two were living in cottages described as brick, mud and thatch. Some villagers inhabited more or less new houses; John Chambers, for example, was described as tenanting a 'new brick built house, barn and stable'. Alongside them were people living in buildings which were in a poor state of repair. William Hopkin farmed 11 acres from a homestead which must have been in many ways typical of this transitional stage. The mud and stud cottage in which he lived was thatched, while his outbuildings included a brick and thatch barn, a mud and stud stable, and a thatched cowhouse.[3]

Some of the houses must have been almost bursting at the seams. Only four people lived alone in 1841 while in eight households there were ten or more people living together. Not surprisingly five were headed by farmers. Richard Harpham lived with his wife and two daughters, two female servants and four agricultural male servants, and William Lee and his wife lived with their three children, two female servants, and three agricultural male servants. Some houses had rooms specially built to house agricultural workers, as was the case at Crosshill where two agricultural male servants and a female servant lived with Michael Saxelby, his wife and three children. Other houses were full of children; William Peatfield and his wife Ann had eight children still living at home. However, the Peatfields were not typical; although the census can only be a rough guide to family size, since it does not record children living away from home, large numbers of children were the exception rather than the rule. In Laxton (not including Moorhouse), in 1841, 45 households contained parents and children, but just 7 had five or more children and 32 (71 per cent) had no more than three.

Finally, with whom did all these people live? The 1841 census enumerators found plenty of examples of the classic nuclear family living together under a single roof, but in addition to those families supplemented with a number of servants there were other households which are more difficult to classify. In a number of cases a man and his family were living under the same roof as an elderly parent – the head of the household – which points to an uneasy transition from one generation to the next. William Nicholson (83) was the head of a household which included his son William (48) and his wife and two daughters, and Robert Weatherall (65) was head of a similarly structured household. These men were described as farmers, but similar instances occurred among agricultural labourers. Maybe they were reluctant to retire. The relationship had obviously been reversed where older people were living as dependants on children. William Bartram (59) and his wife Sarah (67) were

---

[3] NUMD Ma 3 S16.

living with their three sons and a daughter, together with Mary Gibson, sister, and Thomas Gibson (94) father of the wife.

Most relationships seem to have enjoyed matrimonial blessing, although John Keyworth (38), was living in 1841 with his housekeeper and her 10-year old son. A number of children in the village had been born out of wedlock. Martha Hilton (23) and her illegitimate son were living with the blacksmith and his family; while Philip Hooton (54) was sharing a house with his daughter Emma (25) and her two illegitimate children. A handful of young children seem to have been in families to which they had no obvious relationship, presumably adopted for one reason or another. Among these was Charlotte Batley (3), who was living under the same roof as William Dewick, his son Leonard and daughter-in-law Sarah Dewick, and their daughter of three weeks.

Most villagers were involved in farming. Of the people in employment in 1801, 145 out of 171 (85 per cent) were chiefly employed in agriculture, leaving only 26 in trade, manufacturing and handicrafts. In 1811, 113 of the 119 families (95 per cent) were said to be chiefly employed in agriculture, but the proportion later dropped, to 102 out of 122 in 1821 (84 per cent), and to 106 out of 130 in 1831 (82 per cent). Of the 119 heads of household in 1841, 87 (73 per cent) were farmers, cottagers or agricultural labourers. For 1831 and 1841 it is possible to provide a more comprehensive breakdown of occupations (table 6.2). The two lists were compiled on different principles which complicates comparison, but the broader base of occupations is reflected in the number of non-agricultural pursuits. As Laxton grew larger and wealthier it seems to have been able to support not merely the standard tradesmen to be expected in a farming village such as blacksmiths and wheelwrights but shopkeepers and craftsmen. We know that in 1841 Samuel Glazebrook was keeping a shop on the same site as the village shop today. In addition to those listed in the table, members of the Laxtonian Friendly Society included a clockmaker and a whitesmith. Perhaps the most interesting figures relate to female servants. The fact that there were thirty in the village in 1831, and that despite some decline in total population the number had increased ten years later suggests that while Laxton was not immune to the agricultural difficulties of these years it remained relatively prosperous.

LOCAL GOVERNMENT

The prosperity which brought a rising population was not enjoyed by all, and hand-in-hand with improvement for some went poverty for others. The overseers continued to find their time taken up chasing paupers without settlements and pregnant girls without husbands. The Laxton churchwardens complained to the justices in 1822 that George and Sarah Todd and their two children had become chargeable to the Laxton poor rate but lacked a settlement in the

TABLE 6.2 *Occupations in Laxton 1831 and 1841*

Occupation	1831	1841
Agricultural Labourers	62	90
Agricultural male servants		45
Agriculture – occupiers, 1st class	24	
Agriculture – occupiers, 2nd class	36	
Blacksmiths	3	2
Blacksmith journeyman		1
Bricklayers	3	4
Butcher		1
Carrier		1
Cordwainer	1	1
Cottagers		8
Dressmakers		4
Farmers		43
Female servants	30	34
Gamekeeper		1
Grocer		1
Groom		1
Housekeepers		2
Independents	5	
Innkeepers and publicans		4
Joiners		2
Male servant	1	1
Miller		1
Miller's apprentice		1
Milliner		1
Painter		1
Parish clerk		1
Retail trade and handicraft	5	
Schoolmaster	1	1
Schoolmistress		1
Shoemakers		3
Shoe apprentice		1
Shoe journeyman		1
Shopkeeper		1
Tailors		3
Veterinary surgeon		1
Vicar	1	1
Wheelwrights	3	1

Sources: NUMD MaB/174/334 (1831); PRO HO 107/850 Census Enumerators' Books (1841).

PLATE 6.2 *The Post Office. Today this is the only shop in Laxton, and it acts as a general store-cum-post office, run by Miss Margaret Maddison. It has been a shop since at least the 1830s. Samuel Glazebrook was almost certainly the tenant when the tithe map was drawn up. Later it was run for many years by the Laughton family, who kept it as a general store. At one time Laxton had two or even more shops, but today the farmers and their wives travel to neighbouring towns to do most of their shopping.*

village. The case was accepted, but the churchwardens and overseers were still put to the trouble of removing the family to Egmanton. In 1814 they were faced with two cases of bastardy which involved not merely funding the lying-in costs (25s in each case) but time, effort and money in apprehending the putative fathers (one of whom was a farmer in Kirton) to ensure that they paid maintenance. Some families were obviously more of a problem than others. In the autumn of 1831 Fanny Sampson and her sister Hannah both produced illegitimate children, and in addition to paying 10s 6d for midwifery charges, the overseers were faced with apprehending the village wheelwright (in the case of Fanny) and William Extby the village tailor (in the case of Hannah), at a total cost of £1 10s to ensure that they each paid 2s maintenance weekly towards the upkeep of the children.[4] Hannah Sampson married Samuel Dovenor five years later, and by 1841 she was living with her husband, three children of the marriage, and Mary (now 9 and attributed the surname Dovenor), the girl who had unwittingly caused the overseers such a headache.

These were isolated cases, but it became abundantly clear in these years that the cost of relieving the poor was growing out of all proportion, partly as the result of population increase, partly as a result of new expedients including the labour rate and partly, after 1815, as a result of poverty in the countryside. Laxton was no exception to this general rule. One or two individuals left bequests designed to provide help for the poor. John White of the Copthorne family was a Sheffield merchant, but he did not forget his roots, and at his death in 1806 left £40 for the poor to be given out in bread. This capital sum was yielding 40s a year in the 1840s. In 1818 John Hunt left £100, and in 1822 George Lee left a yearly rent charge of 20s for the relief of the village poor. By the 1840s the three bequests were yielding about £9 a year which the churchwardens and overseers distributed in bread at Christmas and on New Year's Day.[5]

Others took precautions against hard times by joining the Laxtonian Society, a friendly society based in the village. It was formed in 1800 with the intention of making sickness and superannuation payments to subscribers. The only record of the society dates from 1846 but it shows membership from 1813 onwards. Sixty-three members are named of whom five are recorded as having died. Two of these joined before 1813: John Rose, a founder member of the society in 1800, died in 1843 at the age of 73; and William Bagshaw who joined in 1805 when he was 25 died in 1844. Both men made small claims on the fund in the years before they died. Not surprisingly the Laxtonian was predominantly an organization for the less well-off members of the village. Of the 63 members, 36 (57 per cent) were labourers while only 5 were farmers. Other

---

[4] NAO PR 4121; PR 4788/10, 11.
[5] White's *Directory of Nottinghamshire* (Sheffield, 1844), p. 733.

occupational groups included 7 servants and a number of craftsmen. No records of payments survive until the 1840s.[6]

These precautions, and the small legacies left to purchase bread for the poor, were a useful supplement but little more to the rising cost of relief. In the later 1780s the village spent about £70 a year on the poor. Costs began to rise from 1790, and they averaged £92 a year during the following decade. A new peak in expenditure of £110 in 1799–1800 set a trend towards much higher outlay. The following year over £200 was spent on poor relief, and the pressure that this placed on the villagers is clear from the fact that insufficient money was raised to meet costs. A subscription for the poor was opened on 31 December 1800, which raised £19 8s, mostly in small contributions, although Charles Doncaster gave three guineas, and several of the more substantial farmers together with the Thoresby agent gave one guinea each. Even so, the church-wardens had to pay more than £34 to the overseers of the poor to cover the deficit.[7] This was an exceptionally bad year, but relief averaged nearly £160 annually in the first decade of the nineteenth century. In 1810 it topped £200 again, and this time it did not fall back as it had done after 1800–1; indeed, in the post-war depression it soared to well over £300, and during the decade 1811–20 the annual average cost was over £285. Such was the complexity of poor relief by this time that in 1821–2, when £388 was spent, £3 10s was given as a salary to the overseers. This was raised to £5 the following year, but when the immediate crisis passed in the middle of the decade the village reverted to the more traditional method of dispensing relief through the work of two unpaid overseers. In 1824 Laxton was among the forty-nine parishes that established the Thurgarton Incorporation, one of the early unions which pioneered the principles later adopted nationally in the 1834 Poor Law Amendment Act. The union had a workhouse near Upton Field, Southwell. Even so during the 1820s poor relief averaged £318, a rise of more than 350 per cent since the 1780s. Nor did the situation change greatly in the final years of the Old Poor Law, with a record £461 spent in 1833–4.[8]

The cost of poor relief was becoming such a burden that a meeting was called in February 1830 to solicit approval for adopting the Roundsman system, whereby men out of regular work could be employed within the village. The meeting considered a proposal to appoint an assistant overseer with a suitable salary, as well as the need to revalue parish property to ensure that assessments were made 'on property not now assessed'. The vicar chaired the meeting, which was attended by agents for the major landowners, and thirteen of the more substantial inhabitants of the village. It was agreed to employ all labour-ing men temporarily out of work as roundsmen, the men being sent by the over-

[6] NAO QDC/4/4.
[7] NUMD MaB/168/161; NAO PR 4119.
[8] NAO DD.M/89/29–30.

seers to the occupiers of land in the parish 'in the proportion of one man to every ten pounds each occupier shall stand rated at to the parochial assessments'. William Peatfield was appointed 'assistant officer for executing the duties of the overseer of the poor, surveyor of the highways and constable' with a salary of £12 a year. The parishioners were to examine his accounts at monthly meetings of the vestry.[9]

The cost of poor relief was rising nationally, but it is still pertinent to consider what the parishioners of Laxton were funding out of their rates. The parish was responsible for relieving individual paupers on a weekly basis, but it also did more than this. A doctor's bill of three guineas for Mary Eyre was met from the poor rate in 1802–3, and £12 14s was paid to a surgeon in 1809–10. Dr Ward's bill in 1816–17 amounted to £14 15s. When Anne Fletcher was committed to the asylum in the 1820s her expenses had to be met from the rates; £4 12s 6d for thirteen weeks in 1828–9, for example. The decision to support a united workhouse scheme in 1824 also cost money. Earl Manvers was paid £25 13s in 1828–9, 'principal and interest of incorporated workhouse', and thereafter the overseers divided poor relief payments between 'resident permanent paupers', 'non-resident paupers', 'occasional resident', and 'bastards'. In addition, regular bills for the purchase of flax point to the efforts made to employ the paupers.

Expenses connected with the poor were hardly surprising, but one reason that the rate rose so rapidly is that other payments were also being made from the poor rate. In one sense this is not surprising; it was common practice, confirmed by legislation in 1739, to raise local and county rates on the same assessment principles as the poor law so that all local taxes became in effect extensions of the poor rate. Almost inevitably however this led to money being raised according to the terms of the poor rate and spent on other causes, but still appearing in the accounts as poor relief. In 1807–8, for example, the overseers paid William Quibell £43 'for militiamen', an allowable expense towards the maintenance of the newly reformed militia at a time of national difficulty during the Napoleonic wars. It was not difficult to move from these beginnings to a more general policy of meeting expenditure out of the poor rate, although under the watchful eye of the JPs such costs were sometimes refused. In 1828, for example, a bill of £5 2s 6d for 'draining tiles' was not allowed. By this time, however, it was regular practice, apparently condoned by the justices, to pay the county rate out of the poor rate. In 1827–8 county rates amounted to £28, the following year to £80, and the year after to £32. By the final days of the Old Poor Law the constables' accounts were also being paid out of the poor rate. The apparently inexorable rise of the poor rate was at least in part a reflection of these add-on costs.[10]

[9] NUMD MaB/168/198–200.
[10] NAO PR 4119.

The number of paupers in Laxton is more difficult to calculate than the cost of their relief. Workhouse bills were paid in the 1780s, although it is not clear where paupers were being sent at that time. In the 1820s Laxton joined the Thurgarton Incorporation but relief in the workhouse was regarded as a mixed blessing, and the village preferred to make its own arrangements. As early as 1810 the Thoresby rental recorded the receipt of £1 annual rent for 'ten poor houses', and a list drawn up in 1830 named fifteen paupers 'who live in Parish Houses and who have small Gardens', together with another ten 'who do not live in Parish Houses but have small Gardens'. Not much is known about these houses beyond the fact that they provided accommodation in the village for the elderly poor. Manvers was requested in 1833 to build more houses for the poor in Laxton, but refused on the grounds that this was the job of the parish officers.[11] The parish gardens were on Westwood Common and have disappeared within living memory.

By the 1830s the cost of poor relief had been a source of national debate for more than a decade, and the problem was finally tackled in the Poor Law Amendment Act of 1834. Under this legislation parishes were allocated to unions, and by centralizing the administration it was hoped to cut the cost of relief. Conditions in the workhouses were deliberately made undesirable, and relief outside the workhouse was supposedly curtailed. Laxton became part of the new Southwell Union, which was formed in 1836 and based on the existing workhouse at Upton. Earl Manvers was elected permanent chairman of the Union. Almost immediately the cost of poor relief fell; from £461 in the final year for which records of the Old Poor Law survive Laxton paid just £76 in 1836–7, the first year in which the new Union operated. This was exceptional, and costs soon began to rise again, to £140 in 1837–8, and to £302 in 1840–1.[12] This increase was largely because the stated government aim of shifting poor relief into the workhouse never really worked. The trend was set in the first three months of the new Union when Laxton paid 14s 7d for the maintenance of two paupers in the workhouse, but £2 5s for out relief. The die was cast, and thereafter out relief constituted a far more important element of cost than poor relief in the workhouse.

One side effect of the New Poor Law was to outlaw housing provision, and the paupers' cottages in Laxton were pulled down. The 1836 Thoresby accounts record '13 old cottages taken down',[13] but since the number of houses in Laxton declined by only seven between 1831 and 1841 some attempt was obviously made to provide new accommodation locally. However, the removal of the cottages was regarded by some contemporaries as a deliberate attempt by Manvers to rid the village of paupers. According to White's 1844 *Directory*:

---

[11] NUMD MaB/218/86–7.
[12] NAO PUS/1/5/2, 4.
[13] NUMD MaB/174/290.

The new poor law, which passing in 1834, was more completely carried out in this than in any parish in the county, for immediately on being joined in Union, the inmates of 13 houses, called poor houses, standing in the carriage road to the parsonage, and the south side of the church, of which ten were very ancient, had three months notice given them to quit, and at the expiration of this notice, these humble dwellings were all taken down, and the inmates left without shelter; many of them were aged men and women, and were removed to the Union house; others, labourers who had been thrown back on their parish from other places, were not willing to go there, and had to sleep in out-houses and barns, for a long time, because there were no empty houses in the village.[14]

Another version of the same story was given to Francis Howell in 1848 by the clerk of the Southwell Union:

About eight or nine years ago in Laxton, Lord Manvers pulled down several cottages; thirty poor persons all came thence in a body to the workhouse, and took it for want of harbour, and not for want of work.

Although Howell claimed to have learnt from other sources that these people were troublesome and dissolute, and that Lord Manvers was considered to have done a good thing by breaking up a gang of bad persons, it did not prevent him from classifying Laxton, in consequence of this action, as a 'closed' village; one where the landlord was deliberately excluding undesirables in order to keep down the cost of relief.[15]

Although it was the poor rate which caused most concern to contemporaries, it was not the only area of local expenditure which was rising. The constable's costs seldom exceeded £30 a year in the late 1780s and early 1790s, but with the reorganization of the militia in the mid-1790s they averaged over £55 annually between 1795 and 1805. Much of this extra expenditure was in connection with the militia. In 1796–7, for example, out of £51, £17 was spent on the milita, and these costs continued throughout the war years. Exactly what they involved is not always clear, although at least one man received a Christmas box of 9s 4d in 1805. Other costs met by the constable included maintenance of the pinfold. In 1800–1 Christopher Rose was paid 6 guineas for building this, and a further £3 18s was spent the following year on 'stone for pinfold'. Fifty tons of stone were bought for Moorhouse pinfold at a cost of £1 9s 2s in 1817–18. The accounts are not complete for the 1820s, but for the years in which they have survived the constable's expenditure regularly exceeded £90 a year.[16]

Road maintenance was also becoming more costly. From the 1780s until 1804 it was quite common for highway repairs to total no more than £20–£30

[14] White's *Directory of Nottinghamshire* (Sheffield, 1844), p. 732.
[15] British Parliamentary Papers (1850), 1152, xxvii. Francis Howell's report, 1848.
[16] NAO PR 4102–4.

a year, which must have meant minimal maintenance along the lines which frequently appear in the accounts of 'hacking ruts'. Little was attempted beyond filling holes in the road with stone, to try to ensure a tolerable surface, but even this became more expensive. In 1804–5 the cost rose to £84, and by the second decade of the nineteenth century more than £100 a year was regularly spent on road repairs. A peak came in 1825 with an outlay of £245, perhaps because a more systematic attempt was being made to improve the surfaces. That year Thomas Broomhead and Company were paid £23 13s for taking up 23½ acres of roadway; James Slaney and Company received £40 10s, and Thomas Cousins and Company £24 for the same work, which related to 88 acres of roadway.[17]

CHURCH AND SCHOOL

The church also became more expensive to maintain, although in the 1790s John Throsby found mutilated effigies, the head of one figure lying neglected on the floor, and the north chapel being used to keep lime, straw, coal, discarded utensils and tools. The graveyard was also in a mess.[18] The cost of upkeep was shared between Manvers, who as impropriator of the rectorial tithes was responsible for the chancel, and the parishioners who paid for maintaining the body of the church and churchyard fences. These costs were met from a church rate and the profits of the church lands, 13 acres scattered through the open fields. In 1809 they were producing £9 a year,[19] but by 1844 the yearly rents amounted to £28 3s 6d. Almost all the land was occupied by John Cook.

The second early spent £54 re-roofing the chancel with lead in 1818 while, perhaps in recognition of Throsby's complaints, the parishioners spent £43 on plumbing and glazing in the late 1790s, and another £11 on repainting in 1810–11. Whitewashing the church cost £6 10s 6d in 1837–8. Much of the outlay was only vaguely accounted by the churchwardens, but more detail was given in the case of the fifty-nine confirmation candidates who each received one shilling in 1806–7, and the £17 spent on mending the bells in 1808–9, Two stoves were put into the church in 1836 and the roof was new leaded in 1843 when the interior was thoroughly repaired.[20] On the other hand the rising costs of maintaining the church must have been particularly irksome to the small band of dissenters who built their own chapel in 1802.

---

[17] NAO PR 4105.

[18] Robert Thoroton, *Antiquities of Nottinghamshire*, 3rd edn, ed. J. Throsby (Nottingham, 1797), vol. III, p. 312.

[19] NAO DR/1/3/2/1.

[20] White's *Directory of Nottinghamshire* (Sheffield, 1844), p. 731.

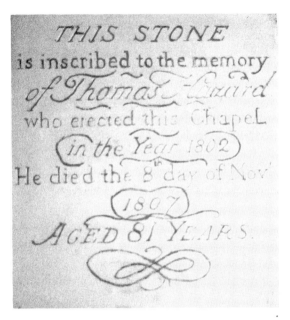

THIS STONE
is inscribed to the memory
of Thomas Hazard
who erected this Chapel
(in the Year 1802)
He died the 8ᵗʰ day of Nov
1807
AGED 81 YEARS.

PLATE 6.3 *The nonconformist chapel. Laxton still has two chapels: a Primitive Methodist chapel on the Moorhouse road, which is now in ruins; and a small Congregational chapel with seating for about fifty people. A monthly service is held in the chapel. This picture shows the plaque in the chapel commemorating the founder William Hazard (see text).*

Relatively little is known about dissent in Laxton at this date except for the Independent chapel built in 1802 by Thomas Hazard. It has since been extended. Thomas Hazard was almost certainly the last of a long line of Hazards in Laxton. There are wills for a Thomas and a Robert Hazard dating from 1534 and 1535,[21] while in 1635 Widow Hazard was paying rent of 2s to Courten and Thomas Hazard was paying £9. During the seventeenth century there were two branches of the family in the village. In the 1680s and 1690s Thomas Hazard was farming 59 acres, while Robert Hazard lived in a house and homestead in the village but paid rent for just under 2 acres of land. Thomas Hazard's farm seems to have remained in the family until 1749 when William Hazard, presumably in disgrace after the cattle plague incident of 1747, and following the death of his wife, vacated the tenancy in favour of William Taylor. Two other Hazards, Thomas and Robert, were cottagers in the village. Of these, Thomas Hazard died in 1765 and his land was transferred to John Petty. From 1745 Robert Hazard was paying £3 14s a year for a cottage and land. He married in 1725 and after his death in 1760 his widow Elizabeth

[21] NAO PR 4143.

held the land until finally Thomas Hazard (1726–1807) succeeded his mother in 1789. It was this Thomas who built the chapel in 1802. He was almost certainly the last of the family in the village. After his death in 1807 the cottage passed to John Chambers and there were no Hazards living in the village in 1812. The Hazards were not dissenters in the 1740s, and when they embraced nonconformity is unknown. What they represent is a long-standing but relatively unambitious family in farming terms, but their memorial is the chapel which has provided them with a place in the history of the village not enjoyed by other more substantial farming families who have passed through over the centuries.

The most pressing recurrent costs in the churchwardens' accounts were for the school. John Truswell held the position of schoolmaster from 1793 until 1847, and part of his salary was met from the proceeds of a £40 charity left many years earlier by an unknown donor. From this, 40s a year was paid to the schoolmaster by Samuel Wheatcroft of Norwell. Other expenses were met by the churchwardens, who had also to maintain the school. Their outgoings included £4 6s 10d in 1808–9 'for school fireplace', as well as an annual salary to Truswell.[22] For this period nothing is known about the number of scholars or the curriculum.

The villagers had to meet the cost of the poor, the constable, the roadways and the church, but this did not mean four separate annual rates. Like many other parishes Laxton was basically rated to the poor, and all other costs were met using the same rating structure. The origin of the Laxton poor rate is unknown, but the valuation in use by the early years of the nineteenth century assessed the parish at £1,333 for local tax purposes. Consequently an 8d rate, as in 1800, raised £44 11s 7d, and a 1s 6d rate, as in 1810, brought in £99 19s.[23] With costs rising by the 1830s a revaluation was called for to try to ensure an equitable distribution of the rating burden. Francis Wharton was approached to undertake the revaluation. He had previously drawn surveys for the Manvers and Savile properties in Laxton, and the churchwardens hoped that Wharton would be able to use his earlier work to keep costs down to about £80–£100. His initial work was completed before the end of 1832 when he

delivered into the hands of Mr Peatfield one of the churchwardens my valuations for the equalization of the poor and highway rates of the Parish of Laxton which before I left had been inspected and comparisons made by several of the principal occupiers and a general meeting was to be held on Friday last for inspection and comparison and for levying rates founded thereon in case such valuations should be approved.

His charge was £100 which he considered to be eminently reasonable in view of the time he had spent on the task.[24] It was not until 1834 that a series of

[22] White's *Directory of Nottinghamshire* (1844), p. 733; NAO PR 4081.
[23] NUMD M.3501, 3506; MaB/174/281; NAO DDSR7/227/42.
[24] NUMD MaB/174/291a.

additional complications mainly resulting from reorganization of the Pierrepont estates were finally ironed out, and his fee was paid in instalments in April and August that year.[25] A copy of his valuation has survived, showing not merely the owners, occupiers and valuations of 1834, but also changes of ownership and occupation down to the later 1860s.[26]

Wharton assessed the rateable value of Laxton at £3,252, although the figure accepted for some years after 1836 seems to have been nearer £3,109.[27] This was the rate that was used to calculate the annual income required to meet the expenditure of the parish over and above the additional sources of finance available to some of the officers. The churchwardens met their costs out of income from church lands leased to villagers, and a church rate raised in conjunction with the poor rate. The overseers of the highways paid for road maintenance by a combination of an annual rate, composition payments, and income from letting the roadside grasses. Composition payments were made by those members of the community who chose to pay a sum of money rather than to do actual work on the roads. Each person was assessed either to do duty or to pay a composition, or some combination of both. In 1834–5 Charles Doncaster was assessed at £195 4s 2d. He provided three teams of workmen for six days each to cover his 'duty', and also paid £2 5s 2½d composition. Finally, the county rate, for the upkeep of county institutions such as gaols, was met partly out of income from the poor rate, and partly from the constable rate. In 1834–5 from £103 spent by the constable, nearly £31 constituted the county rates, and he charged a further 5s expenses for travelling to Retford to pay the money.

The officers worked closely together; it was not unusual for officials to help each other over temporary financial difficulties. In 1815 the churchwardens paid £16 'to the constable to his accounts', and in 1834–5, £25 'to balance the poor accounts', while county rates seem to have been met from both the constable's accounts and the poor rate. A surviving receipt book for the village covering the period 1836–48 records quarterly accounts for the poor, the county rate, and other costs, among them, for the first time in 1841, the new police rate.[28]

WARTIME PROSPERITY

Rising population, house building and more servants point in one direction: while expenditure on the poor was reaching record levels, for many people in Laxton these were years of prosperity. Nationally, between 1793 and 1815, the

[25] NUMD MaB/174/286b; NAO PR 4778/1–2.
[26] NAO PR 4138.
[27] NAO PR 4009–13.
[28] NAO PR 4120.

prices of wheat, barley and oats all increased at a rate not previously experienced by the farming community. Wheat sold at about 48s–58s per quarter in the early 1790s, but averaged 76s in 1795–6 and 119s 6d in 1801. In only ten of the years 1793–1815 did the average price fall below 75s. Weather conditions, and the consequent effects on the supply of grian, were the main factors influencing prices. In these years few seasons were good, and bad years tended to occur in long runs; indifferent harvest followed indifferent harvest between 1795 and 1800, and again between 1808 and 1812. Reserve supplies of grain declined, the size of flocks of sheep and herds of cattle had to be cut, and since population continued to grow, prices soared. Coupled with inflation, and the problems of buying grain from abroad during the long years of war with Revolutionary and Napoleonic France (1793–1815) prices first reached record levels, and then obstinately refused to move back down again.

While consumers groaned under the weight of rising prices farmers generally enjoyed prosperous conditions in spite of the inclement weather and the related problems of sowing and harvesting. Land was in great demand; in England the number of enclosure acts reached a peak, and the boundaries of cultivation were extended to a point not subsequently regained. Landlords sought to enjoy some of the spin-offs from the rise in farmers' profits by pushing up rents during the war years. Rents probably increased two or three times over during the war years, and even allowing for variation across the country increases of between 50 and 100 per cent were common. For the smaller freeholders, squeezed by the economic conditions which had prevailed for much of the eighteenth century, the war years brought relief.

Rents on the lord of the manor's Laxton farms increased rapidly. Charles Pierrepont appreciated the scope for improvement when he inherited the estates, and the survey he immediately commissioned was largely designed to investigate what would be a realistic rent increase; as William Pickin told William Sanday, the surveyor, in December 1789, 'if the Laxton and Kneesall surveys are finished [I] shall be glad if you will bring them with you, as the tenants want very much to know their rents.'[29] In two stages during 1790 rents were increased on the estate. At Laxton the overall rise was from £827 a year to £1,083 (31 per cent), although it varied from farm to farm depending on the surveyor's recommendations; Westwood Farm rent was raised by 15 per cent, whereas Charles Doncaster at Crosshill was obliged to pay a further 48 per cent. The opportunity was also taken to revalue the tithes. The total income had been £217 annually since the 1740s, but following the revaluation this increased to £296, a 36 per cent rise. It slipped back to £290 in 1802.

The consequence of these moves was that Pierrepont's tenants were already paying full economic rents when the steep rise in prices nationally began in 1793, and this may explain why no immediate alteration occurred in the

[29] NUMD M.3315/43.

1790s. No such inhibitions existed at Rufford, and in 1796 the Saviles raised their Laxton rents by 45 per cent. The Honourable Richard Lumley Savile had inherited the estate in 1784 under the terms of the will of his uncle, Sir George Savile. He became the sixth Earl of Scarbrough in 1807. In 1796 the rental of Mary Pinder's 161 acres went up from £74 4s to £110, and of William Newstead's 37 acres from £17 9s to £25. The Laxton increase was slightly in advance of the 38 per cent overall rise for Savile's Nottinghamshire estates.[30]

Pierrepont tenants waited longer for further increases. The overall rental increased marginally in 1799 as a result of various minor changes, but by £344 as the result of a general increase in the second half of 1803. Across the board rents were raised by about 30 per cent between 1802 and 1804, from £1,135 to £1,478. With prices remaining high they were raised again in 1811, this time by up to or in some cases even beyond 100 per cent. William Lee's rent for Westwood Farm increased from £71 10s to £144, while at Crosshill Charles Doncaster's rose from £179 to £343; from 1789, when the rent was £83, the Doncasters had to pay an extra 313 per cent in rent in just twenty-two years. Manvers's rental income in 1812 was more than 260 per cent up on the corresponding figure for 1789. Although sizeable rent increases during the Napoleonic war years were recorded everywhere, these figures partly reflected the neglect of the estate before 1788.

The prosperity of these years persuaded many owner-occupiers and wealthy tenants to stretch themselves, sometimes by way of mortgage, to extend their acreage or to become freeholders for the first time. The result was a resurgence in the number of small-scale owner-occupiers before a final collapse after about 1815 (table 6.3). The surveys point to a resurgence of numbers among the smallholders; individuals with 5 acres or less numbered 48 for 1812, 47 for 1820 and 43 for 1839. The 1812 survey enumerated 114 holders of land; the 1820 survey named 112.

The Laxton Land Tax Assessments are not always consistent, but they also provide an indication of the landownership trend (table 6.4). We would expect to find numbers rising during the prosperous years, but falling away again when conditions deteriorated. The figures may therefore be misleading. Unfortunately, the situation is not clarified by correlating omissions from, and incomers to, the later lists with the Court Rolls. Following the Land Tax Redemption of 1798 a number of freeholders could have been omitted from the lists. This may account for the absence of Thomas Adwick and Charles Doncaster from the 1800 and 1805 lists. In general, the Land Tax Assessments point to an active land market, and here a combination of evidence relating to land transactions and the Court rolls does provide some help.

Beytween 1789 and 1815 the Court Rolls show a ripple effect in the aftermath of the Hinde sale, as several properties came on the market and were split

---

[30] Sandbeck Park MSS, HM 3270/EMR 20, f. 7.

TABLE 6.3 *Landownership in Laxton, 1812–1839*

Owners	1812			1820			1839		
	No.	Acreage	%	No.	Acreage	%	No.	Acreage	%
Lord of the manor	1	2284	63.4	1	2343	63.9	1	2440	62.3
Major freeholders	3	926	25.7	2	828	22.6	2	826	21.1
50–99 acres	–	–	–	1	99	2.7	1	52	1.3
20–49 acres	3	87	2.4	4	114	3.1	6	164	4.2
10–19 acres	9	128	3.6	11	146	4.0	11	150	3.8
5–9 acres	13	108	3.0	7	60	1.6	8	62	1.6
1–4 acres	15	41	1.1	17	52	1.4	14	41	1.0
Under 1 acre	5	2	0.1	4	2	0.1	4	2	0.1
Other	7	26	0.7	6	21	0.6	4	180	4.6
	56	3602*	100.0	53	3667*	100.0	51	3917*	100.0

* As a result of different surveying techniques the overall acreage of the village differs according to the source used.

Sources: NUMD Ma S 7, Ma 4P 15, Henry de Bruyn's survey 1812; M.4918–19, Laxton terrier 1820, prepared by Francis Wharton; NAO AT 70/1A, Laxton tithe apportionment, 1839.

TABLE 6.4 *Number of freeholders recorded in the Land Tax Assessments, 1790–1830*

Year	Number
1790	38
1795	40
1800	33
1805	30
1810	35
1815	36
1820	40
1825	39
1830	39

Source: NAO Q/DDE/1/4, Land Tax Assessments.

up on sale. In 1803 Francis Skinner, Charles Doncaster, Abraham Wright and Robert Eyre bought land from William Thompson, who owned 29 acres in 1803; while in 1806–7 six individuals were admitted for the Moorhouse property lately belonging to Pendock Neale (27 acres). Manvers turned down the opportunity to buy this in 1805 despite a recommendation from his agent that 'some of the land is intermixed and adjoining to your Lordship's and was your Lordship to become the purchaser it would be very convenient for the occupation of those tenants to whom it joins.' Manvers regarded the asking price of £1,833 as excessive for 27 acres.[31] The volume of transactions in the village reached a peak between 1809 and 1815, with the most important sale in 1810 when Charles Doncaster parted with his property.

The rise of the Doncasters in the eighteenth century was not continued in the nineteenth. Charles Doncaster (1736–96) was succeeded by his son Charles who added to the family holdings by leasing part of William Taylor's farm for £14 15s 6d annual rent in 1798 and acquiring land from William Thompson in 1803. Charles Doncaster died in 1808, a relatively wealthy man. In his will, prepared four years earlier, he left several small freeholds and £1,300 to his widow, his estates in Moorhouse and Egmanton to his eldest son Charles; estates in Boughton and Wellow to his second son John; £350 each to his other two sons, and £200 each to his three daughters.[32] The family had come far. Doncaster was buried in Laxton, but he was the last of the family to live in the village. He himself was described as 'of Ollerton', while his heir described himself as 'of Middlethorpe, near Newark', and although he retained the substantial property leased from Manvers in Laxton until the mid-1830s, he disposed of the freehold land in the village. The house was retained for his farm workers.

The details of the Doncasters' sales have not all survived, but coming as they did at a time of prosperity for freeholders, and with no response from Thoresby or Rufford, they offered considerable opportunities to the other Laxton freeholders, if on a more limited scale than the Hinde sale. Ten lots, including Breck Wong and Porter Wong closes which the Doncasters had purchased at the time of the Hinde sale, and totalling altogether just over 43 acres, were sold by auction at the Sun Inn, Laxton on Saturday March 10, 1810. Among the purchasers were George Peck, Thomas Jepson, Robert Weatherall, William Lee and John Cook. Collectively they paid about £1,962 for the land. Further sales almost certainly followed, although fewer details of these have survived. John Chappell is known to have bought 11 acres of Doncaster property and George Kemp 5 acres, while William Quibell and Richard Gray also appear in the manor court records as having purchased land from Doncaster. In 1812 Doncaster owned less than 10 acres in the village, and by 1820 he had sold out altogether.[33]

Perhaps most interesting of all in the course of these transactions was the response of Earl Manvers. Between 1789 and 1810 he seems to have acquired only one property, a house with half an acre of adjoining land, for which he paid £360 in 1810. Even this was not a straightforward transaction. The prop-

[31] NUMD MaB/201/14.
[32] NUMD M.5548; NAO DDM/57/48/9.
[33] NAO DDT/66/16–29; DDM/112/82; NUMD MaB/168/114.

erty had changed hands in 1730 when Samuel Roos sold it to William Moseley. Robert Moseley in turn sold it to William Pickin in the 1790s with an agreement that Manvers should have first option in the event of Pickin disposing of the property.[34] It was this option which Manvers took up in 1810. Otherwise, through all the transactions between the freeholders, Manvers stood apart. His reluctance to purchase land may be significant in view of his interest in enclosure. Possibly he did not see the smaller freeholders as likely to be an obstacle. However, one family did cause him concern: the Denisons of Ossington.

ENCLOSURE PROPOSED

In the mid-eighteenth century the Denisons were one of the two principal merchant houses in the West Riding of Yorkshire. William Denison invested considerable sums in landed property in Yorkshire, Durham, Lincolnshire and Nottinghamshire. The latter included land at Sutton-on-Trent and, in 1768, the 2,403-acre manor of Ossington. William Denison spent little time on the estate, although the large brick house of 1729 may have been partially rebuilt in 1769, and the park and gardens were improved between 1779 and 1781. After he died in 1782 the estate passed to his brother Robert Denison. He had a much stronger attachment to the countryside, as did his successor, a nephew of William Denison who inherited the estate in 1785 and assumed the name of Denison. John Denison employed Sir John Soane to remodel part of the house at Ossington,[35] and he completed the family transition from mercantile to landed wealth. He also had the financial means to consider extending the property.

Ossington lies adjacent to the eastern boundary of Laxton and Moorhouse, and the original purchase almost certainly included at least one small parcel of land in Moorhouse. Denison soon set about expanding this holding. In 1794 he purchased the 23-acre Knapeney closes from William Cook for £269 6s, and he also bought up the 12 acres Thurston Bolton of Rufford had acquired from the Hinde estate. Both these additions were included in the settlement of his estates at the time of his second marriage in December 1796 to Charlotte Estwick. In 1801 he bought 15 acres from the Whites of Copthorne, for which he paid £577 10s, and he also bought a further 6 acres from Pendock Neale. There is also evidence of a land exchange with Francis White in 1811.[36]

[34] BL Egerton 3533, f. 37; NUMD M.4025–6.
[35] R. G. Wilson, 'The Denisons and Milneses: Eighteenth-century Merchant Landowners', in J. T. Ward and R. G. Wilson (eds), *Land and Industry* (1971), pp. 145–62.
[36] NAO De C5/12; DDBG/o; NUMD De C10/10, a, b. Several of these transactions are recorded in the Court Rolls.

By 1810 Denison's intentions were beginning to cause a stir at Thoresby. Manvers was in some financial difficulty, and had to borrow £20,000 in the summer of that year.[37] While he was in no position to buy out the Denisons, Manvers recognized the need to come to some arrangement with them, and he proposed exchanges with both Denison and Scarbrough preparatory to the enclosure of Laxton. As prices and rents rose during the war years, landlords looked forward to even higher rewards by enclosing what was left of open-field England. The surge of enclosing activity in the first decade of the nineteenth century was designed to improve arable output, and it brought into cultivation marginal land, commons and wastes. The failure of the second Duke of Kingston to pursue enclosure on the Pierrepont estates in the second half of the eighteenth century left Charles Pierrepont with considerable ground to make up. Several villages in the vicinity of Laxton were enclosed in whole or in part without Parliamentary sanction, including Kneesall and Ossington. Not surprisingly Pierrepont considered the possibility of enclosing Laxton, not – if his attitude towards land sales is any indication – because he feared the freeholders, but because of the emergence of the Denisons.

In 1810 Manvers instigated exploratory talks with Scarbrough and John Denison, designed to prepare the ground for enclosure. Henry de Bruyn was commissioned to negotiate with Scarbrough an exchange of lands and woods in Laxton and Eakring. The intention was that Manvers should offer his land in Eakring in return for Scarbrough's property in Laxton. The advantage to Scarbrough was to consolidate his family property in the area adjoining Rufford. Even if this proposal was not accepted de Bruyn suggested that at the very least the two parishes should be enclosed and made tithe free.[38] To this end he drew up a survey which was endorsed 'the improvement this estate would experience by an exchange of lands with the freeholders or by an inclosure has been pointed out, on a former occasion and it is to be lamented such great and evident advantages cannot be immediately carried into execution'. No progress seems to have been made with this plan.[39]

Within months of these negotiations beginning Manvers was alerted by William Wilkins, one of his agents, to the importance of negotiating an exchange for any land Denison owned, and on which Manvers had designs, 'for if he gets what he is most desirous of having and it happens afterwards that it is very desirous we should exchange at Lexington he will undoubtedly make us pay dear for it'.[40] This advice was accepted despite Manvers's financial problems. Wilkins met with Denison at Thoresby after which

[37] NUMD M.4167.
[38] NAO DDSR/217/15.
[39] NUMD M.4914; NAO DDSR/217/15.
[40] NUMD MaB/169/230.

I recommended to Lord Manvers to make an exchange of lands with you in the vicinity for the mutual benefit of his Lordship and yourself, and he gave his consent that I should employ a competent person to examine the premises, and my instructions to him were, and which by the enclosed report I believe were implicitly followed, to examine the lands belonging to both parties as impartially as if mutually employed by both.[41]

The proposal was that Manvers should offer Denison land in Sutton and Ossington in exchange for 29 acres in Laxton, of which 19 acres were in '5 closes called Knapeney close and buildings', and the rest was in seven small parcels in Moorhouse. The total holding was valued at £1,865. However, Denison had no intention of parting with Knapeney closes, and his agent was instructed to work out a more acceptable deal. Letters were exchanged between the agents, but it was soon clear that an agreement could not be achieved without considerable trouble. Denison was accused of making unrealistic demands, and in March 1812 Wilkins wrote in exasperation 'I consider the treaty terminated.' The threat worked, and on 10 April 1812 Denison conveyed land in Moorhouse to Manvers. The 1812 rental includes £15 5s 3d, half a year's rent for Moorhouse land bought off Mr Denison. However, Denison had successfully maintained his position by refusing to part with Knapeney closes, and nor had he proceeded with the sale of 38 acres at Moorhouse which he was considering.

The seriousness of Manvers's intentions is clear from the length of the negotiations, and the eventual decision to purchase property, but little progress had been made towards land consolidation or enclosure. The Denisons still owned more than 100 acres in Laxton, and while they showed little further interest in the land market over the next forty years the failure to deal adequately with the problem was to prove costly in the longer term.

With Scarbrough negotiations were resumed in 1815. Plans were sketched out by which Manvers was to part with Eakring, Belle Eau Park Farm, and land in Ompton, amounting to 1,401 acres, and to receive in exchange Scarbrough's property in Laxton (710 acres) together with 663 acres in Egmanton, a total of 1,372 acres.[42] As far as is known, no progress was made on these proposals, perhaps because the first Earl Manvers died in 1816 and agricultural conditions were no longer encouraging. A further scheme for an exchange of land within Laxton between the families was put forward in 1833 when the relevant boundaries were staked out. However, while the major landowners prevaricated piecemeal enclosure continued; between 1736 and 1903 a total of 244 acres of open-field land was enclosed.[43]

---

[41] NUMD M.4171, MaB/169/226, 228; BL Egerton 3533, f. 57.
[42] NUMD MaB/187/954.
[43] NUMD MaB/174/283–90; see below p. 316.

PLATE 6.4 *Westwood Common. The distinctive outline of the western edge of Laxton can be seen clearly on this overhead view of the parish. The area jutting out to the left is Westwood Common, the 80-acre expanse which is today part of the land attached to Westwood, or Common Farm – as it is alternatively known – which can be seen on the picture and in the distance on the inset. Until the 1950s Westwood was the main village common land, and the toft holders (in effect residents) were entitled to graze animals on it during the year. By the 1930s it was no longer much used, and it was 'closed' in 1953. The woodlands (on the left on the inset) can be seen on Mark Pierce's map of 1635. Westwood Farm is one of the independent farms laid out in the 1720s, although the house dates from the 1880s. Today the farmer lives in Kirton, and the house has been sold to private tenants. The land is still owned by the Thoresby estate.*

PEACETIME RECESSION

The prosperity of the war years came to an end with the peace. Grain prices collapsed in 1815–16 and again in the early 1820s. Imports grew steadily, and it became obvious that price levels after the war were not going to be much higher than they had been before it commenced. Adjustments were required, in terms both of the acreage under the plough and the level of rents. Enclosure no longer seemed a relevant issue as landlords sought to placate their tenants with rent abatements, and in some instances, reductions. At Laxton, the Pierrepont rental reached a high point of £3,296 in 1815, the last year of the war, but as demand fell, and agriculture went into recession, these figures could not be maintained. All rents were abated 10 per cent for the Christmas 1816 collection, and 5 per cent at Midsummer 1817. Conditions later improved, and for the next three years rent were paid on time, but this was only a temporary respite. Abatements of 10 and 15 per cent were allowed in the half years to Christmas 1820 and Midsummer 1821, rising to 20 and 25 per cent on the half year rental to Christmas 1821. Finally, with prices severely deflated between 1821 and 1823, Manvers bowed to the inevitable, and in 1822 reduced the rents by about one-quarter. Mrs Lee's rent for Westwood Farm was cut from £200 to £150, while at Crosshill Charles Doncaster's rent came down from £330 13s 4d, to £260. The new rental brought in £2,647 a year, and if this was only 80 per cent of the figure achieved in 1815, it was still more than 200 per cent up on 1788.

After 1822 the situation stabilized. The Pierrepont rental hovered around £2,646 from 1823 until 1832 and there were no arrears. Between 1833 and 1836 the situation again deteriorated as rents nationally went unpaid on arable farms on undrained clays. Earl Manvers's rental at Laxton fell from £2,650 in 1832 to £2,529 in 1833 and to £2,496 in 1834, when, for the first time in over a decade, the accounts record rental arrears. Although rents were held at around £2,470 through the 1830s, arrears often exceeded £200, and in 1836 they topped £500. Recovery was to be long delayed.

The major casualties of economic conditions after 1815 were the freeholders who had done so well from the war years. If the Hinde sale of 1789 marked the high point of their holdings in Laxton the peace of 1815 was like the bursting of a bubble. Countrywide, many who had purchased land during the war years, perhaps by taking on an extra mortgage, found themselves hard pressed. By the time of the government enquiries into agriculture during the 1830s it was clear that many who had ridden on the crest of the wave had since gone under. Following the Doncaster sale in 1810 the volume of land transactions in Laxton continued on a lesser scale to 1832, after which it is not clear whether transactions slowed down or the nature of the information recorded in the Court Rolls changed. Over the whole period 1790–1840 manor court enrolments averaged just over 4 a year, with peaks in 1797 (11) and 1800 (12). Identifiable family successions in the years for which figures are available, ran at about one-third of all admissions.

Although the number of freeholders remained much the same (42 in 1789, 45 in 1812, 44 in 1820 and 1839), the proportion of land they owned did not. Due to discrepancies in the figures the full extent of decline is difficult to measure, but the freeholder acreage measured roughly 10 per cent in 1812, 13 per cent in 1820 and 12 per cent in 1839. By the latter date only six freeholders owned more than 20 acres, and the largest holding was just 52 acres. Many of these freeholds were not viable on their own. Allowing for error as a result of inconsistencies between the surveys, table 6.5 shows that the eighteenth-century trend continued after 1789 whereby the owner-occupiers consolidated their position by renting additional land. The result was a gradual decline in the number of owners occupying only their own land, and a corresponding rise (slightly allayed in 1839) in the number renting additional land. The days of the independent owner-occupier were clearly numbered.

TABLE 6.5   *Landownership and occupation in Laxton, 1789–1839*

	1789	1812	1820	1839
Occupying only land owned	15 (35%)	11 (27%)	7 (17.5%)	5 (15%)
Occupying *more* land than owned	20 (47%)	24 (58%)	27 (67.5%)	21 (62%)
Occupying *less* land than owned	7 (16%)	6 (15%)	6 (15%)	8 (23%)
Unknown	1 (2%)			
	43	41	40	34

Sources: as tables 5.6, and 6.3.

The combinations arising from this confusion of tenure were considerable. In 1820 Thomas Bagshaw owned nearly 5 acres, but he rented another 10 from Scarbrough, and 4 from Manvers; George Merryweather rented 6 acres from Scarbrough and 13 acres from Manvers; while William R. Pinder farmed in total 114 acres of which he rented 101 acres from Scarborough. However, Pinder owned 17 acres, so he must also have let some of his own land to others in the parish. By 1840 the complications were immense (table 6.6); freeholders might be working their own land, or working part of it, and leasing other land, while letting some of what they owned. Elizabeth Berwick, described in 1841 as a cottager, retained in hand 3 acres on which her house, outbuildings and orchard stood, together with a single strip in West and Mill Fields. Altogether she owned nearly 37 acres, and much of the rest was let to George Artcliffe. Samuel Pinder was the tenant of Knapeney Farm, but he was also a freeholder.

TABLE 6.6 *Freeholder tenurial arrangements in Laxton, c.1840*

Owner	Occupier	Holdings	Occupied	Let	Other holdings rented
Bagshaw, Thomas	Not known	9	9	–	16
Baines, Joseph	(Deceased)	2	–	2	–
Baines, William	Farmer	3	3	–	10
Barlow, John	Farmer	14	6	8	8
Bartle, James	Shopkeeper	3	1	2	–
Bartle, John	Cottager	8	6	2	–
Bellamy, George	Not known	2	–	2	–
Berwick, Elizabeth	Cottager	22	4	18	–
Birkitt, John	Cottager	1	1	–	7
Brown, George	Not known	6	3	3	18
Buxton, Robert	Not known	10	–	10	–
Chapman, George	Not known	11	–	11	–
Chappell, John	Not known	1	1	–	–
Clarke, John	Not known	3	3	–	7
Cook, John	Farmer	3	3	–	38
Curtis, Samuel	Not known	1	1	–	–
Dury, Thomas	Not known	2	2	–	–
Gray, Ann	Not known	1	–	1	–
Hill, Benjamin	Agric. labourer	1	1	–	9
Hodson, Joseph	Not known	1	1	–	–
Johnson, John	(Deceased)	2	–	2	–
Keyworth, Thomas	Farmer	16	–	16	–
Lee, William	Farmer	6	6	–	70
Newstead, Thomas	Farmer	6	2	4	23
Nicholson, William	Farmer	8	6	2	80
Peatfield, William	Farmer	1	1	–	51
Peck, Martha	Independent	5	1	4	–
Pinder, George	Innkeeper	7	6	1	14
Pinder, Samuel	Farmer	16	11	5	35
Pinder, William, sen.	Farmer	27	21	6	79
Proctor, Richard	Clergyman	11	8	3	4
Quibell, William, sen.	Farmer	11	10	1	20
Rose, Joseph	Farmer	1	–	1	–
Skinner, Thomas	Not known	16	–	16	–
Skinner, William	Not known	10	–	10	–
Smith, Godfrey	Not known	2	–	2	–
Smith, John	Agric. labourer	9	–	9	–
Taylor, George	Farmer	6	4	2	72
Weatherall, Robert	Farmer	22	16	6	74
White, Francis	Farmer	7	7	–	18
White, Francis	Farmer	6	–	6	24
Woolfit, Richard	(Deceased)	14	–	14	–
Wright, Sarah	Publican	5	5	–	24
Wright, William	Tailor	25	1	24	18

Sources: NAO AT 79/1A Laxton tithe apportionment; PRO HO 107/850 1841 Census Enumerators' Book.

Of the sixteen holdings he owned (31 acres) he occupied eleven and let the other four. Obviously it was not every farmer who had such a complicated arrangement, and table 6.7 looks only at the largest farms in the village. Of the fifteen farms in 1840 which were of 100 acres or more, ten of the farmers leased all their (rented) land from Manvers, and two from Scarbrough. The other three arrangements were slightly more complex. William Wombell rented 50 holdings from Manvers and 2 from William Wright; William Pinder senior rented 78 from Scarbrough and 1 from William Wright; and William Quibell junior rented 45 from Manvers, 2 from the Church, and 1 from Wright. Of the 7 farms between 50 and 99 acres 1 was wholly rented from Manvers, 1 from Scarbrough and 1 from Denison; 3 combined holdings from Manvers and William Wright; and William Glazebrook's 44 holdings were divided between Scarbrough (42), Elizabeth Berwick (1) and George Taylor (1).

TABLE 6.7 *Holdings over 100 acres in Laxton, 1840*

Occupier	Total holdings	Owned	Rented	Acreage
John Keyworth Thomas Keyworth	143	16	159	238
William Wombell, sen.	52	–	52	207
Michael Saxelby	33	–	33	183
Samuel Pinder	44	9	35	165
William Pinder	62	–	62	165
George Peck	34	–	34	154
Richard Harpham	72	–	72	153
William White	26	–	26	142
William Whittington	59	–	59	136
William Lee	76	6	70	126
George Taylor	76	4	72	124
William Pinder, sen.	100	21	79	119
William Quibell, jun.	48	–	48	109
Robert Weatherall	90	16	74	101
William Peatfield	52	1	51	100

Source: as table 6.6.

The second Earl Manvers, who succeeded to the title in 1816, was more interested than his predecessor in acquiring further property in Laxton, and when two of the most substantial freeholding families sold out in the 1820s he was the chief purchaser in both cases. As economic conditions deteriorated after 1815 it was some of the better-off freeholders who found Laxton was no longer a friendly environment, among them the Chappells and the Adwicks.

Perhaps the most poignant of these sales concerned the Chappell family. By the early nineteenth century the Chappells were the longest-established of Laxton's freeholders, and they could trace their heritage and much of their land back into the sixteenth century. John Chappell, who died in 1804, left his land and real estate to his grandson, also John, and bequests of £40 to his daughter Mary, and £120 to his other grandson William. When the young John Chappell married Sarah White of Ossington in 1805 he settled 21 of the 31 acres of his freehold on his new wife. He farmed over 60 acres. Chappell was one of those who purchased land from Charles Doncaster, and by 1812 this had increased the family freehold to 42 acres. Almost certainly he had over-reached himself, and in 1816 he mortgaged the settled land for £800. Although this was redeemed in 1820, Chappell's difficulties remained considerable, and in the autumn of 1821 he sold 23 acres – probably all his unsettled land – to Earl Manvers. The sale price was £1,800, and after Manvers had paid for a new barn Chappell was to lease the land for a rent equivalent to 3 per cent of the purchase money.[44] This did not save the family. By 1839 John Chappell, an owner-occupier with just 11 acres, was living in Moorhouse, but he sold out to John Evelyn Denison of Ossington in 1854 and the family had left the village by 1860.

The Chappells turned to Thoresby in 1821 and five years later the Adwicks also disposed of much of their Laxton freehold to Earl Manvers. The Adwicks were one of the most substantial freeholding families in the village, with more than 100 acres by the early nineteenth century (110 acres in 1812; 104 in 1820). By this time they had moved to Kelham, but they remained interested in Laxton; Thomas Adwick bought 2 acres for £110 in 1802. However, in 1806 Adwick was succeeded by his son, also Thomas, who was less interested in Laxton, and during the 1820s the family disposed of its property in the village. The sales began in 1823 when William Wright bought property from Adwick, but it was in 1826 that the majority of the land went on the market. Adwick's solicitor approached Manvers's agent in November 1825, offering Manvers 26 lots totalling nearly 53 acres, for £3,500, with the proviso that 'we have several parties who are wishing to purchase parts of the estate.' After some negotiation Manvers agreed to pay £3,300. Further property was auctioned on 15 November 1826. Manvers's agent bought nearly 6 acres, including the family house in the village, for £784 19s, and shortly afterwards he paid £55 to William Merrils for an acre of land in the Mill Field. Merrils had purchased this at the auction, and another purchaser was William Pinder who paid £134 15s for 3 acres. When the final deeds were drawn up Manvers had purchased nearly 60 acres (of which approximately 45 acres were in the open fields) for £4,139 10s.[45] By 1840 the Adwicks no longer owned property in the village.

---

[44] NUMD M.5517, 5519–23, 5526–7; MaB/218/14.
[45] NUMD M.5495, 5506, 5539–40; MaB/168/149 a, b, 194/6, 8; NAO DDLK/14/328.

If these were the most notable post-1815 departures, there were other free-holders who also sold property. In a further auction at the Sun Inn in 1828 the late Abraham Wright's 15 acres were put on the market. Rev. Richard Proctor bought an orchard and close, and another purchaser was William Peatfield. No other sale details are known.[46] Peatfield owned 7 acres and Proctor 15 in 1839. Yet another auction at the Sun Inn took place in 1836, this time for the sale of William Pinder's 10½ acres. The land was divided into seventeen separate parcels. From the Court Rolls we know that John Weatherill and Richard Proctor bought part of the land, but although a sale advertisement has survived no details of any other purchasers are known.

One consequence of these various transactions was that by the 1830s Laxton no longer had a small elite of leading freeholders. In 1817 the churchwardens, George Lee and William Lee, owned less than 11 acres between them, and among the leading inhabitants of the village who signed the visitation terriers drawn up in these years were Richard Keyworth and Paul Glazebrook who were not landowners, and Samuel Pinder, George Peck, Thomas Newstead and William Quibell. Samuel Pinder with 22 acres was the largest landowner, and the only owner-occupier in the group. The Lees farmed 149 and 236 acres respectively, and all the others between 42 and 190 acres. The leading men of the village were now substantial tenant farmers.

FARMING IN WAR AND PEACE

The broad trend of prosperity down to 1815 and increasing difficulties for tenant farmers and freeholders alike thereafter had obvious repercussions for the state of agriculture in Laxton. Rising rents point to improving agricultural conditions, and land previously used for grazing was brought under the plough in the later years of the eighteenth century. The pressure to increase cultivation was already growing in the 1780s. In 1783, £3 4s 3d extra tithe was paid for 'fresh land ploughed up', 15a 3r of barley and 4 acres of wheat and peas, in place of grass. At this stage freshly ploughed land accounted for only a handful of acres each year, but in the 1790s the acreages were rather more considerable. In 1790 nine of Savile's tenants and fourteen freeholders paid extra tithe on 260 acres of closes they were ploughing up. In each year down to 1801 a minimum of 170 and a maximum of 293 acres are recorded as ploughed closes.[47] These extra payments cease abruptly in 1802, and it is not clear whether the ploughing up of closes stopped – which seems unlikely in view of the agricultural conditions prevailing over the early years of the nineteenth century – or whether alternative arrangements were made in relation to tithe payments.

[46] NUMD MaB/168/179.
[47] NUMD Ma 2/R6–26.

As for how the farmers worked their land, however, the evidence is poor. For this period there are no inventories to provide a guide to the crops and stock maintained by individual farmers, and nor have any 1801 crop returns survived for Nottinghamshire. There is no reason to believe that any major changes had taken place in the agricultural cycle, and in the early years of ploughing up, during the second half of the 1780s, the accounts record the use to which the grasslands were to be put. Apart from barley, wheat and peas, which we have already met in the Laxton farming cycle, beans were specified in 1784, 1785, 1787 and 1788, oats in 1785, 1786 (15 acres) and 1788, and flax in 1785.[48]

No new crops are mentioned, and the pattern of farming remained traditional. In his survey of Nottinghamshire agriculture prepared in 1798 Robert Lowe found the common course of husbandry in the clay districts north of the Trent (including Laxton) to be fallow, wheat or barley, and peas or beans. Peas were widely grown in this area because they 'smothered the weeds', but Lowe found the crops to be 'very foul'. In a few places clover had been introduced and sown with barley, and Lowe found new rotation patterns on some of the larger estates. Farmyard dung was the major source of manure. Sheep in this area were 'a poor breed' and – confirming the inventory evidence – poultry 'has never been made an object of particular attention'. Fowls, which were 'commonly of a bad breed' were 'raised as much for the diversion of cock-fighting as the table'.[49]

Forty years on the picture had scarcely changed, particularly on the heavy claylands of the county.[50] For Laxton the tithe file, compiled in conjunction with tithe commutation, describes a village where agriculture was competent without being progressive. The assistant commissioner described how:

The soil of this parish is not of the best quality being chiefly divided into two classes – peaty loam, and a sandy loam, and the greater part of the parish is open field, which prevents the cultivation from progressing to its full length. Still the farms are well tilled, and the crops, as far as the character of the soil permits, good.

This hardly suggests a village on the verge of an agricultural revolution, but conditions were more favourable in Moorhouse where 'from being enclosed [it] is tilled better, turnip fallow being introduced and the shifts better regulated.' Clover was sown with barley at Straw Hall Farm, on the eastern edge of the parish.

The tithe valuations give some indication of the farming pattern in Laxton. Of 3,707 acres of titheable land, 1,965 acres were under arable cultivation

[48] NUMD Ma2/R6–13.

[49] Robert Lowe, *General View of the Agriculture of the County of Nottinghamshire* (1798), pp. 37–8, 104, 129, 131.

[50] A. D. M. Phillips, 'Agricultural Land Use, Soils and the Nottinghamshire Tithe Surveys *circa* 1840', *East Midland Geographer* 6, 6 (1976), 284–301.

(53 per cent), 1,400 were meadow and pasture (38 per cent) and 338 acres were woodlands, commons and waste. As we shall see, the proportion of arable had fallen considerably by the 1860s, and this level was not achieved again until very recent times. The most interesting development was in the crop pattern. Information is given in the file relating to 956 acres of cereals, of which 478 acres were in wheat and 237 acres in beans and peas. No barley is specified, and the other 241 acres were in oats.[51] This was a considerable change since the 1790s when Lowe had found few oats grown in the area. The Nottinghamshire tithe files show clearly that by 1840 oats had become a small and somewhat sporadic but none the less significant part of the county's cereal acreage. Almost certainly the acreage under oats expanded from the end of the Napoleonic wars. As wheat prices fell, oats were grown as a substitute crop on both light and heavy land.[52] Although the Court Rolls are virtually silent on husbandry practices, Laxton farmers were obviously able and willing to alter the cropping balance to suit economic conditions, despite the persistence of the open fields.

In the view of the tithe surveyor the failure to enclose restricted husbandry innovation. This did not mean that Laxton stood still. Parcels of land were exchanged between the freeholders and probably also between tenant farmers to create more compact, sometimes semi-enclosed holdings. The scale of this activity is unquantifiable, and one of the most frequent complaints was the near impossibility of keeping track of changes in holdings brought about by exchanges, whether with or without the permission of the lord of the manor. He himself, through his agent, was not averse to engaging in the process; hence Thomas Adwick's letter of 8 March 1820:

I have sent you the particulars of the exchange of lands between the Earl of Manvers, and me, as follows. Exchanged with Mr Doncaster, three lands in Ingar Nook, East Field, Lord Manvers Lands, lying east, and west, now inclosed by Mr Doncaster, for one Land in Kneesall Gate furlong Mill Field (from Doncaster) Lord Manvers land, adjoining South. Thomas Taylor's freehold land North exchanged with Edmund Pearse, three lands in Harwick Nook, South Field, the Hon. Savile lands adjoining East, Lord Manvers West now inclosed by Ed. Pearse, for four lands in Mill Field, on Rushing furlong, the Hon. Savile lands lying East, Lord Manvers West. Please to let your clerk draw up two memorandums of the exchange and we can ratify them when we meet, should you come to Newark Fair on the 17th Inst, perhaps you would be so obliging to bring them in your pocket.[53]

Adwick presumably understood what was going on, but no one seems to have been responsible for recording the transfers that took place (partly because no

[51] PRO IR 18/7459 f. 6, Laxton tithe file.
[52] I am grateful to Dr A. D. M. Phillips for help on this point.
[53] NUMD MaB/194/20.

one in authority, such as the Thoresby agent, could be guaranteed to know about them). In the late 1830s one commentator wrote in scathing terms about the discrepancies which occurred as a result of this laxity:

No correct survey of this parish having been made for the last 30 years and so many exchanges effected among the tenants it will be almost impossible to give an accurate description of each piece of land at length. Then numbers being 1 to 2000, and taken at times from the various surveys of which we have a great number so as to suit the occupier he discovering perhaps that the land contained a rood more than was stated, and in many instances this has arisen from their ploughing away each other's land. Mr Wharton made a valuation of the parish about seven years ago, and he could not make the quantities in the open fields agree in more than one in three.[54]

Problems tended to arise only when land was sold. A terrier of John Chappell's land was drawn prior to sale in the 1820s when someone (probably the Thoresby agent) was careful to add notes about groups of lands which had been enclosed.[55] The sale notice for William Pinder's estate in the 1830s pointed out that eleven lands on Kneesall Lane Flat in the Mill Field had been enclosed and the land tax redeemed.

The root of the problem was that most transfers were small scale and as often as not agreements were verbal rather than written. It was only when a major reorganization was envisaged that efforts were made to keep a full record. One such reorganization occurred in the wake of Benjamin Roos's death towards the end of 1831. Roos was the tenant of Brockilow Farm. Initially carved out at the end of the 1720s, Brockilow changed hands a number of times until Benjamin Hunt became the tenant in 1743. At Christmas 1784 he passed the tenancy to his nephew Peter Roos, and before his death a few months later he appointed Roos as his executor and principal legatee. Roos married Elizabeth Taylor in 1773, and after her death Anne Bartrup in 1782. He died early in the nineteenth century, but his widow, and later his son Benjamin (by his first marriage) continued to farm at Brockilow until the latter's death when there was no obvious successor to the tenancy of the 126-acre farm. George Peck, who applied for the vacancy, was an established Pierrepont tenant, having succeeded his father Joseph to a 100-acre farm in the village. This included 17 acres in the West field, three in the East Field, 11 in the South Field and 20 in the Mill Field, but he was willing to give up this open-field land on condition that the closes which formed the rest of his existing farm were added to Brockilow. The Thoresby agent accepted Peck' argument that his present farm was 'very inconveniently situated', and an agreement was reached allowing Peck to retain 30 acres from his present farm, thereby increasing Brockilow to 156 acres in total.[56]

[54] NAO DD.T/124/45.
[55] NUMD M.5524.
[56] NUMD MaB/168/123; Ma 5E/126.

The tenancy change at Brockilow illustrates the ability of individual farmers to negotiate with the agent to acquire a farm to their liking, but at the same time events conspired to persuade John Pickin of the need for a more substantial reorganization. The death of another tenant, George Lee, provided Pickin with an opportunity to reduce the size of the farm that he had been leasing from 148 acres (together with the Malt Kiln) to 94 acres, 'to admit of the exchanges and alterations being affected with the other tenants'. What this meant was that the 30 acres of Bollam Becks farmed by Lee were added to Knapeney Farm. Knapeney, 109 acres, was in the tenure of Robert Brownlow, who was finding it too much for him. Consequently he vacated the farm, and it was let instead to Samuel Pinder, together with the additional 30 acres from Lee's farm. This was particularly convenient for Pinder whose 20-acre freehold adjoined Knapeney. Robert Brownlow moved back into the village, to 'the public house now occupied by Sarah Wright', which was repaired for him. He was also given the tenancy of a 14-acre farm currently let to John Kelk. Kelk, just 20 and the grandson of the late tenant, was removed 'from any occupation', which appears to have been a rather harsh decision since he was apparently being punished for his grandfather's neglect of the property. The buildings were 'in so ruinous a state that they must be taken down', and Pickin proposed letting the homestead, with the materials, to the village wheelwright, who already had a shop on the premises, and who was prepared to rebuild the house if he was supplied with bricks and timber.

Finally, the wheel came full circle as Sarah Wright was moved to the house left empty when George Peck removed to Brockilow. Several buildings were taken down, and this became the public house.[57] As the Thoresby accounts reveal £114 was spent 'taking down Dovecote, repairs and alterations to buildings attached to it, and alterations at farm premises late Pecks, to admit of their being occupied as a Public House by Sarah Wright'. Thereafter, the Dovecote gradually replaced the Sign of the Sun (or Sun Inn) as Laxton's premier public house, and today it is the only such hostelry in the village. Not everyone was satisfied by the reorganization. Mr Taylor, Benjamin Roos's brother-in-law, does not seem to have been successful in his application 'for a small place for one of his sons as they do not agree at home'.[58]

At the same time as these changes were taking place a new farm was laid out on the east side of the village. John Jepson's buildings in Moorhouse were so dilapidated as to be beyond repair. The house had been 'unfit to stand for some years past'. Replacement buildings were erected near the East Park woods 'with the view of making a farm there as the land in that part of the estate shall become vacant'. Jepson was lucky; though regarded as 'a bad manager', he was provided with a new house and offices – now Brecks Farm – at a cost of £323,

---

[57] NUMD MaB/168/123.
[58] NUMD M.4920.

PLATE 6.5 *Dovecote Inn. The 'Sign of the Dovecot' was one of several public houses in early nineteenth-century Laxton. Its original location is not known, but in 1832 the building shown in this early twentieth century print – which had previously been a farm-house – became the Dovecote. The Thoresby estate converted the house into a pub, and moved the landlady, Sarah Wright, from the previous location. Thereafter the Dovecote became a centre for village meetings and events, and today the jury meet in the pub on the day of their field inspection, and the Court Leet meets here the following week. On the left of the picture is part of Crosshill and in front is the road towards Kneesall and Moorhouse.*

and 94 acres of farmland. William Beans and Valentine Harpham applied for the land previously farmed by Jepson.[59]

As decribed here these changes may appear to have been complex, and such was the fragmentation of land in Laxton that putting them into effect involved reorganization across the parish. The agent's 'account of the open field land in Laxton exchanged among the tenants at Lady Day 1832' runs to eleven pages, and at least eighteen tenants were affected. Francis Wharton, who was then revaluing Laxton for rating purposes was distinctly unamused. He pointed out for the churchwardens' benefit that his fee of £100 was not unreasonable given that 'I had made out all the terriers of the respective farms prior to last Lady Day [1832], that in consequence of the very extensive alterations since made in the occupations of Earl Manvers estate such terriers were rendered useless.'[60] It

[59] NUMD M.4920; Estate Accounts 1832.
[60] NUMD MaB 174/291a, 297a.

was a charge he repeated in 1839 when he was approached with a view to drawing a map of Laxton based on the survey he had compiled in 1820 for tithe commutation purposes:

a terrier of Laxton as it stood in 1820 would be of little use as compared with a plan and terrier of 1833 in consequence of the numerous alterations and almost entire reallotting of the unclosed estate of Lord Manvers about that period, and of other alterations in drains, fences and buildings &c then and previously made of which I obtained a particular account and made several surveys of alterations, from which I constructed and made a finished plan of the parish now in my possession.[61]

It was in Wharton's interest to play up the difficulties but there can be little doubt about the complexity of tenure while the village remained unenclosed, or of the extent to which land was transferred between individuals in the interests of providing everyone with a suitable farm.

LAXTON FARMS

This did not mean a large farm. Little change took place in farm sizes over the period (table 6.8). Farms of 100 acres or more occupied 51 per cent of the non-waste area in 1789, but about 60 per cent between 1812 and 1839. This was

TABLE 6.8 *Farm sizes in Laxton, 1812–1839*

Acreage	1812			1820			1839		
	No.	Total	%	No.	Total	%	No.	Total	%
100+	15	2120	58.6	15	2195	59.5	15	2224	59.0
51–99	10	756	20.9	8	607	16.5	7	497	13.2
21–50	7	242	6.7	10	327	8.9	15	508	13.5
11–20	22	343	9.5	19	276	7.5	12	177	4.7
6–10	11	99	2.7	13	123	3.3	17	146	3.9
1–5	18	49	1.3	11	33	0.9	22	64	1.7
Under 1	30	7	0.2	30	7	0.2	25	6	0.2
In hand					118	3.2		118	3.1
Other		4	0.1	3	2	–		27	0.7
	113	3620	100.0	109	3688	100.0	113	3767	100.0

Sources: as table 6.3.

[61] NUMD MaB/218/68.

largely through an increase in the total number from 12 to 15. William Pinder's 327-acre farm in 1789 had been broken up by 1812, when just 2 of the 15 largest farms were over 200 acres, but neither was as large as the 273 acres held by Charles Doncaster in 1789. In both 1820 and 1839 2 farms exceeded 200 acres, but there is little evidence of any real attempt to follow the advice of contemporary agricultural writers in order to create much larger farms.

Nor were the largest farms consolidated in the manner beloved of contemporary experts. John and Thomas Keyworth farmed 238 acres in 1839, of which slightly less than half was in the open fields – 18 'lands' in East Field (17 acres), 35 in West Field (26 acres), 38 in Mill Field (33 acres) and 41 in South Field (31 acres). Westwood Farm, the only other holding of more than 200 acres in 1839, may have been consolidated by Laxton standards, but William Wombell still had 38 acres in West and Mill Field 'lands'. Only Brecks Farm, laid out in 1832, was entirely enclosed, while of the village farms Crosshill was the most consolidated. The majority of the 183 acres farmed by Michael Saxelby in 1839 were in two groups of closes to the north and east of the village, and only 10 acres were in open-field 'lands'.

The number of farms between 51 and 99 acres declined from 10 in 1789 and 1812 to 8 in 1820 and to 7 in 1839, with the total acreage falling correspondingly from 22 per cent in 1789 to just 13 per cent by 1839. Among farms of 50 acres or less the variation was greater. There were 13 farms of 21–50 acres in 1789, but just 7 in 1812, 10 in 1820 and 15 in 1839. The discrepancy in 1812 may be one of the numerous mistakes made by Henry de Bruyn, which was one reason why a further survey was undertaken only eight years after his work was completed. Possibly surveying errors also account for the changing number of farms of 11–20 acres, which apparently increased in number from 13 to 22 between 1789 and 1812, but then declined to 19 in 1820 and to 12 in 1839.

The number of very small holdings also varied. Those of 6–10 acres numbered 21 in 1789, 11 in 1812, 13 in 1820 and 17 in 1839; while holdings of 5 acres or less – only 14 in 1789 – totalled 48 in 1812, 41 in 1820 and 47 in 1839. Possibly the 1789 figure is an underestimate, but these figures confirm the resurgence of the smallholding during the Napoleonic War period. Robert Lowe noted in 1798 that 'most cottages have a garden and a potato garth, and few of them are without a web of cloth of their own spinning.' In the clay districts, in particular, he found many of the cottagers had 'a few acres of land annexed to their cottage, which enables the cottager to keep a cow or two, and pigs'.[62] Of the sixteen occupiers of between 5 and 9 acres, three were agricultural labourers, two were cottagers, and the others included a shopkeeper, a gamekeeper, an innkeeper, the parish clerk, and a person of independent means. Among the nineteen with between 1 and 4 acres two were agricultural labourers, two were cottagers, two were publicans, and the others included a

[62] Lowe, *General View*, p. 140.

wheelwright, a blacksmith, a carrier, a grocer and a tailor. Most of those with less than an acre were labourers, although their numbers included a shoemaker, a joiner, a miller and a bricklayer. The implication of these figures is that while small changes were taking place over time, the overall balance between larger and smaller holdings in the village altered relatively little.

To ensure the security of the tenant in the absence of leases, a system of tenant right was developed which became in the course of the nineteenth century the standard form of agreement on Laxton farms. The principle of tenant right was that the outgoing tenant should be compensated for his unexhausted improvements by the incoming tenant who could expect to benefit from them. Usually the money was conveyed through the landlord. Such arrangements were beneficial to the tenant in that they gave him security against which he could invest in the land, and for the landlord who could deduct any arrears of rent from sums payable by the new occupier and thereby save himself the trouble of time-consuming and expensive prosecutions for rent default. Tenant right seems to have originated in Lincolnshire during the eighteenth century, and to have been known in parts of Nottinghamshire by the 1770s. When it was first employed in Laxton is not known, but there is a detailed agreement dating from 1832 when George Peck took over the tenancy of Brockilow. Crops, labour, manure and seed were all valued in order to decide Peck's liability.[63] Thereafter numerous agreements survive, particularly from the 1870s after the Agricultural Holdings Acts of 1875 and 1883 gave legal recognition to what was known as the 'custom of the country'. Thoresby adopted standard tenancy agreements which included provision for tenant-right valuations. In the twentieth century these have stipulated that the principles involved should be those of the Nottinghamshire Agricultural Valuers' Association, one year's manure together with seed and labour.[64]

Finally, the Thoresby estate invested rather more heavily and consistently in its Laxton farms than had been the case before 1788. Spending on repairs and improvements was negligible down to 1788, but although Charles Pierrepont spent only £23 in Laxton between 1789 and 1791, the figure then increased steadily. Over the ten years 1792–1801 outlay on repairs averaged £113, and it rose to £218 over the following decade, or 11 and 14.5 per cent respectively of rents. With the onset of problems for the farming community the landlord's contribution increased. Between 1812 and 1821 £2,316 was spent on repairs of which £2,097 was spent from 1817 onwards. From 1818 to 1821 Manvers spent £2,010, 15 per cent of rental income. In 1818 alone he invested £680 on 'taking down old and building new malt kiln', £330 on a new house (almost certainly the one standing today) at Knapeney Farm, and £228 towards new farmhouses for Francis White of Moorhouse and Richard Keyworth. Further

[63] NUMD Ma 5E/153/3.
[64] NUMD Acc 608, Edward Bailey & Son to Colonel D. Holder, 8 November 1949.

payments of £168 (part of a £500 allowance) were made to Keyworth and £60 to White in 1819, while £98 was spent on stabling for Knapeney.

These were the tell-tale signs of a landlord having to help out his tenants, and the second Earl Manvers was not prepared to maintain these levels indefinitely. Nothing at all was spent in 1823 and 1826, and only £1,781 in total, or 6.7 per cent of rental income, between 1822 and 1832. Most of this expenditure was for new buildings on existing farms. In 1827 £290 was laid out on a new farm house in the occupation of William White, and £295 on new buildings on William Lee's farm, while the following year £280 was spent on a new barn and other buildings at Copthorne. During the agricultural depression of the mid-1830s spending increased to compensate, totalling £2,547 between 1833 and 1840, 13 per cent of the rental. In 1836 more than £900 was spent on repairs and rebuilding, and the influence a tenant could bring to bear is clear from the £123 allowed to Michael Saxelby for repairs to Crosshill when he took over the farm in 1837.

Most of Manvers's spending was on improving buildings, but other forms of improvement were not ignored. Land drainage was one of the major developments of the early nineteenth century, much of it designed to increase the agricultural potential of the English claylands. Major improvements to drainage generally postdate the repeal of the Corn Laws in 1846, but individual landlords had long been interested in the likely returns from draining their heavier lands. Fragments of evidence suggest that this was the case in Laxton. In 1836 the Thoresby accounts record payments of £28 to Samuel Smith for drainage at three farms in the village, and from these small beginnings much was to follow during the ensuing decade. As for the fate of the Earl of Scarbrough's tenants in these years no record has survived.

TITHE COMMUTATION

English parishes which had not already commuted their tithes for land or a money payment, either at enclosure, or on some alternative occasion, were subject to the terms of the 1836 Tithe Commutation Act. Tithe payments were converted into a rent charge, with arrangements for each parish being embodied in an agreement, or an imposed award drawn up by assistant commissioners and approved by the Tithe Commission in London. In the 1740s the Laxton tithe was commuted into a money payment, but as this was an informal, local arrangement, the village was subject to the 1836 legislation. Arrangements designed to bring the village into line with the Act began on 24 August 1838 when a notice, posted in the Dovecote Inn and the church, announced that a meeting was to be held in the church on 17 September at 11 a.m.[65] It was none too soon – under the 1836 Act the tithe owners and payers

---

[65] NUMD MaB/175/343.

had until 1 October 1838 to agree a value for the rent charge – but it presaged five years of sometimes bitter conflict in the village.

Initially it seemed unlikely that commutation would be contentious. At the first meeting the vicar, the Rev. Richard Proctor was elected chairman. Also present were agents for the Earl of Scarbrough, Earl Manvers and the Duke of Newcastle (whose interest in Laxton tithes dated back to 1631), and eight freeholders. The proposal discussed was for the vicarial tithes of Laxton to be commuted for £122 and the tithes of Moorhouse for £78. Proctor raised an objection by claiming an extra 20 per cent, but this was not accepted. It was however agreed that the Duke of Newcastle's claim to the Great Tithes on 20 acres in Laxton should be commuted to £4 4s, and that Manvers should commute the Great Tithes for £204 17s. The meeting was then adjourned until 15 October.[66]

An agreement for commutation was drawn up early in November. Manvers, as impropriator, was to receive £383 12s annually in lieu of the Great Tithes. He accepted the vicar's claim and raised the composition payable to him to £143 15s a year from Laxton and £82 7s 6d from Moorhouse, not quite the 20 per cent Proctor had claimed in September, but a reasonable compromise.[67] Up until this point the commissioners were not directly involved, but once they received a draft agreement an assistant commissioner or a local tithe agent was instructed to visit the district and write a report. This was to contain advice as to whether the agreement was fair to all parties, and could therefore be confirmed so that apportionment might take place. The report on Laxton was prepared by Assistant Tithe Commissioner John Mee Mathew, and dated 31 January 1839.

The Laxton agreement did not meet all the stated criteria, and John Parkinson was appointed tithe valuer and apportioner. Disagreements had arisen in the village which were attributed to the lack of an accurate up-to-date survey of titheable land. Parkinson's task was to hold a local enquiry, and this commenced with a meeting on 13 August 1839. The main business was to discuss the making of a map and survey 'for the use of the apportioner of tithes, and to be afterwards copied for being annexed to the apportionment'. To keep down costs it was agreed that

the map in the possession of the earl of Scarbrough shall be adopted by Mr Parkinson for making an apportionment for the commutation; that the survey of Lord Scarbrough's property corresponding with such map shall be adopted, and that the survey of the estate of Earl Manvers and the freeholders furnished by Mr Simpson shall be adopted for the remainder of the parish.

Francis Wharton had already been approached 'to furnish a terrier of the Parish of Laxton to correspond with the Plan made by him in 1820', but his

---

[66] NAO PR 4074; NUMD MaB/175/344.
[67] NAO DD.T 124/49; PRO IR 18/7459.

response was to suggest that a new survey was needed to take account of changes since 1820. For £85 he was prepared to supply a copy of his survey, sketches for valuation, and a terrier relating to the rate valuation map he had drawn in 1833. To supply just sketches and a terrier, Wharton offered to charge only £50, and Parkinson recommended acceptance of the latter terms. He expected to be able to make proper plans from the sketches and from a plan already in his possession. This policy was accepted, though in the event it proved necessary to request further surveying, and the final bill was £63 – 'for sketches and a book of reference to his map made in 1833 and for surveying and making alterations in survey'. To be more accurate, this was what Wharton was paid since 'Mr Wharton's bill of £74 17s being objectionable I submitted it to the Board and reduced the amount to £63.' Once completed the map and terrier was to be left at the house of Mr George Pinder, publican of the Sign of the Sun, for a week so that it could be inspected by all interested parties. Parkinson was to be paid £50 for his work.[68]

It took Parkinson two years to complete the survey, partly because of inconsistencies in the documents from which he had to work. He found, for example, that 'the map furnished by Mr Clutton differs from that made by Mr Wharton in respect to the boundaries of Laxton and Moorhouse, and both are at variance with the statement of the lands charged in the respective townships (having separate rent charges in lieu of tithes) for Highway Rates.' However, he was finally able to report that:

I have viewed all the lands in the parish of Laxton for the purpose of making apportionment of the rent charges for tithes and having taken an account of the tofts and toftsteads and of gaits in open fields from the man who shewed me the lands, I transmit a statement thereof along with sketches of Laxton and Moorhouse, whereon the tofts are referred to by numbers, and think it advisable that a meeting should be held at Laxton to ascertain whether or not the statement is correct, which is important as in the event of an inclosure the claims of parties to rights of common would be strengthened materially by their payment of a portion of the rent charge as owners of tofts or of gaits in the fields.[69]

As a result of Parkinson's efforts a new agreement was reached in August 1841 which looked rather different from the provisional arrangements accepted at the original meeting in September 1838. The reason for this was explained by Parkinson in a letter to William Clutton. The 1838 agreement had contained

a memorandum that the great tithes of the estate of Earl Manvers in the *township* of Laxton shall be commuted for £232, and the Great Tithes of all the other Lands in the

[68] NUMD MaB/175/363–4, 218/65, 68, 71.
[69] NUMD MaB/175/356.

Township (except for the small portion the Duke of Newcastle has agreed to commute for £4 4s per annum) for £151 12s; whereas by the [1841 agreement] the apportionment of the sum of £383 12s for Great Tithes is to be made upon all the Lands subject to such tithes without reference to the respective owners; and which appears to be the most proper mode of proceeding.

Parkinson believed that if accepted in Laxton these arrangements would be passed by the tithe commissioners in London.[70]

Parkinson's map and apportionment gave details of rent payable, and the tithe assessed for all properties in the village. It was lodged at the Dovecote Inn in the hands of William Wright, the publican, to permit consultation, and after some delay, an appeals meeting was held in the public house on 30 January 1843, attended by agents for the main landowners and a number of freeholders. No objections were raised about Laxton, but in regard to Moorhouse questions were asked relating to the tithes of the common, the distinction between meadow and pasture, the boundary between Laxton and Moorhouse, and a claim to tithes by John Evelyn Denison. The vicar denied any knowledge of Denison's claim, even though three witnesses appeared to say that they had indeed been paying tithes to Denison for many years.

These objections meant that a further meeting was required and this was called for 27 October 1843. The first three objections were settled without debate, but Denison's claim proved more contentious. Denison, it transpired, had tithe rights to 8 acres of land in Moorhouse, and consequently £1 19s was deducted from the vicar's rent charge and apportioned to Denison instead. This decision greatly annoyed Proctor, the vicar. He was so incensed by the whole business that he had refused to take services at Moorhouse throughout September and October, and although the surviving account of this meeting is brief he clearly came in for heavy criticism.[71]

The dispute rumbled on until the tithe commissioners eventually imposed a supplementary award on 1 May 1845, which was drawn up by the assistant tithe commissioner (John Mee Mathew). When Parkinson submitted his account for expenses at Laxton in October 1846 he noted 'the great delay and increased expense' caused by two material errors in the original agreement, and 'a frivolous objection [. . .] to the correct line of boundary between the townships, and also by reason of the tithe commissioners having required a new survey of the parish, which, after long correspondence and attendance at the Tithe Office, I satisfied the Board was not necessary and thereby saved to the proprietors an expense of about £200'. The total cost was £382 of which Lord Manvers's share came to £232.[72]

[70] NUMD MaB/218/78.
[71] NUMD M.4009.
[72] NUMD MaB/175/364.

In 1788 Charles Pierrepont inherited an estate which had been neglected for much of the previous fifty years. Laxton was just one part of that property, but perhaps because of the tenurial structure, the new lord of the manor concentrated his enclosing intentions on a number of his other manors. No significant progress was made at Laxton until 1815, and in the post-war years it must have seemed less crucial. The result was a resurgence of the small owners in the wake of the Hinde sale in 1789. Although some were forced to part with their land, particularly after 1815, increasingly the pattern was to combine landownership with the occupation of additional land to make a viable farming unit. The typical independent owner-occupier of seventeenth-century Laxton was succeeded by men and women who combined ownership and occupation in a rather different mixture and, coincidentally, greatly complicated the structure of tenure in the parish. Inevitably this would have made enclosure more difficult than it might have been, but despite the discussions of 1810–15 no immediate progress was made to this end, and in the post-war years the village farmers were probably doing no worse than anyone else in clayland Nottinghamshire. After all, population reached a peak in 1831, many new houses were built, and all the more substantial farmers were able to keep servants. Rents certainly had to be adjusted to changing conditions on the Pierrepont estates, and the cost of relieving the poor also points to economic difficulties (although exactly what the poor rate was funding has to be examined carefully), but there is no suggestion here of real financial problems characterized by vacant tenancies and bankrupt farmers. Laxton missed out on enclosure during the war years perhaps because of tenurial complications, and by the time it was discussed again in the 1840s new problems had arisen.

Chapter Seven

Victorian Village

Victorian England is inextricably linked in the historical imagination with industrial society. This was the era in which the stresses and strains of the Industrial Revolution paid off. Great manufacturing towns full of factories and steam engines, of noise and activity, seemed to encroach relentlessly upon the countryside. Coal mines and iron works scarred its face, and acres of good and not-so-good farming land were taken over to make way for the greatest of all Victorian creations, that dirty, smoke-billowing monster, the railway. Technical achievements of the highest order were celebrated at the Great Exhibition held in the Crystal Palace in 1851: British industry had come of age. This was the age of manufacturing, even if the images are exaggerated and the reality somewhat more sordid than the ecstatic accounts of Victorian apologists sometimes suggested. The towns offered work. The countryside needed fewer hands. The result, almost inevitably, was a movement of population away from staid and conservative rural England, lured to the great manufacturing towns by the seemingly endless opportunities on offer. It was a migration which reached epidemic proportions when farming was gripped by a prolonged and deep depression in the closing decades of the nineteenth century. The countryside was changing just as surely as the towns, but not necessarily for the better. Those who stayed behind were not as well off as their predecessors, and in many instances had to endure living conditions notably less attractive than those of their urban counterparts.

In the countryside the agricultural depression of the mid-1830s was followed by three decades of prosperity for the farming community, partly as a consequence of demand for agricultural produce from the expanding towns. As rents rose new tools and machines – many of them labour saving – were adopted, land was drained, and improved strains of seed were introduced together with carefully controlled livestock breeding, and scientific soil treatment. Unfortunately it did not last. From the 1870s North American wheat and South American meat invaded the market, home prices fell, and for two decades depression ruled in the countryside. Even in 1914 relatively little recovery had taken place. In these circumstances the drift away from the countryside turned into a flood tide of migration, and for those who stayed, the task of making a living from the soil became ever more arduous.

Laxton was no exception to these long-run trends. In the middle decades of the century there was much discussion of enclosure and farm consolidation to exploit the prevailing buoyant conditions, but by the 1870s and 1880s farmers were struggling to make ends meet, the remaining freeholders found the environment increasingly hostile, and the future looked bleak without some form of rationalization. We probably know more about Victorian Laxton than any earlier period, and we can see the stresses and strains under which the community operated as farming conditions changed. This chapter looks at the village from 1840 until the outbreak of the First World War, while chapters 8 and 9 examine, respectively, the agricultural prosperity of the middle decades of the nineteenth century, and the impact of depression on the village farmers from the 1870s onwards.

PEOPLE

At the beginning of the Victorian era Laxton was a populous, thriving village; by 1911 it was substantially reduced in size (table 7.1) and rather less buoyant. In 1841 the village was prosperous: many of the farmers were able to employ female domestic servants, and there was enough work for 107 agricultural labourers and male servants in husbandry. The number of craftsmen suggests self-sufficiency in most everyday requirements. Population, it is true, was declining; the forward movement between the 1790s and 1831 had ground to a halt and slipped into reverse. However, the reversal was relatively gradual until 1861, and the really substantial fall in numbers was largely a feature of the closing decades of the century. Between 1861 and 1901 the population fell by

TABLE 7.1 *Laxton's population 1841–1911*

Date	Total	% decline
1841	642	
1851	621	−3.4
1861	613	−1.3
1871	547	−12.0
1881	483	−13.3
1891	428	−12.9
1901	394	−8.6
1911	389	−1.3

Source: Printed Census Returns.

44 per cent. A village of 613 people in 1861 numbered just 394 at the turn of the new century, two-thirds of its size before the agricultural depression commenced, and probably fewer than at any time since records began.

To find out why numbers were in decline we need to convert these figures into actual people, and this is possible between 1841 and 1881 because the decennial Census Enumerators' Books provide a detailed picture of the village. The population was by no means static (table 7.2); between 29 and 42 per cent of named individuals appeared as resident in Laxton in only one of the five censuses. Only 45 of the 642 people in Laxton in 1841 were still living there forty years later (7 per cent). Another 169 had died, while 168 people born in the village after 1841 were still resident in 1881. In other words 44 per cent of villagers in 1881 had either lived there for forty years or been born in the village during that time. Even those who can be traced throughout the period had usually experienced considerable changes in their fortunes.

TABLE 7.2 *Turnover of population in Laxton 1841–1881*

Census appearances	Number	% of census
1841 census only	270	42
1841–1851	97	
1841–1861	37	
1841–1871	17	
1851 census only	187	30
1851–1861	80	
1851–1871	21	
1851–1881	28	
1861 census only	180	29
1861–1871	71	
1861–1881	48	
1871 census only	191	35
1871–1881	47	
1881 census only	145	30
Two censuses	295	
Three censuses	106	
Four censuses	45	
All five	45	

Source: PRO HO 107/850, 2135; RG 9/2475, 70/3557, 11/3372, Census Enumerators' Books, 1841–81.

Kezia Quibell is a case in point, and she is easier to trace than some because her unusual christian name taxed the orthographical powers of the census enumerators. We first met 'Cassia' Bartle, as she then was, as a 14-year old in

1841, living with her father Samuel Glazebrook (47), her brother Samuel (8) and sister Sarah (5). All three children were illegitimate. Although their father continued to farm in Laxton until he died at the age of 83 in 1874, by 1851 Cassia and Sarah were lodging with Ruth Hooton, and Cassia was described as a general servant. In October 1852 she married William Quibell. She signed herself Glazebrook in the register, but this was crossed through and Bartle inserted. Her husband, described in the marriage register as a farmer, worked 40 acres in Laxton. By 1861 they had a son William, aged 8. William Quibell, senior, died in 1864 at the age of 39, and 'Keziah' appears in the 1871 census as a widow farming 80 acres, presumably with the help of her son who was 18 and living at home. The arrangement was still the same in 1881 when 'Kezia' was 55, and together with William (28 and still unmarried) farming 100 acres. She died at the age of 67 in 1892. In 1877 she held the post of overseer of the poor, on this occasion under the name of Mrs Idezia Quibell. She herself spelt the name Kezia in the marriage register, but it would be interesting to know how it was actually pronounced.

These figures provide endless permutations, but one of the striking points to come out of table 7.2 is that the proportion of people appearing in one census was always higher than those appearing in two or more. Turnover was considerable. In 1851 Laxton (omitting on this occasion Moorhouse) had a population of 534, and in 1861 500. Only 247 individuals can be identified at both dates, including 9 females who had married within the village. Of the 534 in 1851, 61 are known to have died over the following decade. Among these was Henry Pinder, buried in 1853 at the age of 23, for whom the cause of death was given as 'shot'. We do not know under what circumstances this tragedy occurred. Thus 226 individuals appeared only in the 1851 census. Of the 500 people enumerated in 1861, 247 remained from 1851. Of the other 253, 125 were children under the age of 10, who could not have appeared in the 1851 census. Consequently there were 128 people in Laxton who were alive a decade earlier, but not resident in the village. Between 1851 and 1861 in Laxton village the total population declined by less than 7 per cent but this gross figure hides a turnover of individuals amounting to more than half the village. Of the 128 newcomers in 1861, 65 were males and 63 females.

Why did people come to Laxton but then stay for such a short time? In most cases it was because they were hired for a year at the annual Retford, Newark and Tuxford Fairs. Individuals wanting work would congregate in Newark square at the annual fair in mid-May, and wait to be hired. Tuxford Hiring Fair was in November, and Retford Fair was on 11 October.[1] The school log book frequently records the absence of older boys on hiring day at Tuxford. In November 1872 five boys were away at Tuxford, of whom one returned to

[1] *Life at Laxton*, pp. 11–22, describes the various fairs. Hiring as described here went on until the inter-war period: *ex. inf.* Mr Bill Bartle.

school the following week, presumably having been unsuccessful in his quest for work. Absences for both Tuxford and Newark Fairs were recorded in May each year during the 1890s. Once hired, individuals would return with the farmer to the village in which they were to work. In 1824, when he was 14, George Hewitt attended the Martinmas Monday hiring fair at Tuxford, where he was hired for the year by a hat manufacturer at a wage of £2 10s. He was re-hired a year later, and he subsequently lived with a Mr Weightman of Tuxford as a yearly, hired farming servant. In 1835 he married, and by 1843 he and his wife had three small children. He was living in Laxton as an agricultural labourer, and when he applied for poor relief in 1843 it was established that, although he had lived in Tuxford for nearly twenty years, because he had not established a settlement he was entitled to relief in Laxton. He and his family had moved on by 1851.[2]

A similar case was that of John Whittington who at the age of 15 had been hired at Tuxford Martinmas Monday Fair into Egmanton Parish by Richard Johnson. The following year he went to Retford Statute Fair, where he was again employed by Johnson, as a servant, for a wage of £9. By 1841 he was back in Laxton, unmarried, working as an agricultural labourer, and living with his elderly parents. Three years later, when he was 48, and with a wife and young child, he was examined as to his settlement, and found to be chargeable on the poor rate at Laxton. In 1851 the elderly Whittingtons still lived in Laxton, but John and his family had moved on. Chadwick Downs from Sturton was aged about 33 when he was examined in 1844. Like the others he had started work as a servant, in this case hired to William Justice of Sturton for a year at a salary of £5 5s. He stayed there for a year on full wages, and had married at Headon about eight years previously. With his wife Ann, and children George, Mary and Joseph, he had now become chargeable on the parish of Laxton. Ann, incidentally, appears in the 1841 census as living with her eldest child, George, in the household of Thomas Bennet.[3] The family were not in the village in 1851.

Other cases refer to individuals who had once worked in Laxton. Robert Cordell of Tickhill in Yorkshire was examined in 1843. He claimed that at Martinmas 1832 he had been hired to Samuel Pinder of Laxton, farmer, and that he had lodged with Pinder in his house. In 1838 he had married in North Wheatley, and had returned to Tickhill. By 1843 he was in the Union work-house, and claimed that his settlement was in Tickhill. George Bennett was 34 when he applied for relief in 1844. At the age of 15 he had been hired by Mrs Lee of Laxton at the Tuxford Statute Fair, for £4 a year, and he had lived in, but he had not obtained a settlement in the village.[4]

[2] NAO PR 4781/16.
[3] NAO PR 4781/17, 18.
[4] NAO PR 4783/25, 26.

There must have been many similar cases of individuals who for one reason or another spent short periods of time in Laxton. Mostly they are likely to have come from, and possibly returned to, surrounding villages. The 1841 census is not very helpful because individuals were only invited to state their place of birth in general germs, but more specific information was demanded between 1851 and 1881 (tables 7.3 and 7.4). Despite the long-term fall in population, the proportion of people living in Laxton who were born in the village and in Moorhouse, remained almost exactly constant. The proportion born in Nottinghamshire was remarkably high at 94 per cent in both 1851 and 1861, slipping to just below 93 per cent in 1871, and to 86.5 per cent in 1881. The similarity of the 1851 and 1861 figures, despite the fact that the proportions as between Laxton and Nottinghamshire changed, suggests that the assessors had succeeded in establishing a greater degree of accuracy when recording birthplaces. The 1881 figure is also interesting in that during a period of falling overall population the proportion of locally born people also declined, with an influx from neighbouring Lincolnshire, perhaps reflecting the impact of adverse agricultural conditions in the county.

TABLE 7.3 *Birthplaces of Laxton inhabitants 1851–1881*

Place of Birth	1851	1861	1871	1881
Laxton	380 (61.3%)	320 (52.2%)	283 (51.7%)	244 (50.5%)
Moorhouse	28	44	42	43
	408 (65.8%)	364 (59.4%)	325 (59.4%)	287 (59.4%)
Nottinghamshire	177 (28.5%)	213 (34.7%)	182 (33.3%)	131 (27.1%)
Derbyshire	5	3	5	5
Leicestershire			1	2
Lincolnshire	14	21	16	37
Yorkshire	7	4	3	8
Other UK	4	8	15	13
Overseas	1			
Unknown	4			
	620	613	547	483

Source: as table 7.2.

Table 7.4 shows that with the exception of 1861, which does not fit a trend, the proportion of Laxton-born heads of household was on the increase, and the number drawn from the surrounding county was falling. As a proportion of the whole the Nottinghamshire-born heads represented 91.2 per cent, 93.4 per cent, 92.3 per cent and 87.5 per cent, a slightly lower proportion than the

TABLE 7.4 *Birthplaces of Laxton heads of households 1851–1881*

Place of Birth	1851	1861	1871	1881
Laxton	61	58	59	53
Moorhouse	6	3	5	7
	67 (53.6%)	61 (50.4%)	64 (54.2%)	60 (57.7%)
Nottinghamshire	47 (37.6%)	52 (43.0%)	45 (38.1%)	31 (29.8%)
Derbyshire	1		1	1
Leicestershire			1	1
Lincolnshire	4	3	2	6
Yorkshire	3	3	1	2
Other UK		2	4	3
Overseas	1			
Unknown	2			
	125	121	118	104

Source: as table 7.2.

overall population 1841–71, and a slightly higher one in 1881. The trends, however, are similar for those of the population as a whole, with very few coming from any distance. Among incomers to Laxton (not including Moorhouse) between 1851 and 1861 23 had been born in the village since 1851, and 88 were born in Nottinghamshire. Another 13 had come from Lincolnshire, and the only travellers from a distance were the vicar with a married couple who were his groom and house servant. All three had come from Devon.

Between 1851 and 1861 the largest single group of incomers (31) were women who had married into the village, but most of the others had come in pursuit of agricultural employment – 21 carters, 10 agricultural labourers, 8 farmers and 5 agricultural servants (44). Another 10 were domestic servants. In view of these employments it is not surprising to find that the majority of incomers were young; 44 were aged between 11 and 20, and two-thirds of incomers were aged 30 or less. What the census figures are picking up is transient labour, hired short term, and passing through the village. These were predominantly young people, and the pattern was long established. It is hardly surprising to find that Laxton was much more stable in terms of families. Of the 99 households in 1861, 75 can be traced to 1851, and among the heads of the 24 new households were 5 farmers, 8 agricultural labourers and 3 cottagers. Several of these families were either returning to the village or coming into it from only a short distance away. Of the 5 farmers 4 came from surrounding villages and the fifth had married a Laxton bride; while in the whole group of

24, 6 heads of household were Laxton born, and 4 came from neighbouring Kneesall.

These figures for Laxton village between 1851 and 1861 reveal how an underlying stability among families hides a much more significant turnover of individuals, reflecting the marriage market and the demand for agricultural labour. The census data also show that the majority of these people were relatively young. Population pyramids for the whole parish between 1851 and 1881 are given in figure 7.1. Figures collected in 1821 and 1841 (see table 6.1) show remarkably similar trends with the largest group of the population in the 11–19 age range. A gradual narrowing of the pyramid occurred as population began to fall, but the decline in total population, particularly between 1871 and 1881, was across the whole age range. This suggests that it was not just individuals who were leaving the village in search of a fortune elsewhere, but that whole families were migrating. One particular feature is the sudden narrowing of the 21–30 age group in 1871, from 12.6 per cent in 1861 to 9.9 per cent in 1871. This also seems to be reflected in the fall from 11.5 to 9.5 per cent of individuals in the 31–40 age group in 1881, presumably because this particular group had been permanently reduced in numbers by the search for work outside of Laxton.

What these trends meant for particular families can be illustrated from the fortunes of the Roses. In the nineteenth century the Roses were ubiquitous, with five separate households – of which one was in Moorhouse – and five separate Joseph Roses ranging in age from 70 to a few months in 1841. Two branches of the family were bricklayers, two were farming in a small way, and the final branch was headed by an agricultural labourer. When we first meet Joseph Rose (b. 1810) and his wife Ann (b. 1812) he was working in the village as an agricultural labourer. Two years later he succeeded his father, also Joseph, in a farm of nearly 30 acres which he was to work for the rest of his life. Born in Walesby, he had married in July 1835 Ann Lacey, the daughter of an agricultural labourer in Laxton. From the census we know of ten children. Sarah (b. 1837), Ann (b. 1838), Joseph (b. 1839), William (b. 1840), John (b. 1844), George (b. 1845), Mary (b. 1847), Harriett (b. 1849), Thomas (b. 1851), and Frederick (b. 1855). Like many Victorian households this was a family which experienced tragedies as well as happinesses. Three of the children died young: Thomas was only eighteen months old when he was buried in April 1852, while Mary and Harriet were eleven and nine when they were buried on the 5th and 24th November 1858.

What of the other six children? Sarah, the eldest, was living at home in 1861, with her 2-year old illegitimate daughter Sarah Ann. In October 1864 she married Benjamin Clover and by 1871 she was living with him and a growing brood of children under the same roof as his father. Benjamin was described as an agricultural labourer unemployed, and seems to have had few pretentions to follow his father into shoemaking. After Joseph Clover's death in 1879

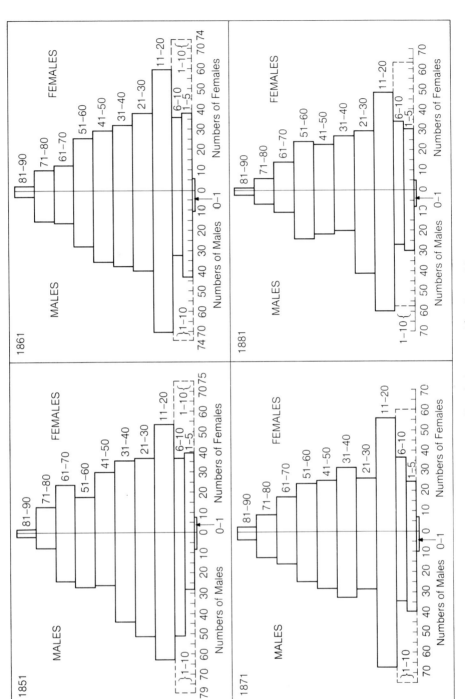

FIGURE 7.1 *Population pyramids, 1851–1881*

Benjamin Clover became head of the household and was described as a carrier. By 1881, in addition to Sarah Ann Rose (still attributed her mother's maiden name in the census even though Benjamin Clover is described as father), the household consisted of George (b. 1866), Mary (b. 1868), Amelia (b. 1870), Lily (b. 1872), Fred (b. 1873), John (b. 1875), and Kate (b. 1877), while Matilda (b. 1865) had already left home.

Joseph and Ann Rose's eldest son, Joseph, was still living at home in 1861, when he was described as a maltster, while another son, George, was a servant in the village. In 1864 Joseph married Elizabeth Pickin, the daughter of John Pickin who farmed about 40 acres in the village. By 1871 they had a daughter Annie (6), and also probably a daughter Harriet – perhaps named after his long dead sister? – who does not appear in the census, but was occupying the same cottage as Joseph junior in 1900. He was working as an agricultural labourer in 1861.

Of the other children we know much less. Ann may have married, although she does not appear in the marriage register. Neither John nor Frederick appear again in the census, although both married in the village: John in 1868 and Frederick in 1875. Both were described as labourers, and their father, in the register, as a cottager. William and George disappear from the records – presumably gone to seek their fortune elsewhere? Consequently by 1881 the now elderly parents were living alone, but Joseph was still farming. With two children and nine grandchildren living in the village, they can hardly have been lonely. Joseph died in 1889 at the age of 79, but Ann was not buried in Laxton.[5]

OCCUPATIONS

Tables 7.5 and 7.6 provide an occupational profile of the village between 1841 and 1881. Table 7.5 was compiled by counting individuals with a stated occupation, and table 7.6 is a similar exercise counting only heads of household. The varying descriptions used between different censuses make comparison difficult. This is particularly evident with servants. Occasionally it seems likely that the enumerator misplaced people. Laxton is unlikely to have had 35 carters in 1851; it seems more likely that these were agricultural workers of one sort or another. The tables only give an individual's first-named occupation, on the assumption that this was his or her major interest. They omit the second and subsequent positions of some interesting combinations including 'Farmer, publican and tailor' in 1851, farmer and maltster in 1871, publican and blacksmith (1851), grocer and saddler (1861), domestic servant and schoolteacher

---

[5] This account of the Rose family, as with other parts of this chapter where few references are provided, has been compiled from evidence in the Census Enumerators' Books and the Parish Registers. The latter are in NAO.

TABLE 7.5 *Occupations in Laxton 1841–1881*

Occupation	1841	1851	1861	1871	1881
Agricultural labourer	62	63	53	36	34
Agricultural labourer's boy				1	7
Annuitant		1		1	
Barmaid		1			
Blacksmith	2	1	5	3	3
Blacksmith journeyman	1	2			
Bricklayer	4	4	3	3	3
Builder		1	1		
Butcher	1	2	1	1	
Carpenter		1		1	2
Carrier	1				2
Carter			35	1	
Charwoman			3	5	4
Cordwainer	1	3	4	2	
Cottager	8	3	13	11	4
Cowman			1		
Dairymaid			6		1
Draper		1			
Dressmaker	4	6	7	3	5
Druggist/grocer		1	1		
Errand boy		3			
Excavator			1		
Farmer	41	51	40	36	34
Farmer's bailiff		1			
Farmer's foreman				1	1
Farm worker		2	5	8	2
Gamekeeper	1		1	3	2
Gardener			2	2	2
Grocer	1		2	2	3
Groom	1	2	2	1	1
Housekeeper	2	12	13	7	3
Independent	5			1	
Joiner	2	1	2		
Labourer				5	
Maltster			1		
Manager				1	
Midwife			1	1	
Miller	1	1	1	2	2
Miller's apprentice	1	1	2		
Milliner	1		2		
Molecatcher				1	1
Nurse		2	2		1

Occupation	1841	1851	1861	1871	1881
Painter	1				
Parish clerk	1				
Pig dealer			1		
Plumber			1		
Publican	4	2	2	3	1
Railway clerk				1	
Relieving officer		1			
Saddler		1			
Saddler's apprentice		1	1		
Schoolmaster	1	1	1	2	1
Schoolmistress	1	1	1		
School monitor				1	1
Seedsman				2	
Servants – agricultural	45		12	22	29
– assistant				1	
– domestic		15		11	17
– farm			3		
– female	34				
– general		51	1	4	3
– house		23	5		
– housemaid			1		2
– male	1			1	
Shepherd			1		
Shoeblack			1		
Shoemaker	3	3	1	2	1
Shoemaker's apprentice	1				
Shoemaker's journeyman	1				
Shopkeeper	1			1	
Stonemason journeyman			2		
Student					1
Tailor	3	5	4	1	3
Tailor journeyman	2				
Tailor apprentice			1	1	
Tile maker		1			
Veterinary surgeon	1				
Vicar	1	1	1	1	1
Waggoner			1		
Watchmaker		1	2	1	1
Wheelwright	1	1	3	3	2
Woodman			3	3	1
	242	274	259	200	181

Source: as table 7.2.

TABLE 7.6 *Occupations of heads of households in Laxton 1841–1881*

Occupation	1841	1851	1861	1871	1881
Agricultural labourer	39	38	35	29	28
Blacksmith		1	2	1	2
Blacksmith journeyman	1	1			
Bricklayer	3	2		1	2
Builder			1		
Butcher	1	2	1	1	
Carpenter		1		1	1
Carrier	1				2
Charwoman			1	3	3
Cordwainer	1	3	3	2	
Cottager	7	3	13	11	4
Dressmaker	1		1	1	2
Druggist/grocer		1	1		
Excavator		1	1		
Farmer	41	50	39	36	34
Farmer (retired)			1		
Farmer's foreman					1
Farmer's wife		2			
Farm worker			1	3	1
Freeholder				1	
Gamekeeper	1			2	1
Gardener			1	1	1
Grocer	1		2	1	3
Housekeeper		3			
Huckster (retired)				1	
Independent	1			2	
Joiner	1	1	1		
Labourer			1	2	
Midwife			1	1	
Miller	1	1	1	1	1
Molecatcher				1	1
Nurse					1
Parish accountant					1
Parish clerk	1				1
Pauper		4	1	1	
Pensioner		1	1		
Pinder			1		
Publican	4	2	2	3	1
Retired				1	2
Saddler		1			
Schoolmaster	1	1	1	1	1

Occupation	*1841*	*1851*	*1861*	*1871*	*1881*
Schoolmistress	1				
Shoemaker	2	1		1	1
Shopkeeper	1			1	
Tailor	2	2	2	1	2
Vicar	1	1	1	1	1
Watchmaker		1	1	1	1
Wheelwright	1	1	3	1	1
Woodman			1	2	1
Not given	5			2	3
	119	125	121	118	104

Source: as table 7.2.

(1871), groom, gardener and domestic servant (1871), and grocer and carrier (1871). A few people described as unemployed, or retired, are omitted, including a Chelsea pensioner in 1861, as are scholars (77 in 1851, 92 in 1861, 126 in 1871 and 119 in 1881), and those with descriptions such as farmer's wife, farmer's son, etc. While these individuals doubtless helped out on farms from time to time, we are left with those who had a full-time occupation, and it is in this light that the structure of employment can be examined, although there are a few entries for which more information would have been helpful. Why, for example, was a theology student from Nottingham Congregational College in the village in 1881?

Since the fortunes of the village depended on agriculture it is natural to look first at employment on the land. The long-term decline in the number of farmers, even allowing for the sharp rise in 1851, suggests rationalization of holdings, and we shall see in later chapters that this was indeed taking place. Even if we add farmers and cottagers together, to allow for some discrepancy of definition, the total rises from 49 to 54 between 1841 and 1851, but then begins to decline, to 53 in 1861, 47 in 1871 and 38 in 1881. The downward spiral continued after 1881; in 1894 Laxton and Moorhouse together had 31 farmers and 16 cottagers, while in 1908 the number was 32 farmers and 4 'cottage farmers'.[6] The changing fortunes of agriculture are also reflected in some of the other figures in this table, particularly the declining numbers of agricultural labourers. Since the majority of these were family men (table 7.6) the effect on population was likely to have been considerable. On a conservative estimate it probably accounts for a loss of perhaps fifty to sixty people

[6] White's *Directory of Nottinghamshire* (Sheffield, 1894), pp. 178–9; Kelly's *Directory of Nottinghamshire* (1908), pp. 104–5.

in the village between 1841 and 1881. Despite these changes, even in 1881 63 per cent of heads of households were directly involved in farming.

The other important group in this context is the servants. Definition is difficult, but if we extract from the figures those groups who were most likely to have been engaged in agricultural work the figures are more easily comparable (table 7.7). The aggregate figures suggest that despite the variation in definition the decline in opportunities for agricultural work was quite marked after 1861. The steep long-run decline in agricultural male servants and agricultural labourers – which is reflected in the age pyramids (figure 7.1) with their narrowing of the 21–30 age group in 1871 – coupled with the fall in the number of farmers, suggests that fewer people were needed to work the land, hence a decline in population.

TABLE 7.7 *Agricultural workers in Laxton 1841–1881*

Occupation	1841	1851	1861	1871	1881
Carter			35	1	
Cowman			1		
Farm worker		2	5	8	2
Labourer				5	
Servants – agricultural	45		12	22	29
– assistant				1	
– farm			3		
– general		51	1	4	3
	45	53	57	41	34
Agricultural labourer	62	63	53	36	34
	107	116	110	77	68

Source: as table 7.2.

These changes reflected agricultural conditions, and further evidence that the economic climate was becoming distinctly chilly is provided by the number of servants who were employed for domestic purposes (table 7.8). The figures for 1841 and 1851 are almost identical except for the increase in housekeepers, but numbers seem to have collapsed in 1861, and although they recovered slightly they were still smaller in 1881 than in 1851. The net loss of agricultural and domestic jobs between 1851 and 1881 was 72. Coupled with a decline of 18 in the number of farmers, this accounts for all but five of the gross losses 1851–81.

It was the fortunes of agriculture which determined the occupational pattern in the village, and which largely explain the population trends. However, a

TABLE 7.8 *Domestic service in Laxton 1841–1881*

Servants	1841	1851	1861	1871	1881
Domestic	0	15	0	11	17
Female	34				
House	0	23	5		
Housemaid			1		2
Male	1			1	
Charwoman			3	5	4
Housekeeper	2	12	13	7	3
	37	50	22	24	26

Source: as table 7.2.

significant number of tradesmen made their living in the village. Throughout these years there were tailors and shoemakers, blacksmiths and bricklayers, dressmakers and wheelwrights, millers and grocers in Laxton, although some of them may have had to supplement their income with farm work. Other occupations appear and disappear in the lists, including the 6 dairymaids in 1861 and the 3 errand boys in 1851, as well as the occasional joiner, midwife, nurse and painter, shoeblack and shepherd, tile maker and waggoner. Some do not appear at all. There are no washerwomen, although in the 1890s Annie Bartram spent enough of her time at the wash tubs of the better-off households – primarily those of the vicar and a few of the farmers – to qualify.[7] Perhaps surprisingly James Lacey, a watch- and clockmaker, was able to find employment in the village, but he also farmed.

As Laxton contracted, the demand for specialist services declined. There were three blacksmiths in the village in 1881, but only one in 1894 and 1908. Thomas Hilton leased the smithy and an adjoining house in 1908, together with 3½ acres of land. The smithy premises included a forge and shoes shed, a store shed, a coal shed and a tool shed. He was succeeded by Arthur Grundy, Laxton's last blacksmith, who arrived in the village in 1912. Grundy used to start at 6 a.m. and would often shoe six horses before breakfast. This was in the days when the larger farms had 6 or 8 horses, the smaller ones 4 or 5, and the village supported anything up to 200. Mr Grundy still found time to farm 45 acres, and to shoe horses in neighbouring villages, among them Kneesall, Egmanton and Ossington. He would travel on his bicycle. Small wonder that there were days on which he scarcely had time to reach the Dovecote Inn before

[7] *Life at Laxton*, p. 64.

closing time: 'just gave meself time to walk there and drink one glass and I had to walk brisk to get there before closing time'.[8]

There were three wheelwrights in the village in 1861 and 1871, two in 1881, and just one in the directories of 1894 and 1908. It is not clear from the census figures how many tradesmen had shops: three are recorded in the 1894 *Directory* but only two in 1908. One was the general store which was already open where the village shop is today in 1841. It sold a wide variety of wares including groceries, paraffin, sweets and toys. Samuel Laughton was the tenant in 1910 when the buildings were in poor condition. The other was a much smaller shop in the front parlour of a cottage, which was stocked with, among other things, pins and needles, soap and starch, and sweets. Laxton had a resident butcher until the 1870s but presumably could not provide enough custom, and thereafter the village had to rely on a man who came each week from Tuxford. He visited the village on a Friday, setting up his stall outside the public house. It was his last call, and he often overstayed his leave when refreshing himself in the Dovecote Inn.[9]

Perhaps the clearest indication of change in Laxton was the demise of the public house. Each farmhouse brewed its own beer, and naturally the taste and quality varied across the parish, but there were also a number of public houses. In the 1840s there were four: in Laxton, the Sun Inn, known alternatively as the Sign of the Sun, the Dovecote (dating as a pub from 1832), and the Volunteer; and in Moorhouse the Ship Inn, a converted farmhouse run by Seth Cole, who also farmed in the hamlet.[10] In addition, Leonard Esam, the village butcher, kept a beer house. Such was the decline that by 1908 only the Dovecote Inn remained.

The Sign of the Sun was the oldest hostelry in Laxton. George Pinder was the publican in 1828 and he was succeeded by William Pinder. For many years William Pinder had farmed nearly 120 acres leased from Lord Scarbrough, but by 1861 he was 80 and had 'retired' to the Sun with its 20-acre holding. He was living there with his wife, his son John – described as his assistant – and John's two children. Pinder sold the Sun in 1863. For a few years it was run by Mrs Maria Ward, but she sold out to Manvers in 1871 for £500. Her son Edward was allowed to retain the tenancy, but in 1873 he was fined £2 for allowing drunkenness on the premises. Shortly afterwards he went bankrupt. The vicar recommended Samuel Sampson for the tenancy: 'he is at present our carrier and has no stabling for his horses. He seems not to care about the licence; indeed he says he would sooner have the house without it . . . steady, honest, conscientious and industrious young man'. Sampson accepted the position. An

[8] Arthur Grundy died in 1987, in his nineties. His memories were recorded several years earlier by Peter Evans, whom I should like to thank for lending me a transcript of this conversation.

[9] *Life at Laxton*, pp. 21–6.

[10] NUMD De/C/7/17.

inventory drawn up in conjunction with this change of landlord lists the rooms of the Sun as a tap room, a bar, and a parlour. The contents of the bar included '17 pitchers, 17 pint mugs, large jug. Ale drainer, 18 glasses, 2 paraffin lamps, 2 globe glasses, 2 hammers, 4 spittoons, 3 spirit kegs and taps, 8 pewter measures, 16 stirrers, 2 trays', and at the end of the list – a teapot. The whole collection was valued at £44 2s. However, the Sun was not destined to remain as a public house for much longer. Falling population must have been cutting demand, and although he recommended Sampson for the tenancy in 1873 the vicar added that

I do not think that the present condition of Laxton (population 547 including Moor-house, having decreased about 10 per cent between 61 and 71) really requires three public houses at Laxton and one at Moorhouse, and so I should be glad if there were one less at Laxton.

Three years later Sampson acknowledged without comment an instruction from Thoresby to close the Sun Inn as a public house on 29 September 1876.[11]

Less is known about the Volunteer Inn. It was located on Crosshill Close virtually opposite the Dovecote Inn, and between 1841 and 1871 the publican was Thomas Hurt. He also worked as a blacksmith in the village. When he relinquished the tenancy is unknown, but in 1881 he was 76 and described in the census as blacksmith out of employment. By 1894 the publican was Thomas Walker. The Inn was owned by the Pinders, but by the 1890s William Pinder had mortgaged the property for £400, and in 1895 he sold out to Manvers for £500. The property included 5 acres of land, much of it in the open fields.[12] Manvers may have closed it down shortly afterwards. At some date after 1881 the Ship Inn in Moorhouse also closed – the premises were still known as Ship Farm until a few years ago – leaving Laxton by 1910 with just the Dovecote Inn.

The present Dovecote Inn dates from 1832. The premises were partially rebuilt in the 1850s, when Charlotte Twibell was the tenant. She was living there with her unmarried son and two daughters in 1861, but shortly after this she ran into financial difficulties, and she and her family left the village by 1866 when Thomas Motley was the tenant. Motley was succeeded by William Merrils in 1880, who was in turn replaced the following year by Mrs Jane Snowden. By 1910 the tenant was J. T. Price, and the premises included a smoke room, a tap room, a kitchen and dairy, a cellar and a clubroom. It was reckoned to dispense annually 80 barrels at 12s each, 150 dozen pints at 4d each and 50 gallons at 2s 6d each. The tenancy included 47 acres of land and a

---

[11] NUMD MaB/168/179; 176/416, 434b, c; 217/145, 155, 158, 160, 161, 167; 5E/130; M.5592.

[12] NUMD M.5695–6.

number of families started with the Dovecote before moving to larger farms in the village.

For many years the pub operated on a 6-day licence, which also came about as a result of the efforts of the vicar, Rev. H. A. Martin. In addition to objecting to the number of pubs in the village, he successfully persuaded Thoresby that the Dovecote should not open on a Sunday. The story is told that, Sunday being the only day of the week when many of the village labourers had a few hours rest, it was common for them to spend some hours in the Dovecote and then to sleep off the effects on Crosshill during the afternoon. This behaviour, together with their raucous comments when the vicar returned from taking the afternoon service in Moorhouse, led to the pub being closed, and a 7-day licence was restored only in the mid-1960s. The village labourers transferred their Sunday drinking allegiance to Egmanton.[13]

PLATE 7.1 *The pinfold. The original pinfold was on a site adjacent to the present pinfold just south of the Dovecote Inn. It was built in 1800–1 by Christopher Roos, possibly as a replacement for an earlier structure. In 1897 a new pinfold, shown here, was built opposite the public house. It was removed in 1969 when the County Council Highway Authority agreed to pay the cost of moving the pinfold back more or less to its earlier location.*

---

[13] *Ex. inf.* Ron Cree. The same story was recounted by Jack Rose on a tape made by Professor Chambers in 1959, and kindly lent to me by Mrs Ann Howard.

HOUSING

In the 1840s Laxton was still predominantly a nucleated settlement. Moorhouse had only a handful of houses, and a number of others lay at a distance from either the village or the hamlet. These included the five independent farms owned by Earl Manvers (Westwood, Brockilow, Knapeney, Copthorne and Brecks), together with Straw Hall, an independent farm on the eastern edge of the parish owned by the Denisons, and smaller houses adjoining Westwood, Brockilow (at Saw Wood) and Brecks (Breck Wong). In addition there were two independent farms at Hartshorn and Laxton Lodge, in the southern spur of the parish beyond the woodlands. These were Lumley Savile properties acquired by Manvers in the 1860s, but administered with his Kneesall estate.

The number of houses had grown as population increased in the early years of the nineteenth century, but once this trend was reversed part of the housing stock was surplus to requirements. In 1841 there were 122 houses in the village, and a decade later the number had risen to 128 with one other under construction. This was the high point and numbers fell to 121 in 1861, 119 in 1871, and 116 in 1881 – of which 13 were empty. A decade later 96 houses were inhabited; in 1901 the number was 95 (another 9 were empty) and in 1911 it was 92. Gross numbers may have reflected population, but they tell us nothing about the size, shape and condition of the buildings.

In 1862 Thomas Huskinson was commissioned by the third Earl Manvers to survey the Pierrepont estates. We shall have cause to return to his agricultural findings in a later chapter, but one of his most frequent complaints as he compiled his report on Laxton was that 'the farm houses in the village are for the most part of inferior character, and the buildings generally ill arranged and in bad repair. Many of the cottages are also very bad, and some scarcely habitable.' Huskinson wanted to see Laxton enclosed, and with that end in view his report made depressing reading about the current state of the parish. Some of his harshest criticisms were reserved for the state of the housing stock. John Birkett, farming 12 acres, was reported to have farm buildings of mud, wood and thatch, 'in ruinous condition, and unfit to stand'; William Cooke farmed his 16 acres from a house 'of mud, brick and thatch . . . so old and dilapidated as to be entirely unfit for residence and incapable of repair'; while Benjamin Hill with just 4 acres lived in 'a wretched house of mud, brick and thatch, unfit to live in, and positively dangerous'. Lest it be thought however that the whole village was ripe for the nineteenth-century equivalent of the bulldozer, Huskinson also noted a number of houses recently built and in good condition. John Keyworth was living in a 'substantial and comfortable dwelling'; Jane Peatfield in a 20-year old house Huskinson considered to be the best in Laxton; and Elizabeth Whittington in a house 'in good repair'. Much the same pattern of good and bad was true of Moorhouse. Robert Booth, in a house 'of mud, brick and thatch, in great dilapidation, not fit for a dwelling' was living alongside William Harpham whose brick and pantile house was 'recently repaired and a comfortable residence'.[14]

What Huskinson was recording was the current state of the long-term rebuilding programme at Laxton which had been proceeding on the Pierrepont property for many years. Almost every year the accounts record payments for replacing or rebuilding village property. In 1844 £240 was spent pulling down and replacing the cottages occupied by Dewick and Johnson, and in 1850 a new cottage and premises was constructed at Moorhouse for George Bartle. Repairs to the Dovecote Inn totalled £113 in 1853. In Huskinson's view, the building programme had not gone far enough, but despite his strictures little seems to have been done in the immediate aftermath of the report, although Philip Hooton's cottage, which Huskinson recommended for demolition, had been removed by 1877.

In the second half of the 1870s, with agricultural conditions deteriorating and tenants more difficult to find and keep, outlay on house repairs by the Thoresby estate began to increase. In 1876 £615 was spent on four properties in the village; in 1877 £1,061 on six properties, and in 1878 £832 on a further four properties. But these sums need to be set against the £2,769 spent building the new vicarage in these years and £814 in 1879 and 1880 on the present farmhouse at Westwood for William Pinder. Why this was built is unclear, unless there was a fire or some such calamity. In 1862 Huskinson described the existing house at Westwood as 'in good repair and adequate to the farm', but the new house was built on a more substantial scale than most Laxton farmhouses; it was described in 1910 as a 'very good and well built house (15 inch walls) but superior to the requirements of the farm'. William Pinder, the tenant, was also provided with new farm buildings in 1885–6, at a cost of £1,040. His successors finally left the farm in 1908, when it was relet to Tom Marrison for whom repairs costing more than £1,000 were carried out over the following years.

Pinder seems to have been particularly well treated, since despite a regular outflow of money on repairs, the state of the housing stock in 1910 left much to be desired. Many houses were described as damp, or in only moderate repair. Samuel Laughton's house and shop were 'very old and becoming dilapidated', and the damp house 'will eventually be pulled down'. With a few houses the story was much the same in 1910 as in 1862. The 'Manor House' farm was tenanted by William Quibell senior in 1862 when Huskinson described the house as 'a very old building generally in bad repair'; by 1910 the tenant, George Cocking, was still having to make do with a 'very old house [. . .] old fashioned rather inconvenient inside'. But it was not always the case. John Birkett and John Cree, Manvers tenants in the bottom of the village, both had

14 NUMD Ma S 16, Thomas Huskinson's survey of 1862.

houses which were not more than 20 years old and in good repair, and a number of other houses were described as being in 'fair repair'. What had certainly changed since 1862 was the demise of the old mud and stud houses. Everyone was now living in a brick-built house, usually under a tile or pantile roof, although there was at least one 'old ruined cottage of brick and thatch' still surviving.[15]

Part of the reason for this rather lukewarm picture by 1910 was that Laxton had not been enclosed. William Huskinson took the view in 1862 that following enclosure the number of farms would be reduced, and the number of labourers' cottages would increase. 'There are at least twice the number' of farmhouses, he wrote, 'that after enclosure will be necessary and after selecting the best of the farm houses for permanent farms, the remainder will make comfortable cottages and allow of the worst cottages being removed.'[16] He earmarked several farms to disappear as separate units and argued that the houses should be converted into labourers' cottages. This did not happen; William Quibell senior's house was marked down for cottages, but was still a separate farm more than forty years later. On the other hand cottage accommodation did become something of a problem in the village over time.

The church owned three cottage properties which were described in 1872 as 'very old and dilapidated'. The vicar wrote to Manvers suggesting that they should be pulled down and rebuilt: 'cottages with proper accommodation are much wanted in the village: there are very few with more than one bedroom and even of them a scarcity. If three good cottages could be built on the ground, they would supply a want, they would be an ornament, instead of a disgrace to the village: and the church property would be greatly improved.' He himself was prepared to put £60 into the project, and he hoped for contributions from some of the freeholders and tenant farmers in the village.[17] The Thoresby agent, John Horncastle, was asked by Manvers to consider the proposal, and he took a less than charitable view of events. The cottages had been allowed to deteriorate, he argued, even though the churchwardens enjoyed an annual income from church lands of £40 a year which should have been more than enough to ensure proper upkeep. Whereas

the first duty of former churchwardens was to keep the property in good repair, and then use the remainder of the rents for the ordinary expenses of the church [. . .] as this would occasionally have involved a church rate, it did not suit them to do so, and now they seek to remedy the consequences of such neglect by a subscription.

In his view former churchwardens had almost certainly neglected the cottages in the expectation that Laxton would be enclosed, and they would 'no doubt

[15] PRO IR 18/55254–5.
[16] NUMD Ma S 16.
[17] NUMD MaB/218/41b.

have been offered to your Lordship for an equivalent in land', as a means of avoiding the expense of repairs. In other words Manvers, and others in the village, were now being asked to make good the deficiencies of former church-wardens. If there was to be rebuilding, however,

Two would be sufficient, and of course cost less money. There is no advantage, but the contrary, in having more cottages in a place like Laxton, than are really required for labourers to be employed by the farmers; and if it was not that your Lordship found work for several of them it would soon be found there were too many cottages already. I am sorry to say many of the cottages in Laxton do not contain the necessary amount of accommodation required for comfort, or decency, but many of them do not belong to your Lordship.[18]

In the absence of enclosure Laxton was still a village of small farms employing relatively little labour and as a result, the need for cottage accommodation foreseen by Huskinson in 1862 had not materialized, although in 1910 there were more than thirty cottages in the parish.

Laxton also had three almshouses, built at the behest of Lady Manvers in 1896. They were described in 1910 as 'very well built' in brick and tile, with a large living room, two bedrooms, and a scullery. Although supposedly for indigent widows, their occupants included Annie Bartram, the village washer-woman, and Jane Dolby, the village midwife.[19] Today they have been converted into two houses.

Farmhouses were accompanied by buildings, and the 1910 survey details each room in the house and each outbuilding in the farmstead. It would be tedious to produce long lists of these but an example helps to give a flavour of the village at this time. William Merrils, the farmer of Crosshill, was living in a brick and pantiled house on two storeys. Upstairs were four bedrooms, a servants' bedroom, and a bacon chamber. On the ground floor were two front rooms, a living room, a kitchen, a back kitchen and a pantry. The house also had cellars, a washhouse, and a coal hole. In the yard were a range of brick and pantiled open sheds including an engine house, a number of looseboxes, a cow shed, and a pig yard.

Inside, the farmhouses were almost as cluttered as in the seventeenth century. When the effects of Joseph Rose were auctioned in 1849, the sale notice listed, among other things, milking gear, a cheese press, a brewing tub, brass and tin pans, a brass saucepan, three feather beds, three bedsteads, a warming pan, an oak chest, 6 tables and 12 chairs, an 8-day clock and a 28-hour clock, a copper furnace, smoothing irons, an Italian iron and heaters and 2 pairs of 'steelyards'.[20] Many of these items would have been familiar to Edith

[18] NUMD M.4010/19.
[19] *Life at Laxton*, pp. 64–5.
[20] NUMD MaB/222/24.

Hickson who was born in Laxton in the 1890s, the daughter of George Weatherall of Bar Farm:

The farm houses are not small, the six or seven bedrooms above the parlours, kitchens, dairies and brewhouses, were all useful and usually all in use. The wash-house too could be under the same upper regions. Always there were a couple of coppers, one for the weekly laundering and the other for the brewing of beer, a pantry, passages, lofts and as a rule, cellars down a flight of stone steps. The large living kitchen had a huge fireplace with oven, boiler, plate-rack and dustpreventer also a fender and fire irons, and in all kitchens, the beamed ceilings were embellished with rows of bacon hooks. The back kitchen, where a great deal of work was done, usually had a brick oven, a huge stone sink with either one or two pumps placed conveniently at each end – one pump yielding well water, the other connected by pipe to a cistern of rain water from the roof. The two coppers might also be there and all were stoked with wood and coal. The huge brewing copper was sufficiently capacious to hold enough water to scald a pig.[21]

The beds were stuffed with poultry pluckings – the feathers were first given 'a good bake in the oven' – and the best beds in the house were brass knobbed. Many homes had a piano: 'it was a poor house that owned no piano, the most important thing in the parlour.' By contrast few families owned books. 'Apart from the Bible, the weekly newspapers and a few books – perhaps Sunday School prizes – the people of Laxton read little or nothing. Novels were considered unsuitable for girls [. . .] precious little money was ever spent on books.' Local news sheets, by contrast, were a necessity, not merely for the information they contained, but also for their later use in fire lighting or in a more delicate employment for which they were considered ideal.[22]

LIFE IN VICTORIAN LAXTON

We have seen how many people there were in Laxton, what they did, and where they lived, but what was it like to live in the village during these years? It was certainly not particularly comfortable. Individuals were frequently exposed to the elements of wind and rain. Often they returned to a damp and not necessarily very warm house. Hardly surprisingly illnesses and accidents were common – and doctors were expensive. Late nineteenth-century Laxton was served by two doctors and a veterinary surgeon, but they lived half a day's journey away, and were called only in the direst emergency. The village had a midwife, a Mrs Dolby, who not only attended at births but also looked after – temporarily – the existing children. For most other purposes home cures were available. Every house had something for constipation and toothache, for sore

---

[21] *Life at Laxton*, p. 27.
[22] Ibid., pp. 43–4.

throats and bad chests. But death, the great leveller, was not to be avoided. Few could afford a hearse, which would have had to come from Retford, and most people were carried to church on a wagon or cart. Everyone attending wore black, and houses along the route drew their blinds as the cortege passed by. The sexton tolled the church bell, the funeral service was read, and another grave was filled in the adjoining churchyard.[23]

If life was hard, it was not necessarily without its lighter moments. There were annual events which diverted the villagers from their usual routine. Earl Manvers was the Master of the Rufford Hunt, which met regularly at the Crosshill. All but the aged and infirm gathered to see the colourful assembly of horses and hounds, scarlet coats and tall black hats. The children were allowed out of school at break time, although the headmaster was not amused when twelve boys absented themselves from school one afternoon in November 1894 after the hunt killed a fox in the village in the dinner hour. On these occasions the villagers were likely to see their landlord in person, although he – and more frequently Countess Manvers – paid periodic visits to the school. A few farmers would take the day off work to follow the hounds on horseback, and many other villagers followed on foot.

The annual celebration of the feast of St Michael the Archangel was an opportunity for everyone to enjoy entertainments in the Green Yard behind the Dovecote Inn. Traditionally, feast week was a school holiday, but after the introduction of compulsory elementary education this was reduced to a couple of half days, although attendance at school was generally poor during the week. Stalls and booths were set up and illuminated and, with visitors from adjoining villages, Laxton was transformed for a few days at the beginning of each October. On the first Monday in January came another important annual event on the calendar, Plough Monday, when the village plough boys tradition-ally performed the ancient play.[24] For the tenants there were the annual dinners. In 1835 Mrs Wright, landlady of the Dovecote Inn, laid on – at the expense of Thoresby – three annual dinners, two (in June and December) asso-ciated with rent days, and the third for the annual tithe dinner. Martha Clark was providing the dinners in 1880. Later, rent day dinners for the tenants took place at the Jug and Glass in Edwinstowe, or in the Hop Pole at Ollerton, although cottagers continued to be entertained at the Dovecote Inn through the twentieth century. When rationing forced the dinners to be discontinued during the Second World War, the villagers were given a sum of money instead.

Then there were the one-offs, the village street decorations, and the tea and sports to celebrate Queen Victoria's Diamond Jubilee in 1897. For the children there were sack and egg and spoon races under the firm hand of Frank Willis the schoolmaster, and the older men and youths competed in a tug of war.

---

[23] Ibid., p. 71.
[24] There is a copy of the Laxton Plough Play in NUMD Ba P 1/26.

With the ending of the Boer War in 1902 the school had a half holiday and 'the children paraded the village carrying flags and singing patriotic songs'.[25] Empire Day was celebrated with a holiday and games in the Hall grounds on the south side of the church. The village mourned the passing of the old queen, but celebrated with vigour the coronation of Edward VII. Once again the streets were decorated; another village tea was arranged with games for the children afterwards, and to round off the evening a torchlight procession moved through the streets.

Finally there was sport. The village cricket pitch was laid out in 1887–8 at Earl Manvers's expense, and the village team was captained by Mr Willis. He had flannels and white boots and wore a flat straw hat, but other members of the team had to play in more utilitarian garb. Matches were played against other village teams, but except for the occasional game at Thoresby the pitches left something to be desired: 'the wickets were terrible, and if you scored 20 runs it was the equal to 100 to-day.'[26]

THE CHURCH

Central to the life of the village was the church, and the parson was a figure of importance in local affairs. During the whole of this period Laxton had only three vicars. Rev. Richard Proctor came to the village in 1826. A native of Yorkshire, he must have been about 50 at the time, and he soon put down local roots by purchasing land. Proctor remained in Laxton until the 1850s, when he was well into his eighties, and may even have died in the village although he was not buried locally. His 19 acres in Laxton and Ompton were sold in 1861.[27]

Proctor's successor, Henry Arthur Martin, stayed for forty years until 1898. He came from Exeter and was only 26 when he arrived in Laxton in 1858. He was later remembered as 'somewhat out of touch, too intellectually inclined to mix with those horney-handed, roughcast sons of the soil and their crude mannerisms'. He had to be 'looked-up-to', so that schoolchildren were taught to curtsey or to touch their cap, and this tradition continued under his successor.[28] When he left in 1898 a subscription raised nearly £48 as a leaving present, including £10 each from Earl and Countess Manvers, and £5 from the Thoresby agent. The rest came from smaller contributions in the village. The presentation was made to him in the school, which he continued to visit until his death in 1911.[29]

[25] NAO SL/106/1/2.
[26] NUMD MaB/197/42; *Life at Laxton*, p. 58; William Beckitt and Jack Cook, *Open Field Recollections* (Laxton, n.d.); Frank Moody, *My Lifetime Memories of Laxton* (Laxton, 1981).
[27] NAO DD.LK/14/331,333.
[28] *Life at Laxton*, p. 62.
[29] NUMD MaB/205/5; NAO SL/106/1/2; PR 4061.

Rev. C. B. Collinson, who came to the village in 1898, was another well-connected young man, although unlike the bachelor Martin, he was married. Both husband and wife were tall and well built, and enjoyed walking around the village streets: 'She had the only fur coat in the district – an unmistakable symbol of aristocracy and wealth;'[30] while he was distinctive because he wore spats or gaiters around the village, and seldom appeared in plain clerical garb. He was also typical of the nineteenth-century clerical scholar, spending many hours in the muniment room at Thoresby working meticulously through papers relating to Laxton, which he brought together into a working history of the village. This was still incomplete when he and his wife left the village in 1916.[31]

The parsons were men of standing in the community, and Earl Manvers recognized their importance by providing a substantial new vicarage in the 1870s 'built to the taste and design of Mr Martin'.[32] The intention was that the existing vicarage (which stands today and is now Old Vicarage Farm) with its outhouses, garden, orchard and croft (1a 2r 7p), should be given to Manvers in return for land adjoining the churchyard (4a 1r 7p), on which Manvers would build a new vicarage. The new house was built at a cost of £2,769.[33] At the same time the Ecclesiastical Commissioners agreed to grant a £30 a year augmentation to the vicar's salary. An estimate drawn up in 1873 showed that the vicar enjoyed an income of £226 a year, almost all of which came from tithes. After meeting the expenses of collection, and paying the rates, this left him with a net income of £195 12s 10d.[34] Small wonder that Proctor was able to purchase land, and that Mr Martin was regarded in the village as a rich man. The vicarage is today in private hands.

If the vicar was an important man in the village, this did not necessarily mean that local people were regular attenders at worship. The 1851 religious census provides a picture of observance in the village. Richard Proctor made the return for the parish church, which had seating for 397 people. On the day of the census (which was Mothering Sunday) he estimated a general congregation of 15–20 in the morning and 97 in the afternoon, with 60 Sunday scholars at both services. These were also the average figures for the past year. Proctor was responsible for the chapel-of-ease at Moorhouse, which had seating for 40, and 15–20 worshippers at the one service a month. The Independent chapel erected in 1802 had space for 105 worshippers. According to the minister, Benjamin Ash, 30 people attended the afternoon service and 70 the evening service, which was below the average of 40 and 85 for the previous twelve months, a

[30] *Life at Laxton*, p. 62.
[31] Christopher Collinson's notes are now in NAO PR 4082–6. They include transcriptions of several documents now missing.
[32] *Life at Laxton*, p. 4. Martin is reputed to have been a cousin of Earl Manvers.
[33] PRO IR/18/7459; NUMD MaB/218/39a–f; M.5609.
[34] NUMD MaB/195/1,57; 210/9b.

discrepancy he attributed to 'a thunderstorm occurring at the time of assembling lessened the number of attendants and left it below the average.' Another 25 people attended a Wesleyan Methodist service held in a private house on the day of the census, while in the Primitive Methodist chapel 'erected about the year 1820' there were 4 present in the morning and 12 in the evening.

If we assume no one went to church more than once, a total of 298, or 48 per cent of villagers, worshipped on census Sunday (table 7.9). However some villagers certainly attended more than one service either in the same church or in more than one place. Benjamin Ash, who was still the preacher at the non-conformist chapel in 1865, told Manvers's agent that year: 'we are on the best and kindest terms with Rev. Mr Martin the vicar, and having our service in the evening of the Sabbath to avoid clashing with the Church service, our object being to help the cause of Christianity and sound morality.'[35] To convert gross attendance numbers into actual people in church we can take the largest attendance and add one-third of the other two, which gives a total of 171. If the 60 scholars (assuming they were the same morning and afternoon) are added we have a figure of 37 per cent of villagers attending church on census Sunday.

TABLE 7.9 *Church attendance in Laxton in 1851*

	Morning	Afternoon	Evening
Parish Church	15–20	97	–
Moorhouse chapel	–	–	–
Independent		30	70
Wesleyan	25		
Primitive	4		12
Sunday scholars	60	60	

Source: M. Watts (ed.), *Religion in Victorian Nottinghamshire: the Religious Census* (Nottingham, 1988), pp. 223–4.

There are no later figures against which these can be compared, but Edith Hickson recalled that in the 1890s 'most of the village children attended Church or Chapel and Sunday School, dressed in their Sunday Clothes.' Older children went to morning and evening services as well. Mothers were usually busy cooking the Sunday dinner in the morning, but would attend the evening service with their husbands, both dressed in their best clothes. When the weather permitted, after church it was common to stroll in the village, and perhaps to return home to a reading of Bunyan's *Pilgrim's Progress* or other

[35] NUMD M.4010/5.

similar literature.[36] Mrs Hickson's memory may be a little rose coloured at this point. The 1851 figures do not suggest a level of attendance in which the whole village, or even a majority, turned out for a single service and nor do the service registers. In 1901 only 34 parishioners received Easter communion, one-tenth of the population, and the church was seldom full. Mr Collinson noted of a service held on the day of Edward VII's funeral in 1910 'practically the whole adult population attended and most of the younger ones, and almost all in Black. A very solemn and impressive occasion.' There was also a full church for a service to celebrate the coronation of George V in 1911, but these were rare occasions. Otherwise the best attendances seem to have been, naturally enough in the countryside, at Harvest Thanksgiving.[37]

John Throsby's comments had obviously been taken to heart, and a number of improvements were made to the parish church. There is a gap in the church-wardens' accounts in the mid-1840s at a time when cleaning and repairing the church was in progress. At an archdeacon's visitation the churchwardens were ordered to have the church properly repaired and whitewashed. At the same time they requested permission to clean up the chancel (Lord Manvers's responsibility). According to Proctor it was 'extremely dirty indeed and the archdeacon said it must be done'.[38] It cost Manvers £25 in 1842, and when this was completed the Rural Dean inspected Laxton church in May 1843 and came away with mixed feelings:

I am happy to find that, on the whole, the work done in the chancel and particularly round the basement or plinth externally, has been executed so well. At the same time I must beg to express my regret, that notwithstanding my very strict and earnest remonstrances to the contrary, the caps of the pillars and the pillars themselves should, after the thorough cleansing they underwent from previous wash, have been again over-laid with another coat of the same. I also feel very sorry that certain portions of oak carving existing in the chancel on the left or north side of it have been removed. True, they were but fragments, yet as those fragments were there, they served at least to show what had been, and a pattern for future restorers of church decoration, and they ought not to have been removed. Perhaps you would be so obliging as to interest yourself so far respecting them as to ask the workmen if they are in existence and endeavour to have them replaced. Before I visit this parish again, I hope you will be so good as to supply a decent door in the door way near the altar rails. The windows in the clerestory of the chancel appear to be in by no means good condition, perhaps I am not asking too much of you to direct your attention to the same. In case you glaze the windows afresh I beg to suggest that the ancient lozenge form of pane be preserved as it is new and not made square. The same mistake in cleansing the pillars has been made in the church as well as the chancel. They have been overlaid with another coat of lime or colour wash, but on

[36] *Life at Laxton*, pp. 45–6.
[37] NAO PR 4061.
[38] NUMD MaB/182/694.

the whole the church is very much improved and much cleaner and less damp than formerly.[39]

When Sir Stephen Glynne visited Laxton church in 1854 he wrote that it was 'a fine church full of interesting features [. . .] the interior fine and solemn [. . .] but unhappily in a state of neglect and decay'.[40]

For half a century money had been spent on the church without noticeable effect in terms of improvement, and at the end of the 1850s Earl Manvers proposed a drastic remodelling of both the church and the churchyard. A special meeting of the vestry was called in February 1859 to consider his proposition that:

in consideration of the dilapidated state of the church at Laxton, Lord Manvers proposes to build [. . .] a new church at his sole cost [. . .] for a sum [. . .] not exceeding £2,000, besides the use and value of the old materials, a certain portion of the old church being retained.

The motion was accepted by a majority of 28 to 1, the lone dissentient being Samuel Pinder junior, the village druggist. A Faculty was obtained, which stated that the church was in a 'state of extreme dilapidation and decay', and that Manvers was 'desirous of building in great part a new church for the more convenient use of the parishioners and the more fitting celebration of the public worship'. He was prepared to spend £2,000 on the project, and to use the old materials on the site.[41]

The church was largely rebuilt to designs drawn by the Nottingham architect T. C. Hine. The tower was taken down, the nave was shortened by one bay – it is still possible to see in the church today where the bay originally began – the aisles were reduced in width and the Everingham chapel was removed. The tower was then rebuilt using the old materials, in a more easterly position adjoining the shortened nave. Seating capacity was reduced from 397 to 295. The restored building was opened by the Bishop of Lincoln on 11 October 1860.[42]

The renovations have not received a good press. In 1916 J. B. Firth referred in the church as having been 'ruthlessly restored [. . .] barbarous deeds were done',[43] and in 1923 another commentator suggested that

It can scarcely be termed a 'restoration' for the tower was pulled down; the proportions of the nave were sadly injured by the abstraction of one of its bays; the north porch was

[39] NUMD MaB/206/22,23.
[40] H. Gill, 'St. Michael's, Laxton', *TTS*, 28 (1924), 97.
[41] NAO PR 4092, 17,391.
[42] NAO DD.846/1/26.
[43] J. B. Firth, *Highways and Byeways in Nottinghamshire* (1916), p. 377.

PLATE 7.2 *St Michael's Church. Built in various phases between about 1190 and 1490, St Michael's became one of the grandest village churches in the county. By the mid-nineteenth century it was in a dilapidated state, as the top picture (taken before 1860) shows. The lower picture shows the result of repair and rebuilding: the nave was shortened and the tower rebuilt, and from outside the church looks Victorian except for Archbishop Rotheram's clerestory – 'the best feature of the exterior':* N. Pevsner and E. Williamson, The Buildings of England: Nottinghamshire *(2nd edn, 1979), p. 164.*

demolished; the south porch and the outer walls of the aisles, where they had gone out of upright, were also pulled down. New outer walls were built in order to reduce the aisles in width and so bring the area of the church more into conformity with the size of the village.[44]

Edith Hickson suggested that the renovations 'caused that grand old church to disappear completely – a great loss to the village and to posterity', although as her account makes clear it was the loss of the old box pews which some parishioners most regretted.[45]

These comments have to be considered carefully. The church was in a poor state of repair by the 1850s and, as Firth commented in 1916, 'the church remains a noble building'.[46] Moreover, for the parishioners, burdened with a church that no amount of money seemed to improve, the restoration had two benefits. First, most of the £2,500 that the work cost was provided by Lord Manvers, leaving the parishioners to fund the restoration of the five bells, and the cost of enclosing and levelling the churchyard. This was met by raising three church rates, of 1s 9d, 4d and 1d in the pound, which brought in £375, and it was supplemented by a donation from the vicar, and the sale of stone to the Highway Office and to one of the farmers, George Saxelby.[47] Second, the church was much less expensive to maintain after 1860. Annual expenditure on maintenance was usually no more than about £30, which normally went on items such as church cleaning (£28s 2s at Laxton and £1 10s at Moorhouse in 1863–4), new bell ropes (£3 3s in 1871–2, and £3 9s in 1889–90), clock cleaning (£4 5s in 1885–6) or coal purchase (£6 7s 9d in 1874–5). Extra expenses were met by forming a committee to organize fund raising! In 1889 it was decided to have a new boiler and heating system for the church, at a cost of £38 17s 6d. The vicar offered to contribute £20, and a committee of seven was appointed to raise the rest.[48]

Simultaneously with the remodelling of St Michael's, Moorhouse Chapel was pulled down and rebuilt from the foundations. At its meeting in June 1860 the parish vestry heard that Mr Denison proposed to build a new church in stone, with a brick lining. This time the proposal was carried unanimously. The Faculty noted that 'the fabric is in a dilapidated condition requiring immediate repair,' and as a result of the rebuilding 'many additional sittings will be gained.' The chapel was 'insufficient for the accommodation of the inhabitants who desire to attend divine service therein'. Plans were drawn by Henry Clutton, and Denison met the whole cost of £890. Not everyone appreciated the new construction – one of the local newspapers described it as having

[44] Gill, 'St. Michael's, Laxton', 97.
[45] *Life at Laxton*, p. 4.
[46] Firth, *Highways and Byeways*, p. 377; *Nottinghamshire Guardian*, 30 July 1949.
[47] NAO PR 4080; 4083; 4766/5.
[48] NAO PR 4082, 4093.

'rather an unfavourable appearance' but 'beautiful outside'. It was opened by
the Bishop of Lincoln on 1 June 1861, with the vicar of Laxton reading prayers.
The benefactor himself was not at the ceremony, having 'missed his train from
London'.[49]

Upkeep of the church was supposedly financed either through the income
derived from the rent paid on the 13 acres of church lands, or a church rate. In
1892 the land was sold to Lord Manvers for £750, and the money raised was
invested in securities. The interest was used to meet church expenses. This
made financial sense given that the rental income from the land declined from
£27 19s in 1862 to £20 4s by 1892 as a result of the agricultural depression.
The capital was invested in consols which were yielding £21 5s 8d in 1893.
The vicar made a donation of £5 and Earl Manvers £11 3s to help clear a
deficit on the churchwardens' accounts. In addition, Manvers made a donation
of £10 annually towards the repair and upkeep of the church. These various
sources seldom yielded enough to do much more than meet running costs, and
capital costs usually had to be met from other sources. New church gates and a
path cost £44 in 1907, and irongates £76 in 1907–8. Another £145 was spent
on church improvement in 1911–12, and £182 in 1912–13.[50]

EDUCATION

At the beginning of the Victorian period educational provision in the village
was minimal. John Truswell, the village schoolmaster, finally retired in 1847
and died the following year at the age of 75, leaving a widow who stayed on in
the village, first as a housekeeper and then in 1871, at the age of 87, as a chair-
woman. The schoolmaster was funded to teach ten poor boys of the parish
reading and writing, and they met in the Everingham chapel in the church.
Truswell's successor Mr R. Brett stayed for only two years, possibly because
the salary was so low. At a meeting in November 1848 the vestry agreed to pay
a schoolmaster and mistress £5 and £2 a year for teaching the 13 parish
(pauper) children, and to pay the same person £6 10s a year for teaching the
Sunday School, and a further £6 10s for doing the necessary business of the
parish apart from collecting the rates.[51] This salary, £20 a year, was offered to
Henry Alvey, who succeeded Brett. He moved to the village with his wife and
two daughters. Alvey did not stay long and in December 1852 the post was
again vacant, and two candidates were nominated for the appointment, Mr
James Woodcock, and Samuel Pinder the village druggist and shopkeeper.
What followed offers an interesting sidelight on the village in the 1850s.

[49] NAO PR 4092, NAO DD/846/1/26.
[50] NUMD M.5432–4; NAO PR 4082, 4094.
[51] NAO PR 4792.

The vicar, who had general oversight of the school, proposed that Woodcock should be appointed, but to his chagrin the vestry – which was the appointing committee – offered the post to Pinder: 'I with many others think him a very improper person for the situation', Proctor wrote to Thoresby, 'his wife cannot teach though very essential that the girls should have a mistress.' To make matters worse, Pinder had no intention of moving into the schoolmaster's house, and intended to continue running his business. William Clutton agreed to attend a meeting in the village at which the issue would be resolved. Woodcock, the defeated candidate, told Clutton he had been 'shamefully abused [. . .] if I should succeed twill prove a triumph of justice over tyranny and malice.' In his view John Keyworth, one of Laxton's leading farmers, had led the faction which opposed his appointment. Woodcock was then living in Tuxford: 'I live here under Mr Keyworth paying a heavy rent, pounds more than he will again get. This is the only reason I can give for his desire to keep me at Tuxford.'[52] In the end it was obviously decided that under the circumstances neither candidate was appropriate, and the vestry approved instead the appointment of William Tomlinson Hand and Mary Ann Hand his wife.[53] They came from Flintham with their two children, although how much teaching Mrs Hand was able to do is unclear since she gave birth to another five children by 1861.

In 1858 the vestry altered the rules under which children qualified to attend the school. Instead of eleven children being educated free, all children sent to the school were to be charged 2d a week, except where more than two children were sent, when the payment was to be 1½d for the third child and 1d for every other child. The schoolmaster's salary was to be made up of £7 paid out of money raised at the annual grass letting (raised to £12 from 1864), £5 as parish accountant, and £2 from Moorhouse, making £14 altogether. This left a shortfall by comparison with the £20 previously raised, but the endowment was increased in 1859 when Mrs Ann Proctor, widow of the late vicar, left £50 towards the school. In 1906 this money was transferred into stock, the interest to be employed for the school.[54]

When the church was restored in 1860 the Everingham chapel was demolished, leaving the school without a home. Manvers spent £483 on a new school building and an adjoining brick and tile schoolhouse. In 1910 this building was described as the upper school, built of brick and pantile, with one large good room in which the girls and boys were separated. The Infants' School, built across the road from the mixed Junior School, was constructed in 1870. Manvers's accounts record payments of £88 in 1870 and £55 in 1871. It was a one-room, brick and pantile building, described in 1910 has having poor

---

[52] NUMD MaB/197/16.
[53] NAO PR 4092.
[54] NAO PR 4102, 4093, 4125.

PLATE 7.3 *The village hall. Until the remodelling of the church in the mid-nineteenth century, the Laxton schoolchildren were taught in one of the side chapels. In conjunction with the remodelling, Earl Manvers financed the new school, shown here. An infants department was built on the opposite side of the road following the introduction of compulsory elementary education in the 1870s. The school closed in 1947 and shortly afterwards this building became the village hall. The infants department is now derelict.*

ventilation and being in only moderate repair. Teaching in the new building began after the summer holiday in 1870.[55]

Hands was succeeded in 1864 by Thomas Reynolds. He stayed for three years, but was not a great success. In February 1866 the school inspectors noted in the log book that 'the success of the school fell below the low point reached last year [. . .] unsatisfactory [. . .] the master has been diligent though unsuccessfully.' In December 1867 Reynolds was succeeded by James Griffiths, 'late student of St Mark's College, Chelsea'. Obviously Laxton did not compare favourably with London, since Griffiths stayed just six months.

By 1870 it was widely accepted in England that the system of voluntary education was failing to meet the needs of a growing population. Forster's Education Act passed that year paved the way for free and compulsory elementary education, both of which followed by 1880. Under the terms of the 1870

[55] NAO SL/106/1/1.

Act voluntary provision for education was insufficient, and the parish was obliged to find sufficient funds. The vicar proposed a scheme whereby the Laxton parishioners would raise about £20 a year, in addition to the salary paid to the schoolmaster as parish accountant; Egmanton was to raise £10, and together with subscriptions, children's payments and a government grant, this was expected to be sufficient to meet the expenses of the school – which was to serve both villages. In March 1871 the Laxton parishioners agreed to pay their contribution through a voluntary 1d rate raised on the same basis as the poor rate and collected by the overseers. The contribution arising out of the grass letting was discontinued. Egmanton agreed to pay its share, but by December 1871 it had contributed only £6 10s, and in 1872 it paid nothing at all. Expenses were £133. The children contributed £31 12s, the government grant £53, Lord Manvers £15, annual interest on the endowment £2 18s, the Laxton voluntary rate £16, and the vicar £6, leaving a shortfall of £11 4s 9d. Martin called a meeting to try to resolve the difficulties.[56]

The outcome of this particular dispute is not known, but by the 1890s the school was funded predominantly from government grants, the endowment of £2 14s 8d, the voluntary rate which raised £10, the Egmanton rate which raised a further £5, and subscriptions from Earl Manvers (£20) and the vicar (£5). Occasional subscriptions were also received from the Duke of Portland, the Duke of Newcastle, and Lord Savile, and collectively these sums were sufficient to keep it solvent.[57] Manvers, from whom the school managers rented the property for £1 12s 6d a year, paid for capital improvements including improvement to the drains in 1896–7 and repairs to the buildings in 1908–9.

The first schoolmaster to operate under the new dispensation was Daniel Pick, who came from Wiltshire in 1868 with his wife Ellen and four children. In 1871 Elizabeth Childs became the infant teacher, and when Pick left in 1873 she became the school's principal teacher. She was aided by two pupil teachers, and by her mother who was the sewing mistress. She in turn was succeeded in 1879 by William Grange. He and his wife Susan moved to Laxton from Norfolk. Their son Cecil was born in the village shortly afterwards. They remained until 1886 when Frank Willis came to Laxton as schoolmaster. He was to stay until his retirement in 1922. His wife, Ruth, worked with him until she retired in 1915.

The major problem for the schoolmasters, and indeed the school trustees after 1870, was to enforce the terms of the legislation on attendance. This was no great difficulty through the winter months, but children were useful hands in the summer, and long before 1870 the tradition had been established of removing them from school to help in tasks about the farms. The master recorded in the school log book on 15 July 1863 that 'many children are now

[56] NAO PR 4093, 4102; SBX/363/5.
[57] NAO PR 4793.

leaving off school for the summer in anticipation of the harvest.' Two weeks later he added that many of the children could not come 'because their parents take them into the fields with them'. The school closed for a month for the harvest holiday, but it still took time to get the children back into school. When it reopened on 7 September, only 17 children attended. The number rose over the following weeks to 28, 45, 49 and finally at the very end of the month to 74. The children were often to be found in September and October either helping out with a late harvest, or gleaning, or potato and fruit picking. Occasionally children disappeared at other times of the year. In February 1869, for example, many children were absent 'bean dropping'.

The tradition was so well established in Laxton that there was no immediate change after 1870. On 17 July 1871 Daniel Pick noted in the school log book that various children had failed to attend: 'many I find are weeding the corn,' and when school resumed in October four pupils were potato picking and 'a great many boys absent plough driving'. The summer break came later in subsequent years in an effort to persuade the parents to keep their children in school, but it made little difference. After the wet summer of 1872 Pick opened the school on 23 September but was obliged to close it for an extra week to allow the children to continue working. Gradually the legislation was tightened up with further Acts in 1876 and 1880, but even moving the harvest holiday made little difference. On 29 July 1887 the master recorded in the log book that 'although the hay harvest is finished the attendance does not improve as the corn has ripened so very rapidly owing to the hot dry weather that some of the farmers have commenced harvest.' As late as 1902 attendance was still poor in mid-September because 'there is a great deal of corn out,' but the problems had certainly lessened during the 1890s; indeed, in 1903 the school reopened on 21 September and on the following day all the pupils were present. Willis obviously regarded it as significant that in 1911 all children were in school on 2 August, immediately before the holiday and despite the harvest, and that they were all there again on 11 September.

The school log books begin in 1862 when there were 62 children on the roll. Numbers stayed at around this level until the passing of the Education Act of 1870, after which they rose rapidly to about 100 early in 1871. (The census records 92 scholars in 1861, but 119 in 1871 despite population decline in the village.) In 1877 97 children were on the roll, and six years later the school was sanctioned by the Education Department to increase to 140 pupils.[58] Numbers probably never reached this figure, although there were 123 on the role in 1897. Two years later the situation changed considerably. With the opening of a new school at Egmanton one-third of the pupils left the school and numbers on the Laxton roll fell to 65. Willis and his wife received an annual salary of £140 based on the assumption that they were teaching 60 pupils, but as

[58] NAO SBX/363/5.

numbers fell due to a 'decrease in the population of Laxton' their income declined accordingly. In 1907 the average attendance was 18 in the infants department and 28 in the mixed senior school, and by 1914 the Willises, together with their daughter Barbara Willis, who received a salary of £15 from 1909, were teaching 50 pupils.[59]

The school day lasted from nine in the morning until four in the afternoon, during which the pupils were taught a variety of subjects. Discipline was exercised by the master. Frank Willis occasionally recorded in the log book the punishment imposed on recalcitrants. Two boys were punished in June 1895 for 'catching a gander and pulling out the feathers, during the dinner hour'. In July 1899 a girl from Egmanton was punished for stealing eggs during the dinner hour. She was locked in the cloakroom for half an hour, which Willis considered a short time, and then caned four times on the hand. In February 1907 seven boys were punished for snowballing a girl, and in October 1908 six boys were disciplined 'for ill using a chicken in the yard'.

School holidays included the 5-week summer break, a week in October for Laxton feast (reduced to a couple of days by the end of the century), a few days at Christmas, and Whitsun week. The school was closed occasionally for other reasons. Epidemics were a frequent cause of closure to prevent the children from coming into close contact. These occasions included a week in February 1878, and 3 weeks early in January 1882 when there was an oubtreak of scarlet fever in the village. The school closed for a week in March 1893 as a result of whooping cough, and for 2 weeks in February 1898 due to measles – although the Rural District Council made an order for a 4-week closure. The winter of 1899–1900 was the worst of all. The school was closed for the last 2 months of 1899 as a result of scarlet fever. Almost immediately after it reopened the village was hit by an outbreak of influenza in January 1900, and in April the school was closed for 3 weeks because of whooping cough. Similar closures were recorded for measles, 5 weeks in January 1903, and whooping cough, 3 weeks in November 1913.[60]

Additional holidays were allowed for a variety of other reasons. In June 1887 the school was closed for a week to celebrate Queen Victoria's Jubilee, but ten years later the Diamond Jubilee merited only a 3-day break. Occasional days were allowed when the school was used as a polling booth, or, as in 1901, 1911 and 1921, when Willis was census enumerator for the village. The coronation in 1911 brought a further break. Holidays were allowed for ploughing matches in 1910 and 1913, and on occasional days when Willis was away in Southwell acting as Assistant Overseer for the Poor Law. Sometimes the school was closed early, in advance of parish council meetings, or for the half-day holiday on 21 December when the syke grasses were paid for, or even for a

[59] Victoria County History, *Nottinghamshire*, II (1910), p. 26; NAO PR 4794.
[60] NAO SBX/363/5; PR 4794.

couple of hours if Willis had to play the organ for a service in the church. Early
closure was also allowed for the annual school feast prior to the summer
holiday, which was usually held in the Hall grounds, although in 1872 all the
pupils were taken to Thoresby for the day in carts sent from the estate. Finally,
the school occasionally had an outing, as in 1910 when the pupils spent a day
in Mablethorpe.

Frank Willis, the schoolmaster from 1886, was remembered as 'the most
influential character in the whole village', hence presumably his role as overseer
and enumerator. In the 1890s children began in the infants' department under
the tutelage of Miss Florrie Bennett, who became pupil teacher in 1892, and
qualified in 1896. They passed from her care into the hands of Mr Willis, a
gifted teacher and administrator who taught a wide range of subjects and was
best remembered for his musical abilities. His wife taught sewing, knitting and
simple dressmaking to the girls. In Willis's time the school was frequently
awarded excellent merit grants, and the inspectors often referred to the good
attendance and the excellent achievements of the pupils. As an indication of
their popularity, he and his wife were presented with a silver teapot on the
occasion of their silver wedding in May 1907.

Laxton provided no secondary education as such, since that was available in
Tuxford at the grammar school. It was a difficult journey, and the school was
for boys only.[61] Maybe this was why Willis established an evening continuation
school in 1900. It met in the autumn and spring only, the quieter agricultural
seasons, and was aimed at older 'lads'. When classes were due to resume in
October 1906, it was noted in the ledger that 'as there are fewer farm servants
in the village than last year attendance is likely to be lower.' The class seems to
have ceased functioning about 1908.[62]

LOCAL GOVERNMENT

By the second half of the nineteenth century the substantial freeholders who
had played such an important part in eighteenth-century village life had largely
gone. There was still something of a village hierarchy, headed by the vicar and
the schoolmaster, and including the wealthier farmers who held the positions
of local government in the village. Owning a freehold of more or less any size
qualified a man for respect. This was so with George Peck, who owned about 5
acres in the 1890s, and was often seen around in 'a tall, somewhat frowsy silk
hat and frock coat', and enjoyed local standing because he owned his own
house and some cottages. He was sometimes asked to draw up wills. Another

[61] *Life at Laxton*, pp. 46–52.
[62] NAO SL/106/1/4.

man respected in the village was Richard Beckitt, who owned 26 acres, and some of the larger farmers also carried weight.[63] Certainly the tasks of running the village had to be carefully handled, especially as these could be time consuming and difficult.

The cost of highway repairs could occasionally rise to more than £100, as in 1843–4 (£192) and 1845–6 (£144). In the latter year 24,500 bricks were purchased from Earl Manvers (and half paid for by him), although the accounts are frustratingly silent on the use to which they were being put. The vestry agreed in 1864 that the roads to the open fields should be kept in good repair and that this should be paid for from receipts at the grass letting. Surviving accounts from the 1880s suggest that Earl Manvers purchased gravel for the road surfaces – more than 360 tons in 1888–9 – and that the parish paid for the work of spreading the materials and making the road. Obviously this was not enough since the August 1890 the vestry voted to make an application to have part of the village highways turnpiked.[64]

The gait-money issue was a particularly sensitive one. Traditionally the sale of grass from the wastes (or sykes) raised money which was distributed among

PLATE 7.4 *Main Street, towards the West Field, early twentieth century. On the left what is today Top Farm, and on the right Town End Farm. Note particularly the gate at the entrance to the West Field – a necessary precaution in the days when animals were grazed in the open fields after harvest – and the unmade road. Older residents remember that animal droppings were once a characteristic of Laxton's roadways. Today the roads are tarmacked, and with few animals moving around the village, they are relatively clean.*

[63] *Life at Laxton*, p. 66; NUMD Ma5E 119.
[64] NAO PR 4107–8, 4093, 4776/1–2.

the 312 gait holders as compensation for their loss of meadow rights. Manvers had acquired the majority of the gaits by the end of the nineteenth century. Each gait conferred 'the right of mowing or taking a portion of the crop of hay two years in every three upon thirty two acres and nine perches of common meadows'. In the course of time, however, instead of a straight division of the gait money between the gait holders, sums were first deducted for other purposes, not merely the fees of the auctioneer but in the 1860s a subscription to the school, and by the 1870s the cost of draining and ditching.[65]

In this way confusion arose over the use of the gait money. By 1907 it was the view of R. W. Wordsworth, the Thoresby agent, that 'the first charge on the value of "gaits" is the keeping the watercourses and roads in good order, and [if] this was properly attended to there would be very little surplus to divide amongst the gait owners.' In fact, this was almost certainly a mistaken view, but it led Wordsworth to the conclusion that 'the recipients of gait money have been little better than thieves and robbers for many years, and that the lord of the manor has a very big bill against them which he will never be paid'.[66] Manvers, through Wordsworth, seems to have been claiming that the gait money should all along have been used to maintain the dykes and roads, but this had certainly not always been the case despite the vehemence of the argument. A distinction had traditionally existed between highway grass sales on Easter Tuesday, and syke sales.[67] From 1908, however, the common and syke grasses were let together, with 10 per cent of the income going towards repairs.

To pay the costs of local government, annual rates were levied, initially on the basis of Francis Wharton's 1834 survey, but over time on slightly amended values. In 1836 the rateable value of Laxton was £3,252 5s. After falling slightly to £3,109 13s in the 1840s, in 1852 it stood at £3,150 10s, and in 1861 at £3,155. Following the rent rise of the 1860s (chapter 8) the rateable value was reassessed upwards, to £4,978 in 1864 and £5,000 by 1871. Since expenditure did not increase proportionately, the rising rateable value meant fewer rates had to be levied to meet parish costs. County rates continue to be paid from the poor rate, and were usually of the order of £50–£75 annually.[68]

Accounts for the Laxtonian Friendly Society for the five years 1841–5 show that 63 individuals were members of the society, of whom 24 received relief. Of these Thomas Hempsall was the most demanding. He was 60 in 1841, and a labourer, and had been a member of the society since 1818. He was on relief throughout these five years. No one else could approach this record. Another labourer, living in Weston, was relieved for 31 weeks in 1844, and for 20 weeks up until his death in 1845, and long reliefs prior to death were also recorded in two other cases. This was not always the case however, since William

[65] NAO PR 4102, 4104; NUMD Ma 2P/96a.
[66] NUMD Ma 2C/162/542, 619.
[67] NAO PR 4102, 4104; NUMD Ma 2C/162/710.
[68] NAO PR 4009–18; PUS/1/7/1–4.

Sampson, an agricultural labourer, received relief for 33 weeks in 1842 and a further 10 weeks in 1843, but he recovered, dying in 1870 at the age of 59. Mostly relief was short term; in 65 per cent of cases the individual was helped for 4 weeks or less.[69]

Those without the benefit of insurance had to rely on the Poor Law. As table 7.10 shows, the majority of relief was paid outdoors, rather than by sending the pauper to the workhouse. Information on parish poor relief survives for only this 20-year period, during which costs were probably relatively low since these were generally prosperous years for agricultural workers. Rates are likely to have risen in the 1870s and especially in the 1880s. The fate of a few individuals is known. In 1853 William Bennett was granted relief of 1s 6d a week. He was an agricultural labourer aged 48, with a wife but no children at home,

TABLE 7.10 *Expenditure on poor relief in Laxton 1848–1867*

Year	Income	Indoor relief	Outdoor relief	Lunatics	Union charges	Other costs*	Total[†]
1848–9	197	14	102	21	41	6	204
1849–50	220	8	78	21	52	89	252
1850–1	296	5	84	21	46	30	255
1851–2	221	8	75	20	42	3	200
1852–3	140	6	76	18	42	1	195
1853–4	206	7	78	18	47	4	209
1854–5	211	3	96	19	50	4	229
1855–6	240	–	82	23	43	4	215
1856–7	230	23	75	23	46	5	243
1857–8	250	35	69	23	48	13	258
1858–9	260	31	77	22	47	11	247
1859 (½ year)	132	19	62	13	28	6	164
1860 (½ year)	236	20	53	10	26	5	166
1861–2	255	31	83	19	53	8	270
1862–3	250	19	71	50	54	15	268
1863–4	275	16	83	19	53	8	270
1864–5	215	8	73	–	68	21	225
1865–6	230	13	73	–	78	22	249
1866–7	250	14	77	–	73	18	245
1867 (½ year)	130	7	39	–	36	12	121

* Includes occasional and smaller items such as registration charges, medical and vaccination fees and, between 1849 and 1850, £106 17s 6d in three instalments on an emigration loan
† Includes payment to county rates, see text
Source: NAO PUS/1/7/1–4.

[69] NAO QDC/4/4.

and he must later have been moved to the workhouse at Southwell, where he died in 1855. A sadder case, but one which points to the harsh reality of village life, concerned Thomas Bartram. He appears in all the censuses, and was farming 20 acres or so. He never married, and by 1881 he was 71 and probably ailing. His brother and sister had both died, and he seems to have had no other direct family in the village. When he himself died, early in 1886 at the age of 75, it was in the Union workhouse.

The records are not sufficiently detailed to work out the overall cost of local government in Laxton during these years. The poor rate was clearly the most costly part of expenditure, but coupled with church, highway and county rates, the total assessed on the village can seldom have been less than £400 annually. In 1849–50 and 1850–51 Laxton rates raised for church and highways, poor and county, £446 and £467. With a rateable value standing at £3,150 this meant an annual overall rate of 2s 10d to 3s. The lower figure may be most accurate because part of the church expenses was met from income from church property. It was almost certainly collected on four quarterly rates, fixed according to anticipated costs.[70] In 1860–1 rates of $3\frac{1}{2}$, $7\frac{1}{2}$d, 6d and 5d raised £289. Sometimes only two or three rates were probably needed, especially since the annual cost of local government did not greatly increase before the 1870s. Rising rents changed the nature of local rating. By 1870, when the rateable value had increased to more than £5,000, three separate rates of 6d, 3d and 9d raised £376.

[70]   NAO PR 4114–18.

Chapter Eight

Prosperity and Improvement, 1840–1873

If the 1820s and 1830s had been uncertain decades for English agriculture, the years from the mid-1840s to the early 1870s are often regarded as one of the most prosperous periods for the farming community. Demand for the produce of the land kept pace with urbanization, and the movement of dairy products and meat was greatly aided by the spread of the railway network. 'High farming', the term coined to describe the improved husbandry of these years, meant the introduction of new fertilizers and the employment of mechanical reapers (among other developments) to bring about a rapid increase in yields. On the heavier soils high farming meant – above all – improved drainage. As late as 1840 in Nottinghamshire, areas like Laxton, on the heavier soils of the county, still relied on traditional forms of farming with small farms because these were the least susceptible to improvement through the new techniques introduced on the lighter soils. After 1846 the situation changed, but not particularly in Laxton. Although some drainage work was undertaken, this was not in the open fields where the traditional ridge and furrow was still the means of running off water. It may have been during these decades that major improvements were taking place on the great Dukeries estates of north Nottinghamshire, and particularly on the Manvers estate, but these did not spread to Laxton. Even so, the farmers enjoyed moderate prosperity in the mid-nineteenth century, and Manvers was able to push up rents quite sharply in the 1860s.[1]

THE ENCLOSURE OF MOORHOUSE

Most contemporaries accepted that to enjoy the full benefits of these agricultural developments land ought to be enclosed. For much of England this was no

---

[1] A. C. Pickersgill, 'The Agricultural Revolution in Bassetlaw, Nottinghamshire, 1750–1873', unpublished Ph.D. thesis, University of Nottingham, 1979, pp. 495–7, 557–90.

longer a problem. Nationwide 86 per cent of all Parliamentary enclosure took place before 1830 and the figure was nearly 94 per cent in Nottinghamshire. Only 3.6 per cent of all open-field arable enclosure by Act of Parliament in the county occurred after 1829.[2] Already by 1840, Laxton was something of an anachronism, and it is hardly surprising to find contemporaries expecting enclosure to take place. Egmanton and Kirton were enclosed by legislation of 1821, Ossington by acts of 1803 and 1836, and Norwell in 1826 and Wellow in 1840. It seemed natural that Laxton would follow. George Chapman, an absentee freeholder living in East Retford, with 30 acres mainly in Moorhouse, wrote to Manvers's agent in 1841 asking whether a meeting of Laxton landowners advertised for 29 June 'has any reference to a contemplated enclosure of the common lands'. If it did, he for one was in favour.[3] As Chapman well knew, this was a meeting in connection with tithe commutation, but it was these prolonged and acrimonious negotiations which brought enclosure back on to the agenda for the first time since 1815–16.

In January 1844 exploratory discussions began with a view to promoting the enclosure of Laxton and Eakring. William Clutton opened on behalf of Manvers by proposing land exchanges with Scarbrough to consolidate the two owners' respective holdings in Laxton and Eakring. Laxton, where Manvers would acquire land, would then be enclosed. Scarbrough's agent countered by insisting that the parishes should be enclosed simultaneously. These conditions were unacceptable to Manvers who was happy to act in the case of Laxton, but unwilling to countenance the idea of simultaneous enclosure for the two parishes. Letters were exchanged over a period of weeks but neither owner was prepared to compromise, and negotiations came to an end when Scarbrough's agent told his opposite number at Thoresby:

[Lord Scarbrough's] view is that by means of previous exchanges, or agreements to exchange in each, such a preponderance and consolidation of property would have been given to Lord Manvers in Laxton and to himself in Eakring as would have enabled each to effect those necessary exchanges with the other proprietors as would have almost amounted to an enclosure of each, and certainly must have decreased both expense and time in making the other divisions and fencing the remaining property.[4]

In truth Laxton and Eakring were the innocent victims of differences between the two earls. Why the eighth Earl of Scarbrough and the second Earl Manvers should have been cool towards one another is unclear. They had certainly had some political disagreements in the 1830s, although neither was usually so passionate about elections as to blind them to their best economic interests. Possibly it was merely a clash of personalities, but whatever the cause of the

[2] Michael Turner, *English Parliamentary Enclosure* (Folkestone, 1980), pp. 190–5.
[3] NUMD MaB/175/337.
[4] NUMD MaB 213.

problems, enclosure was effectively ruled out during their lifetimes. Not that the possibility was ever entirely excluded; in 1849 Thomas Huskinson sent details to Clutton about the terms which would have to be met before the Enclosure Commissioners in London would accept an agreement. The information was sent because 'it may be useful in the application which you contemplate making in respect of Laxton'.[5]

These problems did not apply to Moorhouse where Scarbrough owned no property. According to George Chapman, writing in 1843, there was a 'general desire of the parties interested' to see Moorhouse enclosed, and this was expected to have 'most beneficial consequences'. Moorhouse, or as it was sometimes revealingly known Moorhouse-in-the-Bogs, was poor farming territory. It stood at the junction of two streams which joined up to the east of the hamlet. In an effort to improve conditions Manvers spent £151 in 1841 'cutting a deep drain through the meadows at Moorhouse', but this was only a partial solution to the problems.[6]

Chapman's initiative did not elicit a particularly positive response from Thoresby. William Clutton told him that 'I do not think he [Manvers] will at present entertain the question and for various reasons I should not now feel warranted in advising his Lordship to do so.'[7] Despite this denial of interest, the tithe agreement of 1843 offered the opportunity for a fresh start and the General Enclosure Act of 1845 provided a framework for possible legislation. The Act created an Enclosure Commission which appointed assistant commissioners and surveyors to carry out local enquiries when an enclosure was proposed. They were also responsible for the actual work involved in an enclosure. Even with these encouragements it was not until 1847 that serious negotiations commenced, and then the initiative came from John Evelyn Denison of Ossington.

In July 1847 Denison's agent wrote to Clutton on behalf of his employer 'who has asked me to put the matter of the Moorhouse enclosure in train', enclosing one of the forms of enquiry required by the enclosure commissioners. Manvers's signature was needed or nothing could be done – 'his lordship having more than 2/3 of the interest it cannot be set a going without him'.[8] The response was not immediately encouraging. As Clutton wrote in reply: 'Earl Manvers although he entertains the question of the inclosure of Moorhouse says he will not move in the matter until Mr Denison has talked the matter over with him, and added "You may tell Mr Denison's agent until Mr Denison starts the subject to me I shall do nothing".'[9] Denison can hardly have been elated; after all, it was because Manvers had refused to back him in the 1837 South

5 NUMD MaB/204/1b.
6 White's *Directory of Nottinghamshire* (Sheffield, 1844), pp. 732–3.
7 NUMD M.4009.
8 NUMD MaB/215/76.
9 NUMD MaB/215/89.

Nottinghamshire election that he had withdrawn without a contest. None the less, putting aside the bitterness that he had undoubtedly felt as a result of his treatment in 1837, Denison went ahead with an application to the enclosure commissioners.[10]

The formal application for the enclosure of Moorhouse offers a pen portrait of the hamlet as it was in the 1840s. It covered 114 acres, 'in six different pieces being intersected with inclosures, but it lies remarkably well for inclosing'. There were 17 houses in the hamlet, and a population of 77. The houses were said to be 'generally occupied by small farmers and scattered at different distances on or near the borders of a piece of common land containing about 17 acres'. Everyone living in Moorhouse was engaged in agriculture. Ten individuals owned land in the hamlet, of whom two (owning approximately one-tenth of the land by value) were not party to the agreement. Finally,

the advantages will be great for the quantity of land. The commons are undrained, covered with thistles and so overstocked as to be of little value. The arable land being in scattered pieces in the several open fields subject to the common stock is farmed to great disadvantage. The improvement both to the open and enclosed land will lead to profitable employment for labourers and materially increase the value of the land.[11]

In January 1848 the enclosure commissioners made out a provisional order for enclosure and announced a meeting in March for freeholders to signify their consent or to voice their objections. No record of this meeting has survived, but at a meeting in September 1848 it was agreed that Thomas Huskinson of Epperstone should be appointed valuer, at a fee of 10s an acre. It was also accepted that the tithe survey would not be an accurate enough document upon which to base enclosure, and that a new survey would be needed.[12]

More ominously, a decision still had to be taken about the claim by George Chapman to the lordship of the manor. Chapman had arrived in Moorhouse sometime after 1820 by acquiring a small estate which Manvers had refused to purchase when Pendock Neale put it on the market in 1805. Neale had been holding out for a high price by claiming that the land carried with it the lordship of the manor. Chapman renewed the claim when he heard of the moves afoot to enclose Moorhouse. The Neales, he argued, had obtained the lordship with the property in Moorhouse they bought from Sir Bryan Broughton in 1703. He told William Clutton 'the lordship clearly pertained to the property in my possession, and certain payments were due to former owners of this property as lords of the manor.' However, when Chapman's claim was heard at a meeting in October 1848 it was disputed by the Thoresby agent, who produced

[10] My thanks are due to Dr J. R. Fisher for help with disentangling the political rivalries of these years.
[11] NUMD MaB/215/65.
[12] NUMD MaB/201/37, 215/67, 68, 198/2.

evidence to show that since 1744 'Moorhouse has been treated as part of the Duke of Kingston's manor of Laxton.' Further investigation would have revealed that the precedent was longer established than this, but the point was taken.[13] Chapman's case was dismissed and the Moorhouse Enclosure Act went through Parliament in 1849.[14]

Work was soon in hand improving the hamlet prior to the drawing up of an enclosure award. Thomas Huskinson told Clutton in June 1849 that 'the bore hole and the short drains connected with it, have completely drained that portion of the common crossed by the public road, and that we are now ready to lay in the materials and complete the roads throughout the parish'. Huskinson was satisfied with the work undertaken, and although he had to endure complaints from the freeholders 'that in many points less costly and substantial works would have sufficed' he was not discouraged: 'this of course I expected, and shall feel very well satisfied if I meet with no stronger reproof.' He had spent £490, and bought bricks, lime and sand for £170. He expected the total cost to be £1,060 which would exceed the estimate by £160. By the beginning of 1850 his costs had risen to £854. Despite this enthusiastic beginning it was not until 1859 that Huskinson finished his work. In August that year he drew up the award, which was finally enrolled on 9 May 1860.[15] It had been a costly business at £12 10s an acre, with considerable outlay on dykes, hedgeplanting and fence erection (table 8.1). Although unit costs increased the smaller the amount of land enclosed, Moorhouse was a particularly expensive development.

TABLE 8.1 *Moorhouse enclosure costs,*
1849–1856

Year	Cost		
	£	s	d
1849	916	16	$9\frac{1}{2}$
1850	356	15	$2\frac{1}{2}$
1851	7	10	6
1852	30	10	10
1853	8	7	$11\frac{1}{2}$
1856	107	11	$1\frac{1}{2}$
	1,427	12	5

Source: Thoresby Estate Accounts.

[13] NUMD MaB/201/14, 215/72, 74, 28, 30; 198/2.
[14] 11 & 12 Victoria c. 27.
[15] NUMD MaB/215/85, 198/1/5, 14; Ma 2P/101.

Why the business took so long is not clear, but it may have had something to do with changes in landownership during the 1850s. The apparent threat to the Manvers-Scarbrough duopoly posed by the Denisons in the early years of the century seemed to have passed by 1812, although the family showed no inclination to part with their Laxton property. It was included among the estates settled in 1827 when John Denison's eldest son John Evelyn Denison (1800–73), married Lady Charlotte Cavendish Bentinck, the third daughter of the Duke of Portland.[16] John Evelyn Denison was primarily interested in pursuing his political career. In the House of Commons he represented South Nottinghamshire in the 1830s and North Nottinghamshire from 1857 until 1872. Throughout the latter period he was Speaker of the Commons. This did not mean he neglected his estates, and having instigated the enclosure proceedings for Moorhouse he set about increasing his landed property in the hamlet by buying out the other freeholders. As table 8.2 shows, starting with George Chapman's freehold, he acquired a series of small properties during the 1850s, including the 20 acres which had been owned by the church since Mark Pierce's

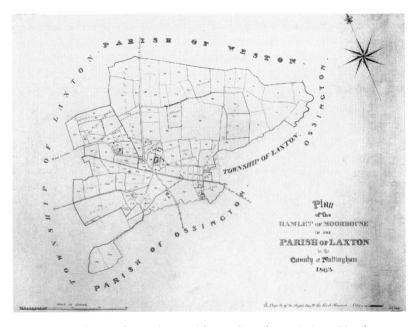

PLATE 8.1 *Moorhouse after enclosure. After prolonged negotiations, Moorhouse was finally enclosed in 1860. This map was drawn in 1863, and shows how the land was divided, and the chief owners. It also shows that the houses were more scattered in the hamlet than in Laxton village and, of course, that there were many fewer. The surveyor was J. S. Long.*

16 NUMD DDBG/10–11.

TABLE 8.2 *Denison purchases in Laxton and Moorhouse, 1849–1865*

Date	Property	Acreage a	r	p	Vendor	Price (£)
1849	Moorhouse	21	3	02	George Chapman	1,450
1852	Moorhouse	2	3	26	William Clarke	165
1853	Moorhouse	20	3	14	Ecclesiastical Commissioners	461
1853	Moorhouse	24	1	02	Thomas Jepson Berwick	980
1853	Moorhouse	10	3	14	Thomas Fowke	660
1853	Moorhouse	13	0	02	William Baines	342
1853	Moorhouse	4	0	04	Thomas Spragging Godfrey	270
1854	Moorhouse	10	3	25	John Chappell	715
1856	Moorhouse	8	2	00	Ann Gray *et al.*	605
1861	Laxton	19	0	12	John Proctor	900
1862	Laxton and Moorhouse	56	2	33	Henry Savile Esq.	3,021
1863	Moorhouse	13	1	31	John Barlow	894
1863	Laxton	19	1	38	William Pinder	1,212
1863	Laxton and Moorhouse	1 4	0 3	12 01	George Bartle	610
1864	Laxton and Moorhouse		3 3	12 12	George Lee	346
1865	Moorhouse	3	3	27	Thomas Smith	158
		237	0	27		£12,789

Note: Some of the purchases included land beyond the borders of Laxton and Moorhouse but sold as a job lot. The acquisition from Proctor, for example, included 7 acres in Ompton. Acreage figures cannot always be ascertained accurately from the deeds.

Source: NUMD Denison of Ossington MSS.

day. Some of these acquisitions included land beyond the borders of Moor-house, but they had the effect of making him the major landowner in the hamlet.

THE 1862 SURVEY

The unwillingness of the two major landowners to reach an agreement which would have led to the enclosure of Laxton's open fields was both a reminder of the opportunity missed by the second Duke of Kingston when the Broughton estate was sold in 1750, and an impediment to improvement, but it did not make change impossible. Outlay on drainage by the Thoresby estate totalled

£1,187 during the 1840s and £1,300 during the 1850s. Only in Kneesall, and during the 1850s in Edwinstowe, was more spent on manors in the Thoresby collection. In 1843 the accounts record a payment of £15 to Michael Saxelby, the tenant of Crosshill Farm, for 'drain tiles', and an allowance against rent of £19 16s 'for draining'. Much greater sums were spent in the years which followed; examples between 1846 and 1864 include £471 at Brockilow, £448 at Westwood, £190 on William Harpham's farm at Moorhouse, and £100 on the Whittingtons' open-field farm. The major outlay was on the enclosed farms. These sums may seem considerable, but drainage was an expensive investment, and by 1862 no more than 13 per cent of the enclosed land (and none of the open-field land) had been drained.[17] Real progress elsewhere awaited enclosure, but this was out of the question without a change of landlords. The opportunity for a fresh start came in 1860: in 1856 Scarbrough died and his Nottinghamshire estates descended to Henry Savile, the second of his illegitimate sons; four years later the third Earl Manvers succeeded at Thoresby.

The new owner of Thoresby was anxious to see just what he had inherited, particularly as rents had not been raised for some years. Thomas Huskinson, who had overseen the enclosure of Moorhouse, was asked to survey the Nottinghamshire estates, and in his report he pointed in no uncertain terms to the urgent need for enclosure in Laxton:

the one impediment to all improvement is the existence of the right of common and the uninclosed condition of the open fields. It is quite melancholy to see so fine a property as this capable of being made one of the best estates in the district comparatively unproductive and left subject to rights and usages so ancient and barbarous that their origin is lost in antiquity, and so adverse to improvement that the only two cases now existing in the Midland counties are Laxton and Eakring.

Yet reading between the lines of the survey it becomes apparent that maybe things were not quite as bad as Huskinson wanted them to be. He admitted that cultivation was 'as good as under the disadvantages of open fields and distance from buildings can reasonably be expected', and that several of the larger tenants practised husbandry which 'would do credit to any estate'. After two decades of expenditure on drainage much of the enclosed land was drained with pipes and tiles. Even without enclosure consolidation had continued. As tenancies became vacant, strips were gradually reallocated within the fields to create larger blocks. such a piecemeal policy was justifiable on the grounds that throughout the years of agricultural depression the level of arrears at Laxton was not as great as on Earl Manvers's enclosed farms at neighbouring Kneesall, which lay on similar soil. Under the circumstances it was arguable that

---

[17] Pickersgill, 'Agricultural Revolution', pp. 845–7; Wood, thesis, p. 386.

enclosure might have been an imprudent course to follow.[18] However, Huskinson was unrepentant: 'the lands are inconveniently allotted, without any regard to the convenience of the tenant, or to the increased rent which would accrue to the owner by more economical management [. . .]. It is a common case that a tenant occupying a farm less than 200 acres would require the greater part of a day to inspect it.' In his view, until enclosure took place no substantial improvement was possible and 'the present miserable waste of time, labour and money must continue.'[19]

The major problem highlighted by Huskinson was the layout of farms:

It is impossible a land owner can derive the full value from an estate so occupied, or that under such conditions land can yield that amount of rent to the owner, employment to the labourer, or produce to the consumer, which is on general grounds desirable, but which is only possible under larger holdings with every appliance which larger capital, the best implements and most economical management of land and buildings can produce.

A comparison of the 1862 survey with the tithe apportionment shows that during the intervening years one farm of more than 100 acres had been broken up, but that the percentage of land in farms of 51 acres or more was the same between the two dates (table 8.3). Both in 1839 and 1862 there were 64 holders of 10 acres or less in the village, occupying no more than 6 per cent of the acreage. Six of the twenty holdings of 24 acres or less included a house or cottage but no other building. All the other holdings had farm buildings in addition to the house, even if many were badly arranged and in a poor state of repair. One of the holdings, which included a shop, was let with 47 acres and the Dovecote Inn. Most of the holdings included common rights. The mainly enclosed farms on the parish perimeters were between 120 and 204 acres, and larger than the main open-field farms.[20]

Equally important was the fragmentation of land as a result of the scattering of the strips. None of the main Manvers farms lay within a ring fence, and most were divided into between 26 and 61 separate blocks of land. The most consolidated were the outlying farms, while Crosshill was exceptional for a village farm in having two blocks of enclosed land – 91 acres in a ring fence adjoining the farm and 83 acres in a ring fence 1 mile east of the village. George Saxelby, the tenant, had just 11 acres in the open fields. By 1910 when the farmer was William Merrils the farm had no strips in the open fields, and the same is true today. More commonly, the medieval fragmentation remained. This did not imply an equal division; the old territorial differences remained. Unenclosed land was not divided in equal proportions between the fields, and in most cases

[18] Wood, thesis, pp. 408–9.
[19] This paragraph and much of what follows is based on the 1862 survey: NUMD Ma S 16.
[20] Wood, thesis, p. 466.

TABLE 8.3 *Laxton Farms in 1839 and 1862*

Acreage	1839 No.	Acreage	%	1862 No.	Acreage	%
100+	15	2224	59.0	14	2105	55.6
51–99	7	497	13.2	8	620	16.4
21–50	15	508	13.5	12	416	11.0
11–20	12	177	4.7	14	212	5.6
6–10	17	146	3.0	20	165	4.4
1–5	22	64	1.7	22	61	1.6
Under 1	25	6	0.2	22	5	0.1
Other		27	0.7		81	2.2
Manvers in hand		118	3.1		118	3.1
	113	3767	100.0	112	3783	100.0
Occupiers of common rights		150			150	
		3917			3933	

Sources: NAO AT 79/1A; NUMD Ma S 16.

the largest proportion of land was located in the field nearest to the farmstead, an arrangement probably reflecting the consolidation of open-field strips during a long period of time before 1862.

The structural pattern was extremely complex overall, and in Thomas Huskinson's eyes capable of much improvement. He regarded small arable farms as unsatisfactory because they were often over-equipped with farm buildings, thus incurring higher estate management and maintenance costs than larger holdings. Huskinson complained bitterly of the bad repair and poor arrangement of farm buildings, and argued that improved farming could be achieved only on substantial farms with adequate buildings. 'In any rearrangement of the estate,' he wrote of Jane Peatfield's holding, 'this farm should be consolidated and enlarged . . . the present site [is] suitable for the erection of better buildings.' Possibly the cost of drainage had diverted money away from farm building repairs over the previous two decades on the Manvers estate, although a new wagon shed was partly financed for John Keyworth in 1847, new farm buildings costing more than £500 were built for William Harpham in Moorhouse in 1857, and £278 was spent re-equipping Richard Harpham's Laxton farm the following year.

Huskinson must have been disappointed by the lack of response to his initiative at least in terms of farm rationalization. Farms which he believed should be discontinued as separate units, with their buildings being pulled down and their houses turned into labourers' cottages, continued to be let on substantially similar terms. One was divided during this period. When the Whittingtons went bankrupt in 1864 their farm, which Huskinson described as being mainly in two compact parts, was split up, but not in the way he had envisaged. 'I recommend,' he wrote in 1862, 'at the earliest possible opportunity the most distant land should be detached from this holding and annexed to William Pinder's farm, where the buildings are adequate and convenient.' With the Whittingtons' demise however, fourteen existing tenants were offered a total of 132 acres, the most substantial parcels were 35 (rather than 60) acres to William Pinder, 32 acres to John Keyworth and 28 acres to Mrs Peatfield. Nine of the fourteen offers were taken up as they stood, two were refused (including John Keyworth), two other farmers received more than they were originally offered, and three tenants not in the original list were added to the group. Of these William Quibell junior took 29 acres, which must have been the bulk of the property offered to Keyworth. It had originally been intended to redistribute 132 acres but in the final analysis 138 were split between existing tenants.[21]

Although Huskinson's major recommendations were largely ignored, some efforts were made as tenancies ended to consolidate the holdings in outlying fields, and strips were re-allotted to increase their size and eliminate the need for farmers to turn the plough on each others' 'lands'. These changes did not necessarily encourage improved farming practices. Here the evidence is frustratingly vague. No papers have survived of individual farmers, and Thoresby tenancy agreements did not stipulate the course of husbandry to be followed in any detail. Consequently we cannot be certain that improved techniques were not introduced, but from what little evidence there is, Laxton was clearly not in the forefront of agricultural progress.

The most obvious restriction on progress was drainage. We have already seen that probably no more than 13 per cent of the enclosed land was drained by 1862, and the open fields, which Huskinson regarded as 'the best portion of the arable land' remained untouched. We also know that the only 'improvements' noted in the tithe papers were some turnip fallows in Moorhouse. Against this evidence we can set the annual returns to the Ministry of Agriculture which began in 1866. The Board of Trade began the annual collection of statistics that year, and it has since taken place each June. Until 1917 the information was collected on a voluntary basis, and although the Laxton farmers seem to have been generally cooperative the early returns probably omitted some parts of the parish. Returns were collected from each farm, and

[21] NUMD MaB/181/644; 206/15.

used to prepare parish summaries. The information gathered from the farmers was then destroyed. The returns covered land holdings, crop acreages, and livestock, and although comparison over time is complicated by changes in the procedures for collecting information, they provide an unrivalled source from which to test long-term trends. Placed alongside evidence from the tithe survey the picture is of a village set in its farming ways.

According to the tithe survey of 1839 the parish of Laxton was divided between 1,965 acres under arable crops, 1,399 acres of pasture and meadow, and 341 acres of common and woodland. The survey detailed the agricultural produce of approximately 2,200 acres, of which 478 acres were in wheat, 240 acres were in oats, and 237 acres were in peas and beans. Apart from 5 acres described as turnip fallow, the rest of the acreage was pasture. These figures confirm the fact that crops were grown in areas outside of the open fields since with consolidation and the gradual erosion of the fields only about 900 acres were left by 1903 (see table 9.5).

The first agricultural return of 1866 suggests that little change had taken place over the previous twenty-seven years. Altogether the return covered 3,044 acres, of which 1,866 were arable, and 1,178 were under grass. (The figure of 1,866 includes 472 acres of fallow, which presumably represented the third field in that particular year, and makes for comparability with the 1839 statistics.) The crops included 536 acres of wheat, 193 acres of barley, 98 acres of oats, 125 acres of beans and 178 acres of peas. Wheat represented 47 per cent of the total, and by contrast with the seventeenth and eighteenth centuries it seems certain from the acreages that the modern practice already operated whereby one of the open fields was in wheat and the other crops were in the second field. In addition, 15 acres of potatoes were grown in 1866, 82 acres of turnips and 166 acres of other crops. The acreage under grass had not changed greatly from the 1,399 acres of 1839. The figure in 1866 was 1,178, but this may have been on the low side since 1,572 acres of grass were returned in 1870. Of this figure approximately 1,000 acres were in permanent grass closes. Only 182 acres were returned as temporary grasses for hay in 1865, but 530 acres in 1870.[22] However these figures are read, they do not suggest a great increase in productivity. Of course they tell us nothing about fertilizers and machinery, but Laxton was almost certainly not in the forefront of progress in this area. The undrained open fields were a barrier to progress, but crops were grown much more widely in Laxton – although on inferior land in Huskinson's view. It was the general prosperity of farming, and the enteprise of a few individuals, which enabled rents to rise and some farms to be consolidated.

[22] PRO MAF/68/51, 52.

THE 1860S LAND EXCHANGES

The third Earl Manvers was ready to revive the dormant negotiations on land exchanges in order to create conditions favourable to enclosure. Where his father had been primarily concerned with the Saviles, the new earl also had to take into account the emergence of the Denisons as substantial landholders on the eastern side of the parish (see table 8.2). In the course of the 1860s Manvers carried through two exchange deals. By the first deal Denison was given land in Moorhouse in exchange for land in Laxton, and the second deal sorted out the disagreements with the Saviles over Laxton and Eakring.

The first deal to be struck was with the Denisons. Horncastle, the Thoresby agent, wrote on behalf of Manvers to Denison's agent in March 1861:

The present impression appears to be that it would not be advisable for Lord Manvers to part with the whole of his lands in Moorhouse, and that if the proposal for an exchange be entertained it should not extend to any of his Lordship's lands lying on the Laxton side of the Weston Road. Also that the equivalent to be given should be confined to the parish of Laxton alone.[23]

This was not a particularly promising opening, and the negotiations proved to be long and complicated. However, in December 1865 an agreement acceptable to the Enclosure Commissioners was approved. Denison was to transfer to Manvers a total of just over 80 acres, of which less than an acre was in Moorhouse and the rest in Laxton. The Laxton property was in 18 separate holdings, of which the largest was William Harpham's 22 acres. In return, Denison received 64 acres from Manvers of which 20 were in Laxton and 44 in Moorhouse. Denison was left with the 74-acre Hartshorn Farm, which lay beyond the open fields to the south of the parish, and Straw Hall Farm (24 acres), together with a close of $8\frac{1}{2}$ acres near to Knapeney, a total of 107 acres altogether.[24]

Before this deal had been completed, negotiations were reopened on the delicate matter of exchanging land in Laxton and Eakring with Henry Savile. In 1846 the family property consisted of 714 acres in eleven separate farms varying between 6 and 165 acres. From this total 57 acres were sold to Denison in 1862 (table 8.2) including a farm of 34 acres and a number of outlying holdings attached to other farms.[25] This left a total holding of 657 acres together with 52 of the 312 gait rights, and various common rights.

Lucius Spooner, acting on behalf of Savile, approached Horncastle in December 1863 to propose a meeting 'to consider the subject of the

[23] NUMD MaB/191/1101.
[24] NUMD Ma 4S 4, MaB/188/1015.
[25] NUMD MaB/187/974.

FIGURE 8.1 *Farm layouts*

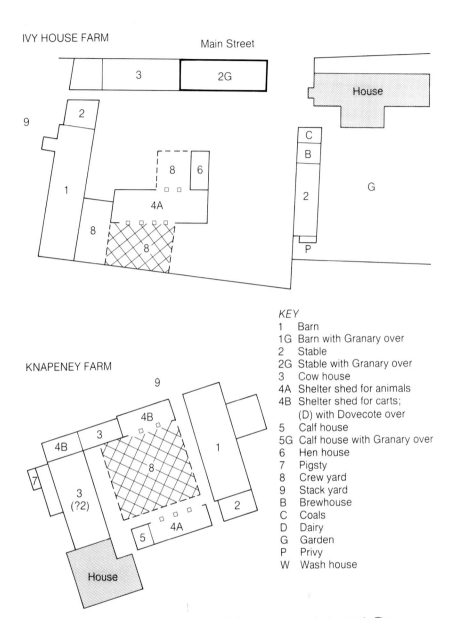

IVY HOUSE FARM

Main Street

3 | 2G

9

2

1

8 | 6

4A

8

8

House

C
B
2
P

G

KNAPENEY FARM

9

4B

3

4B

7

8

3
(?2)

1

2

5

4A

House

KEY
1   Barn
1G   Barn with Granary over
2   Stable
2G   Stable with Granary over
3   Cow house
4A   Shelter shed for animals
4B   Shelter shed for carts;
     (D) with Dovecote over
5   Calf house
5G   Calf house with Granary over
6   Hen house
7   Pigsty
8   Crew yard
9   Stack yard
B   Brewhouse
C   Coals
D   Dairy
G   Garden
P   Privy
W   Wash house

The plans are drawn on the same scale with the compass mark due north. The
buildings are all of brick, and of eighteenth or nineteenth century date. The distinction
between stables and cowhouses is not always clear. With the disappearance of the
work horse after World War Two stables were converted to cater for an increase in
milking herds. Lilac, Crosshill and Ivy House are all located in the village; Knapeney is
one of the detached farms laid out in 1729. On the plans, cross hatching of crew yards
indicates that they were formerly covered. All are now open. Two storey buildings are
shown with heavy outlines.

exchanges with a view to our proceeding if possible'.[26] This time both parties
were anxious to find a solution rather than to give public vent to their
disagreements, and serious negotiations ensued. The complications were
considerable. In September 1865, for example, Spooner wrote one of his
many letters on the subject to Horncastle, requesting information about the
Laxton freeholders:

> I find I have no information of these freeholds of later date than the tithe apportion-
> ment, and no doubt many changes have taken place in them since that time. I need this
> information for insertion of the adjoining ownerships to the Savile lands in the exchange
> plan now preparing. If you have this I make no doubt it will be correct whereas if I
> depend entirely on Laxton people for my information I may go wrong, as I believe many
> of them dont know their own in the open fields.

As a sign of goodwill, and to forward the arrangements as quickly as possible
Spooner offered to supply the same information in regard to Eakring which he
had updated 'to the present date'.[27] Spooner also drew up 'instructions for a
valuation of lands for the purpose of an exchange'. Savile named Thomas
Smith Woolley of South Collingham as valuer, while Manvers relied on
Thomas Huskinson. They were given plans and terriers of the lands it was
proposed to exchange, which they were to value 'for the purpose of ascertain-
ing an equivalent for exchange between the parties'. An exchange proposal was
then drawn up:

> It is proposed that the whole of the Savile lands in Laxton, with the buildings thereon,
> estimated to contain 657a 1r 29p, with the common rights and gates over uninclosed
> lands attached thereto, and the Savile lands in Kirton and Kersal described in the terriers
> and respectively estimated to contain 16a 1r 39p and 5a 2r 34p shall be taken by Earl
> Manvers. It is further proposed that in exchange for the above Earl Manvers shall give
> to the Savile estate the before mentioned lands in Ompton belonging to him and
> estimated to contain 5a 1r 5p, his moiety of the manor of Eakring with the rights
> attached thereto (but not including the advowson of the living if that be attached
> thereto) and such of his lands with the buildings thereon, with the common rights
> belonging in Eakring commencing from the western limit of the parish and extending
> eastwards until the boundary line to be fixed as hereinafter mentioned shall be arrived
> at, as shall be ascertained by valuation to be a fair equivalent for the Lands given up to
> Earl Manvers from the Savile estate.[28]

The transaction was completed in 1867. Savile's Laxton property, together
with land elsewhere – a total of 778 acres – was transferred to Manvers in
exchange for 753 acres in Eakring. The transaction included 52 of the 312 gait

---

[26] NUMD MaB/187/769.
[27] NUMD MaB/187/828.
[28] NUMD MaB/187/860.

rights, together with a number of common rights in Laxton. The land was fragmented even by Laxton standards. One tenant vacated his farm in 1867
because it was too scattered. It proved difficult to relet; as Horncastle told
Manvers:

the farm has been offered to several persons but after viewing its scattered position and
hearing the rent, they all decline it; I therefore thought it would be better to divide it
between the occupiers of adjoining lands.[29]

He eventually managed to let it without pursuing such a course of action, but it
was later combined with the tenancy of Crosshill. The whole transaction was
carefully mapped.[30] It cost Manvers £270, most of which was paid to Huskinson 'for valuing estates and interests appertaining thereto at Laxton and
Eakring'. In effect Manvers, through his acquisition of the Savile and Denison
properties in the 1860s, had effectively put the manor of Laxton back into
single ownership for the first time since the thirteenth century.[31]

As a result of the land exchanges with Savile and Denison, Manvers's
recorded acreage in Laxton increased from 2,462 in 1862 to 3,038. To this
between 1864 and 1871, he added several small freeholds totalling 25 acres, at
a cost of £1,787. In Moorhouse his holding of 93 acres in 1862 declined by 44
acres. However, he did not buy all the freeholds that became available. In 1861
John Proctor's 19 acres in Laxton were sold to Denison (table 8.2).[32] Two years
later when William Pinder put up for sale the Sun Inn together with 20 acres of
land, Denison's agent approached Horncastle to see if Manvers was intending
to buy. Manvers, he was told, would be more than happy for Denison to
acquire it and then to negotiate an exchange with Manvers since 'our trust fund
is not very flourishing just now.'[33] Manvers seems to have bought some land in
the sale – the accounts record the payment of a £58 deposit 'on sundry lots by
private contract', and a £17 deposit 'on lot purchased by Mr Bingham', and the
rentals note the letting of land purchased of William Pinder in 1864. However,
Denison was the major purchaser. Manvers resisted the temptation to pay over
the odds for small parcels of land, possibly because his funds were tight.[34]

Manvers was not only concerned with acquiring land; indeed, land acquisition was merely a prerequisite to enclosure, and in April 1867 Horncastle
approached the enclosure commissioners 'for forms of application for
enclosure', because 'it is in contemplation to inclose a considerable tract of
open field, and commonable lands, in the parishes of Laxton and Kneesall.' To

[29] NUMD MaB/179/567.
[30] NUMD Ma 2P/96a, b.
[31] *Open Fields*, pp. 85–91; Wood, thesis, p. 477.
[32] NUMD MaB/180/590, 602; M.5571,5579; NAO DD.LK/4/331,333.
[33] NUMD Ma 5E 129; MaB/176/416; 5E/130.
[34] NUMD MaB/176/415, MaB/207.

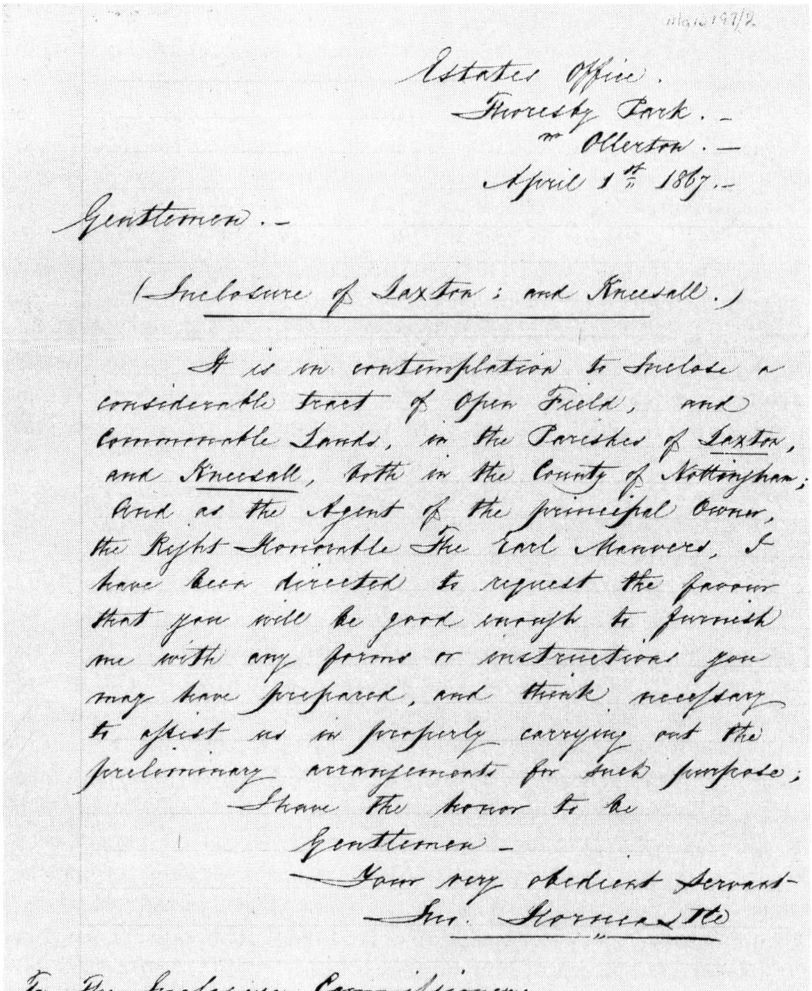

Estates Office.
Thoresby Park. –
nr Ollerton. –
April 1st 1867. –

Gentlemen. –

(Inclosure of Laxton; and Kneesall.)

It is in contemplation to Inclose a considerable tract of Open Field, and Commonable Lands, in the Parishes of Laxton, and Kneesall, both in the County of Nottingham; And as the Agent of the principal Owner, the Right Honorable The Earl Manvers, I have been directed to request the favour that you will be good enough to furnish me with any forms or instructions you may have prepared, and think necessary to assist us in properly carrying out the preliminary arrangements for such purpose;

— I have the honor to be
        Gentlemen –
            Your very obedient Servant
            Jno. Horncastle &c

To The Inclosure Commissioners
    for England and Wales. –
        London. —
    (Inclosure Office. No 3. St James' Square. S.W.)

PLATE 8.2 *The Laxton enclosure proposals of 1867. Following the land exchanges between Manvers and Henry Savile in the mid-1860s plans were proposed for the enclosure of Laxton. This illustration shows a letter written by the Thoresby agent John Horncastle to the Inclosure Commissioners, under whose guidance any enclosure would have had to take place. The information asked for by Horncastle was supplied, but the proposal made no progress.*

the people of Laxton it must have seemed that the long-postponed moment had finally arrived, but once again it was not to be. Yet another start ran into terminal difficulties. The 1869 accounts include a payment of £73 'for plan, references, open lands and commons, Laxton, with reference to enclosure', but that same year. Horncastle confided in the vicar of Laxton that he saw little immediate prospect of enclosure at Laxton, although the public posture remained that enclosure was imminent. This was the line Horncastle pursued when he negotiated in 1870 for some open-field land which was desirable because 'it is surrounded by his Lordship's land', and that 'an enclosure is in contemplation.' He again referred to 'the subject of an enclosure at Laxton' in a letter to the vicar in April 1873, but nothing more was done.[35]

Why did Manvers change his mind? Could he not afford the costs of enclosure or did he choose to direct his financial resources elsewhere? In 1862 Thomas Huskinson had estimated that it would cost £8,555 to enclose Laxton. This included the building of three new farmhouses, and the drainage of the 627 acres of open-field land. The estimated annual return was £548, giving nearly $6\frac{1}{2}$ per cent on the outlay. Borrowed over a twenty-five year period, the investment would give Manvers or his successor an improved estate at no cost and with an increased rental income. By the time the land exchanges were completed in 1867 even sums of £8,500 may have been difficult to raise. In 1864 Manvers began building the present Thoresby Hall, on which he eventually ran up a bill for £170,000. This was no small sum even for the owner of more than 38,000 acres yielding around £35,000 a year annually during the 1860s. The estate accounts do not give much away, but Horncastle's letters contain hints that this outlay was stretching resources to the full.[36] In 1869, for example, he told the vicar of Laxton that 'I think there is little probability of an Inclosure taking place at Laxton, until the great and expensive works at Thoresby are nearly completed.'[37]

Other evidence also suggests financial problems. When two small purchases of open-field land were being considered in 1870 Horncastle pointed out to the solicitors that it would be necessary to borrow the purchase money from 'Lady Manvers's trustees'. In 1871 Manvers bought the Sun Inn for £500, and the following year he paid £40 for a cottage in the village. His only other ventures into the Laxton land market before the 1890s came in 1879 when he exchanged land to facilitate the building of a new vicarage, and 1880 when he

[35] NUMD MaB/197/2, 23, 56.

[36] The estate accounts include payments annually between 1864 and 1877 on the rebuilding of Thoresby and related projects, with a balance of several thousand pounds to Earl Manvers. On this evidence Manvers was not in any difficulty. However, the building accounts show that each year a substantial part of the cost was met by sums of money, often running into five figures, received from Lord Manvers. It may well be that finding this money was a problem and that Manvers therefore requested that outgoings at Thoresby on the estate be kept to a minimum.

[37] NUMD MaB/197/56.

acquired $2\frac{1}{2}$ acres of open-field land. Expenditure on improvements and repairs on the Manvers estate also fell.[38]

PROSPERITY ON THE LAND

Manvers may also have lost interest in enclosure because Laxton joined in the general prosperity of agriculture during the 1860s. This was not what Huskinson had anticipated, but although few of the 1862 proposals were implemented Laxton thrived. The difficult years of the mid-1830s had seen the build-up of rent arrears on the Pierrepont estates, and a slight fall in the overall rental from £2,650 in 1832 to £2,467 by 1838, just over 7 per cent. There were a few minor fluctuations through the 1840s and 1850s, but no substantial movement of rent, even though arrears remained at a level not previously tolerated; over £500 between 1850 and 1852 for example. After that the rental gradually increased, from £2,458 in 1850 to £2,686 by 1861 (9 per cent).

The 1862 survey was partly designed to enquire whether the tenants could afford to pay more rent, and before the end of the year all the Laxton farmers were notified of the increases they could expect.[39] They were asked to submit a written acceptance. One tenant failed to notice this requirement and had to ask the vicar to give him a reference, while William Johnson complained bitterly:

I did think that you would not raise my rent for during a period of forty years I have been paying a rental of 6s per acre more than my neighbours, taking them on an average which in that time amounts to more than five hundred pounds, a very considerable sum for a poor man like me. My land is also in the worst furlongs, and lays on the farther side of every field, a circumstance which renders it a great deal inferior to that which is gainer [sic], and worse to farm. And now, after a life spent in hardships and toil, cares and trouble, I have arrived at the age of 61, and have not been able during that period to lay a single pound by, and it has been with the greatest difficulty that I have paid my way; and this from a man that has not spent a day in idleness from his extreme youth is a case that I think you must consider a hard one. And whilst my neighbours have been laying by yearly I have been spending my own private income on your farm to keep the doors open. It is now in better condition than it ever was before, and I do not like to leave it now, seeing it as my birth place, a thing which I fear I shall be obliged to do ere long unless you allow me to stop at the old rent. I keep no servants my children do the work, and I am robbing them to keep myself.[40]

Despite a touch of flattery – 'you [Horncastle] are a kind gentleman, and willing to listen to a poor man' – it did him no good and the rent was raised.

---

[38] NUMD MaB/217/14, 167, MaB/176/413; M.5592, 5608; Pickersgill, 'Agricultural Revolution', p. 553.

[39] NUMD MaB/177.

[40] NUMD MaB/178/517a.

The most sustained resistance came from John Keyworth, who held the largest farm in Laxton. The family arrived in Laxton in 1798 when Richard Keyworth (23) married Elizabeth, the daughter of George Lee of Westwood Farm. Almost immediately he became the tenant of what is today Town End Farm, where Thomas Jepson (and more recently his widow) had farmed for half a century. It was 134 acres in extent and was rented for £67 a year. In 1818 Keyworth built the present house on the farm for which he was allowed £500 by Manvers.[41] Richard died in 1839 at the age of 64, when he was succeeded by his son John (b. 1803), who almost certainly worked in tandem with his younger brother Thomas (b. 1807). The situation is not entirely clear, but in his father's lifetime John Keyworth had taken the tenancy of a 96-acre farm, and with it a lease of the malt kiln. After 1839 the two farms were worked together by the brothers. In addition the younger Keyworth had inherited 8 acres of freehold from Robert Lee in 1833, and this was worked with the two farms as a single unit. By 1862, however, Thomas was living in his brother's house but no longer farming, and John Keyworth was working the whole 240 or so acres as a single farm. Huskinson reported Keyworth to be 'of a somewhat churlish and discontented temper', though 'on the whole a good tenant', so it is perhaps not surprising that Keyworth was less than happy about the rent rise. In November 1862 he told Horncastle that the new terms were unacceptable and he would quit both farms. After some negotiation, Keyworth and his 'nephew' George Bennett were invited to Thoresby early in December 1862. Bennett (36) was a wheelwright, and the illegitimate son of Keyworth's wife Frances. It was agreed that Keyworth would keep the 135-acre Town End Farm – which, having no children, he finally gave up to John Bagshaw in 1880 – at the revised rent, and Bennett would become tenant of the 96-acre Bottom Farm. They were to enjoy equal shares in the malt kiln.[42]

With these differences resolved, the rental increased to £3,307 in 1863, a 23 per cent advance on the 1861 figure of £2,686. In 1860 the gross rental value of the parish was £3,620, and all non-Manvers property was assessed at £947. This may have been out of date, but after the lord of the manor raised his rents, the parish reviewed the valuation on which rates were based, and raised it to £5,048 in January 1864, and to £5,302 in April 1864, and £5,333 in 1871–3.[43] By the last of these dates Manvers had acquired the Savile property and his Laxton rent stood at £4,138, approximately 78 per cent of the total.

Rent rises were an indication of prosperity, and even Huskinson had to admit that Laxton had some reasonable tenants. Both land and buildings on Richard Harpham's 152-acre estate were 'creditable to the tenant'; George Pinder 'appears to me to have done more towards the improvement of his farm,

---

[41] NUMD MaB/208/20ff.
[42] NUMD MaB 178/507–8; 195/2; M.4010a,b.
[43] NAO PR 4115–18.

which is naturally poor land in a bad situation, than any other tenant in the parish'; and William Pinder was 'a young and energetic man, and the cultivation and condition of his land and buildings very creditable to him'. Of course the two Pinders were at Knapeney and Westwood Farms respectively, and Huskinson was anxious to stress the advantages of consolidated farms. Elsewhere he found problem cases. William Childs, the blacksmith, came from a family established in the village for more than seventy years in the 1860s, but this did not prevent Horncastle from taking a firm line of action with a defaulting tenant. He was unmoved by a letter from the vicar in February 1868 requesting that Childs be permitted a year's trial in his house and shop as an opportunity to improve his situation: 'William Childs has frequently deceived me, and particularly on the last occasion by making himself a bankrupt after inducing us by his representations to take possession that I have completely lost all confidence in him.' Three days later Childs was served with notice to quit at Lady Day, and Horncastle took steps to recover £16 16s unpaid rent from his bankruptcy receivers.[44]

Another problem case was Elizabeth Whittington, who had succeeded her late husband in 1860 as tenant of a 136-acre farm described by Huskinson as in particularly bad shape: 'the buildings are ill-arranged and inadequate [. . .] the farm is generally in a discreditable state of cultivation [. . .]. Mrs Whittington has been tenant 24 years and has a son at home, 26 years of age, assisting her, but the farm is at present in worse condition than any other upon the estate.' The son was Henry, described as 21 in the 1861 census. A decade earlier one young man who might have testified to the less than ideal conditions on the farm was a 20-year old agricultural labourer who the census enumerator found sleeping 'in a barn'. Perhaps not surprisingly the Whittingtons went bankrupt in 1864.[45]

On the other hand some individuals were tolerated almost beyond the call of duty. George Lee is a case in point. He was an owner-occupier who rented additional land from Manvers. By the 1860s he had run into considerable financial difficulties. In January 1864 provisional agreement was reached between Horncastle and Lee for the purchase of three properties Lee had inherited: East Kirk Ing in Moorhouse (3a 2r 2p), which had been purchased by George Lee (d. 1798) from Pendock Neale in the 1790s; Crouchill Close in Laxton (3a) which George Lee's son William bought at the sale of Charles Doncaster's property in 1810 for £260 8s; and land in the West Field inherited by the same William Lee (3a 3r 8p). William died in about 1822 leaving the property to his widow, Mary Lee. She died in 1834 leaving it in trust to her grandson George. It was this George Lee who by 1861 was in difficulty. That year he mortgaged the land for £450, and two years later he borrowed a further

---

[44] NUMD M.4010/8, 9, 11, 13a.
[45] NUMD MaB/189.

£100. These sums were paid off only after he had sold the land to Manvers for £700. When it became clear that East Kirk Ing was predominantly in Moorhouse, Denison was persuaded to acquire the property for £345 12s 6d. Manvers paid the balance of the £700 for the other land.[46]

While these negotiations were in progress Lee requested the tenancy of Knapeney Farm in place of George Pinder. This posed a problem in relation to 'your conduct at Treswell which was heard before the magistrates at Retford'. Lee had farmed in Treswell during the 1860s, and it was here that his eldest son John was born in 1862. No details are known of the case, but Lee was asked to explain himself, and character references were requested. The rector of

PLATE 8.3 *Knapeney Farmhouse. Knapeney was one of the four independent farms laid out in 1729. Among the farm buildings is a barn, part of which could be an original structure dating from the 1720s. Nothing is known of the original house; the present one dates from 1818 when it was built at a cost of £330. George Lee was tenant here in the 1860s. Between the First and Second World Wars it was a difficult farm to let, and for many years it was managed from Thoresby. It was sold into private hands in 1950, and today the house is empty and semi-derelict.*

[46] NUMD MaB/180/590, 592, 602; M.5560, 5563.

Treswell wrote in no uncertain terms to say that Lee was 'scarcely ever sober and his associates anything but respectable'.[47] By contrast the vicar of Laxton was disposed to write to Horncastle in more favourable terms after a conversation with Lee and his mother.

He assures me that he is thoroughly resolved to give up all his bad habits and to strive to be steady industrious and high principled. If under these circumstances and with this promise on his part you should feel justified in still recommending him to Lord Manvers as a tenant, you would be giving him one more chance, and be doing a great kindness to his wife and two children, and to his mother. And I feel that his being thus accepted as a tenant with no circumstances hidden, and under his own promise to try and turn over a new leaf would be a different thing both as regards Lord Manvers and the wellbeing of the parish.

Apparently satisfied, Horncastle admitted Lee as tenant of Knapeney farm.[48]

This was not to prove a happy decision. In 1866 Lee was fined by the Court for tethering his cattle in the open fields before they were broken, and two years later Horncastle found himself caught up in a family quarrel. George Lee's mother Elizabeth farmed in the village. Huskinson described her in 1862 as '60 years of age but an active person, and has a son 22 years of age, who assists in managing the farm'. The son was William, who was offered the tenancy of the farm in Laxton on condition that he supported her financially, and found her houseroom. According to George Lee, his brother had other ideas which he chose to keep quiet. 'I had my tea with him Sunday week before Laxton rent day, and we had nothing wrong all comfortable together to all appearance' but that same night William, allegedly, told Mr Taylor, his 'great friend', that he was to have the tenancy 'and then he should turn his mother out and send her to me'. George Lee, by his own account, then went with his mother to Thoresby to report the matter. Horncastle had little time for family feuds, and he warned Lee to reach an agreement with his brother or both of them would be turned out. It did not help George's case that he owed money to his brother – and his landlord – nor that Horncastle had discovered from other people in Laxton that Lee 'has again become very unsteady, and indulges much in drinking to excess. He is also much in debt, and has, I fear, got through the greater part if not all his money.' In the circumstances Horncastle was reluctant to accept George Lee's version of events, and he decided to give him notice to quit Knapeney Farm the following Lady Day and not to expect to succeed to his mother's farm in the village; indeed, Horncastle 'to protect Lord Manvers' interests' was also giving Mrs Lee notice.[49] He told George Lee,

[47] NUMD MaB/226/9.
[48] NUMD MaB/226/8; 180/598.
[49] NUMD MaB/176/376, 226/11, 14.

Independent of your having resumed your habits of drinking to excess, at times, and being much in debt, I fear it is not intended to use your brother William fairly. It appears to me that if the present disposition to quarrell amongst ourselves is indulged in, ruin to all will be the consequence. In order therefore to protect Lord Manvers interests I have felt it my duty to give both your mother and yourself notices to give up your frams at Lady Day next.

But Horncastle also provided a let-out. He made it clear that if the proposal from William Lee was accepted he would reconsider his decision, and Lee seized on this to patch over the troubles. A few months later he was warned for selling straw and hay contrary to the terms of his agreement which produced another contrite letter to Horncastle about how it was only 'a little straw', and how even that 'I did ignorantly. I did not know I was going wrong (as I have known others do so) or I would not have sold it.'[50]

Two years on and Lee was again served with notice to quit because he had run into excessive debt. A further supplication followed:

I should have been over with the money before now but have had such a serious loss in my horses and was obliged to buy more to get my work done and another reason wheat being so low I thought I would keep it a little time and pay you both half years together. I do hope Sir you will allow me to stay. I will pay you all at the next rent day at Laxton or one half year's sooner if you wish it [. . .]. I have five little boys the eldest not nine years of age for the sake of my children I beg to stay do please look over it this time. I will pay all up at the rent day [. . .]. I have lost two working horses, 2 yearlings foals, 2 beast and 12 pigs. It makes it very serious altogether.[51]

Again he was allowed to continue, and the saga resumed. In 1872 he wrote to apologize for his rent arrears, and two years later he was again bemoaning his losses – 12 horses, 7 foals, 2 good bullocks and over 20 calves in the past year. And when Horncastle finally pulled the rug from under him in 1875 Lee complained about the low valuation for tenant right placed on his farm; but Horncastle had had enough: 'a place left in a more disgraceful state than you left it in I never saw.'[52] George Lee and his family were no longer living in Laxton in 1881, but his maligned younger brother was farming 136 acres.

In this case the tenant fought his battles with the landlord, but other men who ran into difficulties looked for help to their relations and friends in the village. The Saxelbys are a case in point. Michael Saxelby took over the tenancy of Crosshill from Charles Doncaster in 1837. By 1862 he had moved to a smaller farm and his son George was the tenant of Crosshill. Huskinson described George, aged 34, as 'a very good farmer'. Unfortunately this promise

[50] NUMD MaB/226/10, 13, 15, 16.
[51] NUMD MaB/226/18.
[52] NUMD MaB/226/20, 23, 55a, 56.

was not maintained. By 1869 George Saxelby was confined to bed by gout, and in financial difficulties. As a result he assigned over his property to his brother-in-law William Birkett who agreed to pay the debts and to ascertain the value of the property. William Harpham took over management of the farm. Both men were acting for the benefit of Saxelby's son, who was 6, and daughter, 8. In 1871 Saxelby's wife Sarah was recorded in the census as head of household and tenant of the farm. George Saxelby is not mentioned, although he died in 1875. His widow and friends kept the farm going, and by 1881 the tenancy had passed to the son, George, who was just 18. He married in 1883 and left the farm the following year although he returned to take on another Laxton tenancy in the 1890s.[53]

[53] NUMD M.4010/14; MaB/193/52. *Ex. inf.* Mrs Margaret Ilyott.

Chapter Nine

―――――◆≫⊛≪◆―――――

The Agricultural Depression and the Reorganization of the Open Fields

In the 1860s and 1870s it was possible to be optimistic about the future of agriculture. The doubts which had surfaced in the later 1840s following the repeal of the Corn Laws in 1846 seemed unfounded. Free trade in grain had not led to a collapse in prices, and the farming community enjoyed considerable prosperity in the era of 'high farming'. The future seemed assured until in the early 1870s dark clouds began to gather on the horizon. In 1874–5 wheat prices fell, bringing what many expected at the time would be an uncomfortable break in the general level of agricultural prosperity. As it transpired this was not a short-term interruption, but a radical change for the worse. Adverse season followed adverse season down to 1882, with 1879 particularly disastrous in that all types of farming were badly hit. Farmers blamed the wet weather, but foreign competition had the effect of preventing prices from rising as they would normally have done in years of bad harvests. The impact of competition was even more apparent in the 1880s when prices continued to fall despite average or better than average seasons. Further acute depression followed in the early 1890s. With changes in both land use and output – as many farmers became processors of corn into livestock products – and falling rents, the picture by the closing years of the century was rather less sombre, but it was the 1940s before agriculture once again became prosperous.

THE AGRICULTURAL DEPRESSION

Arable-livestock areas like Laxton were the most severely hit by the depression. As Edith Hickson recalled many years later 'that period of prosperity known to our grandparents was already a legend handed down as something we could not possibly experience, for them there had been unbelievable plenty of everything, even luxury.' For her generation 'a state of real privation had settled on all [. . .] farmers and their workmen suffered alike and that decline of fortune was reflected in the lives of their children, who all had to work from the earliest possible age.'[1] Of course we all tend to look back to a golden age which may or may not have existed in the past, but there is plenty of evidence – including the decline of population and the shortfall in work opportunities – to suggest that the Laxton of the 1890s was considerably changed from even twenty or thirty years earlier. As we shall see, significant land-use changes were possible to counter the impact of depression, but the open-field farmers in Laxton were locked into an annual cycle which could not be drastically altered without a massive reorganization of the farming system. The consequences were severe for freeholders and tenant farmers alike.

The clearest single guide to the depression in Laxton is provided by the Thoresby rental. As we have seen, in the 1860s rents had soared upwards. With the acquisitions from Savile and Denison, Manvers's rental income exceeded £4,000 in 1870 and reached £4,138 two years later, but then came the cold winds of change. Ostensibly all was well, although the rental had slipped back gradually to £3,990 by 1883, but this disguised the extent to which Laxton was by then deeply in the grip of the depression. From the later 1870s returns of rent were made to farmers in difficulties. These amounted to £397 in 1877 (nearly 10 per cent of the rental), and £227 the following year. In 1879 10 per cent of rents was returned on the first half yearly rent, and 20 per cent on the second half year, together with a 10 per cent tithe abatement, while the 1881 accounts record a payment of £88, 'donation towards stock losses'. In all, the sums of money effectively given back to the tenants during these years amounted to 13.5 per cent of the rental in 1879, 18 per cent in 1880, 24 per cent in 1881, 22 per cent in 1882, and 21 per cent in 1883. Despite this, arrears totalled £826. Nor was it merely the Thoresby tenants who were in trouble. The vestry agreed to return 10 per cent of Wiliam Cook's rent for his church lands in 1879, 1881, 1882 and 1883.[2]

By 1883 it was evident that rents could not be maintained at the levels they had reached before the depression, and the accession of a new agent at Thoresby produced a wholesale reorganization of the accounting procedure. In June 1883 Robert Walter Wordsworth was appointed to the position of land agent for a considerable slice of the estates of the third Earl Manvers. A great-nephew of the Lakeland poet he was only 34 years old at the time, but he was remembered locally as 'a thorough gentleman who was to be looked up to'.[3] He was certainly not faced with an easy task, especially as one of his first jobs was to reduce rents across the estates. At Laxton virtually all rents were reduced by 30 per cent, with the overall rental falling from £3,990 in 1883 to £3,075 in 1885. John Bagshaw's rent for Town End Farm came down from £177 to £133, and William Lee's was reduced from £181 to £134. A few dropped even

---

[1] *Life at Laxton*, pp. 5–6.
[2] NAO PR 4093.
[3] *Life at Laxton*, p. 58; J. V. Beckett and B. A. Wood, 'Land Agency in the Agricultural Depression: R. W. Wordsworth at Thoresby, 1883–1914', *Trent Geographer*, 11 (1987), 16–23.

faster; Richard Harpham's rent fell from £191 to £100. But if Wordsworth hoped these changes would halt the slide he must have been sadly disappointed. In 1887–8 and 1888–9 arrears stood at over £1,000, and in both years £600 of the rental was effectively written off. The rental was down to £2,664 in 1888–9. The turn of the decade proved to be the low point, with some rents falling even further. William Lee clearly could not afford £134, and by 1891 his arrears had reached £380, and his rent had dropped from £134 to £105. By 1896 the rental had recovered to £2,777, with a few rents even showing an increase. On Robert Weatherall's farm the rent rose from £80 to £86 between 1891 and 1895. Although arrears remained at more than £900 in the early 1890s, the sums of money lost annually as a result of prevailing economic conditions had fallen to under £50.

The great depression flattened out after 1896, but little recovery had taken place in Laxton by the time war broke out in 1914. Apart from occasional fluctuations, the rental hardly changed, and at £2,891 in 1913–14 it was still only 70 per cent of the levels achieved in the early 1870s, and less than the income received from a substantially smaller acreage at the end of the

PLATE 9.1 *Horse ploughing in West Field (late 1940s?). This picture sheds interesting light on the local farmers' knowledge of Laxton. Despite the bare landscape – and even the trees have now gone – most of today's farmers who saw this picture could recognize not merely the field in which it was taken (West Field), but also whereabouts in the field (Kirton Gate), the strip which was being worked (Albert Rayner's), and the make of plough. It was the identity of the ploughman which almost defeated them. Several possibilities were ruled out on the grounds that the man involved did not have a grey in his team. Finally, he was recognized as Arthur Frecknell, who was hired by Bill Sampson, the farmer, for a year in the late 1940s.*

Napoleonic wars a century earlier. It also seemed impossible to reduce arrears below £400 a year.

Behind every falling rent was a distressed farmer, and Wordsworth was inundated with requests for rent rebates or reductions. John Atkinson wrote in September 1882:

> I have told you several times I have lost money on my farm for a good many years which I think one good reason for wishing you to lower my rent. The seasons and the price of wheat have been very serious, but it is the quality of the land and the game which I ask you to consider. About two thirds of my arable land is very strong clay it takes many horses to work it (which are very expensive keeping) and seldom grows more than half a crop. In such a case there is but little corn to make money or straw to make manure.

Wordsworth's response was to ask Atkinson what he thought would be fair and reasonable. The tenant responded: 'if we have no better weather strong clay land will be of little value of which I have an extra quantity. If you will reduce my farm to £100 a year I think it will be a fair value for it.'[4] This was accepted.

Some families ran into severe financial difficulties. The Peatfields were a notable example. Samuel Peatfield came to Laxton in about 1740 and leased a farm of 29 acres. Gradually the family fortunes improved; by 1812 they were farming 66 acres, and in 1840 William Peatfield lived in the bottom of the village (Ide Farm today) and farmed 100 acres. During the 1850s William Peatfield senior passed the farm to his eldest son William, who had spent some years during the 1840s and 1850s away from Laxton (most of his children were born at Chilwell near Nottingham). He died in 1861, at the age of 43, leaving his widow Jane with six young children and a farm now expanded to 111 acres to run. All went well until the depression, when the family ran into trouble, as is clear from the warm testimonial written on their behalf by the vicar in 1883:

> The Peatfield family have been long tenants of Earl Manvers and I should be sorry that the family here should be obliged to leave their farm; the widow whose husband died 22 years ago has had a hard battle to fight, and many difficulties to go through, and the one unmarried daughter was for many years our church organist, giving her services gratuitously, and only resigning the post a year ago when she became incapacitated through a spinal affliction which still renders her an invalid and unable to walk. I have a great regard for her. The two sons who are still at home and unmarried (there are two more sons, married) have worked hard and under great difficulties latterly. If they are really able to carry on the farm I should be glad that they should do so.[5]

The sheriff had taken possession of the farm, presumably because the tenants were bankrupt, but a solution was found. Jane Peatfield's son Samuel, just 20, who was effectively managing the farm, was permitted a rent reduction from

---

⁴ NUMD MaB/206/48.
⁵ NUMD MaB/217/57.

£129 to £100 and, when this still proved too much, to £90 in 1891. It recovered to £94 by 1895 and Peatfield was still farming 101 acres in the village in 1900, and (at a rent of £92) 1910.[6]

These are just two cases, and there were many more families who suffered during these years. The gravity of the situation demanded further action, and once again enclosure seems to have been considered by Thoresby. This was Wordsworth's first intention in regard to Laxton, and he proceeded to consolidate strips whenever tenancies ended. By fixing things in 1883 so that a number of tenancies fell in at the same time he thought it would be possible to bring about a re-allocation of the strips. 'Fixing' is the right word, because Wordsworth needed to persuade a number of tenants to hold on to their land as it stood for a further year, and this was where the plan came unstuck.

Wordsworth's master scheme began with an offer to Richard Beckitt of first refusal of the lease of John Birkett's farm. However, there was a condition: 'I must ask you and Mr Keyworth to retain your present holding for one year longer, when I would release you, and I would try to get Mr Whitworth to take the far off land from you at next Lady Day.' Birkett however proved less obliging when asked to stay in his farm for a further year. Despite Wordsworth's proposal 'as a personal favour to a brother agent who has to undertake an arduous post in most unfavourable seasons', the offer was declined. Consequently Wordsworth was forced to proceed in a more piecemeal fashion than he had hoped, although he took the opportunity whenever possible to rearrange the enclosed areas most distant from the village farmsteads. Some of the outlying fields in a tenancy which came vacant in 1884 were added to neighbouring farms. But the wholesale enclosure Wordsworth had envisaged eluded him. He remained optimistic, writing of Laxton in 1885 that 'it is one of the few parishes still unenclosed in the Midland Counties and its inclosure is now contemplated.' This was part of an attempt to persuade the Ordnance Survey to produce a 25-inch sacle map of Laxton, in addition to the 6-inch map already produced, to help him speed up the process.[7]

Discussions with the Ordnance Survey did not ensure that the rent was paid, and Wordsworth was left with little alternative but to proceed in a piecemeal fashion. This made for laborious progress, although the mean size of the principal Manvers farms increased by about 10 per cent between 1862 and 1891 and the number of smaller holdings declined. The figures conceal the complex gross change in the structural pattern brought about by a variety of exchanges, purchases, amalgamations, divisions and re-allotments. Thus, the increase of mean holding size was not merely because small holdings were amalgamated into larger ones, but also because land acquired after the exchanges and purchases was integrated with existing Manvers tenancies.

[6] NUMD MaB/218/59.
[7] NUMD Ma 2C/152/15, 20, 26, 383.

Something of what this meant for the estate can be seen from tenant right valuations for the period, which reveal not merely the turnover of farmers during the depression but also the way in which some properties were re-allotted. There are several examples but none clearer than the case of George Bennett whose 71-acre farm was divided at his death in 1893 (table 9.1). Bennett – not to be confused with the other George Bennett, whose case was discussed in chapter 8 – was a Laxton man who spent most of his working life as an agricultural labourer, finally acquiring a tenancy only in his sixties. He died well into his eighties, when the farm was divided fourteen ways. This was an exceptional case, but there were other instances in which parcels were taken from even the largest farms. When George Saxelby vacated Crosshill in favour of William Merrils in the 1880s the majority of the tenant right (£306 1s 6d) was paid by the incoming tenant, but two small pieces of land were taken off for other tenancies. In these ways Wordsworth gradually brought what he considered to be a greater sense of rationality to the farm structure without making any fundamental alterations to the pattern of farming.[8]

TABLE 9.1   *The division of George Bennett's farm, 1893*

New tenant	Acreage			Tenant right			Rent		
	a	r	p	£	s	d	£	s	d
F. Bennett	10	2	26	42	17	5	16	0	0
W. Wilkinson	14	3	30	7	12	9	9	5	0
G. Bennett	1	0	13	1	14	6		15	0
W. Atkinson	4	0	24	25	11	9	3	0	0
G. Johnson	1	3	29	6	8	11	1	10	0
G. Moody		1	39	2	19	9		8	0
J. Laughton	1	1	19	7	14	9	1	2	6
J. Bagshaw		2	05	2	8	3		7	6
W. Merrils	11	2	37	13	3	9	10	10	0
E. & A. Small	8	2	01	27	8	7	7	10	0
S. Sampson	8	3	03	14	2	7	8	0	0
J. Rose	1	0	28	6	13	2		16	0
S. & J. Peatfield	5	3	00	19	0	8	4	0	0
Bramford			12	2	13	0		10	0
	71	0	05	180	9	10	63	14	0

Sources: NUMD Ma 5E/119/1; Acc. 608 'Tenant Right valuations'.

[8] NUMD Acc 608; Wood, thesis, p. 416.

These figures show only the Manvers tenancies, but the whole village was affected (table 9.2). Between the start of the depression and the outbreak of the First World War the overall number of occupiers in Laxton declined by 40 per cent. The most notable reduction was in the number working 50 acres or less, down from 49 before the depression began to just 27 by 1910 with, at the same time, a slight increase in those working 50 acres or more. Large arable farms were better able to withstand the depressed conditions than middling farms. However, small farms were in greater demand during the depression, partly because there were too few tenants available with the necessary resources to take on larger farms. Under the circumstances Laxton became more rather than less attractive as a place to farm because the smaller tenancies which were most sought after in the prevailing conditions were to be found in some numbers in the village.

TABLE 9.2 *Occupiers of land in Laxton 1870–1915*

Date	Number	1–5	5–50	50–300	300+	Acres rented	Acres owned
1870	73	16	33	22	–		
1875	70						
1880	69						
1885	61						
1890	60	10	24			3387	39
1895	61					3446	30
1900	59					3330	161
1905	55	10	19	26	–	3462	25
1910	53	8	19	25	1	3588	17
1915	52	5	22	24	1	3592	5

Sources: PRO MAF/68/254, 425, 710, 995, 1280, 1565, 1850, 2135, 2420, 2705.

Despite the tenancy rationalizations Wordsworth also found it necessary to increase the level of expenditure on farm property in Laxton. As rents fell and tenants left, landlords had little option but to increase spending on their estates in order to attract farmers. At Laxton between 1870 and 1874 the landlord reinvested the equivalent of 4.5 per cent of the rental; between 1910 and 1914 the proportion was 35 per cent. The accounts are not specific enough to show precisely how this money was being spent, but most of it must have been to improve existing farmsteads. Even with this considerable outlay it was no easy task to find and keep tenants, a point which is clear from the turnover of families and names in Laxton in the decades after 1873.

A comparison of the 1873 and 1900 rate books shows that during these years fourteen or fifteen surnames disappeared which can be found in village records dating back into the eighteenth and sometimes the seventeenth century, among them Baines, Glazebrook, Lee, Newstead, Nicholson and White. In 1842 there were four branches of the Pinder family in the village, all owning land and three of them farming in excess of 170 acres; by 1900 Jane Pinder, farming 284 acres at Westwood, and Joseph Pinder, with a house and garden leased from Manvers, were the sole representatives. With Jane Pinder's departure in 1908 only Herbert Pinder, living in the cottage rented by Joseph in 1900, remained of this once vast clan. Of course the story was not always the same. In 1900 there were still Bartles, Bagshaws and Moodys, Peatfields, Pecks and Quibells, Roses, Weatheralls, Laughtons and Crees, several of which are still reprented in Laxton today. Even so, the turnover was considerable. Of 52 holdings for which the start of tenancy is given in the 1910 survey, 32 were of no longer date than 1901, and just three predated 1890. John Bagshaw, who had been farming 145 acres at Town End since taking over the tenancy from John Keyworth in 1880, could boast the longest tenure of a single property.

THE FARMERS' RESPONSE TO THE DEPRESSION

Farmers in the midland counties responded to the depression by altering the balance of agriculture away from arable production towards livestock. Pastoral farming was best suited to the claylands, and made more sense in price terms. Consequently, in the last quarter of the nineteenth century the acreage under cultivation declined while the acreage under permanent grass increased. Permanent grassland in Nottinghamshire increased from 152,000 acres in 1870 to 208,500 in 1895 (37 per cent). Conversely arable cultivation declined from 289,000 acres to 240,000 acres over the same period, a fall of 17 per cent.[9]

The continuation of open-field farming obviously complicated the situation in Laxton, and in the absence of enclosure mixed farming continued. The agricultural returns provide a picture of farming in the period, from which it is apparent that most farms must have looked in the 1890s much as they had done in the 1860s.[10] There were usually around 200 horses in the village, anything between 100 and 250 pigs, and large numbers of cattle, sheep and poultry. When a full enumeration of animals was called for in 1885 the total came to 3,660. Close analysis, however, reveals that the village did experience change, and here the flexibility of the closes enabled the farmers to respond to

---

[9] K. C. Edwards (ed.), *The Land of Britain*, part 60, *Nottinghamshire* (1944).

[10] PRO MAF/68/51, 52, 254, 425, 710, 995, 1280, 1565, 1850, 2135, 2420, 2705. The discussion which follows is based on these returns.

the prevailing conditions. If they continued to mix arable with livestock, the Laxton farmers gradually changed the role of each. In 1870 2,001 acres were in corn, green crops and fallow (assuming fallow to be uncultivated arable), but by 1895 the figure was 1,730, a decline of 13 per cent. Over the same period the proportion of land in permanent or temporary grass increased from 1,572 acres to 1,716 acres, 8 per cent. In fact, 1870 offers a rather high base for the latter calculation; if we take 1875 as the base year, when depression was still setting in and before very much alteration had occurred in acreages county-wide, 1,402 acres were under grass in Laxton, and the increase by 1895 was nearer to 22 per cent.

Changing the use of land brought benefits only when accompanied by other developments. Grassing down was partly to save on labour costs, hence the falling number of agricultural labourers in the village, and the continuing need for children to help out in the fields during the busy parts of the agricultural cycle. It was also to accommodate an increased head of cattle so that farmers could benefit from the more stable prices of dairy products. The number of cattle in Laxton rose from 514 in 1870 to 660 in 1895 (28 per cent) and the overall rise down to the First World War was 56 per cent. The change was a mixed blessing; Edith Hickson noted that 'the cows and young beasts were apt to display rather apparently their bone formation beneath a scruffy hide,'[11] and Laxton was too far from the railway to benefit from urban milk sales, hence the importance of butter production.

Arable farming could be made more efficient by using machinery. Reapers and binders were introduced on Laxton farms, and the village had a steam threshing machine in the 1890s.[12] Wheat constitued about half the crop, reflecting the rigidity of the rotation, while barley, oats, beans and peas accounted for the other 50 per cent, but in varying proportions through time. Across the country after about 1870, farms responded to grain imports from the United States by becoming processors of corn products for livestock, a trend which was to continue (except in the war years) down to 1939. The effect in Laxton is clear in figure 10.2. Oats, once despised on the claylands, came to play an increasing part in the arable economy because they made less demand on soil fertility than wheat and were more suitable as a livestock feed. In the 1880s oat began to displace peas, but the longer-term trend was for oats to replace barley in the crop pattern. From only 5 per cent of the Laxton corn crop in 1875, oats regularly exceeded 20 per cent from the 1890s onwards. Peas, beans and barley were all victims of this changing pattern. Potatoes, turnips and swedes, vetches and tares, usually occupied about 200 acres, but no other crops figured significantly in the village. About 20 acres in the village was devoted to orchards and fruit growing, but Laxton was not a centre for one of

[11] *Life at Laxton*, p. 8.
[12] Ibid., p. 2.

PLATE 9.2 *Village fête. This undated print is thought to depict either a float at a pre-First World War feast, or celebrations marking the coronation of Edward VII. On the left is Frank Willis, long-serving school master and church organist, who was doubtless responsible for organizing the children on this occasion. In the middle is Sam Bartle and on the right is Harold Bagshaw.*

the growth areas of this period, horticulture. While the open fields did not encourage change, Laxton farmers managed to alter the balance between crops and livestock and to change farming practices in an attempt to come to terms with the depression. None the less, without rent reductions the village farmers could not have made a living, and even with them some struggled.

THE CHANGING PATTERN OF LANDOWNERSHIP

If the tenant farmers suffered in the depression, at least they could hope for some protection from the landlord. Not so the freeholders, whose long struggle against adverse conditions finally came to an end in the bleak conditions of the late nineteenth century (table 9.3). The sources do not all agree, but a combination of data from the rate books and surveys provides a clear indication of the trend. Figures drawn from the *Return of Owners of Land* of 1872–3 are notoriously unreliable, and the table takes no account of 269 acres wrongly

TABLE 9.3 *The decline of the freeholders in the late nineteenth century*

Date	Number	Acreage	Source
1860	44	312	Rate book
1862	45	413	Estate survey
1873	30	218	Rate book
1873	17	140	*Return of Owners*
1889	23	175	Tithe survey
1900	19	163	Rate book
1910	13	76	'Domesday' survey

Sources: NAO PR 4109–18, PR 4073; NUMD Ma S 16; Ma 5E 119; *Return of Owners of Land 1872–3* (2 vols, 1875); PRO IR/55254, 55255.

attributed to John Keyworth, since this land is known to have been rented and not owned. Only Thomas Keyworth is attributed the same acreage as in 1862. All the other figures point to the same conclusion, a long term decline in both numbers and acreage which was aggravated by the economic conditions prevailing after 1873. The chief beneficiary was Manvers, whose acreage grew from 3,135 in 1873, to 3,220 in 1900 and to 3,500 in 1910.

The third Earl Manvers had gradually increased the size of his Laxton holding since Huskinson measured the total at 2,322 acres in 1862. The exchanges with the Saviles and Denisons increased his holding by 716 acres. Between 1864 and 1880 he spent a further £1,897 acquiring six small freeholds totalling 27 acres.[13] Manvers made no further purchases until 1892, but between then and 1908 he acquired property from eleven of the twenty-three freeholders listed in 1889. In total this amounted to about 120 acres. The effect was to reduce the freeholders to little more than a nominal acreage in the parish, while consolidating his hold on the open fields. In 1891 freeholders owned about 45 acres in the four fields, but Manvers gradually cut into this figure, and with his acquisition of Primrose Farm on the eastern edge of Laxton in 1906 he became sole owner of all the arable land in the open fields. Primrose Farm was a 27-acre holding he bought from George Pinder of Edwinstowe for £600, and Wordsworth recorded that 'the acquisition [. . .] will make Lord Manvers sole owner in Laxton open fields.'[14] In theory this paved the way for enclosure of the open fields, but Manvers had not acquired all the gait rights and these remained an obstacle to enclosure.

By the time the third earl died in 1910 the freeholders had been largely excluded from Laxton (table 9.4). These figures are an overestimate because

[13] NUMD Ma S 16.
[14] NUMD Ma 2C/161/165, 166.

TABLE 9.4 *Landownership in Laxton, 1910*

Owner	Acreage			%
	a	r	p	
Earl Manvers	3501	2	38	86.1
W. E. Denison	464	0	22	11.4
John Rose	32	3	29	0.8
John Bagshaw	16	2	00	0.4
J. Stevens and A. Broughton	10	3	31	0.2
W. Quibell	10	3	18	0.2
Harriet Brant	7	1	00	0.2
George Bagshaw	6	3	06	0.1
Execs Handley	4	1	24	0.1
William Taylor	4	1	01	0.1
G. Newbert	1	0	00	0.1
Hewitts		1	00	
Vicar	5	2	00	0.1
Schools		1	03	
	4066	1	32	99.8

Source: PRO IR/55254, 55255.

the maximum size of the parish (including roads), as measured by the Ordnance Survey, was 4,007 acres. However, the survey attributes 259 acres to Moorhouse, which must include land outside the parish boundary. In any case Moorhouse was largely a Denison preserve. By contrast, in Laxton Manvers owned 3,493 acres, 92 per cent of the total, although this may include some land beyond the parish boundary.

THE REORGANIZATION OF THE OPEN FIELDS

Manvers's policy of acquiring freeholds was largely designed to permit consolidation of holdings and to ease the path towards enclosure. When Primrose Farm was purchased in 1906 the tenant promptly offered his notice, but Wordsworth tried to dissuade him with offers of improved buildings and a rearranged holding. That same year he proposed an exchange with the Denisons of land at Knapeney which lay more conveniently for them.[15] In the end enclosure did not take place, but between 1903 and 1908 the most com-

---

[15] NUMD Ma 2C/162/316, 329; Wood, thesis, p. 427.

plete reorganization of the farming structure was implemented since the partial enclosure of the 1720s. It was a transformation which has continued to shape the nature of farming to the present day.

In 1903 Wordsworth wrote to all the tenants explaining how he hoped to restructure the open-field system to make it 'more convenient for the tenants who hold land'.[16] It turned out to be a complex, time-consuming and taxing task since it could be done only with the agreement of freeholders and tenants alike – and Wordsworth (wisely, as we shall see) insisted from the beginning that his proposals should be accepted unanimously. It also required delicate negotiations both to purchase a number of awkwardly placed freeholds, and to placate the holders of common rights. He intended to begin with a trial run by enclosing East Field. If this succeeded he proposed that, as each of the other fields reached their fallow year in the farming cycle, part would be removed from the common-field system and enclosed while the rest would be consolidated into larger plots. The benefit of waiting for the fallow year was that cropping and stocking was not interrupted, and Wordsworth avoided the expense of tenant right valuations of standing crops as well as the numerous disagreements to be anticipated in making such valuations.

For the East Field scheme to work Wordsworth had first to negotiate three purchases of land. These cost £721.[17] He also ascertained from the independent owners of common rights that they did not object to the fencing of East Moor Common, which he intended to carry out simultaneously. By mid-April this was achieved, and Wordsworth called a meeting in the village at which 'everyone was unanimous' in favour of enclosing the East Field and fencing the common. Within a couple of weeks work began on the East Moor Common fence, and by June Wordsworth had informed the tenants of their revised East Field holdings.[18] He tried to ensure that existing tenants retained as much of their original land as possible, and that their total holding was roughly commensurate with their pre-reorganization acreage. The 100 strips were consolidated into 23 holdings which although still farmed without fencing were effectively removed from the open-field system.

Since he had unanimous backing Wordsworth was prepared to take a tough line with dissentients. When wind of George Birkitt's criticisms reached him the response was direct:

I stated perfectly plainly when I met the tenants at the Dovecote and before the agreement was signed that for the purposes of hedging and road making I should have to take small strips of land, but no one who has the smallest amount of common sense can fail to appreciate the vast benefit the inclosure will be to all holders in the Little [i.e. East] Field, or to be grateful to Lord Manvers for doing what he now is. In your case you have

[16] NUMD M.5842.
[17] NUMD Ma 2C/160/508, 550; M.5709, M.5760.
[18] NUMD Ma 2C/160/527, 559, 570, 597; Ma 5E/141; Wood, thesis, p. 419.

in addition been given seeds and bone to make a grass paddock, and for all this you give us nothing but abuse. If you are dissatisfied, please take the straightforward course and give up your holding, and try and get some other owner from whom you think you can obtain better treatment.[19]

Doubtless others complained, even if less audibly in the comfort of the pub, but Wordsworth succeeded in removing the East Field from the open-field system and re-allotting it in closes.[20]

Inspired by this success, in 1905 Wordsworth undertook the rather more complicated task of reorganizing the South Field. He informed the tenants in the spring:

I have reason to believe that my efforts [vis a vis the East Field] were not wholly unsuccessful. I am prepared to try and adopt a similar course in the 'South Field', coming fallow this year, if it be the wish of those that hold land in it that I should do so – only, if I do undertake this, I must have a reasonable assurance from the tenants that they will accept whatever re-arrangement I propose [. . .]. I suggest that the tenants meet and discuss whether they will accept my suggestion or not. If they accept it, I will promise them on my part that I will do my utmost to make it a success and a help to every tenant in the field.[21]

Wordsworth's scheme involved calculating the total area held by each tenant in the field, and then working across the furlongs enlarging the largest of the original strips in each tenancy and eliminating the smallest when possible.[22] The tenants held a private meeting in the village at which they agreed to accept the scheme. The vicar tipped off Wordsworth about possible troublemakers, to which he responded: 'I will do my best to deal gently with Laughton. It is really too amusing to think of old Tom Bennett having something to say, he has only two acres in the field scattered in six different places! But then he is of course one of the very old order.'[23]

With this assurance Wordsworth met the tenants. As he wrote afterwards,

I held a meeting today of our Laxton tenants relative to some rearrangement of the open fields. And of their own accord they, with one exception, gave it as their wish and opinion that Lord Manvers should, and could enclose such portions as were his freehold so long as no commons were encroached upon. And some of the older tenants stated that they knew that inclosures on these lines had taken place during their lifetime.[24]

---

[19] NUMD Ma 2C/160/666.
[20] NUMD M.5435.
[21] NUMD M.5842.
[22] NUMD MaB/195/7, 219/1–3, 220/1–20, 225/1–15.
[23] NUMD Ma 2C/161/585.
[24] NUMD Ma 2C/161/593.

The events which followed moved the vicar to write in the following year's parish magazine:

What a sight it was on Thursday 4th May to see all the tenants of Laxton in the South Field, when Mr Wordsworth undertook the difficult task of reapportioning the various holdings so that every tenant might have his land as much as possible in one piece! The enclosure of Stubbin Side for the purpose of sowing it down, and the cleaning and bridging of the Long-Syke dyke are notable changes. Let us hope that the stackyards of Laxton will tell a tale in the course of time, and that the effective drainage of so much land will make things better.[25]

Of course not everyone agreed with this panegyric. Once again George Birkitt complained, and once again Wordsworth countered in no uncertain terms.

I thought you were about the last person in Laxton who had any cause to complain of the re-allotment of land, for you have it all in one place, and that nearest to home – of itself sufficient to make up for any slight deficiency of acreage, had there been any. But there is none, as I can show you.[26]

Joseph Merrils, another dissatisfied tenant, was reminded that he had been a party to the original agreement:

I cannot move in any direction without it being clearly understood that you will loyally carry out the resolution carried at the meeting of the tenants before I began to reallot the field that all tenants would abide by my decision, whether they liked it or not. To attempt to do otherwise, as you spoke of doing yesterday would really not be honourable, and I am sure that upon consideration you will see this.[27]

Eventually everyone was placated, and the 398 strips were reduced to just 78, while enclosures more or less halved the size of the field (figure 9.1).

Early in 1906 the tenants voted to approve a continuation of the scheme to the West and Mill Fields. Wordsworth was happy to continue – 'I will do my best to reallot the land without delay.' However, following the complaints he received after the South Field reallocation he again insisted that decisions should be unanimous, particularly as some of the most notorious grumblers were absent from the meeting: 'I however notice that J. Merrils, J. Cook, S. Sampson, J. Dewick, G. Birkitt and B. Moody, were not present. I ought to be given some assurance by these tenants that they will accept my reallotment. I know one or two who may raise difficulties at the last moment, and this must not be.'[28] The necessary assurances were forthcoming, but before Wordsworth

25 NAO PR 4760/14.
26 NUMD Ma 2C/161/617.
27 NUMD Ma 2C/161/621.
28 NUMD Ma 2C/161/988.

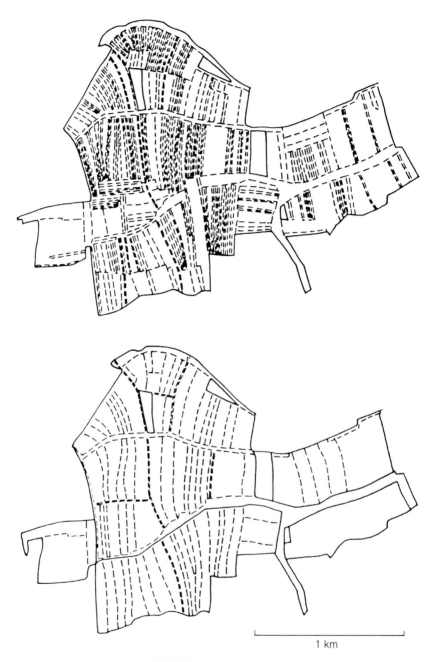

FIGURE 9.1 *South Field before and after reorganization, 1905*

could complete the reallocation he had to negotiate the acquisition of just over 6 acres from three freeholders. He paid £275, a price he regarded as over the odds, but worth paying because they made Manvers sole owner of two of the three remaining fields. With the purchase of Primrose Farm in the autumn of 1906 the monopoly was complete, and West Field and Mill Field were re-allotted in 1906 and 1907 respectively.[29]

From 1908 Laxton took on a rather different appearance, and one which can be seen on the ground today. The basic features of the open-field pattern were preserved, although the furlong boundaries disappeared completely. Some of the long narrow strips of the past disappeared, and the strips became broader, with a few roughly square in shape. The average size of the remaining strips increased from about three-quarters of an acre to slightly over 2 acres, which made it possible to promote the more efficient use of corn drills and reapers. The binder was first used in Laxton about 1904.[30] The total was reduced from 1,162 to 263, and some of the latter, including the 27 in East Field, were effectively outside the common-field system. The unenclosed area was reduced from 899 acres to 508 acres, which remained unfenced (table 9.5). The sykes and lanes remained virtually unchanged, although some roads were re-aligned and new roads made to improve access. New ditches were cut, brick culverts were constructed along the main drainage channels into the open fields, and

TABLE 9.5 *The reorganization of 1904–1908*

| Field | Before reorganization | | | After reorganization | | | |
	Date	Strips	Acres	Date	Strips	Enclosed (acres)	Unenclosed (acres)
East	1903	100	67	1903	23	67	none
South	1905	398	321	1905	78	135	143
				1911		43	
West	1906	264	217	1906	65	54	155
				1912		7	
Mill	1907	400	294	1907	97	75	210
				1913		9	
Total		1162	899		263	390	508

Sources: After C. S. and C. S. Orwin, *The Open Fields* (Oxford, 1938), p. 192; B. A. Wood, 'Laxton in the Twentieth Century', *East Midland Geographer*, 7, 6 (1980), 232.

[29] NUMD M.5774, 5775, 5777; Ma 2B/162/44–6; Ma 2C/161/165, 166, 162/316; Wood, thesis, p. 427.
[30] Wood, thesis, pp. 422–3.

the existing ditches were thoroughly scoured. The grazing and cropping rules were updated in 1908.

The areas removed from the open fields became new enclosures, and this process continued until 1913 (figure 9.2). In some instances enclosures continued to be farmed in strips. Of these, some of the larger ones were relatively close to the village and easily accessible. The tenants received freedom of cropping within their tenancy agreements, but the areas involved could no longer be used for grazing because the enlarged strips within them were not fenced. The exception was Stubbinside, on the south side of the South Field, an area for which an agreement was reached allowing it to be seeded down so that the tenants would be able to graze stock in proportion to their land holding. The furlongs enclosed may also have been chosen because they were roughly equal in extent, and could be fenced with the minimum of expense, which would also explain why the strips within them remained unfenced.[31]

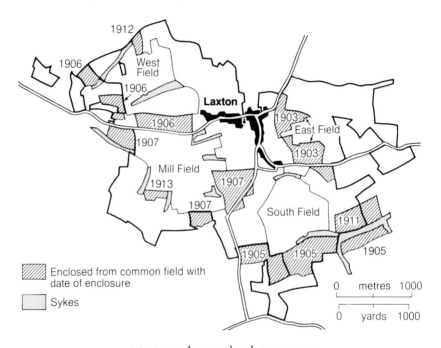

FIGURE 9.2 *Areas enclosed, 1903–1913*

The reorganization was a remarkable triumph for Wordsworth. With relatively little friction he managed to reorganize the open fields without seriously damaging the farming system, and to provide many of the benefits of

---

[31] NUMD Ma 2C/161/617; Wood, thesis, p. 424.

enclosure without incurring the full cost.[32] Wordsworth himself was impressed with all the activity. He wrote in 1913 of 'the very great expenditure which has been going on now, for 30 years to my knowledge, in the improvement of Lord Manvers' property in that parish, and is still continuing [. .] no parish in the whole of the Southwell Union has had the same amount done for it as Laxton.'[33] The accounts record expenditure of £439 on the open fields during the years of reorganization.

As a result of his efforts, by 1910 the total number of holdings had increased since 1891 from 40 to 42, with the mean size of the larger ones falling from 114 to 111 acres. The number of less than 25 acres remained unchanged at 14. This was made possible partly because some of the small holdings acquired by Manvers were already farmed by existing tenants, and these were simply integrated with their current tenancies. Consequently the main change was in the shape rather than the size of the fields because while the strip pattern changed considerably the field pattern remained substantially unaltered. This also meant that the mean distance between the village and the open-field strips in each holding did not change significantly, while, even after enlargement, the strips remained much smaller than the enclosures.[34]

Some of the smaller newly enclosed furlongs were added not to village farms but to the existing outlying farms. Knapeney was completely enclosed, while Brockilow, Primrose (purchased 1906) and Copthorne (by 1911) almost so, their only strips being in enclosed furlongs. Westwood was the only one of the outlying farms to retain some land in the open fields. Even today the tenant has a single strip in the West Field. In the case of Knapeney, Primrose and Copthorne, which lie contiguous to each other on the eastern side of the parish, Wordsworth took the opportunity to reallot territory whenever possible in order to consolidate the farms. In 1907, for example, when the tenant of Copthorne was given notice to quit for failing to pay his rent, and for poor farming, Wordsworth added outlying meadow from Kanpeney to the Copthorne holding, while the block of outlying fields in Copthorne were added to Knapeney. Primrose was enlarged by adding adjoining fields which had previously been farmed from the village. Even so, there was still room for further manoeuvre since a number of strips and enclosures in the vicinity of Westwood and Brockilow Farms continued to be farmed from the village, and an outlying meadow in Brockilow was well over a mile from the farmstead.[35]

For all Wordsworth's efforts, the fundamentally fragmented pattern of open-field farming persisted, but the question remains: why go to such lengths and yet leave open fields in Laxton? Unfortunately we do not know, although a few

[32] Wood, thesis, pp. 418–25; *Open Fields*, pp. 191–2.
[33] NUMD Ma 2C/167/132.
[34] Wood, thesis, pp. 425–8, 488–9.
[35] Wood, thesis, pp. 427–8, 492–3; NUMD M.5437.

suggestions can be made. First, the unpopularity of large farms during the agricultural depression must have ensured that there was little or no incentive to enclose merely to increase farm sizes. At the same time the introduction of machinery, for which the narrow strips were unsuited, made some form of reorganization imperative. Second, the prevailing climate of opinion favoured land reform rather than further enclosure, and legislation might not easily have been obtained. Thirdly, the reorganization was achieved without a great financial outlay on legislation, surveying, fencing and other necessary expenditure, and these economies may have appealed to Manvers given the reduced state of the Laxton rental. Finally, the recognition that Laxton was one of the last places where open-field farming was still practised was already beginning to dawn. It was in May 1906, in the middle of the reorganization, that the vicar published a short article on Laxton in *Country Life*, under the headline 'A Survival'. It was the first public acknowledgement that Laxton was unique.

Not surprisingly there were some who thought even these reforms were a travesty. A correspondent of the vicar's told him in 1905, when the reform programme was scarcely under way:

I grieve for the future of Laxton, it is like old wine losing its flavour, you will blot all out of special interest and begin again with a clean slate. I could see a difference on my last visit, the open field at the east end fenced in, and the squatters cottage swept away and the site converted into an apple garden. *I do not like it*.[36]

Despite these misgivings there was one great advantage in the change; the farmers could be more certain which of the wider and less numerous 'lands', as they continued to be called, were in their tenure. With so many 'lands' in the past, and with great numbers of labourers passing through the village, mistakes were inevitable. Farmers, or their labourers, would plough or even seed the wrong strip, and then there would be trouble over compensation. During the exchange negotiations of the 1860s Lucius Spooner pointed out to Horncastle that 'many of them dont know their own in the open fields.'[37] There were some of course who claimed never, or nearly never, to make a mistake. In the 1930s one Laxton farmer recalled to C. S. Orwin that as a young man he had known every one of his father's twenty strips in the Mill Field, and the only time he had made a mistake was when ridge and furrow were obliterated by snow and he had carted manure on to a land adjacent to that of his father.[38] Since 1908 such memory has been much easier. The bailiff claimed in the 1950s that he knew every strip of every farmer, and most of today's full-time farmers would have little difficulty identifying different tenures.

[36] NAO PR 4079.
[37] NUMD MaB/187/828; J. B. Firth, *Highways and Byeways in Nottinghamshire* (1916), p. 380; *Life at Laxton*, p. 11.
[38] *Open Fields*, p. 126.

Victorian Laxton was a village in decline. Population fell steadily after 1831, and rapidly after 1861. Houses were pulled down and not replaced; public houses were closed. Work opportunities faltered, and domestic servants were in less demand. It was agricultural conditions which were the cause of these reverses. The prosperity of the middle decades, with rising rents and optimistic talk about enclosure (at Thoresby if nowhere else) was followed by deep depression, falling rents, bankrupt tenants, and a necessary change in the farming pattern. The remaining freeholders were bought out; tenancies changed hands and out went some long-standing village families; and finally the open fields were reorganized, although not enclosed. Not that any of this meant the village was a depressing place in which to live. Conditions could he hard, and for some the workhouse was the final destiny, but there was plenty of activity with hunt meets and feast weeks, jubilee celebrations and Sunday School parties. The church was partly rebuilt (and Moorhouse chapel almost entirely so), and Lord Manvers funded two school buildings and a schoolhouse. But he lived at Thoresby and exercised only limited influence in Laxton, which may explain why the villagers were not over-conscientious attenders at church worship. Agricultural depression may have plunged some families into financial problems – particularly, perhaps, the freeholders with no landlord to help them out – and forced young people to seek their fortunes elsewhere, but it did not destroy the community. The village was still largely self-contained in terms of the services on offer, and the farmers helped each other through difficulties. By the early years of the twentieth century, the depression had partially lifted, the farming cycle had been adjusted to cater for more livestock and the demand for animal feeds, and the open fields had been reorganized to improve efficiency. When the plough boys performed their play in January 1914, and the young girls danced round the maypole on May Day, few could have foreseen just how much the village was destined to change as the twentieth century unfolded.

Chapter Ten

Twentieth-Century Village

In August 1914 the First World War broke out, and rural life was never to be quite the same again. When the village school reopened on 8 September after the summer break, Frank Willis recorded in the log book that 'the Great European War broke out during the holidays. This afternoon the girls began to knit caps and scarves for our soldiers.' In place of history and geography lessons he instructed the children about the War, and the immediacy of the conflict was brought home when Herman van Batenburg, a Belgian refugee, was admitted to the school in December 1914. He was just 6, and was to be one of three Belgian children who spent the war years in Laxton school. In December 1915 Willis's son Oscar taught a lesson in the school on 'the English soldiers' equipment at the Front'. The children watched an airship pass overhead in October 1917, and they were encouraged to write to the soldiers on active service. Their contribution to the war effort consisted of planting potatoes and blackberrying.

A number of Laxton men went to the front. One or two were regular soldiers, while others volunteered for Kitchener's army.[1] Many did not return; the Roll of Honour in the church contains thirty-two names of those who served, of whom nine died. It reads like a roll-call of the village families – Bagshaw, Cree, Laughton, Maddison, Moody, Rose and Saxelby among them. Frank Willis recorded in the school log book the names of former scholars killed on active service, which included his own son Oscar. Families were split by the War; from Bottom Farm Charlie and Clifford Whitworth went to the Front, Charlie died and his brother came back. For the families that lost sons and husbands the memory was to linger for years, but finally the War ended. In November 1918 Willis recorded in the log book how 'the children paraded the village and sang patriotic songs on the occasion of the Armistice,' and Alice Bailey (now in her eighties) can still recall the tea that was laid on, and the games on the vicarage lawn to celebrate the end of hostilities. The school was

[1] William Beckitt and Jack Cook, *Open Field Recollections* (Laxton, n.d.), pp. 3, 11.

closed for the day in December 1919 when Lord Manvers unveiled the village war memorial, on which are engraved the names of those who fell in the Great War.[2]

No community escaped the Great War, but in some ways Laxton was remarkably untouched by the conflict. Like every English village, it has changed during the twentieth century in ways which must have seemed scarcely possible to the young men of the generation that went to war in 1914, but in agricultural terms the War made little impact on the long-term development of the village. A few heavyweight hunters were commandeered for army use (and a few others were conveniently hidden out of sight), but the tractor and the combine harvester – which have together transformed village agriculture – arrived only with the Second World War. Since then there have been all sorts of experiments: kale and sugar beet (but not oil seed rape) in the spring corn field; the disappearance from the village of working horses and a sharp reduction in numbers of sheep and other animals; the demise of the fallow field; and landlord changes with a swiftness unmatched since the early years of the seventeenth century. The estate which the Pierrepont family had gradually pieced together over more than 300 years was broken up in the early 1950s. About 800 acres were sold to tenant farmers, and 1,760 acres and the lordship of the manor passed to the Ministry of Agriculture. The Ministry sold its holding to the Crown Estate Commissioners in 1981. The Thoresby estate retained about 900 acres in the village, but the big house means much less nowadays. The sixth and last Earl Manvers died in 1955. In 1980 Thoresby Hall was sold to British Coal, who resold it in 1988 to a hotelier. The nominal owner of the family's remaining acres in Laxton does not even bear the name of Pierrepont.

The change which has taken place in Laxton during the century has been largely to do with agricultural practices and, consequent upon them, declining population. In 1914 the village was largely self-sufficient, but today this is certainly not the case. In this chapter the story comes down almost to the present day, through a period of change which has been as rapid and profound as in any previous century.

PEOPLE AND PLACES

The steep decline in population after 1861 was temporarily arrested during the first two decades of the twentieth century, but it resumed again after 1921 and continued until 1971. Between 1971 and 1981 a rise of 9 per cent restored population to its level of 1961 (table 10.1). The 1981 figure was just 45 per cent of the maximum achieved in modern times, in 1831. However, the nature of this decline needs to be kept in perspective. In 1881 there were 104 families

[2] NAO PR 4145.

TABLE 10.1 *Laxton's population in the twentieth century*

Year	Total
1901	394
1911	389
1921	396
1931	348
1941	No census
1951	312
1961	293
1971	264
1981	294

Source: Printed Census Returns.

in the village; in 1981 the number had fallen to 99. In other words the size of households had fallen considerably, from 4.6 in 1881 to just 3 in 1981. This partly reflected the triumph of machinery over labour. Most of the farmers work their holdings with family labour, hiring in extra help at busy times of the year. As a result, the number of people employed on the land is now much smaller than it was even in 1914, and the decline has been particularly rapid since 1945. With little demand for young male labour the village age structure has altered considerably. During the nineteenth century roughly half the villagers were aged 20 or under; in 1981 just 21 per cent were under 16. In the nineteenth century the number of people over 60 in the village did not exceed 10 per cent; in 1981 the number of pensionable individuals was nearly 16 per cent.

As population declined the village lost its services. The mill was blown down in 1916 and not rebuilt, although two millstones in the churchyard are a reminder of this once important village institution. Arthur Grundy was the last blacksmith. He was still shoeing a few horses twenty years ago, but his services were required only occasionally once the tractor replaced the horse in farming. 'Cobbler' Laughton was the last village shoemaker. Today there is a district nurse living in the village, but no millers, blacksmiths, wheelwrights or cobblers. Only the village shop-cum-Post Office survives. The shop dates back at least to the 1840s and in the 1920s it was kept by Florence Barnes.[3] Her husband was the resident bricklayer for Laxton and the surrounding villages. In those days the Post Office was run separately by Mary Moody from a house where the telephone box now stands, but when she married Percy Maddison

---

[3] Kelly's *Directory of Nottinghamshire* (1928).

PLATE 10.1 *The Mill. This wooden post mill stood on a site in the Mill field until it was destroyed in a gale during 1916 and not replaced. In 1635 Laxton had mills in both the South and Mill fields. The first of these was probably used primarily by the people of Moorhouse. The latter site continued in use until the twentieth century, and can still be seen today.*

the business moved with her to his farm (now known as New House). Margaret Maddison, the present postmistress, was born there, and the family transferred the business to the village shop at the end of the 1930s when Maddison had to give up farming. Today's farmers and their wives visit Newark for the market, or Tuxford and Ollerton for shopping. Falling population, the bus and the motor car, have together transformed a largely self-sufficient village into one which is almost bereft of services.

The school was also a victim of falling numbers and an ageing population. Frank Willis retired from the headship at the end of November 1922, when he was succeeded by Granville Cartledge. Willis's daughter Barbara also ended her connection with the school, although she continued to live in the schoolhouse. Willis had been a popular teacher, although the school became rather old fashioned in his later years. In June 1922 the inspectors noted that it needed to be 'worked on more modern lines'. For his funeral in 1927 the children were given a half-day holiday, and the death of Mrs Willis three years later was also recorded in the log book. Granville Cartledge was a popular teacher, still remembered by many of the villagers today, but he contracted tuberculosis and died in the summer of 1934. His successor, Constance Cox, stayed until 1947 when, reputedly after an argument with the vicar, she moved to Thurgarton school.

School life continued much as before. There were regular holidays for the November ploughing matches, and for royal weddings. When the Duke of York was married in April 1923 the children were provided with a 'sumptuous tea in the parish room', while on the occasion of George V's Silver Jubilee in 1935 there was a tea, maypole dances and country dancing. The school closed for the king's funeral in 1937, and took three days off to celebrate the coronation of George VI. Old Mr Marrison at Westwood Farm arranged parties on his 80th and 86th birthdays, and there were Christmas festivities to be enjoyed. After his retirement Frank Willis undertook the role of Santa Claus. Other events were less fun. In June 1931 the log book records that 'the dentist visited on Tuesday and treated 22 children for dental defects. Some of these had to go home and some had to be absent the next day.'

By the time the Second World War broke out the school's days were numbered. In 1921, 73 pupils were on the role, but the total declined to 47 in 1927 and to 38 by 1941. The teaching staff was cut to accommodate this alteration. In 1921 the school had four paid staff, but by 1939 the headmistress was working with only an uncertified assistant. With the outbreak of the Second World War the children were instructed in the use of gas masks, and the detection of air raids. For their Christmas party in 1939 they were entertained by troops billeted in the village, and as part of the war effort they were encouraged to pick blackberries and potatoes. In 1942 Manvers leased the school to the Southwell Diocesan Board of Finance, but with just 26 pupils on the role it closed at Christmas 1947 and the children transferred to Kneesall.[4] The old infants' department is now derelict, but the main school building has become the village hall.

The church has also changed in the course of the twentieth century. When the First World War broke out the Rev. Christopher Collinson was still the vicar of Laxton, and a respected figure in the village. He resigned at Michaelmas 1916 after eighteen years in the parish, and was succeeded by the Rev. James Tunbridge, who had been a CMS missionary in India. Tunbridge still lived in the style of a country parson, with two maids at the vicarage, but he stayed only four years. He was succeeded in 1921 by the Rev. Samuel Bleau, who retired in 1930, but continued to take services periodically until the early 1940s. Rev. P. M. Daubney was appointed to the living – the Thoresby estate paid his £15 10s removal expenses to Pickfords – but he in turn was succeeded by the Rev. W. J. Thurston, then curate of Newark, in 1932. Thurston was offered the post at £341 a year, but it was agreed that he should receive £365 a year with Manvers funding the difference. Assured of this income he set about installing central heating and electric lighting in the vicarage, but by 1938 he had run into financial difficulties. The living was yielding only £300, and Thurston was short of money because the family business in which he had

4 NAO PR 4089; SL/106/1/2–3.

shares had stopped paying dividends, and this had reduced his income by £180 a year. He found himself unable to pay off the debts on the heating and lighting of approximately £70. Although the living yielded £404 15s, of which £209 was tithe annuities, and £126 came from the Ecclesiastical Commissioners, after various outgoings had been met the net income was only £341 10s 5d. Earl Manvers paid £23 9s 8d to make up a guaranteed stipend of £365.[5]

Thurston also set about the church with energy. In 1933 he gained approval for a new boiler and radiators as well as various changes within the church such as the distempering of the walls to obliterate modern texts and the erection of a new oak pulpit in memory of Christopher Collinson. Two years later electric lights replaced the old oil lamps, and an oak screen was erected to commemorate the king's Silver Jubilee. An electric blower for the organ was installed in 1946. The advowson was transferred from Manvers to the Southwell Diocesan Board of Patronage in 1942.[6] The days of the Victorian parson who became part of the village community were now long passed, and since 1942 Laxton has had eleven different clergy. Today Laxton does not have a resident parson and the vicarage belongs to an estate agent.

We have some indication of church life from the service registers and a survey of parochial work carried out in 1921 and subsequently updated. Easter communicants are an indication of attendance, and these peaked at 101 in 1912. They fell away during the war years, recovered in the mid-1920s and have gradually declined since. Of course they are only a rough guide to attendance. In 1920 51 parishioners took communion, but there were 42 at the morning and 76 at the evening services. A year later 60 villagers were on the electoral roll. There were 17 members of the choir in 1921, and 6 bellringers. Church expenses amounted to £46, and £6 11s 10d was raised for home and overseas mission work.[7] Frank Willis completed forty years as organist in 1926, shortly before his death. The first-fruits communion service continued until recently, usually at the beginning of August. In 1938 25 attended the 5.30 Holy Communion. By 1955 it was held at 6.30 a.m., and by 1968 it had slipped a further hour to 7.30 when it was a sung mass with 22 attenders. Today there are 43 on the electoral roll, and average congregations are about 12. Elsewhere in Laxton services are still held in the Old Independent (now Congregational) chapel and in Moorhouse chapel (although it was closed during the Second World War). The old Primitive Methodist chapel in Moorhouse is in ruins.

Poor relief remained a parish responsibility until the end of the 1920s, and the charities were dispensed each year. On Christmas Eve bread was customarily distributed to the village poor; in 1925 35 individuals received a total of 174 loaves.[8] Table 10.2 gives the annual cost of relief in the last days of the Poor

---

[5] NUMD Ma 3E 2064–5; 5E/122/1.
[6] NAO PR 4084–7, 8487.
[7] NAO PR 4089.
[8] Frank Moody, *My Lifetime Memories of Laxton* (Laxton, 1981).

TABLE 10.2 *Poor Law payments 1912–1927*

Year	Opening balance	Outgoings: contributions to common fund/county rate	Payments to the Union Treasurer	Balance in favour end of year
1912–13	86	221	216	91
1913–14	59	238	226	71
1914–15	77	246	254	69
1915–16	84	264	270	78
1916–17	124	231	248	97
1917–18	136	244	246	133
1918–19	122	297	298	121
1919–20	162	373	386	150
1920–1	192	643	654	181
1921–2	204	697	710	191
1922 ($\frac{1}{2}$ yr)	105	362	368	99
1923	224	659	638	232
1924	93	209	206	97
1925	91	447	444	93
1926	96	473	478	91
1927	101	496	500	96

Source: NAO PUS/1/8/1–3.

Law. Individuals were paid relief either due to illness or to lack of income. Annie Priest, aged 66, was receiving 3s a week relief in 1923 and 1924 to supplement her weekly earnings of 4s, while George Sampson (45) a crippled labourer, was paid relief to supplement whatever wages he could earn. On the other hand Ann Lacey's application for relief was refused in August 1924 because although she was 87 and unwell she had three sons who were expected to support her. William Rose and his wife Florence were allowed 15s each for fourteen weeks in October 1924. They had six dependent children and were unable to make ends meet because he was awaiting hospital admission for treatment for an ulcerated stomach. In 1928 the overseers allowed £2 16s expenses for the removal of Edward Wightman (52) to Radcliffe asylum.

Applicants for relief were usually old and poor, and often infirm, but the enquiries about family members who might be able to support them is an indication of prevailing social attitudes. When Edmund Musgrove (36), imbecile, was awarded relief in 1927 the overseers noted that his father Benjamin was a county council roadman earning 32s a week. However, although there was a tendency for contributions towards the common union fund to increase after about 1920, the real reason for the increase in outgoings was the county rate. This was between £165 and £199 between 1912–13 and 1917–18, but in the aftermath of the war it soared to £295 in 1919–20, and to £531 the following year. Although it fell back in the mid-1920s it was still nearly £400 in both 1926 and 1927. The Poor Law was reformed by the Local Government Act of 1929. The guardians were swept away and their powers vested in the local authorities.

Today's roadways follow the routes of paths and tracks which can be traced in the seventeenth century, but during the twentieth century they have undergone considerable change. In the early years of the century the roads were mainly cart tracks – an cart track-widths. Older people in the village today can still remember how filthy the roads were because no one cleared up after the cows had been moved into and out of the village for milking. Upkeep was primitive. The roads had a gravel surface which was raked to fill in the ruts. A local farmer Sam Whitworth, who left the village in 1916, used to haul about 200 tons of granite from Tuxford station each summer, which he left along the roadside for the village roadman Tommy Walker to fill in the ruts. Roads around the farms were occasionally improved. In 1923–4 the Thoresby estate spent £53 14s 4d on making Knapeney Road. At Church Farm, Moorhouse, in 1928 George Saxelby's 132–acre farm was still served by a lane, which was often impassable in winter. Saxelby argued that this damaged his implements and harness during the winter period, and he pressed for a 10-foot road – which would cost £400 – and a rent reduction.[9]

As traffic increased improvement became imperative, and in 1929 the County Council took over responsibility for road upkeep. The gates which barred the roads into Laxton were removed in the 1930s, partly because motorists failed to shut them. In 1933 a fence was erected along the northern edge of Mill Field to separate it from Acre Edge Road. The Thoresby agent hoped that the County Council would be persuaded to erect the fence because it was 'most unreasonable that the Lord of the Manor should be called upon to spend large sums of money in fencing, as this trouble is all due to motor traffic and funds should be available to pay for these fences from motor taxation'. Since the road had to be a minimum of 50 feet wide some encroachment was necessary on the arable strips along the northern edge of Mill Field. Thoresby proposed to let the County Council have the land at a nominal figure.[10] Co-operation between landlord and Council also occurred in 1949 when, to ensure the improvement of the road between Laxton and Moorhouse, Manvers agreed to donate a parcel of land, on condition that the Council planted a quick hedge or suitable protective fences, and paid any necessary

[9] Beckitt and Cook, *Open Field Recollections*, p. 6; NUMD Ma 3E/2042.
[10] NUMD Ma 2C/182 f. 790, 822.

legal costs. The same terms were proposed for improving the road to Egmanton two years later.[11]

Other developments beyond its borders also affected Laxton. During the 1920s the Nottinghamshire (Dukeries) coalfield was opened up, and with it came the building of New Ollerton. Coal was found at the bottom of Cocking Hill in 1920, and three Dutch children were admitted to the school because they lived in the village while their fathers undertook trial borings at Ollerton. Since the 1930s a number of villagers – including one of the current part-time farmers – have found employment in the colliery. From the late 1930s oil was produced in central Nottinghamshire, around Eakring, Bothamsall and Egmanton. Prospecting took place in Laxton where the D'Arcy Exploration Company were given permission to drill on a number of farms during the 1930s and 1940s including Westwood Farm where they prospected in 1942–3. Since the 1940s a number of villagers have been employees of the Butterley Brick Works at the bottom of the hill west of the village towards Ollerton.

In 1939 came the Second World War, and by contrast with 1914–18 the village was considerably affected. Local farming practice had to be altered to conform with government requirements; troops were billeted in the village; and German prisoners of war worked on the land in the last years of the War. For those villagers old enough to remember the War, the event which made most impact occurred on 28 August 1940 when eight bombs were dropped on the village. It was a hot day and a group of village ladies had been on a visit to Southwell. Just as they returned to Laxton, late in the evening, a bomber, presumably lured by the uncovered headlights of the bus, dropped its cargo. Several of the bombs landed directly on the village, and at least one fell in West Field, where it left a large crater. Barbara Willis was killed outside the door of the schoolhouse, and damage to the village was considerable.

Nineteen Thoresby tenants were affected by the air raid. Pantiles had to be relaid, and glass – most of the village lost its windows – replaced. A number of houses required new plasterwork or guttering. Two properties took the full force of the explosions. Mr G. W. Laughton's farmhouse required extensive repairs both externally and internally, while the covered crewyard, the cowhouse and the barn were described as a total loss. Repairs and renewals cost £459. The schoolhouse, where Miss Willis was killed, was severely damaged. The outbuildings were a total loss, and the roof, windows, doors and plasterwork all required extensive renovation, costing in all £125. The Thoresby estate spent three guineas on immediate clearing up after the bombing, and £521 6s 7d on repairs in 1940–1 and £332 17s 3d the following year. This was rather less than the estimate of £1,038 to repair the various damaged properties, and less even than the £945 which Manvers was

[11] NUMD Ma 5E/161/1–5.

prepared to accept in settlement of the claim. He finally agreed to take £817 compensation.[12]

This was not the only war-related damage in the village. In 1941 the Air Ministry took over a 3-acre plot of land from Knapeney Farm, to become part of Ossington Airport. Landing lights were positioned in Laxton woods and a search light at Knapeney Farm. The site was valued at £37 10s. Compensation was claimed for the damage to pasturage, and after it was de-requisitioned in 1945, £24 was paid as compensation for dilapidations.[13] The proximity of the air strip may explain why an RAF plane crash landed in the village in 1942.

Change has been considerable in Laxton during the course of the twentieth century, but this does not mean that it has been an unpleasant place to live. Ron Cree, now retired but still living at Old Vicarage Farm, looks back over his life-time in the village with considerable satisfaction. There were whist drives and dances every two weeks or so; it was not too difficult to cycle to Tuxford to the cinema, or even to Newark or Retford. He recalls spending evenings chatting in the stables, or playing cards around the fireside. Since working hours were long, bed time was early, perhaps 10 p.m. But he has no regrets. 'It were heaven,' as he recalls; Laxton was a 'grand place to live in'. In the 1920s and 1930s the village had a thriving Amateur Dramatics Group. Even today there are pig roasts and dances, but Laxton Feast, with its swingboats and coconut shies, did not resume after the Second World War. The villagers no longer take the law into their own hands by causing affrays in the alehouse as their seventeenth-century predecessors did, perhaps because the Dovecote Inn is a pleasant village pub patronized from the local towns and villages. Today's village is not in the commuter belt, but it is more cosmopolitan, less self-sufficient, and less isolated from the community round about.

FARMING IN LAXTON, 1914–1939

On the eve of the First World War British agriculture remained, if not depressed, certainly far from buoyant. The long-term shift from arable to grass and from corn to cattle, which had been proceeding through the last quarter of the nineteenth century was still ongoing; indeed, it was to continue with hardly any interruption down to 1939. The acreage in permanent grass in Laxton had gradually risen, enabling farmers to keep more cattle, while the proportion of land under the plough had fallen slightly with some recovery after 1900 (figure 10.1). The Great War itself brought relatively little change to the farming pattern in Laxton, apart from a temporary decline in permanent grass and a fall in the number of cattle and sheep. Emergency wartime powers were used by the

[12] NUMD Ma 5E/174–90.
[13] NMD Ma 5E/175/3–9.

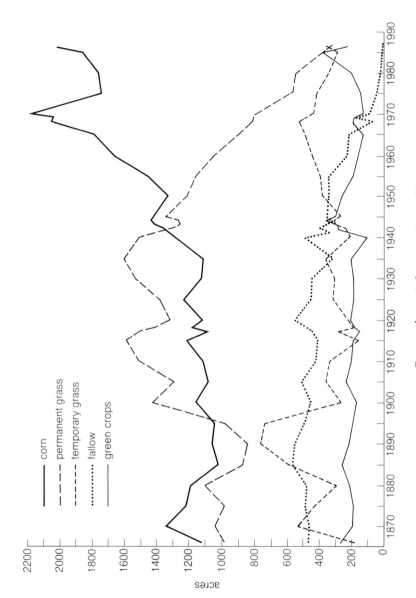

FIGURE 10.1 *Crops and grass in Laxton, 1866–1986*

government to persuade farmers to plough up grass in order to increase arable output. Between 1914 and 1918 in the north Midlands (including Nottinghamshire) the proportion of land devoted to arable produce increased by 10 per cent.[14] Laxton was only marginally affected since in June 1918 the acreage under crops was less than in 1915 and only slightly (46 acres) in advance of 1910. Possibly because the acreage cropped declined in 1917, in March the following year 24 Laxton farmers were issued with orders to plough up specified land which was to be cultivated as arable in order to grow corn and roots in the 1918 harvest. The burden was shared around. No individual was asked to plough up more than 13 acres, but the overall total was 255 acres.[15] Rent arrears remained substantial through the war years, although there were few discharges or abatements before 1917–18, when they totalled £185.

After 1918 the trend towards grass was resumed, partly as a result of the collapse in corn prices in 1921 and almost continuous depression in agriculture through the 1920s. In the north Midlands the arable acreage declined by 20 per cent down in 1939, and nationally the proportion of land in grass peaked in 1938. The acreage under permanent grass in Laxton increased after 1920 to reach a new level of more than 1,600 acres in 1935. The Thoresby estate accounts give occasional hints of farmers turning land down to grass. In 1921–2 £8 4s was spent 'preparing land given up by F. Sampson for laying down to permanent pasture', and in 1928–9 Mark Bailey was allowed £23 10s on a $9\frac{1}{2}$ acre field 'left to grass'. In the course of the 1920s, part of the former East Field was fenced to provide a larger area of grazing land adjoining the Step Farm steadings on the eastern side of the village, and in 1931 the strips at the western end of Stubbinside were added to Brockilow. These had not been cultivated for many years. A boundary fence was erected, and a water trough introduced at Brockilow Corner 'to serve this field and also a considerable area in Stubbinside, which is being put down to permanent pasture'.[16]

Together with this increase in land permanently under grass came other significant alterations in the farming pattern. These included a slow but perceptible rise in the acreage under temporary grasses, a shift out of barley as farmers concentrated on growing oats as a fodder crop (figure 10.2), and a steady increase in the number of cattle (figure 10.3). A recovery also occurred – although not to pre-1914 levels – in the number of sheep. Deep littering was introduced for poultry production. The acreage under crops in the parish hardly changed between the wars. The Wheat Act of 1932 encouraged farmers to increase arable cultivation and national output rose by 2 to 3 per cent annually in the years immediately prior to 1939. In Laxton the acreage under wheat increased by 60 acres between 1930 and 1935 to represent virtually

[14] E. H. Whetham, *The Agrarian History of England and Wales, vol VIII 1914–39* (Cambridge, 1978), p. 116.

[15] NUMD MaB/216.

[16] Wood, thesis, p. 494; NUMD Ma 2C/182/100, 2C/181/939.

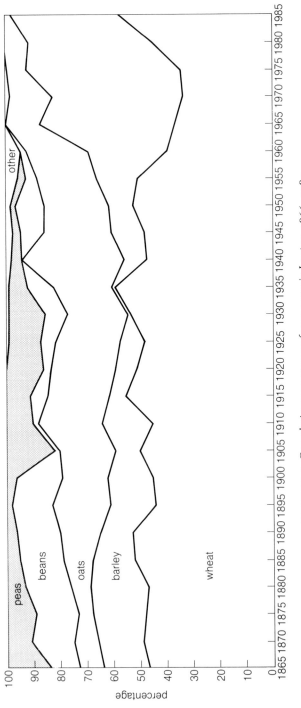

FIGURE 10.2 Cumulative percentages of corn crops in Laxton, 1866–1985

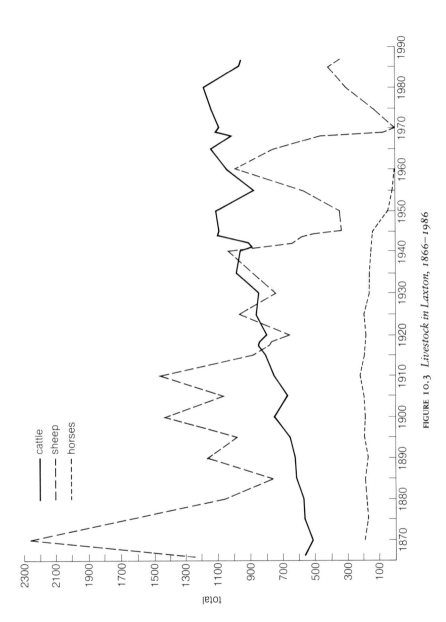

FIGURE 10.3 *Livestock in Laxton, 1866–1986*

60 per cent of the overall corn crop. Oats represented a further 22 per cent of the crop in 1935, and barley a mere 1 per cent.

The most important change of the 1930s was in milk production. The Agricultural Marketing Acts of 1931 and 1933 provided the legislative framework for establishing Marketing Boards. The Milk Marketing Boards set up in 1933–4 offered a secure outlet for the production of milk by guaranteeing to find a buyer and by organizing the allocation of supplies, with the result that dairy farming became a relatively secure enterprise and one with a bonus to the farmer of a regular monthly milk cheque to aid cash flow. Whereas the Laxton farmers had kept a handful of milking cows and their wives had made butter for sale at Newark and Tuxford markets, from the 1930s they turned their attention instead to the sale of fresh milk. Between 1930 and 1940 the number of cattle described in the agricultural returns as cows or heifers in milk or calf, rose from 244 to 368 as a direct consequence of this change of practice. Sidney Johnson at Brockilow is remembered as the first farmer to sell fresh milk out of the village. It meant rising early since the cows had to be hand milked, and the milk had to reach the station at Carlton-on-Trent 5 miles away by 6 a.m. Once the practice developed of churns being picked up in the village for transport to Mansfield Co-operative, or to Lincoln and Nottingham, all the farmers began to keep dairy cows.

The consequences were considerable, none more so perhaps than the need for suitable buildings. In every year from 1914 to the end of the 1940s the Thoresby estate spent at least £400 on repairs to farms and farmsteads. The estate accounts are not all that helpful because they merely record sums of money spent on particular farms rather than detailing the way in which the money was employed. In 1928–9, however, some of the account entries are annotated, and as a result we know that out of the £945 spent that year the roof and floor repairs at Brockilow cost £61, fencing at Primrose Farm cost £27, a new granary floor at Richard Clark's farm (Town End) cost £42, and a new roof for Jack Cooke's farm cost the estate £57. Farms were put into repair for new tenants. When George Saxelby took over Church Farm, Moorhouse, in 1921 the repair bill for Thoresby was £175, and £25 was spent in repairs to the house E. J. Rose took over in 1934. Covered roof yards were provided for two farmers in 1936–7, sheds were boarded in 1937–8, and a water supply to the fields was established at Kanpeney in 1944–5. The outlay at Knapeney was probably exceptional, but substantial investments were made in other farms as well. In 1930, for example, it was agreed to spend money on draining and extensively repairing Church Farm, although to save money it was to be undertaken by estate workmen over a number of years.[17] From the 1930s the Thoresby estate was busy knocking stables into cow houses, a trend which gathered momentum when tractors began to replace horses. In 1914–15 the

[17] NUMD Ma 3E/2046.

repair bill represented 16 per cent of the rental, but this was a low point, and a decade later in 1934–5 it was nearly 36 per cent. The figures fluctuated but the proportion remained at about 30 per cent. From 1933–4 (the year the Milk Marketing Boards were established) the repair bill always topped £1,000.

By the 1930s the landlord was committed to maintaining the open-field system but the cost was rapidly threatening to become prohibitive. Laxton was becoming more expensive to keep up at a time when the Thoresby estate was poorly placed to fund investment. Like many great landowners, the earls Manvers found themselves in deep financial difficulties after 1918, and the family fortunes were not helped by the long illness of the fifth earl. When the fourth earl died in 1926 the estate passed into the hands of trustees because Evelyn Robert, who would have been the fifth earl, was debarred from succeeding to the title by mental illness. He died in 1940 when Gervase Evelyn became the sixth and last earl. Extensive land sales took place between 1899 and 1952, and the family was reluctant to acquire additional land. Apart from two small closes measuring little more than 2 acres, the Pierreponts did not venture into the land market at Laxton between 1918 and 1939, and their only serious acquisition before 1950 was Straw Hall Farm, a 24½ acre holding acquired from the Denisons for £750.[18]

What had occurred between the wars was a subtle shift of emphasis in the farming pattern, without interruption to the basic pattern. Laxton may have been spared some of the worst problems of these years because of the mix of holdings. After all, mixed farming was common in the pre-1939 period partly because diversification reduced risk. Thus in 1935 the Laxton farmers cropped 1,324 acres, while leaving 1,974 acres under grass and 322 acres fallow. Between them they had 986 cattle, 888 sheep, 163 horses, 356 pigs and over 5,000 fowls, ducks, geese and turkeys. If mixed farming kept them in business it did not guarantee profit, and here the tenants had to look for support to the landlord and his agent.

Rents of Manvers farms in Laxton provide a yardstick against which to measure the conditions under which farming took place between the wars. The rental increased between 1908–9 and 1919–20 from £2,766 to £2,989. Arrears had fallen to £153, the lowest figure since the 1870s, but discharges and abatements totalled £168 in 1919–20. Presumably the agent was confident about the future since in 1920–1 the rental rose to £3,478, and arrears fell to £116. This optimism seems to have been justified in the 1920s. Rent arrears fell below £100 during the middle years of the decade, and there were few abatements or discharges. This may have reflected the slip back in the rent from £3,478 to just £3,280 by 1924–5, at which it remained until 1928–9 when it declined further to £2,950. That year rents returned and discharged topped £100 for the first time since 1921–2, and arrears crept up to £249.

[18] NUMD M.5855, 5871–5.

If the rental is taken at face value, farming during the 1930s was not unprofitable. The rental stayed at or about £2,900 until the war, and arrears topped £100 only in 1933–4 and 1938–9. However, this was partly achieved by allowances against anticipated rent. In 1930–1 rent returns amounted to £311, and the following year they were £314. These were the worst years, but abatements still totalled £135 in 1932–3, £212 in 1933–4, £110 in 1934–5, £120 in 1937–8, and £284 in 1938–9. Some tenants had difficulty raising their tenant right payments, and others remained in arrears with them for several years.

Several farms stayed in the same tenure for many years. Town End Farm passed from John Keyworth to John Bagshaw in 1880 and to Richard Clark in 1913. He in turn was succeeded by George Woolhouse in 1941, whose son still farms there today. Copthorne was tenanted by the Quibells from 1908 until they purchased the farm in 1950. Crosshill was leased by William Merrils in 1888 for a tenant right valuation of £306. It remained in the family until 1945 when C. W. 'Tim' Ward became the tenant. He stayed until the present tenant, Michael Jackson, took the farm in 1974. Ward had previously been the tenant of Brecks Farm which he took over from John Turner in 1939. He gave up Brecks to the Hoggards when he left in 1945 and they subsequently bought the property in 1950. Many of the tenants in 1950 had been in the village for ten or twenty years. Several of today's tenants are the sons and grandsons of men who came into the village between the wars, among them the Hennells (1919), the Godsons (1932) and the Nobles (1933), the Sayers (1940) and the Woolhouses (1941).

These examples of longevity are not necessarily typical since on average between the wars three or four farms changed hands annually, usually as single entities although when Mark Bailey vacated Step and Bottom farms in 1928 one went to John Cree and the other to Walter How. Tenants were sometimes difficult to attract. Elmer 'Jack' Rose claimed in later life that he and his family returned to Laxton in 1934 when the Thoresby agent 'begged' him to take over nineteen strips which were then uncultivated. Rose's first job was at 13 when he worked as a dayboy at Westwood Farm. Later he worked on the Thoresby estate as a drainer. The holding he took over in 1934 had not been ploughed since the First World War, and he started out with a capital of £100, a spade and a wheelbarrow.[19] His son Edmund remembers being brought up in a tiny cottage. Later Rose acquired more land as smallholders gave up farming, and by the time he retired he was working 67 acres.

The turnover of tenancies on other farms suggests that unsuitable tenants may from time to time have gained a toehold on the ladder, or that some farmers could not make a go of the farms they had leased in the prevailing economic climate. When the Pinders left Westwood in 1908, the new tenant

---

[19] *John Bull*, 21 December 1957.

was Tom Marrison. The farm remained in his family for two decades, but in 1929 Hawksworth Marrison left and the new tenant was George Trickett, who paid a tentant right of £780 and rent of £225. But he did not stay; two years later he passed the farm to J. W. Price, this time for a valuation of £510. Price and his family have retained the farm ever since, although the present tenant, Tom Price, lives across the parish border in Kirton and the farmhouse has been sold.

The clearest example of agricultural difficulty was at Knapeney farm. This was difficult to let in the inter-war period because of the ratio between grass and arable. For many years the tenancy was held by the Bartles but the farm changed hands in 1917 and 1920, and again in 1924 when Edward Chapman took the tenancy. By 1933 he had reached the end of his resources. He was overdrawn at the bank to the tune of £160 and could raise no further money or credit. He was also £115 in arrears with his rent, and still owed £152 15s 4d on the tenant right valuation which had been payable when he came into possession of the farm nearly a decade earlier – which suggests that he was admitted without adequate financial security. Chapman clearly could not continue, and the Thoresby agent agreed to take the farm in hand on condition that the stock would be sold at auction with proceeds going towards the payment of rent and valuation arrears. The parting was far from amicable. Hubert Argles, the agent, told Chapman in July 1933 that in twenty-four years at Thoresby 'I do not think I have ever received such an unpleasant letter as I received from you four days ago.' None the less he agreed, 'in due course', to 'put your case before Lady Manvers and Captain Gervas Pierrepont and then write you further'.[20]

In the agricultural conditions of the time Argles was far from sanguine about the possibility of reletting the farm, largely because 140 of the 207 acres were in arable. He suggested that the Thoresby estate should provide £2,000 (£10 per acre) to pay wages, buy stock and implements, and to allow receivers to run the farm. He also intended to reduce the arable acreage. These terms were accepted, three teams of horses were bought to work the farm, and for the next few years it was managed by the agent through a foreman, John Jones. He initially lived in the house but moved up to the village and lived in the school-house (after it was repaired following bomb damage) for much of the war because Knapeney was alongside Ossington aerodrome. Argles was aware that the whole farm had fallen into a state of dilapidation, and that considerable improvements were required to the buildings and water supply, and to farmstead access. It was costing considerable amounts of money: £451 in 1933–4, £185 in 1934–5, £223 in 1935–6, and £253 in 1936–7. Part of this went on the construction of a new access road from the Ossington Road.[21]

[20] NUMD Ma 2C/182/831.
[21] NUMD Ma 3E/205b, 2048–9, 2057, 2062.

Finally attempts were made to improve farming conditions by further consolidation of landholdings. Much depended on the agent, and for most of the period down to the later 1940s the post was held by Hubert Argles who had served his apprenticeship under Wordsworth and had doubtless strengthened his position by marrying a daughter of the fourth Earl Manvers. Ron Cree remembers him as a 'grand bloke', and Frank Moody recalled that he was 'a very active person, to be seen on horseback, or his bicycle as he carried out his duties'. Argles was not prepared to countenance major changes in an effort to improve farming incomes, but he did make some alterations to farm sizes. Between 1910 and 1933 he pushed through a number of exchanges in order to complete the consolidation of Brockilow, while strips in enclosed areas farmed from the village were added to Westwood and Brockilow as opportunity arose at the end of tenancies. This did not end complaints about the time taken to cart to and from the distant fields and strips, but the farmers found it possible to adapt within the existing structure, hence the adoption of two-furrow ploughs from 1921 onwards.[22]

Nor, despite Laxton's acknowledged historical importance, did Argles regard the open-field strips as sacrosanct. Table 10.3 shows how rationalization of strips continued after 1910, and has been held in check since 1952 only by deliberate policy. In Mill Field the reduction was achieved by merging existing strips.

TABLE 10.3 *Number of strips in the open fields during the twentieth century*

Date	West	Mill	South	Total
1904	65	97	78	240
1952	51	68	47	166
1985	50	68	46	164

Also during the inter-war period a number of the very small holdings disappeared (table 10.4). Those of between 1 and 20 acres declined from fifteen in 1920 to nine at the outbreak of war. The smallest of these were no longer viable in twentieth-century agricultural conditions, and the Manvers papers make a clear distinction between farms and cottages. Most cottages had only a garden, although in 1925 the blacksmith's shop had 3½ acres of land attached and three others had more than an acre. The number of large farms had scarcely changed since the eighteenth century, and only Knapeney and Westwood exceeded 200 acres. The latter, with 281 acres, was by far the largest of the Manvers tenancies. On the other hand there were still twenty holdings of less than 100

[22] Beckitt and Cook, *Open Field Recollections*, p. 5.

TABLE 10.4 *Size of Manvers farms in Laxton, 1925 and 1950*

1925				1950			
Size	No	Acreage	% of total acreage	Size	No	Acreage	% of total acreage
100+	14	2102	66	99+	15	2298	70
51–99	10	794	25	49–98	10	731	22
21–50	6	223	7	24–48	6	235	7
11–20	2	24	1	12–23	–	–	
6–10	4	34	1	Under 11	4	32	1
1–5	1	1	–				
Cottagers	24	14	–				
	61	3192	100		35	3296	100

Source: NUMD Ma 2B 65/2; Wood, thesis, p. 466.

acres, which indicates the continuing importance in the village of the small farm. Town End, the largest of the open-field farms, was 146 acres.

These figures are for the Manvers estate, but they can be compared with a listing for the whole parish dating from 1929 and prepared by the Orwins, presumably on the basis of information they collected locally since none of their manuscript references fit this information (table 10.5). Their list confirms the trend towards the consolidation of the larger holdings at the expense of the smaller ones, although the longer tail may reflect the inclusion of Denison

TABLE 10.5 *Number and size of Laxton holdings, 1929*

Size of holdings (acres)	Number	Acreage
200+	2	487
70–200	20	2333
40–70	9	478
20–40	6	139
9–20	4	54
5–9	6	42
Under 5	12	16
	59	3549

Source: *Open Fields*, p. 192.

property and one or two remaining small holdings. In any case the twenty-two holdings of under 20 acres occupied a mere 112 acres, or 3 per cent of the land area.

One of the advantages of retaining a range of farm sizes in Laxton was that it enabled men with little capital to step on to the first rung of the farming ladder as smallholders and part-time farmers. Those who proved their worth could count on Argles to help them climb the rungs to larger farms. As a land agent in the 1950s noted:

most Laxton farmers started as farm or estate workers, and the range in size of the holdings provides an almost perfect 'farming ladder'. The smaller holdings can be taken by a man with relatively little capital, for he will be helped to a great extent by the open field grazing rights which are available to him, while the custom of the away-going crop means that he does not have to find a large amount for ingoing expenses.[23]

Among the farmers who benefitted from this system was Herbert Godson who came to Laxton in 1932 by leasing a farm previously tenanted by Mrs Price. The tenant right valuation was £118. In 1937 he gave the farm up to Henry Cooke for a tenant right of £52 12s and took over Percy Maddison's farm. This was 118 acres and was rented at £100 a year. The Godsons are still at New House Farm. Several of those who stepped on to the ladder clearly intended to acquire one of the larger, consolidated farms. Sidney Johnson first arrived in Laxton when he took over Francis Gale's 4-acre holding in 1909. Manvers had acquired this the previous year, and Johnson paid a tenant right valuation of £14 3s 3d to Gale and £4 annual rent. He later took over other land and by 1915 his rent was £83 18s 6d. In 1917 he left his original farm, accepting tenant right valuations of £74 12s 10d from William Sampson and £18 11s 11d from Manvers. He then took over Knapeney farm from George Bartle, paying a valuation of £349 12s 19d. His rent was £154. Three years on and he was ready to move again. He passed on Knapeney for a tenant right valuation of £472 7s 6d and in turn took over the 167-acre Brockilow Farm, for which the valuation was £311 2s 3d and the rent £165. Here he stayed, eventually passing the farm to his son, who retained it until 1961 when he retired across the road to Saywood.

FARMING IN LAXTON, 1939–1980

Towards the end of the 1930s the long years of depression in agriculture, which effectively dated back to the 1870s, came to an end. Government concern about the possibility of another war with Germany resulted in livestock and

[23] J. R. Rundle, 'Laxton Today', *Agriculture*, LXII (1955), 172.

fertilizer subsidies. The 1937 Agriculture Act introduced a Land Fertility Scheme under which subsidies were paid to farmers towards the purchase and transport of lime and basic slag. Then in the spring of 1939 the Agricultural Development Act provided a subsidy of £2 an acre for ploughing permanent pasture. During the War the national acreage under the plough increased by about 50 per cent while most types of livestock – cattle apart – were effectively discouraged because of a shortage of feeding stuffs. After 1945 the recovery was continued, but prosperity also brought change on the land.

In farming terms the changes in agriculture were very much more profound in Laxton during the Second World War than they had been in 1914–18. The County Agricultural Executive Committee requisitioned and ploughed up Westwood Common, and several farmers took advantage of the subsidies on ploughing enclosed grassland. As a result of the plough-up campaign the corn acreage increased from 1,283 acres in 1940 to 1,440 (the highest figure since records began) in 1944. The overall crop acreage increased by about 30 per cent during the War, and several hundred acres of permanent grass were ploughed up. The major increase was in wheat, up from 605 acres in 1940 to a peak of 865 acres in 1943, but the quantities of potatoes, sugar beet and flax also increased significantly. Labour-intensive work was partly aided by the availability in 1944 and 1945 of a number of German prisoners of war and several full-time members of the Women's Land Army. With a considerable fall in the number of sheep (from 1,027 to 331 between 1940 and 1945) enough grassland was available for an increase in the head of cattle, which in 1943 exceeded 1,000 for the first time since records began. The number of pigs and poultry declined.[24]

The War brought a considerable increase in yields, which was partly a consequence of the spread of machinery – tractors, seed drills and combine harvesters – and of inorganic fertilizers. The first tractors arrived in Laxton at the end of the 1930s, and six were in use in 1940. Until the 1920s the agricultural returns record up to 200 horses in the village, most of them engaged in agricultural work. The total was 150 in 1939, 130 in 1945, but only 16 in 1955, by which time the horse had effectively disappeared from farming.

The legacy of the war was prosperity on the land and technical advance in agriculture, and for Thoresby this meant that rents could be raised and farms let. Although the rental altered only marginally through the war years, arrears almost disappeared, and rent returns and abatements topped £100 only in 1941–2. With that one exception they were insignificant for the whole period down to 1950, and in 1948–9 the rental was increased from £2,853 to £3,313.

After the War, it proved possible at last to let the problematic farms which

---

[24] The post-1945 agricultural returns are in the following: 1945–65, PRO MAF/68/4138, 4323, 4508, 4693, 4943; 1968–86, Ministry of Agriculture, Fisheries and Food, Chalfont Drive, Nottingham.

had come in hand since the 1930s. In addition to Knapeney, which had not been tenanted since 1933, Primrose Farm came in hand in 1940–1, and Straw Hall in 1942–3. The latter was leased from the Ossington estate until it was purchased by Lord Manvers. The house was demolished in 1940 to make way for the aerodrome. The three farms were probably designed as a single tenancy but they were not let until 1948, when Straw Hall was added to the Knapeney tenancy and Primrose separately tenanted.[25] John Jones, the Knapeney foreman, took the tenancy of Knapeney at £300 a year for the 227 acres, and his son Emrys Jones agreed to take Primrose Farm (55 acres) for £70 a year. The agreement was not entirely amicable because John Jones and Colonel Denzil Holder, the Thoresby agent appointed to replace Argles in 1949, were hardly on speaking terms. Holder accused Jones of being 'extremely rude to me without any cause', but Jones refused to acknowledge that he had anything for which to apologize. His wife told Holder: 'you will neither gain nor retain the tenants' respect if you try to bully which I am sure was not your intention.'[26] She herself complained of the leaking roof: 'The rain comes through the ceilings on to my beds, also the tiles have slipped into the spouting over the front door, causing the rain to splash on the door, and is rotting door and boards inside, and it simply pours through the roof of the scullery.'[27] Since Holder had undertaken to provide improved dairying facilities on the farm, Knapeney continued to cost the estate money; repairs and running costs totalled £341 at Primrose and £226 at Knapeney in 1948–9.

The situation at Knapeney pointed to the root cause of Holder's difficulties, money. While expenditure on repairs and improvements had reached new levels in the inter-war years, Laxton consumed ever increasing amounts of capital. Outlay reached new peaks of £2,481 in 1947–8 and £3,050 in 1948–9 (87 and 92 per cent of the rental respectively). Admittedly these high figures seem to have been spent partly in response to the legislation of these years, and the fact that by 1948 virtually everyone in the village was milking, but the Thoresby estate's net income from Laxton in 1947–8 and 1948–9 was a paltry £50, and this on an estate which was considered in the early 1950s to have been badly neglected. The consequences of this financial position were to be severe.

After 1945 in Nottinghamshire the level of arable output was maintained, with a considerable increase in barley as a substitute for wheat and oats, and farm sizes grew. Between 1952 and 1962 the number of agricultural holdings of more than one acre in the county decreased from 5,474 to 4,655. Average acreage rose from 74 acres in 1952 to 85 acres in 1962. Large farms became more common. The number with 300 acres or more increased in

---

NUMD Ma 3E 2048, 2049, 2053, 2056; Ma 4S 6, M.5875.

[26] NUMD Acc.608, Holder to Jones, 22 July 1949, Mrs Jones to Holder, 3 October 1949.

[27] NUMD Acc.608, Holder to Jones, 25 April 1949, Mrs Jones to Holder, 22 September 1949.

Nottinghamshire from 227 in 1922 to 285 in 1962, while holdings of between 1 and 50 acres decreased over the same period from 4,165 to 2,694. Livestock were integrated within animal farming systems.

Laxton reflected these trends. After the war came a temporary decline in grain production, but it then increased rapidly during the 1950s (see figure 10.1). In 1950 the village had 1,334 acres under corn crops, but by the late 1960s the figure topped 2,000 acres. This high point was not sustained, but once again in 1986 more than 2,000 acres were under corn crops. The acreage under corn in 1986 was twice the level of a century earlier. The rise in productive acreage was partly achieved through a change in cropping. In the inter-war period about half the Laxton corn crop had been wheat and another quarter oats. The final quarter consisted of barley, beans, peas, and mixed grains. Barley had accounted for anything up to 20 per cent of the corn crop in the late nineteenth century, but it fell below 10 per cent after 1920, and in 1935 only 13 acres of barley were grown in the village. In the 1950s and 1960s the acreage under corn expanded because more barley was being grown. The peak was in 1969 when 1,383 acres were in barley. In that year it represented 68 per cent of the corn crop, and wheat and oats were 14 per cent each.

With entry into the European Economic Community at the beginning of the 1970s, and the adoption of the Common Agricultural Policy, British farmers were encouraged to concentrate on 'corn' rather than 'horn'. Until very recently two crops have been particularly favoured, wheat and oil seed rape. In 1970 wheat represented one-third of the Laxton corn crop, barley nearly one-half, oats and beans 18 per cent. After that the balance shifted with oats and beans virtually disappearing and wheat once again representing more than half the village corn crop. In 1986 1,309 acres were in wheat and 703 acres in barley. Oil seed rape was first introduced in Laxton in 1975 when 54 acres were grown. Since then the acreage has increased considerably, and in 1985 350 acres were under rape, which was almost certainly the most substantial acreage in a non-corn crop over the past century, and possibly ever.

These changes in cropping have also meant a decline in permanent grass and fallow. Since 1945 the acreage under permanent grass has fallen steadily. From more than 1,600 acres in the mid-1930s it fell to just over 1,000 acres in 1960, and to 323 acres in 1986, the lowest figure since records began. The fallow has also gone. Until World War Two more than 400 and sometimes more than 500 acres were left fallow each year, but from 1940 the fallow was gradually eroded, falling below 300 acres in 1960 and finally disappearing in 1968. Only 3 acres were officially designated fallow in 1986. The decline in permanent grass was partly offset by an increase in temporary grass during the 1950s and 1960s, although this has tailed off since 1970. In 1935 2,296 acres in Laxton were under temporary or permanent grass or fallow (63 per cent), and 1,324 acres were cropped (36 per cent); in 1985 675 acres were under grass (23 per cent) and 2,282 acres (77 per cent) were cropped.

These changes have had little impact on the number of cattle in the village (although not, as we shall see, in the open-field farms). The overall figures have seldom fallen below 1,000 head of stock since 1943. This has been possible because of an increase in temporary grasses to provide feed, and the introduction of artificial feeds. Sheep numbers recovered after the war, to reach 989 in 1960, but they fell again during the 1960s and collapsed in the foot and mouth outbreak of 1967–8. Today sheep represent only a tiny part of the village economy by comparison with their role in the past. Agricultural horses have disappeared since 1945 (which has also helped the feed situation), and in recent years poultry have become much less important to the village economy.

THE BREAK-UP OF THE ESTATE, 1950–1952

After World War Two it was clear that everything was not well at Thoresby. Denzil Holder carried out an inspection of the estate following his appointment in 1949 and he concluded that an extensive programme was required to improve the farmhouses and buildings, under the terms of the 1948 and 1949 Agriculture Acts. One possibility was to consolidate the holdings – this, perhaps, the last serious suggestion of enclosure – but the village was now celebrated for its open fields, and the Thoresby estate was pledged not to enclose. An alternative course of action was needed, and in the event it was decided to raise the necessary capital by securing a bank overdraft, and then selling a number of the farms to repay the loan.[28]

After some deliberation in the autumn of 1949 six farms and a cottage were selected for sale and the tenants informed in November.[29] The auction took place on 24 May 1950 in Nottingham, and the outcome is given in table 10.6. Knapeney, Primrose and Brecks Farms lay within ring fences. Copthorne included 18 acres in the open fields. Church Farm lay in Moorhouse although 56 of the 139 acres were in Laxton, and the property included Brecks Cottage on the Laxton side of the parish boundary. Laxton Lodge Farm also lay within a ring fence, in the south of the parish with 8 of its 129 acres straddling the Kneesall boundary. Manvers had acquired the farm in the exchange with the Saviles during the 1860s, and it consisted predominantly of a series of arable and grass closes beyond the woodlands. It lies contiguous with Kneesall rather than Laxton.[30] The boundaries of the lots put up for sale were almost those of the boundaries of the tenancies although some rearrangements were made by including in the sale parcels of land farmed from the village, and by leaving out two others in the Primrose Farm tenancy but distant from the main farm.

---

[28] Wood, thesis, p. 431; NUMD Acc.608, Westminster Bank to Colonel Holder, 4 November 1949.

[29] NUMD Acc.608, Holder to the Laxton tenants, 7 November 1949.

[30] NAO DD/405/9; Turner, Fletcher and Essex, *Sale Catalogue* (Nottingham, 1950).

PLATE 10.2 *An unchanging village. For all the changes described in the text since the Ministry of Agriculture took over the open field farms in 1952, Laxton remains surprisingly untouched by the passage of time. The picture at the top dates from c.1910, while that at the bottom was taken in 1988. One house, of which two side windows can be seen just beyond the couple in the gig in the top picture, has now gone. This was the old house for what is today Smithy Farm, and it has been replaced by a modern building somewhat out of character with the general tone of the village.*

TABLE 10.6 *The six farms sale of May 1950*

Farm	Acreage	Rent (£)	Purchaser	Consideration (£)
Copthorne	131	125	W. G. Quibell	3500
Knapeney	227	300	Mr and Mrs John Jones	6800
Primrose	55	70	Mr and Mrs Emrys Jones	2050
Brecks	120	154	George Watkin Hoggard	4500
Laxton Lodge	129	110	Mr B. Pickering	5350
Church Farm	139	155	George Saxelby	4000
Brecks Cottage	0.5	20	George Saxelby	525
	801.5	£934		£26725

Source: NUMD Manvers collection, uncatalogued papers relating to the six farms sale.

Five of the farms were bought by sitting tenants, and Laxton Lodge went to one of Earl Manvers's Kneesall farmers. These farms drop from our view hereafter, but it is worth noting what has happened to them since 1952. Five of them have changed hands at least once since then, and only Brecks had the same acreage in 1977 as at the time of the sale. Knapeney was amalgamated with Chestnut Farm, Eakring, and today the farmhouse stands empty and the buildings unused. Laxton Lodge was amalgamated with Caunton Common Farm, and both Church Farm and Primrose Farm have been expanded. Church Farm, Moorhouse, is the only one not to have changed hands. The Saxelbys, who own and farm Church Farm, come from a long line of Laxton farmers dating back to the early nineteenth century.

The 1950 sale left Thoresby with 24 farms at Laxton, ranging between 12 and 145 acres and totalling 1,753 acres (table 10.7) and 22 cottages, and four

TABLE 10.7 *Manvers farms in Laxton after the 1950 sale*

Acreage	Number	Total acreage	%
100+	7	820	47
51–99	9	677	39
21–50	6	234	13
11–20	2	23	1
	24	1754	100

Source: NUMD Ma 5E/159.

almshouse tenants. The farms had between 1 and 52 acres in the open fields with a total of 28 per cent in the open fields.

Economic conditions were such that the smaller farms, particularly those with less than 50 acres, were scarcely viable. As a result the long-term future of the remaining farms was a matter for serious concern. The secretary of the County Agricultural Executive Committee suggested that the National Trust might be persuaded to buy the farms 'in order to retain their unique character for posterity', because of 'their exceptional educational value, and their interest to overseas visitors'. In the event, when Earl Manvers sold the property on 28 February 1952, the new lord of the manor was the Minister of Agriculture.[31]

Almost simultaneously with the six farms sale Manvers opened negotiations for the sale of the open-field farms. It was clear that at his death, whenever that might be, considerable land sales would be required to pay death duties, and Manvers took the view that it would be better to ensure the future of the village in advance of that event (which finally occurred in 1955) in the hope of protecting the open-field farms. Negotiations with the Ministry of Agriculture commenced a few days after the six farms sale.[32] Manvers, apart from conducting some of the discussions in person, kept the Laxton tenants informed as to his reasons for the sale. It was two years before negotiations were completed, but finally Manvers sold to the Ministry 1,761 acres for £51,500. The transaction included the open-field farms, as well as the lordship of the manor, the first such change for 300 years.

This was not the end of the Pierrepont interest in Laxton. The family retained (and still retains) three farms, Brockilow (143 acres), Westwood (375 acres) and Crosshill (175 acres), all of them enclosed holdings, although Westwood still has a single strip of $5\frac{1}{2}$ acres in West Field. Tom Price, the Westwood farmer, was in trouble in 1974 for growing rape on the strip when the field was in grass, and again in 1981 for breaking the cropping rules. Thoresby also retained one other strip (currently let to Robert Grundy), the small holding at Saywood on the south side of the village, and the woodlands, a total of 900 acres.[33] Out of 3,456 acres in 1950 the Thoresby estate had sold 802 acres to tenants (23 per cent), 1,761 acres to the Ministry (51 per cent) and retained 900 acres (26 per cent). They also kept eighteen cottages, including the wheelwright's shop, which was let to Wilf Saddington, the schoolhouse, and the village Post Office. A number of these have since been sold to private owners, including the farmhouse at Westwood Farm. Today Thoresby retains a handful of cottages in the village and the two cottages in the woodlands at Saywood. A terrier compiled in the 1960s measured the estate at nearly 896

[31] Wood, thesis, pp. 434, 476.
[32] Thoresby Estate Office, minutes of meeting 9 June 1950.
[33] NUMD Ma 5E/162.

acres, of which 767 was farmland and 116 acres was woodland. The 2-acre
Stubbins Close was bought in 1963, the same year as the schoolhouse was sold
to a private tenant.

The Ministry of Agriculture had effectively taken over control of the manor,
and of the open-field farms, and almost immediately the new landlords carried
out a comprehensive survey of their acquisition which provides a broad view of
the estate that they had acquired. They counted 22 farms, the difference since
1950 being that two 11-acre holdings were downgraded to smallholdings. One
of the farms – Primrose – was in Moorhouse and beyond the open fields. The
21 full-time open-field farms ranged between 37 and 145 acres. In addition, 4
cottages and 3 almshouses are listed. The whole property totalled 1,754 acres
and the rental income was £2,012. This, however, was only part of the story.
The survey also examined the farm buildings and the farmland, and the results
suggested that much work was required on the estate.[34]

All the farms had some of their land in the open fields, but how much varied
considerably and one-third was considered a reasonable average. Several farms
were described as 'very scattered' including those of Jack Rose and Ron Cree;
William Rushby's open-field land was 'not unduly high'; while at Manor Farm
Joe Pashley was fortunate that his land was 'more compactly arranged than
most of the others'. Horace Hennell's farm was described as 'reasonably
compact, and the proportion of open field land is low'. By contrast at Step
Farm Jack Cree's open-field land was 'rather high', at Holme View Farm Albert
Rayner had 'a high proportion of land' in the open fields and at New Bar Farm
George Rushby's open-field land was 'above the average'. Ernest Jones at Bar
Farm had 'several good sized fields conveniently grouped near the homestead
and the proportion of open field land is not unduly high'. Arthur Grundy's
farm had the distinction of being 'less inconveniently laid out than some of the
others'.

At least two farmers had alternative interests. A. E. Frecknell farmed 50
acres in addition to running the Dovecote Inn. The trade was said to be 'fairly
regular but small', selling about 18 gallons of beer a week. Arthur Grundy, the
blacksmith, held 3½ acres with the smithy, and a separate farm of 44 acres. The
house belonging to the farm was occupied by Mr F. James 'who works part-
time for Mr Grundy'.

The farm buildings were almost entirely brick and pantile, with the occasional mention of slate and timber. William Rushby's implement shed was a
galvanized nissen hut. The buildings were still geared mainly for keeping cattle

---

[34] Ministry of Agriculture Survey, 1952, now in NUMD.

and horses, although J. Walker had a tractor house. Some had been enterprising. At School Farm Bill Bartle had converted two loose boxes into a dairy and milking parlour, and he had also taken steps to increase the number of cow standings.

The facilities of the houses were primitive. Water had been piped into the village at Lord Manvers's expense in 1913,[35] and most of the houses had running water although often only in the scullery and not in the adjoining buildings. Reg Rose, when he took over the tenancy of Bottom Farm in 1953, had neither water nor electricity in his farm buildings. It was agreed that with the commencement of the tenancy a new cooker and power point should be installed and that electricity should be supplied to the buildings. E. Noble at Twitchell Farm was the only farmer with no electricity supply, although Mrs Rushby had none in her smallholder's cottage. Some farmers had improved their facilities. William Rushby had installed a kitchen grate, a hot water system and a bathroom. Only Holme View Farm, where Albert Rayner took over the tenancy in March 1951, had a water closet. Three farmers, Jack Cree at Step Farm, George Rushby at Bar Farm and Albert Rayner had telephones.

The Ministry of Agriculture retained the lordship and the Laxton properties from 1952 until 1981. Laxton was run by the Agricultural Land Commission until 1963, and thereafter by the Ministry. It was clear that improvements were needed, and once again the thorny question was raised of drianing the open fields. Little progress was made. The capital costs were held to be prohibitive while the benefit to the farmers was likely to be minimal. In other words the Ministry would have had to lay out thousands, and possibly several hundred thousand pounds, but the strip sizes were such that the tenants were not ready to pay increased rent because they could see no major advantage.[36]

With farm buildings the situation was rather different. Despite the outflow of money from Thoresby much work still needed to be done. Many of the farmhouses were up to 200 years old, and the farmsteads had been designed for a system of mainly arable farming with some rearing and winter feeding of cattle in partly covered yards. Buildings and stackyards were rather congested, and little room was available for additional equipment. Neither the buildings nor the distribution of the fields was particularly suited to dairy farming. The structure of Laxton, with the farms in the village, produced a serious shortage of home pastures near to the farm buildings. In addition, cow sheds were often substandard, and dairies were a rarity even though most of the farmers had a milking herd.[37]

In these circumstances the Ministry was faced with a major renovation task. In twenty years three replacement farmhouses were built and thirteen were re-

[35] NAO PR 4760/25.
[36] *Ex. inf.* Peter Evans.
[37] Rundle, 'Laxton Today'.

roofed; £100,000 was spent on capital works and £50,000 on repairs and maintenance. One of the first necessities was the provision of bathrooms for the farmhouses. A modernization programme was put into practice which affected virtually all the units.[38] Outside, new barns, lean-to sheds and cattle yards were needed. Cowsheds were brought up to the higher standards of modern hygiene requirements, and stables and loose boxes converted for similar use. Better grass mixtures enabled farmers to carry more cows and cattle per acre on their enclosed land, and as a result they needed more storage for hay and housing for cattle. In addition, many of the older buildings were unsuitable for modern machines. They were narrow, high, and with small doors, making it impossible for a tractor to move in and out to muck out from one end to the other. The aim was to achieve labour- and time-saving buildings.

Many of the old layouts dating from the village rebuilding of the years 1720–80 disappeared. This did not please everybody; indeed, the Ministry's efforts were thought by some to pose a threat to the future of Laxton because the visual appearance was changed when prefabricated Dutch barns were erected which clashed with the local building style. These worries were slightly eased when Laxton was designated a conservation area by the County Council in 1971. Since then local authority planning controls have prevented demolition, although this has created its own problems. Modern farming demands modern buildings, and to build new in old brick was impossibly expensive. Old pantiles and bricks from derelict buildings were retained for use in repairs. Otherwise, in the 1970s conservation meant a modest tree-planting programme; overhead power cables were put underground at the expense of the County Council, and successful resistance was mounted to bizarre schemes for building a half-size replacement for the old wooden mill blown down in 1916. The Council rebuilt the pinfold in its present position in 1969. It is near to, but not on the site of, the original pinfold, which was moved in 1897. On the other hand conservation has not prevented the demolition of one or two older and unsafe buildings, while two or three of the modern farmhouses in the village are discordant with the local architectural style.

The need for improved buildings has been connected with the streamlining of farming and the use of machinery in place of manual labour. In Nottinghamshire in 1955 there were 24.5 workers per 1,000 acres of crops and grass, but this figure declined to 20.7 per cent by 1963. The number of tractors and combine harvesters in the county increased from 3,116 and 19 respectively in 1946, to 6,720 and 1,120 in 1963. No longer was it necessary for men to rise at 4 a.m. to prepare the horses for a day's ploughing, and to set off shortly after 6 a.m. to spend eight hours ploughing a single acre.

More efficient farming meant fewer men employed on sheer manual labour, and the Laxton farms became family farms. Between 1925 and 1950 there were

---

[38] J. F. Hoare, 'The Laxton Open Fields Estate', *Agriculture* (March 1972), 93–7.

normally 50 or more labourers in the village, the majority of whom were full time rather than casual workers. Machinery cut into these numbers, which declined to 39 in 1955, and to only 23 at the end of the 1960s. In 1985 and 1986 the number was 13, and even when farmers, their wives and families, are added, only about 50 people are now required (full, part time and casual) to farm Laxton. In the circumstances it is hardly surprising that when ten council houses were built in 1951–2 some of their occupants worked outside the village, although among the current generation of farmers Colin Cree lived in one for a number of years while working with his father who had the tenancy of Step Farm until the mid-1960s.

The Agricultural Land Commission sought a balance between maintaining the essential features of the open-field system and the need to ensure that the land was farmed as efficiently as possible within these constraints. It was particularly important to make efficient use of mechanical cultivation, and to this end enclosed land in the open-field farms was rearranged and consolidated, while the more fragmented pattern of the unenclosed strips was maintained. As a result, the open fields remain in 1988 as they were in 1952 at 483 acres in extent, now with 164 rather than 167 strips in total. The major limitation to the landlord's interest in investment was the comparatively small acreage of the farms, but the general trend during the Ministry's years was towards more efficient buildings and consequently towards making the farms economically viable as family units despite their relatively small sizes. Initially the number of farms was not affected. There were twenty-one in 1961 by which time two of the smallholdings and one of the cottages had gone. However, it was clear that 80 acres was an inadequate size for a full-time holding, and the Ministry proceeded to reduce the number by redistributing land at the end of tenancies, while retaining a number of smallholdings. Consequently the number of smallholdings, and the number of holdings over 100 acres have both increased whereas the number in between has been reduced. By 1972 the number of full-time farms had been reduced to 16, with 5 others becoming part-time or retirement holdings of 7–10 acres. Most of the farms were of about 110 acres, with approximately 30 acres each in the open fields, conforming to the average of about one-third which the ministry noted in 1952.[39] Since 1955 the number of individuals occupying land in the village has steadily declined, from 41 to 28 by 1975 and to 23 since 1980. Although these figures are for the whole village, they largely reflect the efforts of the Ministry to rationalize holdings.

To achieve the required balance various alterations took place in the field and strip pattern during the 25 years after 1952. Many of the strips in the enclosed furlongs were enlarged, by contrast with those in the open fields which remain largely unchanged. Most adjoining strips remain in separate hands, although when the open-field land was removed from one of the

[39] Ibid.

holdings in 1976 several strips were given to the tenants of adjoining strips, on the clear understanding that they would continue to cultivate them as separate units. In the enclosed areas, by contrast, boundary removals and amalgamations have made a considerable difference. As land has been re-allotted between farms, considerable enlargement has been possible of the areas of strips, particularly in the cases of those in the old East Field, Stubbinside and Hunger Hill, which now contain some of the largest fields in the parish. The increase was brought about by the elimination of many of the smallest fields and the strips which were still worked separately in enclosed areas such as Stubbinside and Brockilow Corner; a policy deliberately pursued by the Ministry's agent in the 1960s.[40]

Much of the change has been brought about in the hope of finding a solution to the most intractable of the village problems, the distance between house and land. In 1952 18 per cent of the acreage was more than 1.4 miles from the farmsteads, with consequent time loss in the movement of equipment and machinery. The tractor, of course, helped, but did not overcome the problem of moving cows to and from the farmsteads. A possible solution was suggested in 1961 with a plan to erect three new farmsteads outside the village, but this was abandoned when the impact that it would have on the traditional open-field structure was realized. A proposal to consolidate the land by exchanging outlying areas on the irregular boundary with the Thoresby Estate in return for the outlying block of Crosshill Farm east of the village, also failed. Under the circumstances, the best that could be achieved was a re-allotment of land when tenancies ended, and the negotiation of exchanges of land between sitting tenants. To prevent complaints among the tenants that good land was being swopped for bad, the ploughing of permanent grass, and the installation of efficient underdrainage, helped to bring about acceptable change. However, although the holdings became more consolidated as a result, the area adjoining the farmstead on each holding increased by only a small amount, and the distance to the fields was not significantly reduced. The resulting changes affected a large proportion of the village, with considerable repercussions for individual farms.[41]

The number of farms was further reduced to fourteen by 1980, at which it remained (along with four part-time holdings) in 1988. These fourteen farms ranged between 93 and 148 acres. Each farm had approximately 80 acres of enclosed land, and another 30 in the open fields, giving an average of 114 acres, well below what is normally regarded as economically viable in modern farming conditions. Structurally these changes have had an important effect in the village, because what might be termed the middle rung of the farming ladder has now been kicked away. Several of the tenants farming today

[40] Wood, thesis, pp. 436, 496–7.
[41] Wood, thesis, pp. 450–1, 498–501.

benefitted from being able to start with a small farm, and next-to-no capital. The ingoing valuation was often negligible with the custom of an away-going crop, and many farmers gradually built up their capital and stock before moving to larger farms making the smaller ones available to their own sons and other young aspirant tenants, but new tenants must today start with a considerably larger holding – and a considerably larger capital.

Since the First World War Laxton has continued to decline in numbers. Far less labour is now required to work the land – in the 1980s 50 people can do the work which in 1851 required 166 (50 farmers and 116 agricultural workers) – and this has had an effect both on population (through smaller households) and age structure. More people work out of the village, and with no school, no resident parson and few services, Laxton has changed considerably. Farming has also altered. In the adverse conditions of the inter-war period the concentration was on arable fodder crops, and, from the 1930s, dairying. With a return of prosperity to the land after 1945 the area of permanent grass has been reduced, and the arable increased. One consequence has been a relative decline in the role of the open fields in arable production. In 1903, before the reorganization and with a reduced arable acreage due to the agricultural depression, the open fields represented 56 per cent of the parish arable. This declined to 30 per cent after the reorganization and associated enclosures, to 24 per cent in 1950, and to just 16 per cent in 1986. Since 1950 considerable changes have taken place with several large farms sold into private hands, and the open-field farms passing to a new landlord. The number of tenancies has been reduced and the smaller farms have disappeared. No farmer now has more than about 30 acres (or slightly less than one-third of his acreage) in the open fields. Despite these changes, agricultural economics have moved even more quickly, and today's open-field farmers still struggle to make a reasonable living.

Chapter Eleven

Epilogue: the Survival of the Open Fields

This book began with a question, why have the Laxton open fields not been enclosed? As the preceding chapters have shown, part of the answer is that large areas of the parish *have* been enclosed. Laxton may always have had a considerable acreage outside the open fields. Even the 1,892 acres in the open fields in 1635 represented just 47 per cent of the parish acreage, and strictly speaking this was an overestimate. Mark Pierce included 80 acres of common or waste, and in a number of instances he noted where furlongs had been made into closes. These included Harwick closes in South Field (three closes of 32 acres) and some 300 acres of closes in Mill Field. This process was ongoing (table 11.1). In 1730 164 acres were removed from the fields during the partial enclosure, and nearly 250 more came out intermittently between 1736 and 1903. Today the 483 acres left in the open fields is rather less than the whole of South Field in 1635. However, today's open fields are rather different from their predecessors. The furlongs are no longer significant, and the strips bear little relationship even to the seventeenth-century 'lands'. In 1635 Mark Pierce counted more than 2,200 'lands'; today just 164 strips remain (figure 11.1): in 1903 the average strip was three-quarters of an acre; today the average is 3.75 acres. Other important changes have also taken place. As far as we can tell all

TABLE 11.1 *Acreage in the open fields 1635–1988*

Field	1635	1635 (adjusted)	1725	1736	1903	1908	1988
West	418	346	318	300	217	156	146
Mill	833	488	433	374	294	210	196
South	508	460	428	335	321	143	141
East	135	135	134	134	67	–	–
	1894	1429	1313	1143	899	509	483

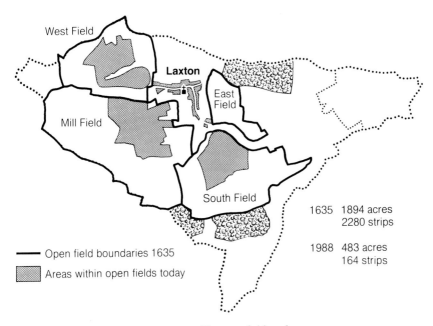

West Field

Laxton

East Field

Mill Field

South Field

1635 1894 acres
      2280 strips

—— Open field boundaries 1635

▨ Areas within open fields today

1988 483 acres
      164 strips

FIGURE 11.1 *The open fields today*

the arable land was in the open fields in 1635; in 1986 the open fields represented a mere 16 per cent of the parish areage cropped for cereals. In 1635 there were no fewer than 103 separtae farm holdings with a median size of 15 acres; today most of the fourteen full-time open-field farmers work around 110 acres.

The initial question needs therefore to be rephrased – why has enclosure in Laxton taken place in this piecemeal fashion and not resulted in enclosure of the whole parish? Part of the answer is straightforward. Parishes throughout the country went through various stages of enclosure. In many cases it culminated with an Act of Parliament sometime after 1750, but more often than not the legislation was to regularize earlier arrangements and to permit the enclosure of what was left of the open fields rather than to start from scratch. What is unique about Laxton is not the phases of piecemeal enclosure over time, but the failure to complete the task. No single explanation can be suggested for this failure. For hundreds of years the pattern of piecemeal enclosure both within and beyond the open fields was entirely predictable. Full enclosure would certainly have been difficult; plenty of evidence has now been collected to show that across the country it was almost invariably delayed where freeholders were numerous. Since the Laxton freeholders – rather against the expected national trend – actually increased both their numbers and their collective acreage during the period 1635–1789, delay was almost inevitable. On the other hand the lord of the manor's attempts to buy them out had been less than wholehearted, and an opportunity to pave the way for enclosure was missed in the 1750s.

Formal enclosure of the whole parish was seriously considered for the first time in about 1810, but the negotiations made little headway, and were abandoned in the post-1815 agricultural difficulties. Further discussions in the 1840s foundered on the rocks of disagreement between Manvers and Scarbrough. Meantime the enclosure of Moorhouse went ahead, and the land exchanges of the 1860s seemed at long last to have removed the obstacles to enclosing the rest of the parish. But it was not to be. A combination of agricultural prosperity in Laxton, and the potential cost of enclosure at a time when the third Earl Manvers was busy funding the new house at Thoresby, led to yet another postponement. Consequently Laxton entered the agricultural depression in the 1870s with open fields, but with enough land enclosed to adjust the farming balance in favour of animal husbandry. By the time enclosure was seriously considered again in the early years of the present century the landlord was prepared to fund only the cost of a more limited exercise, and once the vicar alerted the nation to the uniqueness of Laxton in 1906 the emphasis moved from enclosure to preservation. Possibly the extensive acreage in closes gave Laxton a flexibility in farming practice which made enclosure less crucial for the economy than elsewhere.

Of course what has been preserved must not be mistaken for a typical medieval open-field system. Laxton is not a museum, and the nature of farming has altered over time to provide optimum conditions from which the farmers can profit. The communal meadow lands were enclosed as long ago as the 1730s. At that time the principle was also abandoned whereby all the farmers worked from and lived in the central settlement. More recently the strips have taken on a size and shape unknown in medieval England in order to cater for modern farming equipment; common rights have ceased to be a major debating area as the demand for communal grazing has come to an end; Westwood Common has been removed from the system and cropped, and since 1967 even the fallow field has disappeared.

On the other hand much survives. Although shorn of some of its powers the court retains an important role in regulating husbandry in the open fields. The annual cycle over which it presides continues to bear many of the hallmarks of earlier generations. The crop rotation is still the same as it was in the seventeenth century, even if the fallow field is no longer left bare in the traditional manner. The grass is still sold for hay as it has been for 250 years (an important tradition in the village although not a medieval practice); the jury still makes its annual tour of inspection; the crops are still rotated through the fields; and the court still holds its annual meeting in the Dovecote Inn. But how long can this continue?

In September 1981 the Crown Estate Commissioners became the lords of the

PLATE 11.1 *Jury Day in the 1980s. The jurors are seen here in the Dovecote Inn discussing the fines to be imposed on offenders. On the left are Bob Grundy of Smithy Farm, Brian Morton of Brockilow and Ernie Kent of Ide Farm. The brothers Albert and Alec Rayner (of Holme View and Bar Farms) are in the far corner; and on the right hand side are Edmund Rose – holding pen – of Moorgate Farm (the court crier or bailiff), Colin Cree of Step Farm, Bill Haigh of Manor Farm, and – back to camera – Reg Rose of Bottom Farm.*

manor of Laxton, and the terms of the agreement by which they assumed control stated that they would maintain the system of open-field farming just so long as there are tenants willing to work the strips and to conform to the rules of the manor court. The Commissioners had no great desire to take over Laxton. Having decided to sell the farms, the Ministry of Agriculture was forced by political pressures to lay down terms and conditions which effectively excluded potential purchasers who might have hoped to introduce commercial farming. Since bodies such as the National Trust showed no interest in the village it was left to the Commissioners to relieve the government of a particularly contentious sale. In many ways, however, the Crown Estate Commissioners were a bizarre choice of landlord. Managing Laxton is almost impossible to square with their statutory duty to increase income and enhance the capital value of properties under their control, on behalf of the Chancellor of the Exchequer.

However, having acquired Laxton, and having undertaken to maintain the system of open-field farming, the commissioners had no intention of ignoring the estate. For all the efforts of the Ministry since 1952 Laxton was still in need of considerable investment, and there was scope for greater efficiency. The key to improving yields was, in the Commissioners' view, underdraining of the open fields. Some areas were almost too wet to farm at one time, including parts of the South Field near Long Syke. The cost of draining, and the limited returns to be expected while the fields remained in strips, had deterred both the Thoresby estate and the Ministry of Agriculture, but the Commissioners were determined to attempt underdraining in the hope that outputs would rise and the farmers would be better able to make a reasonable living. The tenants were expected to make a contribution. Underdraining took place in both enclosed and unenclosed areas of the estate but it is not yet finished; indeed, it has slowed down as a result of agricultural conditions, but some of the worst problems have been solved. Not all the farmers are convinced of the value of the drainage scheme because the returns are small. Overall, however, the improvements seem to have helped to make the new landlord more popular than at first, when the Commissioners were viewed with considerable caution, although some villagers still believe it was a dark day for Laxton when the Ministry sold the farms.

The Crown Estate Commissioners remain committed to their undertaking to keep Laxton as it is just as long as tenants are available and willing to work the system. With fourteen full-time farmers in the village and with the three Thoresby tenants liable (and in two cases willing) to serve on the jury despite their lack of open-field land, the numbers problem is not yet serious. This could change if Thoresby were to sell its farms at some future point, while more serious problems are posed by current agricultural economics and tenancy successions.

Several of the Laxton farmers have a relatively low standard of living as a result of the size and type of farms and farming that they are engaged in, which has changed substantially in the past ten years or so. In 1948 virtually everyone produced milk, but today only Bill Haigh at Manor Farm still has milking cows. Farmers began to change in the mid-1970s, partly due to a grass shortage in the dry summers of 1975 and 1976, and partly as a result of other changes which have discouraged the small producer, including tuberculin testing and the ending of churn collecting from outside the farm gate. The farmers could not afford parlour systems and bulk tanks, and so they moved out of dairying. Nine farms in the village (including the enclosed farms) were mainly dairying until 1970 but the number declined to three in 1975, and to one today. With only one open-field farmer still milking the village crew-yards are for the most part silent, deserted places. The change in practice, however, has done nothing for the farmers' incomes. Even with low rents few of them are making such profit, and in the future direct funding may be needed to give them a chance of making a reasonable living.

Other ways of improving the farmers' incomes have of course been considered, but most have been rejected as impractical in view of the small size of holdings and the fixed nature of the agricultural cycle. There has been discussion of having oil seed rape in the open fields but this has been firmly resisted by the court. Peas are a chancy crop on sticky land like Laxton, and are hardly grown now. The result is that the cycle today is wheat, spring or winter barley or second wheat, and, in the third field, hay. Although the hay is less valuable to today's farmers because they keep relatively few animals, it can at least be sold profitably for horseculture.

The second threat to the open-field system is the next generation of farmers in the village. Many of today's tenants have come up the hard way and retain an affection for their holdings. The brothers Albert Rayner of Holme View and Alec Rayner at Bar Farm, started life as farm workers, and moved on to tenancies while having very little capital. Albert Rayner, now in his seventies, took over Holme View farm in 1951 with £200 he had saved, and £300 borrowed from his mother. He celebrated by getting married and buying a tractor. The Rayners' elder brother Wilfrid, who farmed in Laxton until he died in 1982, made his way in much the same fashion. At 14 he began as a stable boy at Thoresby, and moved on to become a groom. In this role he travelled widely, even crossing the United States in the 1920s with Lord Manvers's polo team. Then he turned to farming, with 40 or so acres. In retirement the acreage drifted down to under 12. Others have also been around a long time. Reg Rose took the tenancy of Bottom Farm in 1953; Ernie Noble has been at New Bar Farm for thirty years; and Edmund Rose took over a small farm with his father in 1948 which they worked in tandem until 'Jack' Rose died in the 1960s.

It is the length of time that some of these men have been in Laxton which raises doubts about the future. The farmers are on ordinary agricultural agreements. They have the same rights of cropping – except in so far as these are governed by the court – and the Succession of Tenancy Act allows them to pass the farm to a son or daughter. Some have successors who are following in their footsteps. Edmund Rose has already handed on control of Moorgate Farm to his son Richard, and Reg Rose's son Stuart, who lives at Lilac Farm, is gradually assuming control of Bottom Farm. On the other hand the Rayner brothers are both near to retirement age, but although both have sons, in neither case does the son intend to follow the father into the tenancy.

So how are these problems to be tackled in the future? Most of today's farmers hope to see the system maintained. As Edmund Rose has put it, they want to see Laxton conserved for the future as the present generation of farmers have maintained it in the past. But the tenants are apprehensive about whether or not it can be. Why, as Ted Sayer of Top Farm put it, should any young man want to take on a Laxton tenancy with all its built-in disadvantages? Most are uncomfortable about new tenants coming from outside the village, and do not believe the open-field system can be successfully maintained if tenancies are given to people without a feel for the open-field system. One or two outsiders have been successfully integrated over the years, including Bill Haigh who came to Manor Farm from Normanton-on-Trent nearly thirty years ago and now his son Robert at Ivy House Farm. Everyone is aware however that two or three vacant tenancies, or two or three tenancies taken over by outsiders with no commitment to the system, and it could easily collapse for the lack of jurymen and court officers. Possibly the next generation of tenants will need to have special clauses written into their agricultural agreements about abiding by the rules of the manorial court and keeping to the rules of the open-field farming system, but this would not solve the economic problems of the tenants.

In terms of agricultural economics there seem to be only two possibilities for the future. One is further amalgamation of the farms, but then the problem arises of maintaining sufficient tenancies to keep the jury system going, and the farmers might be reluctant to work farms jointly. They have always been willing to help each other out. Alec Rayner worked for many years in cooperation with George Woolhouse of Town End Farm, and Horace Hennell helped Bill Haigh when he first came to the village. Today Colin Cree works with Johnny Godson, and Ernie Noble works with Ken Woolhouse. At the same time the farmers like to retain their independence and they are willing to pay each other for any help that may be given. There is some borrowing and hiring of specialist or expensive tools, but wherever possible farmers prefer to have their own machinery because they all want to work when the weather is fine, and not to have to watch the sun shine while they wait idly by for their neighbour to finish.

The other possibility is part-time farming. One or two farmers already have interests outside farming. Reg Rose has his agricultural machinery business and Edmund rose is one of the farmers who offers bed and breakfast facilities. Extending these interests is almost certainly going to be necessary for farmers to make a decent living in the future, but they may need to go further and think of farming as merely one interest. There are four part-time smallholders at present, but there is a temptation to regard them as being not really proper tenants (because they are part-time and smallholders), and similar problems may arise if any of the present full-time holdings are turned into part-time ones. In other words an incomer with 100 or more acres, but still part time, may find it just as difficult to integrate into the system, and the consequence might be to split the village.

Over time much has changed in Laxton but today's farmers walk the same paths and tracks, and follow the same agricultural routines as their predecessors of the seventeenth century and earlier. No one today remembers the wealthy Francis Green who died in 1712, or the formidable William Doncaster in the eighteenth century. The graveyard offers evidence of names now long gone, the Pinders and the Weatheralls among others, and today's families believe they have a heritage to carry into the future. The villagers are as concerned about the future as their predecessors in the 1620s and 1630s, when the lordship of the manor changed hands several times in a couple of decades, or in the nineteenth century when enclosure was so frequently under discussion. It is not easy to be optimistic, but Laxton has survived numerous attempts to enclose it, or to alter the way of farming, and it will doubtless resist a few more in the future. However attenuated, it remains as a monument to an agricultural system which can be seen nowhere else in England, and as such it is unique.

Appendix The Population of Laxton

For the period before the decennial census returns (1801 onwards) the population of Laxton has been estimated from the parish registers using the technique known as aggregative analysis (figure A1.1). The parish registers begin in 1563, but there are a number of gaps:

Baptisms   1572–7, 1612–14, 1621–7, 1683–6, 1726–7
Marriages 1563–1629, 1685–7, 1709–10
Burials   1563, 1571–9, 1589–98, 1611–16, 1626–31, 1677–86, 1727

These gaps, together with the relatively small size of Laxton, ruled out family reconstitution on quite the lines developed in Keith Wrightson and David Levine's book, *Poverty and Piety in an English Village: Terling 1525–1700* (1979).

Natural increase has been estimated as births (approximated as baptisms) less deaths (approximated as burials). Although some families seldom appear in the registers, the various dissenting groups in the village seem – in the absence of evidence to the contrary – to have gone to the parish church for their baptisms, marriages and burials. This means that coverage should be more or less complete. As a check on the figures derived from this exercise the results can be compared with other population estimates (table A1.1). No comparison has been suggested here with the figures given in the text which are derived from estate surveys.

Natural increase, uncorrected for migration, suggests a continual population increase which could not be accepted on the basis of these other estimates. A migration factor needed to be built in to the figures to correct the imbalance. When net migration away from the parish of four per annum was assumed between 1603 and 1676 the change in population fitted quite well within the ranges of estimates between these years. This fit with the non-parochial data made it possible to scale the population estimates from natural-increase data. In the absence of similar non-parochial data after 1676 the same method was

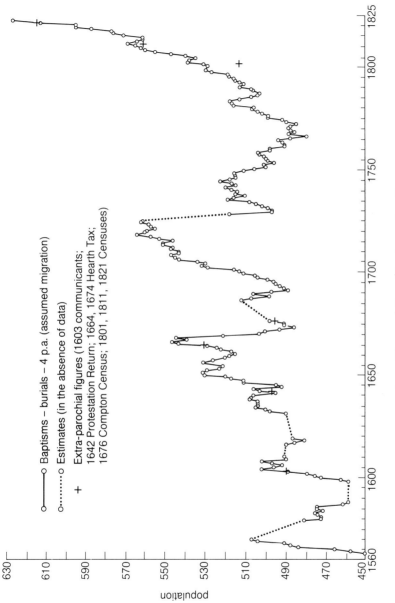

FIGURE A1.1 *The population of Laxton, 1563–1801*

TABLE A1.1 *Population estimates from various sources*

Year	Source	People/ Households	Multiplier	(Estimated) Population
1603	Communicant Returns	310	1.60	496
1642	Protestation Returns	153	3.25	497
1664	Hearth Tax	127	4.75	603
			4.25	540
1674	Hearth Tax	102	4.75	485
			4.25	434
1676	Compton Census	314	1.50	471
1801	Census			513
1811	Census			561
1821	Census			615

Sources: A. C. Wood, 'An Archiepiscopal Visitation in 1603', *TTS*, 46 (1942), 11; W. F. Webster (ed.), *Nottinghamshire Protestation Returns 1642–3* (Nottingham, 1980), pp. 18–19; PRO E 179/160/322, E 179/254/30; Anne Whiteman (ed.), *The Compton Census of 1676: a Critical Edition* (1986); Printed Census Returns.

used to continue the population estimates down to 1801. In other words the formula adopted was number of baptisms less number of burials, less four. Although such constancy of emigration is unlikely, the results derived from using it give population estimates which fit reasonably well with the census totals of 1801–21 (differences of +18, +8 and −2 respectively). This suggests that as a proxy for average emigration over the period it is reasonably accurate.

It is difficult to quantify the likely error in these population estimates but the error of 18 in 1801 may be representative. A maximum is likely to be the ±60 range of the mean Hearth Tax estimates with which the estimate on the basis of natural increase −4 shows good agreement. A check with the Cambridge Group for the Study of Population and Social Structure has suggested that while this methodology is rough and ready, it is unlikely to contain serious errors.

Select Bibliography

MANUSCRIPT SOURCES

Bodleian Library, Oxford
  Mark Pierce Survey and Map, 1635
Borthwick Institute, York
  1764 Visitation Returns
British Library
  Egerton Papers
Cheshire Record Office
  Delves-Broughton Papers
Hodgkinson and Tallents, Solicitors, Newark
  Laxton Court records
Ministry of Agriculture, Nottingham
  Agricultural Returns 1968–86
Nottinghamshire Archives Office
  Laxton Parish Records
  Quarter Sessions Papers
  Poor Law Records
  Land Tax Assessments
  Laxton Tithe Apportionment
  Laxton School Log Books
  Wills and Inventories, Archbishopric of York
  Records relating to the 1910 Finance Act
Nottingham University Manuscripts Department
  Manvers Papers
  Tallents Papers
  Denison of Ossington Papers
  Ministry of Agriculture Survey 1952
Public Record Office
  Feodaries Surveys
  1910 Domesday Return
  Agricultural Returns 1866–1965

Laxton Tithe File
Census Enumerators' Books
Records relating to the 1910 Finance Act
Sandbeck Park
Earl of Scarbrough's Papers
Thoresby Park, Estate Office
Papers re the sale of Laxton to the Ministry of Agriculture, 1952

PRINTED SOURCES

Unless otherwise stated, place of publication is London.

Beckitt, William and Jack Cook, *Open Field Recollections* (Laxton, n.d.).
British Parliamentary Papers (1850), 1152, xxvii. Francis Howell's report, 1848.
Census Returns, 1801–1981.
Copnall, H. H. (ed.), *Nottinghamshire County Records of the 17th Century* (Nottingham, 1915).
Firth, C. H. (ed.), *Memoirs of the Life of Colonel Hutchinson* (1906).
Glasscock, R. E. (ed.), *The Lay Subsidy of 1334*, British Academy Records of Social and Economic History (1975).
Kelly's *Directory of Nottinghamshire* (1908).
Kelly's *Directory of Nottinghamshire* (1928).
Moody, Frank, *My Lifetime Memories of Laxton* (Laxton, 1981).
Nottinghamshire Guardian, June–September 1949.
Thompson, A. Hamilton, 'Chantry Certificate Rolls for the County of Nottingham-shire', *TTS*, 17 (1913), 61–4.
Walker, P. C. and S. L. Ollard (eds), *Archbishop Herring's Visitation Returns 1743*, Yorkshire Archaeological Society, Records Series, 77 (1930), IV.
Webster, W. F. (ed.), *Nottinghamshire Protestation Returns 1642–3* (Nottingham, 1980).
White's *Directory of Nottinghamshire* (Sheffield, 1844).
White's *Directory of Nottinghamshire* (Sheffield, 1894).
Whiteman, Anne (ed.), *The Compton Census of 1676: a Critical Edition* (1986).
Wood, A. C., 'An Archiepiscopal Visitation in 1603', *TTS*, 46 (1942), 3–14.
Wood, B. A., Charles Watkins and C. A. Wood (eds), *Life at Laxton: the memories of Edith Hickson* (Nottingham, 1983).

INTERVIEWS

In the course of researching this book, the following were kind enough to talk to me, at greater or lesser length, about Laxton in the past and the present: Mrs Alice Bailey, Mr Bill Bartle, Mrs Janet Cooke, Mrs Annie Cree, Mr Colin Cree, Mr Ron Cree, Mr Peter Evans, Mr Michael Jackson, Mr Graham Laughton, Mr Rowan McFerran, Mr Denzil Newton, Mr Edmund Rose, Mrs Margaret Rose, Mr Reg Rose, and Mrs Marjorie Sayer.

I was also loaned two tape recordings: J. D. Chambers and E. J. Rose, 1959; and P. W. Evans and J. E. Rose, 1975.

SELECTED SECONDARY SOURCES

Beckett, J. V., 'England's Last Open Field Village under Threat?', *Trent Geographer*, 11 (1987), 24–5.
Beckett, J. V., 'Laxton, England's Last Open Field Village', *The Historian*, 20 (1988), 13–16.
Beckett, J. V. and T. Foulds, 'Beyond the Micro: Laxton, the Computer and Social Change over Time', *Local Historian*, 16, 8 (1985), 451–6.
Beckett, J. V. and T. Foulds, 'Landholding and Society in Laxton in 1841', *TTS*, 89 (1985), 108–21.
Beckett, J. V. and T. Foulds, 'Reconstructing an English Village in the Eighteenth and Nineteenth Centuries using FAMULUS 77: Laxton, Nottinghamshire', in P. Denley and D. Hopkin (eds), *History and Computing* (Manchester, 1987), pp. 45–9.
Beckett, J. V. and B. A. Wood, 'Land Agency in Agricultural Depression: R. W. Wordsworth at Thoresby, 1883–1914', *Trent Geographer*, 11 (1987), 16–23.
Beresford, M. W. and J. K. St Joseph, *Medieval England: An Aerial Survey*, 2nd edn (Cambridge, 1979).
Cameron, A., 'Laxton before 1635', *East Midland Geographer*, 7, 6 (1980), 219–26.
Chambers, J. D., 'The Open Fields of Laxton', *TTS*, 32 (1928), 102–25.
Chambers, J. D., *Laxton – the Last English Open Field Villages* (1964, 1979).
Chambers, J. D., *Nottinghamshire in the Eighteenth Century*, 2nd edn (1966).
Collinson, C. B., 'A Survival', *Country Life*, XIX, 789 (19 May 1906), 713–14.
Colvin, H. M., *History of the King's Works*, 2 vols (1963).
Crook, D., 'The Early Keepers of Sherwood Forest', *TTS*, 84 (1980), 14–20.
Delano Smith, Catherine, 'Laxton in 1635', *East Midland Geographer*, 7, 6 (1980), 226–30.
Dodgshon, Robert A., *The Origins of British Field Systems* (1980).
Firth, J. B., *Highways and Byeways in Nottinghamshire* (1916).
Foulds, Trevor, 'Laxton: Field Names as Evidence for the Ancient Landscape', *Nottinghamshire Historian*, 42 (1989), 4–11.
Fox, H. S. A., 'Approaches to the Adoption of the Midland System', in T. Rowley (ed.), *The Origins of Open-Field Agriculture* (1981), 64–111.
Gell, J. A. J., 'Laxton – Network Analysis of an Open-field Parish', unpublished BA dissertation, University of Nottingham, 1977.
Gill, H., 'St. Michael's, Laxton', *TTS*, 28 (1924), 96–105.
Groves, Colin, 'Gazetteer of Minor Moated and Fortified Sites in Nottinghamshire', unpublished MA thesis, University of Nottingham, 1987.
Hoare, J. F., 'The Laxton Open Fields Estate', *Agriculture* (March 1972), 93–7.
Hoskins, W. G., *The Midland Peasant* (1957).
Keeton, A. W., *Laxton and its Past* (Nottingham, n.d.).
Lowe, Robert, *General View of the Agriculture of the County of Nottinghamshire* (1798).

Mingay, G. E., 'The Duke of Kingston and His Estates', unpublished BA dissertation, University of Nottingham, 1952.

Mingay, G. E., 'Landownership and Agrarian Trends in the Eighteenth Century', unpublished Ph.D. thesis, University of Nottingham, 1958.

Mingay, G. E., *English Landed Society in the Eighteenth Century* (1963).

Orwin, C. S. and C. S., *The History of Laxton* (Oxford, 1935).

Orwin, C. S. and C. S., *The Open Fields* (Oxford, 1938).

Pevsner, N. and E. Williamson, *The Buildings of England: Nottinghamshire* 2nd edn (1979).

Phillips, A. D. M., 'Agricultural Land Use, Soils and the Nottinghamshire Tithe Surveys *circa* 1840', *East Midland Geographer* 6, 6 (1976), 284–301.

Pickersgill, A. C., 'The Agricultural Revolution in Bassetlaw, Nottinghamshire, 1750–1873', unpublished Ph.D. thesis, University of Nottingham, 1979.

Rieley, J. O. and P. R. Tomlinson, *Woods, Hedgerows and Grasslands of the Parish of Laxton, Nottinghamshire* (Nottingham, 1987).

Rundle, J. R., 'Laxton Today', *Agriculture*, LXII (1955), 170–2.

Slater, Gilbert, *The English Peasantry and the Enclosure of Common Fields* (1907).

Storey, R. L., 'A Fifteenth-century Vicar of Laxton', *TTS*, 88 (1984), 39–41.

Thirsk, Joan, 'The Common Fields', *Past and Present*, 29 (1964), 3–25.

Thirsk, Joan, 'The Origin of the Common Fields', *Past and Present*, 33 (1966), 142–7.

Titow, J. Z., 'Medieval England and the Open Field System', *Past and Present*, 32 (1965), 86–102.

Thoroton, Robert, *Antiquities of Nottinghamshire*, 3rd edn, ed. J. Throsby (Nottingham, 1797), vol. III.

Train, Keith, *Nottinghamshire Families* (Nottingham, 1973).

Upex, S. G. and B. A. Wood, 'A Survey of Relict Open-Field Landscape Features at Laxton', *East Midland Geographer*, 7, 6 (1980), 238–46.

Victoria County History, *Nottinghamshire*, I (1906), II (1910).

Watts, M. (ed.), *Religion in Victorian Nottinghamshire: the Religious Census of 1851* (Nottingham, 1988).

Wheeler, P. T. and B. A. Wood, 'The Reorganisation of the Open Fields at Laxton, Nottinghamshire, 1900–1910', *Trent Geographer*, 11 (1987), 2–15.

Wilson, R. G., 'The Denisons and Milneses: Eighteenth-century Merchant Landowners', in J. T. Ward and R. G. Wilson (eds.), *Land and Industry* (1971), 145–62.

Wood, B. A., 'Laxton in the Twentieth Century', *East Midland Geographer*, 7, 6 (1980), 231–7.

Wood, B. A., 'Land Management and Farm Structure: Spatial Organisation on a Nottinghamshire Landed Estate and its Successors, 1860–1978', unpublished Ph.D. thesis, University of Nottingham, 1981.

Wood, B. A., 'Teaching Sources: Laxton, Nottinghamshire', *Trent Geographer*, 14 (1983), 1–7.

Index